FORTY-SEVEN STRAIGHT

Bud Wilkinson

FORTY-SEVEN STRAIGHT

THE WILKINSON ERA AT OKLAHOMA

TOLD BY HIS PLAYERS
AND BY HAROLD KEITH

UNIVERSITY OF OKLAHOMA PRESS : NORMAN

BY HAROLD KEITH

Forty-seven Straight: The Wilkinson Era at Oklahoma (Norman, 1984)
*Oklahoma Kickoff: An Informal History of the First Twenty-five Years of
    Football at the University of Oklahoma, and of the Amusing Hardships
    That Attended Its Pioneering* (New York, 1948; Norman, 1978)
The Obstinate Land (New York, 1978)
Susy's Scoundrel (New York, 1974)
The Runt of Rogers School (New York, 1974)
The Bluejay Boarders (New York, 1972)
Go, Red, Go! (Nashville, Tenn., 1972)
Brief Garland (New York, 1971)
Komantcia (New York, 1965)
Rifles for Watie (New York, 1958)
A Pair of Captains (New York, 1951)
Shotgun Shaw (New York, 1949)
Sports and Games (New York, 1940)
Boys' Life of Will Rogers (New York, 1936)

Library of Congress Cataloging in Publication Data

Keith, Harold, 1903-
    Forty-seven straight.

    Includes bibliographical references and index.
    1. Wilkinson, Bud, 1916-   . 2. Football—United States—Coaches—
Biography. 3. University of Oklahoma—Football—History. I. Title.
GV939.W48K44   1984   796.332'092'4 [B]   84-40274
ISBN 0-8061-1898-9 (alk. paper)

The paper in this book meets the guidelines for permanence and durability
of the Committee on Production Guidelines for Book Longevity of the Council
on Library Resources, Inc.

The frontispiece is reproduced through the courtesy of the Sports Information
Department, University of Oklahoma.

Dedication
to

PORT ROBERTSON

Academic Counselor and Freshman
Coach, University of Oklahoma

*"He kept scores of kids of various
egos and personalities in school.
Nobody ever said anything derogatory
about Port. He was highly respected."*
— ROSS COYLE.

*"Port was the best thing that ever
happened to OU football. He could
make the players keep their noses in
their books."* — TOMMY MCDONALD.

*"Port was rough and stern, but when
my grades came in, I loved him like
a father."* — CHARLEY MAYHUE.

*". . . a man I would learn to despise,
then respect, then love — Port G.
Robertson."* — JOHNNY TATUM.

GOMER JONES

Associate Athletic Director and
Line Coach, University of Oklahoma

*"You played hard for Gomer
because you loved the guy.
You wanted to make Gomer look
good."* — DOC HEARON.

*"A great, great coach and a
great, great guy. He taught
me more technique than I ever
thought about learning from
the pros."* — STAN WEST.

*"I always had the feeling that
he knew totally what he was
doing."* — PRENTICE GAUTT.

*"A dear guy. He had a charm
that everybody felt."* — EDDIE
CROWDER.

CONTENTS

ILLUSTRATIONS

Young Bud as a Senior at Shattuck Military Academy. Photo from the 1933 *Yearbook,* Shattuck School, Faribault, Minnesota.

PREFACE

A biography of Bud Wilkinson with Tim Cohane, sports editor of *Look* magazine, joining Wilkinson as coauthor, was the original plan. We were all enthusiastic about it. And Cohane could get the book serialized in *Look.* When Coach Wilkinson decided to run for the United States Senate, the project was sidetracked. He could not give Cohane the necessary interviewing time.

Several years later it occurred to me that this book still deserved to see the light of day. Some of Wilkinson's coaching feats have never been equaled by any other coach in the history of college football, and books had been written about them all. For this project I had advantages no other writer had: I had seen every game, 178 in all, that Wilkinson's Oklahoma teams had played. More important, I knew all his players. Why not write the book from the viewpoint of the former players themselves, traveling about the country to interview them personally?

I got in touch with Tim Cohane, now Executive Director of Corporation Communication Seminars. He was enthusiastic about my plan to undertake the project and mailed me much of his material. Then I wrote to Wilkinson. I told him that I wanted to write an honest, graphic, and entertaining book; that the University of Oklahoma Press had offered a contract; and that the University of Oklahoma Foundation would provide a grant in support of it.

Wilkinson replied that he was "somewhat surprised." He thought that the book should be a forthright, candid report of what actually occurred, describing the personal qualities and skills of the men who created the record. "Inevitably I am a part of the story," he wrote, "but I would not want the book to be biographically inclined to me or our coaching staffs." This was precisely what I had in mind. He said that he would talk to me at my convenience, and he has done so.

I am grateful to many besides the coach and Cohane. I am indebted to Ron Burton, Director of the University of Oklahoma Foundation, without whom there would have been no book; to Mrs. Addie Lee Barker, my former associate in sports information at the university; to David Burr, Vice-President for University Affairs, University of Oklahoma; to Frank ("Pop") Ivy, Eddie Crowder, and Bill Jennings, former assistant coaches, University of Oklahoma; to the late Dal Ward, former coach, University of Colorado;

to Don Faurot, former coach, University of Missouri; and to George L. Cross, emeritus President of the University of Oklahoma, who graciously gave me permission to quote from his book *Presidents Can't Punt: The OU Football Tradition.* My wife, Virginia, gave valuable counsel.

I am also grateful to Walter Byers, Executive Director of the National Collegiate Athletic Association; J. R. Morris, Provost of the University of Oklahoma; Tom McCurdy, copublisher of the *Purcell* (Oklahoma) *Register;* Mary Wilkinson, the coach's first wife; Ken Farris, former Athletic Business Manager, University of Oklahoma; and Art Wood, Hall Haynes, Port Robertson, Sharon Beery, Ned Hockman, Jimmy Stewart, C. L. ("Curly") Sloss, Charles Parker, John Keith, Bob Connor, Don Bryant, Robert Smith, Mike Treps, Jan Burton, and Ken Neptune.

I especially acknowledge the sixty-one Oklahoma players of the Wilkinson era whom I personally interviewed, Claude Arnold; Dr. Paul Benien, Jr.; George Brewer; Dr. Newt Burton; Paul ("Buddy") Burris; Jim Byerly; Gene Calame; Jimmy Carpenter; Dr. George Cornelius; Bob Cornell; Ross Coyle; Leon Cross; Eddie Crowder; Monte Deere; Merle ("Red") Dinkins; the Reverend Donald M. Fletcher; John Garrett; Prentice Gautt; Bobby Goad; Tommy Gray; Myrle Greathouse; Jim Grisham; Jimmy Harris; Darlon ("Doc") Hearon; Brewster Hobby; Doyle Jennings; W. D. ("Buddy") Jones; John E. ("Buddy") Leake; Phil Lohmann; Mike McClellan; Tommy McDonald; Norman McNabb; Willie Manley; Charles Mayhue; Jack Mitchell; Harry Moore; Jay O'Neal; Pat O'Neal; Buddy Oujesky; Bob Page; Homer Paine; Jerry Pettibone; Billy Pricer; Joe Rector; John Reddell; Mike Ringer; Darrell Royal; Jakie Sandefer; Johnny Tatum; Clendon Thomas; George ("Junior") Thomas; Pete Tillman; Ken Tipps; Jerry Tubbs; Jim Tyree; Colonel Jack Van Pool; Billy Vessels, Lieutenant Colonel Dennis Ward; Jim Weatherall; Stan West; and Calvin Woodworth.

It was impossible to learn the present-day occupations of all the Wilkinson players. I could not find them all. I apologize to the ones omitted.

Norman, Oklahoma

HAROLD KEITH

FORTY-SEVEN STRAIGHT

1. JIM TATUM'S PRIZE RECRUIT

Jim Tatum, Oklahoma's football coach in 1946, was a big, bossy, hard-nosed fellow who didn't think he was doing a good job unless he had everybody mad at him.

"And he was gifted at that," says Jim Tyree, the team's cocaptain and left end that year. "He knew that if the team was all mad at him, they'd be together in the game. For example, before the Oklahoma Aggie game, he made us practice on Thanksgiving afternoon when we wanted to have the day off and work Friday instead. But Tatum saw we were mad about it and made us work Thursday. We were so mad at him that we took it out on the Aggies 73-12. Darned if I don't think he planned it that way."

Don Faurot, Missouri mentor who coached the Iowa Pre-Flight and Jacksonville, Florida, Naval Air Station service teams during World War II and had Tatum as his line coach at both places, put it succinctly and well when he said, "Tatum was the best recruiter and defensive coach I ever saw."[1]

Let's follow Tatum for a moment in recruiting action at the University of Oklahoma, where his aggressive player procurement program would be of enormous value to the dynasty that would follow his. It was the summer of 1946, and the August sun was frying the playing turf at Norman's Owen Field. George Brewer, a Lubbock, Texas, boy who had just won the 100-yard dash in the Border Conference track and field meet in his first semester at Texas Tech, was visiting Tatum's Sooner watering hole, where hundreds of players just back from war service were trying out. For most of them it was their first football in three or four years.

"All my family had played football at Texas, but I wanted to be different," says Brewer today. "I visited everywhere, even at Notre Dame. I'd almost decided to go to SMU." Eddie Chiles, of Fort Worth, a personable Oklahoma graduate in petroleum engineering, persuaded Brewer to at least take a look at the revitalized program at Norman. World War II was over, and the National Collegiate Athletic Association (NCAA) had no rules penalizing athletes who changed schools after the war.

"They picked me up at the university airport and drove me to Coach

---

[1] Bob Broeg, *Ol' Mizzou* (Huntsville, Ala., 1974), p. 181.

3

Tatum at the stadium," Brewer recalls. Tatum grinned, shook hands, and looked Brewer over admiringly. "Want some football shoes and shorts to run around in?" Tatum invited. He pointed to a nearby locker. Brewer opened it and discovered that it was full of game gear—helmet, pads, pants, jockstrap, the whole shooting match.

Brewer put it all on and went outside. Although he hadn't worn a uniform for months, everything fit. Somebody knew all his sizes.

A single-wing tailback at Lubbock High School, he watched Oklahoma's new split-T formation with curiosity. "How'd you like to take some handoffs?" Tatum presently inquired. A center and a quarterback were provided, and Brewer tried some handoffs along the sideline, away from the scrimmage.

"I had a heck of a time trying to field those split-T handoffs without looking at the ball," he laughs today.

The next day was Saturday, and there was hitting all over the premises. Again Brewer climbed into his new togs. Again Tatum accosted him. "How'd you like to run a few plays?" the big coach purred with his disarming grin. "We know you're not used to our new formation, but we thought you might enjoy seeing what it's like."

He put Brewer on the starting unit quarterbacked by Jack Mitchell with Joe Golding at right halfback. The rookie from Lubbock didn't know it, but he was traveling with Sooner royalty.

With Mitchell telling him his assignment before each play, Brewer forward passed two touchdowns, ran for two others.

"Next morning was really funny," Brewer remembers. "We were at Jeff House, and I was having breakfast with Coach Tatum. The *Daily Oklahoman* of Oklahoma City had spotlighted my scrimmage feats of the day before in a story that said, 'Texas gridder tears the gate off the OU practice field.' That fired me high as a rocket. I was only seventeen."

Tatum looked at him over the ham and scrambled eggs. "What we need here at Oklahoma is one more halfback with good speed," he said. Brewer blinked. Things were moving pretty fast.

"I can't do anything or make any decisions until I talk to my parents," he said.

Big Jim's hairy hand reached out and swooped around a nearby telephone. To the operator he said, "I want you to try now on that call I placed to Lubbock, Texas."

"He talked to my folks right there in front of me," recalls Brewer. "Then I talked to them. I never went home at all. I stayed right there in Norman, Oklahoma. He was slicker than a whistle."

As a sophomore in 1947, Brewer started all of Oklahoma's games and led the Big Six Conference in scoring. Tatum could pick them. So could Eddie Chiles.

Paul ("Buddy") Burris, a 215-pound Muskogee farm boy who had played guard as a freshman for Coach Henry Frnka's Sugar Bowling Tulsa Hurricanes, was home from the war, in which he'd been an army staff sergeant and won three battle stars in Europe and the Philippines. Mrs. Jewel Ditmars, an Oklahoma sports enthusiast living in Muskogee, tried to interest him in the new Oklahoma football program that was becoming the talk of the state.

"I went to Norman to watch their spring practice," Burris remembers. "Tatum conned me into scrimmaging. I hadn't played football in three years, but I blocked three punts that day and stuffed their quarterback keeper. I slipped home fast after the workout. I knew he'd be after me. I wanted more time to think things over. I knew I could make any team in the country, even if I had to walk on and show 'em."

A week later Burris was plowing on his father's farm. "In those times we did most of our plowing with horses and mules. I was driving 'em and walking barefoot behind the plow in the soft dirt. That was great for my legs.

"I saw a black Cadillac parked down at the end of the furrow. The lady in it looked like Jewel Ditmars. A big, well-dressed man stood outside the car door. He looked almost bigger than the car. It was Jim Tatum. He had driven clear to Muskogee and come out to the farm to see me. That impressed me.

"I crawled over the fence and talked to 'em. He invited me down for summer practice and offered me the full load—room, board, books, tuition, and fifteen dollars a month for laundry. I took him up. I was ready."

Burris became the only Oklahoma player in history to make first-team All-American guard all three years he played at Norman.

Tatum could pick them out of the small high schools, too, after only a long-distance telephone introduction. Jess Fronterhouse, coach at Fairland, up in the northeastern Oklahoma lead and zinc country, drove to Norman to watch an early Sooner spring practice. He brought with him George ("Junior") Thomas, also nicknamed "Jug," and Ronald Dry, two senior-high-school backs. Both were still attending Fairland High School, Fronterhouse had explained over the phone.

"Bring 'em over anyhow," Tatum insisted. "We'll try 'em out."

"Seeing a couple hundred OU players cavorting about Owen Field was kinda awesome," Thomas remembers today. "At Fairland, population 682, we had only 17 boys out for football. That was our whole squad. But after watching OU run, I thought I could play with 'em."

5

At first, Tatum didn't scrimmage Thomas and Dry. Fronterhouse mistook this for waning interest. On the sideline he regaled the OU staff with stories about the feats of his two stars. They had led Fairland to 9 football victories in 10 starts. In basketball they had sparked Fairland to 30 victories in 31 games. "These boys can go," Fronterhouse insisted. "They won't let you down." The Sooner coaches listened politely. They were hearing lots of stories about high school boys.

With the sun slanting low over the pink tile wall of the Sooner stadium, Tatum finally waved Fairland's one-two punch in. On the second play the 170-pound Thomas snatched up a poorly pegged lateral from under his feet. Accelerating beautifully and weaving like a snake, he ran 50 yards. On the next play the 195-pound Dry bucked 8 yards down the middle for a touchdown.

"What a swell lawn they got here to fall on!" Thomas told Dry in the end zone. He was thinking of Fairland's gravelly field and Grove's rocky rectangle. "Yeah, only you guys haven't fallen on it yet," corrected a panting varsity player.

Tatum soon pulled Thomas and Dry and invited them to attend further drills. "These boys can go," Fronterhouse told Tatum. "I told you they wouldn't let you down."

Thomas enrolled in summer school at OU, passing six hours. Late in August, Coach Henry Frnka, who had switched from Tulsa to Tulane, phoned Thomas, inviting him to visit Tulane. Fairland was a lot closer to Tulsa than to Norman, so Thomas knew Frnka much better than he knew Tatum. He went to Tulane and promised Frnka that he would attend school there and play football. He returned to Fairland to get his clothes, flying to Joplin, then traveling the rest of the way by bus. He arrived home in the morning.

"I saw a car parked in front of our house at Fairland," Thomas says. "Coach Tatum was sitting in the living room waiting for me. He looked tired and sleepy, but he was grinning. He'd driven nearly all night.

"I decided to go with him to Oklahoma," Thomas recounts. "After having seen New Orleans, I knew that I wasn't a big-city boy anyhow. I thought of the Sooner split-T and how exciting it was to run off it. An eighteen-year-old boy changes his mind every fifteen minutes anyway." Three years later Thomas, a Sooner All-American, led the nation widely in scoring, amassing 19 touchdowns and 117 points.

Sometimes Tatum missed on his judgments, but when that happened it didn't take him long to reverse his field. In 1946, Myrle Greathouse, of Amarillo, Texas, who had played as a substitute blocker-linebacker for

Coach Dewey ("Snorter") Luster's Sooners of 1942, came home from service and called on Tatum to determine the status of his scholarship. Greathouse had just got off the ship. At 170 pounds he was in no condition to try out in 100-degree weather for any football team.

Tatum didn't offer him a scholarship. He told Greathouse that because he was so small he would have to try out. He wanted linebackers in the 200-pound category. So Greathouse tried out. For three days Tatum watched the pale Panhandle marine level his best ballcarriers in the July heat.

"Don't worry about that scholarship," Tatum told Greathouse. "You'll get one. But I'd like to have you stick around awhile, get used to the split-T, get acquainted with the fellows."

"He did everything he could to put weight on me," Greathouse laughs today. "He even sent a case of beer out to my house. But I gave it all away because I don't like beer.

"Coach Tatum was a man with lots of university money which he was passing out that summer to married players," Greathouse went on. "He told me that I didn't need any money because back home my father was so well off that we had a swimming pool in our backyard. He didn't know that it was the town commercial pool and my dad only managed it in the summer."

For the next three years Greathouse backed Oklahoma's lines in stabbing fashion. And after graduation he became a diligent recruiter for his school.

There were others. Stan West, a pass-catching end from Enid, reported to Norman for discharge from the navy. A few days earlier he had received a telephone call from Tatum, whom he had never seen. "I'll meet you at the interurban station when you report at Norman," the coach said.

West adds, "I found out in a hurry that he was an operator. He met me at the trolley station, just as he said he would, and drove me out to the navy base. I had just finished a leave, but he said he'd get me another one, and in ten minutes he had it. I don't know how he did it so fast."

West became an All-American guard at Oklahoma and later twice made the all-pro team at that position. His style was just playing soft. "If you bust through, you might miss the guy," he said.

Jack Mitchell, a quarterback from Arkansas City, Kansas, had spent a freshman season at Texas before entering service. When he returned home from the military, the first man he saw at the depot was a big stranger named Tatum. The coach invited Mitchell to Norman for spring practice. Although he had intended to go to Texas, Mitchell obeyed his father's wishes and came to Oklahoma.

Tatum liked to keep his players happy. Before Oklahoma's Gator Bowl

7

victory over North Carolina State, he called a squad meeting and told them they were each to receive a gift. "Which do you want, a gold watch or $125 cash?" he asked.

"We all voted for the money," Merle ("Red") Dinkins, end from Blackwell, laughs today. "I'd give anything now to have the watch."

Another financial nuance in which the new coach indulged was to assign an Oklahoma City businessman to some player as a "sponsor." That gave the sponsor, or "sugar daddy," as the players called him, the right to enter the Sooner dressing room after a game and visit with the player.

"Once my sponsor slipped me a twenty-dollar bill," recalls Dinkins. "I almost fainted. To me it looked as big as a hundred."

At the end of the season the sponsor telephoned Dinkins. "You had a fine year," he said. "Come up to Connolly's and get yourself a new sports coat."

Dazed, Dinkins wandered into Connolly's, in Oklahoma City, and found that the going price of sports coats there was $125. Dinkins almost panicked. He phoned the sponsor. "I need shirts and socks and shorts lots worse than anything else. Can I substitute them for the sports coat?" he asked. His sponsor said okay.

"That's the only time in my life—before or since—that I ever wore a pair of seven-dollar silk underpants," Dinkins laughs.

Everybody worked hard at Tatum's spring and summer camps, but first they had to survive them. Bodies glistening with sweat, they blocked and tackled vigorously on three gridirons flanking Oklahoma's stadium. All drills were permitted by the NCAA.

"I never saw so many college football players in my life," Leon Manley, later a Sooner tackle, vows today. "They were swarming in and out carrying suitcases. I never saw so many different styles of suitcases, either." David Wood, an ardent Sooner fan in the state legislature, said, "Tatum was hired at lunch and by supper he had a backfield and half a line."

The assistant coaches directing the one-on-one worked fast. "You block him" or "you tackle him," they would order. If somebody physically creamed his opponent, they'd stop the drill, ask his name, and write it on a pad.

One of the candidates was 26-year-old Jake McAllister, a balding tackle from Okmulgee who in 1941 had strayed away to Alabama for his freshman season then put in 40 months overseas with the combat engineers battling the Japanese. For half an hour McAllister watched the proceedings with a mingling of amusement and disgust. Finally his turn came. Facing his opponent, he took his stance.

"Hit that guy," directed George Radman, one of Tatum's young lieutenants, pointing at McAllister's opponent. McAllister wiped him out.

"What's your name?" Radman asked. Pencil poised, he hurried to Mc-Allister's side.

"My name's Jake McAllister," replied the veteran. "What's yours?"

The laughter rang out merrily. Radman's, too. The incident eased some of the tension.

Brewer, Burris, Greathouse, Thomas, Mitchell, Dinkins, and West were only a few of the standouts Tatum brought to Norman with recruiting tenacity that bordered on the fantastic. But his prize catch of all wasn't even a player. He was the Sooners' backfield coach, a tall young Minnesotan everybody called Bud.

Bud Wilkinson's parents were Charles Patton Wilkinson, a successful Minneapolis real-estate mortgage dealer, and Edith Lindbloom Wilkinson, a Swedish girl who with her sister was brought to the United States when she was quite young. Bud's given name was also Charles, but his middle name was Burnham, and "the Burnham kind of got changed into Bud," the coach explained later.

His father (hereafter referred to as C. P.) was English and Scotch-Irish. His paternal grandfather, William Alfred Wilkinson, was a successful builder of sawmills through the upper Middle West and also patented inventions for improving sawmill equipment. Tim Cohane researched much of this early phase of the Wilkinson family history.[2] He writes, "I suspect that it is from his grandfather that Bud derived much of his inventiveness as a coach, and from both his father and his grandfather his tremendous organizational qualities and dedication to excel."

From his mother, Edith, Bud got his handsomeness. His probing blue eyes were his father's; however, he looked very much like his mother and she was blue-eyed, too. Edith was very industrious and at one time held two jobs, working both as a secretary and as a style model. When Bud grew up he, too, was seldom without two jobs, sometimes more.

His father, C. P., was a dominant person who was described by Bud's late brother, Bill, as "a charger." For much of the last two decades of his life he suffered from reduced peripheral vision, but that did not slow him in the slightest or prevent him from driving his own car.

Bud lived in an upper-middle-class home in an attractive residential area of south Minneapolis. Next door on the left lived his paternal grandparents.

---

[2]Cohane declares that his most helpful source on Bud Wilkinson's early family life was Mary Wilkinson, the widow of Bud's brother, Bill, whom he interviewed in Minneapolis. Not only did she introduce him to Bud's stepmother, Ethel, but she drove him to Faribault, Minnesota, home of Shattuck Military Academy, where Bud had attended prep school.

From the maiden name of his maternal grandmother, Mary Lydia Burnham Wilkinson, Bud got his middle name. On the right lived his mother's sister, Florence Pinger.

When Bud was eight, his mother, Edith, died. Her death resulted from a train accident complicated by a heart-liver ailment. C. P., who was deeply in love with her, was terribly shocked. In due time, however, he wooed and won a second wife, Ethel Grace. A delightful person, Ethel Grace had to take over the Wilkinson home with Wilkinson relatives and in-laws all around her. Despite being under constant inspection, she proved adequate to all tests. Between Ethel and her stepsons, Bud and Bill, a warm rapport grew.

Ethel recalls that as a youngster Bud had not yet developed the coordination that later made him a standout athlete. He often dropped dishes and tumblers while helping set the table. He became handy, however, at concocting homemade ice cream, handier still at eating it. Incidentally, the C. P. Wilkinson home was one of the last in Minneapolis to install an electric refrigerator. C. P. blocked the purchase for years with the remarkable explanation that "these mechanical things usually don't work."

C. P. loved music. Edith was a soloist in a church choir. Later the father and two sons often serenaded Ethel with their harmonizing. They were especially partial to "She Was Only a Bird in a Gilded Cage." After Bud began coaching at Norman, he and C. P. sometimes greeted each other by bursting into the refrain of "Oklahoma!"

When Bud was thirteen, he was enrolled at Shattuck Military Academy, in Faribault, Minnesota, fifty miles south of Minneapolis. During his first few weeks there he suffered all the keen loneliness of a youngster living away from home for the first time. It was the custom on Sunday for families to pack a picnic lunch and drive to the academy to visit their sons. During the first visit of the Wilkinson clan Bud cried, and Mary Wilkinson, his grandmother, said, "We should take the boy home." C. P. took Bud aside that first Sunday and talked to him sternly. And Bud stayed.

When he began playing football at Shattuck, Bud quickly forgot his homesickness. He began as a second-string center on the Badger intramural team but quickly developed into a signal-calling tackle on the academy eleven, which was coached by Carl A. Anderson. At Shattuck, "Wilky," as he was called there, captained the 1932 football team and also won four letters at center field on the baseball team and three as goalie on the ice-hockey team. He played center on the basketball team his senior year. In addition, he was graduated cum laude, became a first lieutenant in the cadet battalion, vice-president of his class, and business manager of the yearbook and had a part in the senior play.

Wilkinson played his college football at the University of Minnesota. Those were the middle 1930s, when Coach B. W. ("Bernie") Bierman's hard-twisted Gophers won the national collegiate championship all three years Wilkinson played. Bud was a guard in 1934 and 1935, but as a senior in 1936 was moved to blocking back and signal caller in Bierman's single-wingback formation. He also played defensive halfback.

Bud's football intelligence was proved in the 1936 Minnesota-Washington game, his first at quarterback. The score was tied 7-7. It was late in the fourth quarter. He called a running play. Coming out of the huddle, he saw that Washington, expecting it, had drawn in its defense. So Wilkinson checked signals, and Andy Uram pegged to Ray King for the winning touchdown. Later Bierman described this play as a "fine example of a quarterback's keen observation."[3]

Bierman's system emphasized drive and power. His boys crashed on every play, always hitting somebody in the foe array. They aimed to punish the enemy with everything they had, wearing him down for the kill late in the game. If you stopped Bierman's inside stuff and his weak-side stuff, you'd stop him because that was where he liked to go. His teams threw perhaps ten passes a game and averaged hitting six. He used only sixteen men in the tough games. In a cold climate he could do that; in Oklahoma's southwestern heat, it would not have been possible.

Bierman's men weren't big, the line about 200 pounds and backs 190, but they were superbly conditioned. In practice he drove them to the point of quitting. When the weather was bad, they worked indoors on the soft dirt of the Minnesota fieldhouse. He'd line them up and blow his whistle. They sprinted hard until he blew it again, when they trotted to the wall. When they turned around, they were greeted by another toot of that maddening whistle and repeated the maneuver.

After he had sprinted them into virtual exhaustion, Bierman would say, "Well, let's relax a little and jog," and they would trot around and around the enclosure. When they became spent from doing that, he would say, "Well, can anybody here still sprint a little?" and start the dashes again. They would do this over and over until they were on the verge of mutiny. But they never mutinied. Finally, being driven relentlessly to promote their own condition became fun. They learned to take it.[4]

[3] B. W. Bierman, *Winning Football* (New York, 1941), p. 171.
[4] Bud Wilkinson to author, August 30, 1946.

11

Wilkinson recalls the evening training-table meals at Minnesota. He remembers the scholarship job they got him at a men's clothing store and says that he really worked his hours there. He doesn't remember what he was paid. At Minnesota, Wilkinson also played goalie on the ice-hockey team, captained the golf team, and won the Minnesota Big Ten medal as the outstanding senior in scholarship and athletics. He also learned to play handball by squaring off against George Quam, who was born with only one arm yet twice became a semifinalist in the national championships.

As a graduate in 1937, Wilkinson quarterbacked the College All Stars to their first victory of all time at Chicago's Soldier's Field over the professional champions, the Green Bay Packers. The hero of the game, in Bud's view, was Johnny Drake, Purdue back, who covered Don Hutson, Green Bay's fine pass receiver, holding him scoreless. In a column written by Hal Middlesworth, sports editor of the *Daily Oklahoman,* Wilkinson also praised Sammy Baugh, the Texas Christian forward passer.

"We scored the only touchdown on a pass, Baugh to Gaynell Tinsley" (Tinsley later became the Louisiana State coach whose team Oklahoma met in the 1950 Sugar Bowl), Wilkinson recalled: "Baugh was superb. I've never seen a passer like him. All he wanted was four men down, and he'd take care of the rest. If one receiver was covered, Sammy was very apt to pass to another. His great gift was spotting an open receiver.

"I remember late in the game we were on our forty-five-yard line with only a few seconds left to play. It was second down and one yard to go, a good time to pass. So we called a pass. I was the blocking back, and blocking backs are rarely thrown to. So when the ball was snapped I faded out into the left flat and trotted down the sideline, hoping to stay out of the way of our regular receivers.

"Suddenly some sixth sense made me look up. There was the ball, looking me right in the eye. I had to catch it to keep from getting hit in the face. That's how Baugh could throw."

Wilkinson revered Bierman, his Minnesota coach. "He was honest, forthright, and the hardest-working individual I have ever known. He wasted less time than any coach I ever saw. There never was a greater coach."

Meanwhile, Ossie Solem, the Iowa coach, became so impressed with Wilkinson's quarterbacking in the 1936 Iowa-Minnesota game that when he took the coaching job at Syracuse he hired Wilkinson as an assistant. Bud stayed four seasons with the Orangemen. He developed a tremendous respect for Solem, one of the few coaches who abided by both the spirit and the letter of recruiting and subsidy rules. Bud did the same thing later to a remarkable degree at Oklahoma.

Phil Allen, one of Wilkinson's ends at Syracuse, says that Bud was "just out of Minnesota and was, more or less, our age and able to communicate better with us than the older coaches." He added, "I don't know if it was Bud's idea or Ossie Solem's, but halfway through Bud's first season during home games he would go into the gym, which was behind the end zone at Archbold Stadium, and phone information down regarding the opponent's offense and defense."[5]

Bierman frowned on posting an assistant coach in the press box to scout the opposition. "I feel I get more accurate information from sources closer to the field," he wrote in *Winning Football.*[6] Bob Zuppke, veteran Illinois coach, also made sport of the custom. "Why put football coaches in the grandstand?" Zuppke asked. "The game's greatest strategists are already there." But Phil Allen is sure that Bud's upstairs surveillance "won the Penn State game for us that year." Today, of course, the custom is widespread.

Allen also credits Wilkinson with teaching him and Wilmeth Sidat-Singh, Syracuse's skilled black halfback from Harlem, a play they called the pivot pass. In those days offensive ends ran directly at a halfback and then suddenly cut in over the middle or broke to the outside. Allen says: "Bud taught Wilmeth and me that I should run at the halfback, then stop and turn around directly in front of him. Wilmeth would fake his throw. I would then turn and run by the halfback and Wilmeth would throw over his head to me. This worked for a number of touchdowns and long gainers."

Earlier, at the University of Minnesota, Bud had met Mary Shifflett, who had transferred from Carleton College. She was the daughter of Glenn Shifflett, a Grinnell, Iowa, lawyer. On August 27, 1938, they were married at her home in Grinnell. After Bud accepted the Syracuse job, Mary was graduated from Syracuse with a B.A. in philosophy. They had two sons, Pat, born August 16, 1940, and Jay, born April 11, 1942. At Syracuse, Bud also earned a master's degree in English (his B.A. from Minnesota was in English).

In 1941 Bud left Syracuse and went into the navy preflight program—but not until he'd had a tiff with his father, who wanted him in his mortgage investment business. Sensing Bud's growing interest in coaching, C. P. called his friend Charlie Johnson, executive sports editor of the *Minneapolis Star and Tribune,* and asked him to take Bud to lunch and try to talk him out of coaching. Johnson arranged the luncheon.

No sooner had they sat down than Bud grinned and said in his friendli-

[5] Phil Allen to author, November 26, 1980.
[6] Bierman, *Winning Football,* p. 153.

est manner, "Charlie, if the idea of this luncheon is my father's, to try to talk me out of coaching, forget about it, and let's enjoy the food. I've made up my mind that coaching is what I want to do."

Then came the war. Although Wilkinson as a prep schooler had leaned toward the army because of his matriculation at Shattuck, when he enlisted for World War II, he chose the navy and became a hangar-deck officer on the aircraft carrier *Enterprise.*

First, however, he went to Iowa Pre-Flight, where he tutored the centers and quarterbacks on the nationally famous Iowa Pre-Flight Seahawks coached by Don Faurot, of Missouri. Jim Tatum, of North Carolina, whom Wilkinson had met when Tatum was an assistant coach at Cornell while Bud was at Syracuse, became Faurot's line coach. That's where Wilkinson and Tatum were introduced to the new split-T formation taught by the man who devised it, Faurot. They couldn't have had a finer teacher.

During the war Wilkinson saw action in the engagements at Iwo Jima, Tokyo, Kyūshū, and Okinawa. The commanding officer of the *Enterprise* commended Wilkinson for his high performance of duty on May 14, 1945, while his ship was under attack and had been hit by the enemy. He "organized fire-fighting equipment and men in a most efficient manner, thereby enabling the fires to be brought under control quickly," the citation read.

Early in 1946, after his discharge from the service, Wilkinson acquiesced temporarily to C. P.'s wishes and joined him and brother Bill in the investment business. But it was much too pedestrian a life for Bud.

In the meantime, after coaching the Jacksonville, Florida, Naval Air Station Jax Fliers to an 8-2 season, Tatum worked hard to get the Oklahoma job, which had become available with the resignation of Snorter Luster, who was too ill to continue coaching. In his five years as Sooner mentor, Luster had won two Big Six Conference championships and never finished lower than second.

When Tatum was invited to come to Norman for an interview, he asked whether he could bring with him a young man whom he would like to hire as assistant coach, Charles ("Bud") Wilkinson. Permission was granted. Both men came. President George Cross and the regents were very much impressed by Wilkinson. They offered the head coaching job to Tatum but attached the condition that he bring Wilkinson to Oklahoma as assistant coach. After some fencing, Tatum agreed.

C. P. knew that he was licked. Too good a strategist not to beat a dignified retreat, he took Tatum hunting and even professed to be enthusiastic about Bud's decision. Yet a decade later C. P. remarked to a friend, "I wonder when my son will get over this impulse to coach football."

14

Although Wilkinson, while at Iowa Pre-Flight, was aware that cadets regarded Norman, Oklahoma, as their least desirable option when selecting their preference in flight stations, the young coach discovered that impression to be totally erroneous and found Norman "a beautiful town."

Vitalized by Tatum's recruiting, Oklahoma in 1946 finished 8-3, losing only to Army, Texas, and Kansas and playing terrifically against all three. The Sooners defeated North Carolina State 34-13 in the Gator Bowl. Tatum's defense against rushing topped the nation that year with its average yield of 58 yards a game. Faurot knew whereof he spoke when he said that Big Jim was "the best recruiter and defensive coach I ever saw."

Tatum ran a wide-open show at Oklahoma. Tim Cohane says that "the postwar atmosphere encouraged a liberal approach in everything. Big Jim, a complete individualist, was never known to be neurotic over ethics or the feelings of others." When Maryland offered him its head job—he jockeyed both Maryland and Oklahoma into raising their salary offers before going to the Terrapins—he had left the Oklahoma department in considerable disarray.

It was then that President Cross offered Wilkinson the job of head football coach at Oklahoma. When the regents dismissed the popular Lawrence ("Jap") Haskell as athletic director for permitting Tatum to spend departmental funds recklessly, President Cross asked that Wilkinson be named interim athletic director until a full-time director could be hired. The regents approved.

Yet the university owed a debt to Tatum, the big North Carolinian, not only for bringing Wilkinson to Norman but also for personally recruiting the flower of the state's four-year accumulation of playing talent back from World War II. For his first three years as head coach Wilkinson would have this nucleus from which to structure his Oklahoma program.

2. "GENERAL JACK"

Bud Wilkinson was a big, blond, articulate man with a soft, modulated voice and a smile that would charm the birds out of the trees. When he was standing talking with somebody, he would sometimes shuffle his feet, bob his head, and, clasping his hands in front of him, rub them softly together. You felt comfortable in his presence and drawn to him even before you were introduced.

On the sideline at games he usually wore a gray flannel suit, a white oxford cloth shirt with a button-down collar, a red four-in-hand tie, and a snap-brim hat. If the sideline was muddy, he wore black coaching shoes with cleats. The players called him "the Great White Father," though he was only a few years older than they.

"He insisted upon perfection," remembers guard Norman McNabb. "Mediocrity was a dirty word to him. His players were disciplined and unselfish, a brotherhood I've never seen equaled." Stan West, another guard, says, "He always had us extremely well prepared. His practices were short, about 1:45 to 2:15, and no waste motion. You were always going." End Bobby Goad says, "The overall intensity he put into his work was contagious. He was a man in a hurry, disciplined, highly organized."

The new head coach had excellent relations with the returned war veterans. He never set a curfew during the week; he knew when to be insistent and when to close his eyes. "We'd all been to war," points out Stan West, "and we knew we had to obey the man at the top."

Wilkinson believed very thoroughly in players continuously pushing themselves to physical limits they never dreamed they possessed. Every team he coached was taught the value of excruciating effort. "Remember," he told his Oklahoma teams, "that it's been medically proven that when your body is telling you to quit, you have gone only half as far as you can go."

Although Wilkinson's silky offenses would soon become the talk of the nation, defense was the game's most important element in his view. "I have always felt that defense was the key to winning," he declares. "If you play sound defense and couple this with a fine kicking game, you will be able to control field position. You can then scratch around on offense and put some points on the board."[1]

Jack Mitchell, Wilkinson's first quarterback at Oklahoma, once said,

16

"I could always tell when he was really worried about a game because then we'd work hard all week on kicking and defense."

Wilkinson's first task was to engage a line coach. He chose Gomer Jones whose Nebraska line had given Tatum's Sooners their toughest opposition in the conference. Jones had played center for Coach Francis Schmidt of Ohio State. Wilkinson had known Jones in the navy. "I was very impressed with Gomer and all the things we had in common," he says.

Gomer, as the Sooner players called him, was a short, thick-necked, 210-pounder whose round shoulders sloped a trifle forward as he walked with short, fast, purposeful steps. He had alert blue eyes, curly hair, and wore horn-rimmed spectacles with crystal fronts and black temples. A superb tactician, Jones wouldn't let his linemen free-lance. Everything had a special skill or technique. On the practice field he donned a red baseball cap and a red jacket.

"If you did good, he'd tell you on the field in front of everybody," says tackle Willie Manley. "If you fouled up, he'd snatch that baseball cap off his head and throw it on the ground. 'Run the play over!' he would order in a hoarse, raspy growl."

"You know a boy's got it, but how do you get it out of him?" he once described a coach's biggest problem.

Jones quickly won the hearts of the Sooner forwards. "We all loved the guy," says left tackle Homer Paine. Guard Stan West rated him a "great, great coach and a great, great guy. He taught me more technique than I ever thought about learning from the pros." Norman McNabb remembers, "He wanted every guy he coached to love him like a brother or a dad, and we all did." Pete Tillman says, "He was a super individual, a quiet, dedicated, loyal assistant to Bud."

The most plainspoken man on the squad was guard Buddy Burris. He was very frank and not always diplomatic. If you'd had a bad game, he might walk up to you in front of everybody and say, "You didn't play too well last week, did you?" Or he might even harpoon himself. "I didn't play well last week," he might say. And then give you the details.

One of the first things Burris did in fall workouts was get crossed with the new line coach, Gomer Jones. "Here I was already a football player, and he was from Nebraska, and he was trying to change my stance," Burris laughs today. "He didn't like my feet being so far apart on offense. I was stubborn but he stayed with me. 'Try it my way for two or three weeks,' he said, 'then if you still don't like it, we'll go back to your way.'

---

[1] Bud Wilkinson to author, June 20, 1980.

"So I did it his way and found that I had better lateral control, better balance, and a little more power straight ahead. I found out Gomer was a good old boy. I'm the type that can't like a guy too soon anyhow. They have to prove themselves to me."

Another of Wilkinson's first acts was to raise Bill Jennings, a Tatum student assistant, to full coaching status and use him heavily as a recruiter. After the Big Six freshman rule had been voted back into effect May 1, Oklahoma again started signing high-school players. "Texas shut us out in their state in 1947," Jennings remembers. "We had a tough hassle with Oklahoma A&M for Oklahoma boys, too. When we began winning on the field, the recruiting got easier, especially in West Texas."

In 1947, Wilkinson was not yet thoroughly acquainted with Texas geography. "I'm going to Wichita Falls to see a boy," Jennings once said in staff meeting.

"Good," said Wilkinson. "On your way back stop off at Amarillo and see . . . ."

"And Tatum was just as bad," Jennings laughs today. But both learned quickly.

One of Jennings's best hauls was at Hollis when he snared both Leon Heath and J. W. Cole. "Another Hollis kid, Ted Owens, wanted to come so badly that I got him a job at McCall's Grocery in Norman," Jennings says. "Bruce Drake, our basketball coach, soon learned that Owens could play that game, so he was glad to take him over." Later Owens became basketball coach at the University of Kansas.

Seven years earlier the Sooner marching band, directed by Professor William R. Wehrend, unknowingly recruited still another Hollis player, a 12-year-old grade-schooler, for the Sooners. It happened in the late 1930s when Coach Tom Stidham's Sooner powerhouses ran rampant.

The grade-schooler waited eagerly for those Saturday afternoon games at Norman. "I'd put a radio on our front porch at Hollis and have me a solo game in our front yard," he says today. "The play-by-play of the OU game wasn't so important, but that 'Boomer Sooner' played by the Oklahoma marching band was. It lifted me right out of my socks. I thought they were playing it for me while I was having this game all by myself out in our front yard. Jump those fire hydrants! Dodge those trees! When I got older I wasn't hard for Oklahoma to recruit even if Jack Baer was the only man from the Sooner staff who came to Hollis to see me." Baer got a good one while he was at it. The twelve-year-old's name was Darrell Royal.

Thirty-one of Wilkinson's top 33 players, including Royal, were war

veterans, a situation common all around the nation. Most of Oklahoma's were older, married men who wanted an education. The war was behind them now and they wanted to get on with their lives. But they loved football so passionately that during a summer volleyball game they would run around the net and elbow each other.

Pass defense was Royal's dish. He liked to cover the ends coming down. He had learned the art in 1945 from Bob Andridge, the old Tennessee star, while playing as a substitute for the Third Army Air Force team of Tampa, Florida. Andridge showed Royal how to stay agile and nimble, how to change direction right and left while retreating swiftly. "I learned that if I lost half a step backing up, the receiver would be open," Royal recalls today.

Royal never forgot Andridge's teaching. Before every Oklahoma game or practice session, he would warm up in reverse gear by going through all the correct retreating action. He still holds the all-time Oklahoma school record for intercepting enemy passes, 15 for three seasons, 17 for four.

The most determined scholar on the football squad was Ken Tipps, who had played at Wilson High School and Oklahoma City Central. In 1946, the Tatum year, Tipps was enrolled at OU but did not play football. "I thought I was too old and too busy," he explains. After four years as a bombardier-navigator on B-29s in Guam and the Pacific theater, he wanted "to get on with my profession" as he puts it.

As a matter of fact, he had already got on with it. Married and twenty-six years old, Tipps was majoring in petroleum engineering and working on a Phillips Petroleum Company oil rig besides. The derrick was near Maysville, and Tipps was driving to his job 150 miles daily, round trip, seven days and nights a week. Despite the lack of study time, he made good grades.

"But in Oklahoma you grow up with football from the second grade on," Tipps says today. "I knew I was missing something. When Bud became the coach I let Tyree, Plato, and the others talk me into coming out. I still worked eight months a year on the oil rig and graduated in three and one-half years, but I didn't have much time to study. I listened."

Fullback Eddy Davis was wounded in the Battle of the Rhineland, tripping a Nazi land mine and suffering injuries to his right hip. For six months he lay in various army hospitals, but when the war ended, he returned to Norman, enrolled in the University, bought a half interest in a restaurant, and eating his own steaks, averaged 8.5 net yards per carry through the last six games of 1946.

Another Sooner who had a singular connection with cooking was De-

19

mosthenes Andros, right guard from Oklahoma City Central High School. Enlisting in the marines, Dee became a field cook and won the Bronze Star at Iwo Jima for heroism beyond the call of duty. Taking off his apron, he helped wipe out three Japanese gun emplacements.

Big John Rapacz, of Kalamazoo, Michigan, Wilkinson's first Sooner center, found size a handicap in the war. When his marine outfit stormed the tiny island of Roi in the southwest Pacific, Jap bombers began seeking them out. In less than five minutes Rapacz dug himself a foxhole as big as a buffalo wallow and lost no time scrambling into it.

The prize walk-on of the squad was Wilbur ("Buddy") Jones, who weighed only 155 pounds. Jones had a brilliant high-school football career at Maud and Holdenville. After a tour in the navy he was offered football scholarships by Tulsa and Oklahoma A&M, but no offer came from Oklahoma. Wanting a geology degree, he came to Norman anyhow, trying for a track scholarship.

Although Jones emerged from the war unscathed, he nearly became a fatality in the pole vault. His aluminum pole broke, and down went Jones between the jagged points. He could have been impaled. Landing flat, he had the breath driven from his body. John Jacobs, the Sooner track coach, who always saw humor in everything, said mildly, "Buddy, those aluminum poles are pretty expensive. Wish you'd be more careful about breaking them."

When Wilkinson became football coach in 1947, he opened practice to all comers. "Somebody in my history class talked me into going out," says Jones today. Jones blocked and tackled so furiously that Wilkinson quickly gave him a scholarship.

The smallest gladiator in the starting line was Bobby Goad, right end from Muskogee. Sensitive about his lightness, he came to me before the 1947 fall practice and asked me to list his brochure weight at 175 pounds, though all he actually hefted was 160. He was afraid the coaches might find out his true weight and not play him. I was glad to accommodate him.

"Too small to be a football player, but nobody ever told him," was Stan West's chuckled characterization of Goad. "Boy, he wanted to play! And he *did* play!"

Others wanted to play too. There was tackle Wade Walker, one of the captains. Walker was a finesse player. He could tie up his man with a high block in the hole, then vamoose into the secondary for deadly down-field duty. He was cranky about speed. To help get it, he wore light back-field shoes. Each fall he'd ask Sarge Dempsey, OU equipment man, for "low quarters," as he called them. He was probably the only lineman in the United States wearing low-top shoes. Walker never wore hip pads either until manufacturers began building them into the playing pants. Then Wilkinson made him wear them.

Of Walker, Stan West said, "I had the reputation of being the laziest man of all in our calisthenics drills, but I was chain lightning compared to him. 'Lord,' Wade used to say, 'you get warm enough out here anyhow.'"

Norman McNabb, the guard from Norman, was three years a marine and saw some savage fighting at Saipan and Iwo Jima. His only wound was a skin burn across the back. "All they gave me for it was a couple of jiggers of brandy," he remembers. McNabb played two years of service football with the Fourth Marine Division. Jap Haskell, the Sooner athletic director, wrote him once a month all the time he was in service. "He was like a dad to me," says McNabb.

Homer Paine, Enid tackle, who had transferred from Tulsa University, was the luckiest of all the returning war veterans. A football injury probably saved his life. Before the war Paine had lamed a knee in a high-school game, nursed it carefully through a freshman season at Tulsa University, then injured it again after entering the army. He was transferred from the infantry to an antitank unit, where everybody rode instead of walked. Later, in the Battle of the Bulge, Paine's old infantry outfit, the 99th, lost nearly all its 200-man unit. All but 7 were killed, wounded, or taken prisoner. Paine's knee held up fine for the Sooners.

Earl Hale, who had played six-man football at Markham, Texas, and Nute Trotter, of Borger, Texas, also reported. The Sooners returned their two-man ambush that in 1946 had overpowered an Army punt for a touchdown, McNabb, who blocked it, and tackle Bill Morris, who fell on it behind the Cadet goal. Tatum had also persuaded Charles Sarratt, a rugged halfback from Belton, South Carolina, to leave Clemson and join him at Oklahoma. In Oklahoma's Gator Bowl victory, Sarratt passed to Jim Owens for one touchdown, threw a long pass to Merle Dinkins to set up another, and ran 54 yards to a third touchdown on a play recalled by penalty.

"We didn't have any poor athletes," says Bobby Goad.

Before the war Stan West's brother, Cooper, went to college at Northwestern Normal, at Alva, and while there acquired a pair of secondhand football shoes, which he gave to Stan. "I loved these old brogans," West says today. "They had oblong leather cleats. I even wore those old things to milk in."

The oldest of the 1947 freshmen was Harry Moore, center from Blackwell. There was reason for his late arrival at the University. In 1940 his father died, and Moore worked two years at the zinc smelter caring for his mother and two sisters. In 1942 he enlisted in the marines and served on the USS *Idaho,* which was very busy with the Japanese. Moore became

21

the admiral's orderly. A first lieutenant marine torpedo plane pilot at his discharge, Moore wanted two things: (1) petroleum engineering and (2) football. So he came to Norman.

The offensive formation off which Oklahoma operated was the split-T, originated by Don Faurot of Missouri, a coach from Oklahoma's own conference, then the Big Six. Faurot first loosed it on opponents in 1941, and his Tigers that year led the nation in rushing, won the Big Six championship, and played in the rain-drenched Sugar Bowl.

Previously the only splitting of offensive linemen was done by offensive ends, who varied the distance they lined up outside their tackle. Faurot's idea of moving his guards away from the center and his tackles away from his guards forced the defense to spread out too, giving the split-T blockers the angle and creating the seams through which the split-T backs could gush. The duty of the blockers was to meet the opponent high in the hole, just hooking him and standing him off while the ballcarrier zipped past.

The nicety of the new formation lay in its handoff. The halfback had to learn to take the ball from the quarterback by feel, without looking at it, and concentrate instead on watching the blocking develop in front of him. The quarterback placed the ball in the halfback's hands as the latter whizzed past looking for the open route. The offense hit the hole so quickly that its offside linemen, those on the opposite side of the center, only shadowed their opponents, then swung across field to block downfield ahead of the play.

Players sometimes contrived techniques. The refinement of the split-T block used by Oklahoma was developed in 1946 by Wade Walker, youthful right tackle from Gastonia, North Carolina, hub man of Tatum's Sooner blocking shield. Always leading with the shoulder and foot on the same side, a simultaneous movement that propelled him squarely into the middle of his opponent, Walker opened the hole at a definite place or stuck his head in the middle of the defensive man and took him the way he wanted to go.

"The secret of the split-T was the charge count, beating the other side to the jump," says Walker. "Hut-two! Hut-two! Hut-two! Every one of our practices started off with 20 to 25 minutes of starts and stances. We did it against live bait or with the dummies or in the open field. But we darned sure did it. Every signal drill was full speed."

"I loved it," said Merle Dinkins. "It gave you so much angle on the blocking. You just brushed your man, and if you did it right, your ball carrier was through the line and gone." Center Alonzo ("Pete") Tillman liked it too. "I didn't have my head down between my legs all the time," he remembers. "I could watch the man on my nose and block him easier. The snap was just a lift, not a throw."

The most discouraging thing about fall practice was that Wilkinson's first Oklahoma team had lost two fine players to professional football, halfback Joe Golding and guard Plato Andros, each a second-team All-American. Each would have had two years left of college football. Warren Giese, All-Conference end, did not return either. The most cheerful aspect was that the Sooners had gone back to Ma's cooking. Mrs. A. S. ("Ma") Richter, famous on the campus for her family-style meals, fed the Sooners at training table.

Detroit, Oklahoma's first opponent, held two advantages. Coach Chuck Baer's Titans had started workouts two weeks ahead of Oklahoma, which could not begin until August 30 because of Big Six Conference rules. Also, the Titans scheduled a game a week before they met the Sooners. Detroit was destined to lead the nation that year in rushing with 319.7 net yards a contest.

In their dressing room at the Detroit stadium the Sooners sat quietly on benches along the wall. Outside, the small stadium was jammed with 25,375 fans, many of whom sat 8 and 10 deep in chairs around the playing field. Several hundred Sooner supporters had come on a special train.

Bud and Gomer were sitting together on a wooden bench off to one side of the dressing room, staring gloomily at the floor while they awaited the call to battle on the rough, poorly mowed field. The expression on their faces reminded me of something that Donn Byrne, the Irish author, once wrote. Byrne said that nobody is as lonely as the fighting man who stands alone in his corner of the ring, his seconds having just climbed out, waiting for the bell that starts the first round. Bud and Gomer looked exactly the same way.

It had been Bud's idea that fall to write on each Sunday after an OU game a newsletter about the game to our alumni all over the nation. The report was sponsored by our alumni association and went to all paid-up members. It was my duty to phone him each Sunday morning, write down his comments, then, leaning heavily on the play-by-play I had typed in the press box, blend the whole into an account of the game. I always showed it to Bud before giving it to the printers Sunday afternoon so that it could be dispatched promptly by mail to our alumni. I was careful to weave the feats of linemen as well as backs into the account, especially their vital blocks and tackles. I got this information by talking to them on our team plane coming home Saturday night after each game. If it was a

Norman game, I would go to their dormitory and find them.

Burris kicked off, and after Rapacz and John Husak, junior guard from Curwensville, Pennsylvania, piled Detroit plays, the Titans punted, and it was Oklahoma's ball on its 32. Then the Sooners gave their new coach an unforgettable thrill when they moved 68 yards for a touchdown. Royal's darts behind blocks by Walker and Goad and Mitchell's sneaks behind the blocking of guards Dee Andros and Buddy Burris and center John Rapacz were vital. Mitchell swung around end for the touchdown.

In Jack Mitchell, Wilkinson had an extraordinary quarterback who could take his team down the field and score. John Cronley, *Daily Oklahoman* sports editor, would later pin a new nickname on Mitchell, "General Jack." A gaunt-cheeked, Roman-nosed, low-slung, 175-pounder, Mitchell seemed to move the team by the force of his personality. He had other talents too. He was Oklahoma's finest quarterback runner of the Wilkinson regime and also its best punt runbacker. He wasn't above doing a little persuading of his own in the huddles.

"Twenty-two on two," he would announce positively to the circle of sweaty faces. Then he might turn to Plato Andros, mighty Greek guard. "Plato, this play depends entirely on you. If you knock your man out of there, this touchdown will be yours."

Mitchell always had control of his team. He had their confidence, too. He called signals in a sharp, insistent, far-carrying voice. Even when he called a bad one, which was seldom, the other players thought it was their fault if the play failed. They didn't think Mitchell could call a bad one.

Off the field Jack was an extrovert and a natural psychologist. You could hear his belly laugh clear down to the campus corner. He always laughed loudest when he himself was the goat of some quip or wisecrack. He was a sharp dresser, usually going around in slacks, white bucks, and a white sports shirt open at the throat.

As a runner the best thing Mitchell did was go at full speed toward the sideline, as if running up against a wall. At the last second he would cut at almost a 90-degree angle by first digging his heel in the grass and pushing off downfield. The key to this was to plant the heel—not the toe— in the grassy turf, the only playing surface available at that time.

He had an interesting variety of ball-carrying tricks. He could fake one way and go another. He could fake one way and without losing momentum continue in the same direction. Or he could start fast toward the left side-line as if running around a tackler, then baffle the opponents by retreating left in a big half circle back toward his own goal and continue circling until he got strung out down the opposite sideline. Giving a little ground to gain a lot, he could do this to either right or left.

24

Tough and underrated, Detroit countered with a 56-yard run down the left sideline on a fake handoff, and the score stood 7-7. The Sooners kept going out in front, 10-7 on Dave Wallace's 23-yard field goal and 17-7, when Mitchell plucked a punt out of the sky, crossed the field laterally, faked a handoff to Charley Sarratt, and dashed 60 yards to score. Detroit pulled up to 17-14 on a 41-yard run by Len Rittof. Mitchell bubbled 15 and 10 yards on sneaks to the Titan 1, from which Sarratt boomed over for the decisive touchdown, Oklahoma leading 24-14.

Kaysserian of Detroit bucked across their final touchdown. When Jim Owens blocked the conversion, the Sooners had won 24-20.

"Some old Detroit boy was beating me with his fists," remembers Buddy Burris. "He knocked my tooth out, bloodied my nose. I had to call time. The game went on. I hit him three times with my fist. He fell. Our guys grabbed me. He had it coming but nobody knew it but him and me. He'd been following me everywhere. Bud jerked me off the field, made me sit on the end of the bench. "'I thought you were smarter than that,' Bud said. But he apologized to me Monday when he saw the films."

In his Monday noon talk before the Oklahoma City Quarterback Club, Wilkinson revealed a coaching error that few had seen. When Myrle Greathouse, Sooner fullback, came to the sideline for a chin strap, Kurkowski of Detroit ran 56 yards to a touchdown. Wilkinson took the blame. "Typical behavior by a starting coach," Bud disclosed. "We had only ten men on the field."

The Detroit game showed what Wilkinson's sideline behavior would be for the next seventeen seasons. The new Sooner mentor paced the sidelines tirelessly, staying on top of the action. Sam Lyle, a later Sooner assistant coach, said of Wilkinson, "Bud is the greatest leader on the field I ever saw. Many coaches tell their boys, 'I can get you ready five days a week but what you do on Saturday is up to you.'

"Bud led on Saturday too. His Oklahoma boys knew he was with them every second of the game. They could see it in his sideline demeanor. They reflected his burning interest with their own trick of kneeling along the sideline behind him and rooting for their team on the field."[2]

Rallying from behind an eight-point deficit, Oklahoma defeated Texas A&M, coached by Homer Norton, 24-14. Oklahoma led 6-0 when quarterback Jack Mitchell flipped a buck pass to Bobby Goad. Then Norton's Cadets pulled ahead 14-6.

The rest of the game belonged to Oklahoma. Royal lateraled to Mitchell, who ran 33 yards for a touchdown, with Jim Owens rubbing out the last

[2] Sam Lyle to author, November 3, 1955.

tackler on the 5-yard line. Then George Thomas hit off tackle behind Walker and Goad for 3 yards and another touchdown. Mitchell passed to George Brewer for 24 and the finale. John Rapacz, Oklahoma's big center, intercepted two passes and recovered a fumble, and Oklahoma had the victory, 26-14.

That took the Sooners to the Texas game in the Dallas Cotton Bowl. Coach Blair Cherry's Longhorns had overwhelmed Texas Tech 33-0 and Oregon 38-13 and had just scored the nation's number 1 upset with a 34-0 annihilation of North Carolina, ranked number 7 in the polls. Oklahoma hadn't beaten Texas for seven seasons. Bob Sumter, Oklahoma's Indian tackle of 1926, put it well when he said, "It has been a bloody thing each year, with us furnishing the blood. We're the ones in the Alamo."

The 1947 Texas-Oklahoma game, and its altercation involving the officiating of referee Jack Sisco, has never been told from the viewpoint of the Oklahoma players on the field.

"Early in the fourth quarter, Texas was on our 40," recalls guard Buddy Burris. "Bobby Layne, their passer, dropped back to throw. West and I rushed him but I was in front and hit him just as he threw the ball. I hit him clean. Layne was tough. He just jumped up, grinning. But down the field Royal intercepted the pass, and when the referee hung a penalty on me for roughing Layne, we lost the interception and the ball too, and Texas went on down and scored."

Another Longhorn touchdown is still argued. With the clock showing that the first-half time had expired, Texas had failed to score. Before the game it had been agreed that the Cotton Bowl clock would be the official one. However, Sisco quite properly ruled that Texas had time for one more play, explaining that Texas had sued for time out with three seconds left and that there was no way to so inform the clock-keeper.

Bobby Goad, Oklahoma's right end, relates his version of the touchdown play. "It was a handoff, Bobby Layne to Canady," says Goad. "Our line stopped it. Stopped it too hard, I guess. We either knocked the ball loose from Canady or there was a mix-up on the Layne-Canady handoff because the ball was bounding on the ground in the Texas backfield. I was right on top of the play when it happened. "Layne picked it up and while on one knee yelled to Clay, pitching to him. Clay ran wide to his right and scored. But I thought Layne's knee was down, and the film showed it."

In the fourth quarter, when the officials took Royal's interception away from Oklahoma, Sooner fans began throwing pop bottles. "I'll never forget those bottles sailing out on the field," says Homer Paine grimly. "Mitchell and I hurried to the center of the gridiron. 'It'll take a long throw to get us away out here,' we reasoned."

26

Jack Mitchell goes 33 yards to score against Texas A&M at Norman in 1947, with Jim Owens rubbing out a tackler. Photo by Oklahoma Publishing Co.

im Tyree running, after fielding short pass from Mitchell. Photo y Sports Information Department, University of Oklahoma.

Wilkinson (right) congratulates Blair Cherry, Texas coach, following the Texas victory in 1947 at Dallas.

Darrell Royal sweeps Nebraska's end in 1947 as Oklahoma won 14-13. Photo by Sports Information Department, University of Oklahoma.

Sooner cheerleaders appealed to their fans to cease firing bottles and it was the cheerleaders of both schools who finally cleared the debris off the turf.

Oklahoma scored when Mitchell faked a pitch but kept inside, and again in the fourth quarter after Tom Landry, now the Dallas Cowboy coach, punted over the Sooner goal. On the first play thereafter, Thomas ripped 8 yards on the handoff then turned and lateraled to Mitchell, who ran 72 more for a touchdown. Oklahoma's penalties and three lost fumbles were costly. Texas made no turnovers and won 34-14.

The game itself was waged cleanly, and at the close the Texas and Oklahoma players shook hands while some of their followers were punching each other in the stands. Both bands marched off the turf in orderly fashion, and the rival student bodies seemed under control. The Sooners had long since learned that Texas was the best team they would meet, year in and year out.

Kansas, coached by George Sauer, had defeated Tatum's Sooners the year before and tied Oklahoma for the Big Six title. Some of their men had played with the formidable Fourth Air Force team in wartime. It was a Kansas team that would go undefeated and narrowly lose 20-14 to Georgia Tech in an Orange Bowl game the Jayhawkers almost won in the final seconds.

Although Oklahoma outyarded the Jays 339 to 155, Kansas fought magnificently and earned its 13-13 tie. Royal's punting had begun to jell. He kicked four out-of-bounds against the Crimson and Blue.

Oklahoma's option play was conceived in this battle. The Sooners were down on the Kansas 30, and they were moving. It was fourth down and 1. Mitchell called the Sooners' bread-and-butter play, the handoff by George Thomas. Ray Evans, playing left defensive half for Kansas, left that position and ran up and became a linebacker, filling the handoff hole. Mitchell gave Thomas the ball. Evans met him at the line of scrimmage. No gain.

"That bugged me," Mitchell says today. "I didn't sleep all night. In those days, when we called the dive, we ran the dive even if they had it stopped. I was sick. By faking the ball to Thomas and keeping it and going wide, I could have run through Evans's vacant halfback spot for a touchdown and we would have won the game. Nothing there but green grass. I remembered that."

The schedule gave Oklahoma no surcease. Texas Christian, coached by Leo ("Dutch") Meyers, the crafty mentor who brought out Sammy Baugh and Davey O'Brien as great college passers, was next. Meyers's Frogs had nearly toppled Tatum's powerful 1946 Sooners the year before, losing 14-

12 in a sweeping rain. Tatum had tried to get Meyers to postpone that game 24 hours until Sunday afternoon.

The Dutchman had glanced at all that nice mud that would dull the Sooner speed, then rolled his eyes piously. "Play on Sunday? Nothing doing! We're a denominational school. What are you trying to do, Jim, get me fired?"

Meyers didn't need a wet field at Norman. Defensively his Froggies were the best Oklahoma had met all season. In the first half alone they came into possession of the ball through a total of six Sooner turnovers, intercepting four forward passes and falling on two Oklahoma fumbles. Oklahoma's players recall that the Frogs employed a 4-4 defense to throttle Wilkinson's rushing offense.

Texas Christian's 20-7 lead as the two teams walked off the field at the half was money in the bank, and the Sooners couldn't make them spend any of it in the last half, which was scoreless and featured a thrilling punting duel between the rival bantam kickers, Carl Knox of TCU and Darrell Royal of Oklahoma. Sarratt scored Oklahoma's touchdown with a buck off left tackle after a 48-yard Oklahoma drive.

Meyers departed from coaching custom when he and his squad didn't leave Fort Worth until the morning of the game, traveling by special railroad train and arriving at Norman two hours before the kickoff. They were accompanied by a 75-piece swing band and hundreds of Fort Worth followers.

With the season half over, the Sooner record stood 2-2-1 and a state sports columnist wondered in print "if the Sooners were missing the mature leadership of Jim Tatum." But Wilkinson had already begun a vigorous shake-up of his own. On Monday, the usual day of rest, the soft-talking, gentle-mannered coach threw the weary Sooners through a stiff two-hour scrimmage, "the roughest of my life," as tackle Homer Paine described it. Several starting players were demoted. In an effort to provide player leadership, Bud told the squad to elect a pair of cocaptains to serve the rest of the season. They chose Jim Tyree, the 1946 honor captain, and Wade Walker.

The wisdom of these moves became evident as Oklahoma faced four consecutive Big Six Conference foes. Iowa State had a new coach in Abe Stuber, and no opponent that year beat him badly. The Sooners didn't either, but they won 27-9 even though Stuber's team put them in retreat all through the third quarter.

As the game unraveled, George Thomas moved on stage. He intercepted a pass and brought it back 48 yards, and Brewer scored in two bucks. Then Thomas bore off tackle for 12 yards and, turning, scooped the ball out to fullback Ed Kreick, who fielded it off his shoe tops and ran 73 additional yards to score. Thomas also caught Wade Halbert from behind after a 58-yard chase that saved a touchdown. Later Brewer used a magnificent open field block by Walker to reverse 41 yards for a fourth touchdown.

West blocked a punt. Burris blocked an extra point. Royal had punts of 71 and 65 yards besides booting out on the Cyclone 6 and again on their 7. Benched with a sprained neck, center John Rapacz scowlingly sat out the game, the only one he had missed in nine years.

Kansas State at Manhattan was next. Wilkinson looked warily at the Wildcats, and no wonder. Kansas State had lost 23 straight. Oklahoma was in its most wretched physical condition of the season because of injuries and influenza. Upsets were polka-dotting the college football fabric from coast to coast. Kansas State always played inspired football at home.

Sure enough, they did it against Wilkinson's Sooners too. The result seemed to pivot on a sequence of bone-bending defensive plays early in the second quarter. Oklahoma led 7-6, but its play was ragged. The Wildcats had a first down on the Sooner 4.

Like a concrete dam containing a freshet, the defense, tutored by the new line coach, Gomer Jones, held. West stopped Grimes for no gain. Tyree failed Christopolous after a yard advance. Walker, wearing his low-cuts, broke through fast to nail Grimes for a loss of 4. On fourth down the Wildcats forward passed, but John Rapacz, still wearing his busy scowl but back in the lineup, shot across the flight of the ball, intercepted, and fought back 24 yards to run the Sooners out of the hole. Homer Paine tackled the Wildcat ballcarrier four times in the first five plays of the last half. Oklahoma won, 27-13.

Next came the championship game with Missouri at Columbia, a duel between Faurot, father of the split-T, and Wilkinson, his pupil. The Tigers were fresh from wiping out Duke 28-7 at Durham. In that game Faurot's split-T scored the most points ever made against a Wallace Wade–coached Duke team. Missouri stood 4-0 in Big Six play, but the Sooners were in their best physical condition in a month.

It was a cold, foggy day. Oklahoma scored first on a double-safety punt return. Brewer caught the punt, crossed in front of Mitchell, faked the handoff to him, and helped by a timely shoulder nudge on a Missourian by Rapacz was on his way down the right sideline. Goad obliterated another Tiger to free Brewer in front of the Sooner bench, and, as George went flying past, all the Sooners, players and coaches alike, stood to watch and cheer the final cooperation, Burris bumping another Tiger out of the way on the 40 and Paine screening still another down on the 25. The Missourians, never giving up, gamely chased Brewer every foot of his 70-yard touchdown run, their breath trailing behind them like streamers of steam.

Wilkinson's double-safety punt runbacks were carefully organized. Before the kick the Sooners always knew to which side of the field the runback would go, regardless of the faking between the two safeties. It was the job of the line to hold up the opponents' coverage, then get outside it and converge as blockers to the sideline down which the runback was coming.

Mizzou's forward passing bore fruit in the second period, when quarterback Bus Entsminger hit big Mel Sheehan for one touchdown and snapped another aerial to Sheehan that helped set up another, but Walker blocked one conversion, and Dawson missed the second, so Missouri led by only five at the half.

Nobody could have guessed that two exquisitely placed punts would decide the issue. On the second play of the fourth quarter Royal toed a punt out of bounds on Missouri's 1-yard line. When Husak tossed Quirk for a loss, the Tigers had to kick. Then they stopped Oklahoma, and again Royal dropped back to kick, this time from Missouri's 38.

Again he arched the ball prettily over the sideline chalk, this time on the Mizzou 4. The stands gasped. Missouri was having to play the fourth quarter largely from their own end zone. The Tigers launched a buck by Howard Bonnett, but Frankie Anderson, Sooner substitute guard from Oklahoma City, playing the first college game of his life, knocked the ball loose from him, Husak recovering on the Tiger 4.

Two bucks by Eddy Davis put the ball on the 1. As Mitchell brought the team out of the huddle on third down, he saw a Missouri tackle edging in toward the center. Mitchell checked the signal, sending the play outside the tackle, where Goad, given a good blocking angle, put him away, and Brewer scored. Dave Wallace kicked another goal, and Oklahoma was on top 14 to 12. The Tigers launched a desperate passing rally from kickoff, but Myrle Greathouse put a solid hit on Quirk, the Gold and Black fullback, and Rapacz recovered on the Sooner 20.

Oklahoma felt a great surge of stimulation. Mitchell moved the Sooners 80 yards to a touchdown in 12 plays, and Wallace kicked his third goal.

On this drive occurred the incident that illustrated Mitchell's powers of persuasion. The ball was at midfield. It was third and 8. Mitchell called Brewer's handoff over tackle. He turned to Brewer in the huddle. "George, this is the biggest down of the game. We gotta make the yardage or give 'em the ball. We're depending on you. Above all, *hold onto the football!* Don't drop it!"

Two versions exist of what happened. First let's hear Mitchell's. "I fully intended to give the ball to Brewer," says Jack. "But when I got up to the scrimmage line, I saw that both Missouri's tackle and linebacker had moved into our handoff hole. And they'd been stopping my checked signals by changing their alignment after I'd checked.

"I remembered the Kansas game, when Ray Evans had filled the hole and stopped our handoff cold. I decided to fake to Brewer and keep it myself outside. I wasn't sure I'd make it, but I knew George wouldn't. The snap came back. I faked the handoff to Brewer. Both the tackle and the linebacker busted him. I kept the ball and ran 41 yards."

Now Brewer's account of the play. "Jack had me so fired up about not fumbling that you couldn't have taken the ball away from me with a blowtorch. Our line blocked. Turf spewed from my cleats. I went down under a big pile of Missouri bodies. Then I had a sickening sensation. I didn't have the ball! I knew I'd fumbled it. I looked down the field. There was Mitchell, the ball under one arm, still running. They finally stopped him on their 6.

"He hadn't intended to give me the ball. He had conned me into making a good fake. He'd given me a limp hand and put the ball on his hip. But later he let me carry it in for a touchdown, although he and I were then tied for the Big Six Conference scoring leadership."

Oklahoma won 21 to 12. After the game Faurot rode in the Sooner team bus back to the hotel. "Your guards ate us up," he told Bud.

Twenty years later, when Putt Powell, sports columnist for the *Amarillo* (Texas) *Globe-News,* asked Wilkinson to name the most important play of his coaching career at Oklahoma, Bud chose three—Royal's out-of-bounds punts and Anderson's forcing of the Tiger fumble in that Missouri game of 1947. "That was my first year as head coach," Wilkinson explained. "If we had lost, I am quite sure a number of Oklahoma fans would have felt that I, a stripling only 30 years of age, was not mature enough to handle the head coaching job at a major university."

Climate, Tom Novak, and Carl Samuelson were problems in the Nebraska game at Lincoln. The mercury stood at 25, and a cold north wind stiffened the fingers of the players. But the sun was shining, and, most amazing of all, a crowd of 32,000 jammed the stadium. Wearing boots and galoshes and carrying blankets, those Nebraska fans always came no matter what the weather.

Novak, Nebraska's roaming linebacker, was the outstanding defensive man in the game. "We tried to send our plays away from him," Mitchell remembers. "He was tough." So was Samuelson, a gorilla of a man at left tackle.

On a quarterback keeper in the first half it was Samuelson, jamming the end and holding his ground, who reached out and caught Mitchell across the mouth with his swinging forearm, driving the quarterback's lower teeth through his lower lip. "Helmets quit then at the forehead," Sooner players describe the lack of facial protection. Mitchell's teeth were sticking outside through his lip. Blood was running down his jersey. He couldn't speak plainly while calling signals.

At halftime Mitchell lay on his back on a table in the Sooner dressing room. Dr. Mike Willard, Sooner team physician, was sewing him up, 16 stitches inside the lip, 16 more outside. The other Sooners were walking past laughing at the quarterback. Wilkinson was standing nearby reproving Mitchell for not calling more strongside plays.

Then Wilkinson's face softened. He patted Mitchell on the head. "Well, Jack," he said, "I guess if I had thirty-two stitches in my lip I wouldn't be running plays toward that guy either. Don't worry. We'll start moving this next half."

Oklahoma did move better thereafter. Soon the Sooners broke George Thomas loose for 45 yards on a handoff. "That made my stitched lip feel better than anything," laughs Mitchell today.

An interception by John Rapacz and Greathouse's linebacking helped stand off the Cornhuskers. So did another punting feat by Darrell Royal. On fourth down with 13 yards to go, Royal punted out on the Scarlet 18. But Nebraska was penalized 5 yards on the play. Royal walked up to Stan West, Oklahoma's acting captain. He said, "Stan, let's run that thing again."

West stared at him. "What?" he said, unbelievingly.

"Stan, take the penalty, I can beat that."

On the sideline Wilkinson was vigorously crossing his hands in the referee's refusal-of-penalty gesture. West blinked. "Bud's gonna kill you and me both," he said. But he took the penalty, giving Royal another shot at the coffin corner. This time Royal coolly kicked out on the Cornhusker 10, a trap from which the Nebraskans could never extricate themselves. Oklahoma won 14-13.

Later, after he became coach at Texas, Royal agreed with Wilkinson. "I should have let it stand," he says today. "Players and coaches have different temperaments. On fourth and one from the middle of the field, players always want to go for it. Coaches don't."

One game was left. Oklahoma A&M, which had beaten Texas Christian 14-7 and lost only 14-21 to all-victorious Southern Methodist, had scheduled a two-week rest before the Sooner battle. Coach Jim Lookabaugh and four of his staff drove several hundred miles round-trip to scout the Sooner noseout of Nebraska. They were determined to avenge that 73-12 cudgeling

33

applied by Tatum's Sooners at Stillwater the year before.

Right from the start the pace was furious. Not until their fifth possession did the Sooners lay out a scoring march. It was a typical OU offensive, 79 yards in 15 plays with every play a rush. Mitchell bluffed a lateral and swung around end for the touchdown.

In the third period the Aggies came out after the Sooners. Jack Hartman, their quarterback, who is today the Kansas State basketball mentor, drove them 38 yards to one touchdown and 34 to another, Bob Meinert plunging for both.

The Sooners rallied fiercely in the fourth quarter. Thomas swung wide to his left, a pitchout from Mitchell nestled under his left arm. Watching him like hawks, the Aggie defense swung with him. Suddenly Thomas made a sharp cut to the right, exploded into the clear, and ran 38 yards to score. That tied things 13-13, but Oklahoma still had Wallace. With the heat on, Wallace notched his kick, and OU led 14-13 with 12 minutes left.

The Aggies, however, were full of fight. Up the field they came, a football team that trailed narrowly in the score but courageously refused to dip its colors. From the Sooner 48, Hartman tried a long pass, but Dinkins leaped to intercept it, a timely play. The Aggies held for downs, but the Sooners still had Royal.

Royal did his thing, coolly belting a punt out on the Aggie 10. Charley Dowell, reserve center from Tulsa, came in to roll Roof for a loss, and with three minutes left Oklahoma took the ball on downs on its 43. Everybody seemed reconciled to a 14-13 Sooner win. But everybody was wrong. On first down, Walker and Goad opened the Orange and Black line, and Thomas spilled through the rent and ran 58 yards down the west sideline for a touchdown. Wallace kicked goal, and the Sooners won 21-13. Royal further contributed to the result with three pass interceptions.

The 1947 Oklahoma team finished 7-2-1, a slightly better record than Tatum's the year before. They had had to come from behind in eight of their ten games. They again tied Kansas for the Big Six crown. They swept their last five games. They placed sixteenth in the Associated Press poll.

Although some Oklahoma City backers complained to President Cross that "Wilkinson is too nice a person to get the job done" and that he (Cross) had better be looking for a coach more like Jim Tatum, the president's reply was to recommend to the regents in April that Wilkinson stay on as coach and also be given the full title of athletic director.

Wilkinson's answer was to craft Oklahoma teams that would win thirty-one consecutive games.

1947 SENIORS TODAY

Myrle Dinkins is president and owner of the Lamar Company of Shawnee, Oklahoma, specializing in water-treatment plants, pumping stations, and waste-water treatment in Kansas and Oklahoma.

Bill Morris, later employed by Kerr-McGee, died in Oklahoma City in April, 1983.

Charles Sarratt is chairman of the board of Astro Drilling Company of Oklahoma City. He is also president of Astro Energy Corporation of Oklahoma City. In 1983 he was appointed by Governor George Nigh a regent of the University of Oklahoma.

Jim Tyree is president and chief executive officer of Oneck, Inc., a diversified energy corporation of Tulsa, Oklahoma.

3. SUGAR BOWL CHAMPIONS

In the spring of 1948, Wilkinson hired a new assistant coach, Frank ("Pop") Ivy of Skiatook. Tall, affable and quiet-spoken, Ivy had played end with the Chicago Cardinals, champions of the National Football League. Before that he had been an All-American end at Oklahoma.

On the first day Ivy reported, Wilkinson handed him a list of names and a map. In the division of recruiting territory Ivy was assigned Oklahoma City and the northwest "clear to Siberia," as he puts it. "Go out and see if we have any players," Wilkinson told him.

One of the first places Ivy visited was White Deer, Texas, where Jim Weatherall, an excellent tackle prospect, had already made up his mind to go to Texas. A big, shy kid, Weatherall actually preferred a third school. In November of 1945 he had ridden to Norman on the bus and watched Oklahoma A&M annihilate the Sooners 45-0. "From then until I graduated, Oklahoma A&M was where I wanted to go to college," remembers Weatherall, "but all they ever told me was 'we'll keep an eye on you.'"

The more Ivy eyed Weatherall, the more he wanted him. "He looked awfully big and strong to come from White Deer, Texas," Ivy chuckles today. He persuaded Weatherall to at least visit Norman before he announced his choice, and Weatherall agreed.

Ivy leveled with the Panhandle phenomenon. "Jim, I'm just as scared as you are," he confessed. "You're the first guy I ever tried to recruit."

Weatherall did visit Norman. Afterward Wilkinson, Gomer Jones, and Ivy flew to Hooker, near White Deer, to visit him. "That did it," Weatherall grins today. "They were such nice people. I knew I'd be happier playing for them."

In Santa Clara University's Broncos, Oklahoma drew a formidable opening-day opponent. Hall Haynes, their top back, was an offensive gem. Haynes had glided through California's Rose Bowl-bound Golden Bears for three touchdowns, two of them thrilling runs of 51 and 38 yards. Incidentally, Haynes was an Oklahoman, born in Duncan and moving to Wilson at the age of six. "We lived a few miles outside Wilson on an oil lease, and there were always make-up football games," Haynes remembers today. "Since I usually was the youngest and smallest, I was most often the everlasting center for both sides."[1]

Oklahoma's 1948 backfield upon arrival at Santa Clara, California, for the Santa Clara game. Left to right: George Brewer, Bud Wilkinson, Jack Mitchell, George Thomas, and Darrell Royal. Copyright Oklahoma Publishing Co.

With so many lettermen returning, Oklahoma's two-a-day workouts in September were savagely waged. A new sophomore back, Lindell Pearson, of Oklahoma City Capitol Hill, who in the fall of 1947 had strayed off to the University of Arkansas but had been recovered by a swift counter-raid, was on the second team at left half. A strapping 185-pounder who could move and throw, Pearson was gradually improving his bucking and blocking.

Wade Walker, back from his honeymoon in Wisconsin, not only practiced football twice a day but began playing golf between morning and afternoon

[1] Hall Haynes to author, November 22, 1980.

37

workouts until Wilkinson found out and made him stop. Pete Tillman, who had missed spring practice after breaking his arm in an automobile accident, had fought his way to the starting team at center. As a senior at Mangum High, Tillman had played center on offense, linebacker on defense, and called all the plays, both offensive and defensive. As the autumnal heat worsened, the competition for a starting spot in every position became keen.

In spring practice Wilkinson had installed a new formation, a delayed trap that had little relationship to the split-T. He moved Royal to quarterback and Mitchell to halfback. The coach was concerned that other teams might begin to defense the the split-T more successfully. He doubted that Oklahoma was throwing enough passes.

"I loved the new deal because I got to run with the ball more than ever," said Mitchell. "I even played some at fullback and as a wide pass receiver. Royal could throw the ball long."

Against Santa Clara, Oklahoma won the first half. The Sooner secondary intercepted four passes. Two were by Ed Lisak, a Kalamazoo, Michigan, sophomore, who also slapped down two others. The Sooner line, robustly backed by a couple of rough oldsters from the shortgrass country, Greathouse from Amarillo and Tillman from Mangum, smothered the Bronc running attack and stopped Haynes. Bill Remy, Norman sophomore, and George Thomas ran the ball down to the goal. Brewer bucked across. Les ("Bingo") Ming, who had played at Chickasha and Oklahoma City Central, toed a 27-yard field goal. Oklahoma led 10-0.

The Broncs countered when Martin passed 18 yards to Osborne, but Wilkinson moved Mitchell to quarterback, and on the first play Mitchell called a buck by Thomas over guard. A Santa Clara linebacker took a step inside to stop the play. That was fatal. Mitchell checked signals. Walker and Goad clicked perfectly on their blocking duty, and Thomas ran the new hole for 82 yards and a touchdown. Oklahoma led 17-7 at the half.

"We had only four basic plays, so our quarterbacks had no trouble with audibles," recalls assistant Pop Ivy. "Bud seldom put in a new play unless it had been tested on the practice field in full pads. In 1948 nobody else in the United States, college or pro, was using audibles as well as Oklahoma."

The last half was a Santa Clara story. Coach Len Casanova's Broncos won with forward passing and superior hustling. Undismayed by Oklahoma's interception of four of his aerials in the first half, quarterback Bill Sheridan pegged the game winner, a long heave. Haynes found a wide-open spot in the Sooner secondary and fielded it for the decisive touchdown. Final score: Santa Clara 20, Oklahoma 17.

On the following day Wilkinson found Buddy Jones, whom the Sooners called "Light Foot" because he ran like a deer without seeming to put his feet down.

"Buddy," said the coach, "we need a safety. There's no way you can make our team on offense. I'd appreciate it if you'd play only safety."

Jones cheerfully made the sacrifice. "We had a strong pass defense," he says. "Lisak, Royal, Tommy Gray . . . ."

On the plane coming home Wilkinson told the team, "You looked great the first ten minutes." The next day Paine and Walker, the cocaptains, went to Wilkinson's office.

"Coach," they said, "if we looked good for the first ten minutes, why don't you play us ten minutes—and we'll go twice as hard—then put in a fresh line while we come out and rest. Then put us back in." Wilkinson agreed.

"The next game we began alternating lines," recalls Willie Manley, alternate left tackle. "I wish we'd had three," he added. "Look how hard we could have gone then." Wilkinson had always believed that his linemen should play both offense and defense. Now they could block and tackle with sustained ferocity.

One week later Coach Harry Stiteler's Texas Aggies were warring very evenly with the Sooners at Norman. "With the score tied in the second quarter, Coach asked me if I could take some center snaps," Mitchell recollects. "'Let me practice a little,' I replied."

While Texas A&M had the ball, Mitchell and center Pete Tillman practiced snaps on the sideline. "Pete was a good snapper," Mitchell recalls. "He had a good solid butt. Coach sent us in. Texas A&M's defense began giving us all kinds of daylight for quick split-T handoffs. All I did was check to the holes, and we went right on downfield and scored." Wilkinson also ran Royal some at quarterback in the last half, and the versatile Hollis product moved the Sooners to three more touchdowns. Oklahoma, helped by liberal use of its reserves, won 42 to 14.

Texas, the most climactic foe of the season, was next. What formation would the Sooners employ, and who would be the quarterback? Wilkinson talked it over with his staff. Royal had the qualifications, but the players believed in Mitchell and in the split-T he jockeyed so adroitly.

With Brewer out for a month with a broken fibula, Wilkinson vitalized his team by inserting three sophomores, halfback Lindell Pearson; fullback Leon Heath, of Hollis; and guard Clair Mayes, of Muskogee. All year in practice Wilkinson had refined Heath's blocking from fullback, teaching him to get close to his opponent—right up in his face—before uncoiling on him. "Make up your mind to flatten him every time," the coach instructed. "It isn't at all hard if you do it right."

At Hollis High, Heath had started out as a double wingback guard, whose job it was to pull and lead the interference. He also led the rush to the dinner table while driving one of his father's combines during the summer wheat harvest in the north. This was good for his weight. Soon he was crowding 180 pounds.

"Who were the best cooks you encountered on your harvest travels?" I once asked him.

"The Nebraska farm wives," Heath answered without hesitation. "I especially liked their creamed potatoes, fried chicken, and home-frozen ice cream." He also liked their fourth meal, the midafternoon snack.

Texas was no snack, the Sooners discovered before 70,000 in the Cotton Bowl. Although they'd won eight straight from Oklahoma, the Orange was always up for the Sooners. And the Oklahomans still remembered the "Sisco game" of the year before.

Right from the start the Sooners ran a front race, taking the track away from the Longhorns. Both Sooner lines swarmed over the Texas backs. Bobby Goad twice tossed Campbell of Texas for losses on bootleggers. The Sooner defense yielded only two first downs in the first half.

Soon the Sooners were off to their first touchdown, a split-T advance of 73 yards with Mitchell at the controls. Pearson's 17-yard sweep was the longest gain. Heath pounded over from the 2 after a 10-yard dart by Royal. Oklahoma led 7-0 at the half. Again Mitchell swung the Sooners into a long overland march. Again Oklahoma scored, George Thomas bucking over Mayes, Walker, and Goad. Now Oklahoma led 14-0.

Texas put a passing drive into gear and scored. Oklahoma replied when its line blocked Heath loose down the middle on a 68-yard buck to the Texas 12. On the next play George Thomas rode his blockers into the end zone. Now Oklahoma led 20-6.

Texas fought hard, Tom Landry scoring on their fourth play from kickoff. The kickoff itself was most dramatic. Halfback Perry Samuels, a sprinter in track, returned the Oklahoma boot 65 yards before Royal postponed the touchdown by dragging him down from behind. Oklahoma won 20-14.

After the game Blair Cherry, the Texas coach, praised Mitchell, the Sooner helmsman. Cherry particularly liked Mitchell's signal checking. "He's the best in the country at making the split-T work," said the Texas coach. "He worked our defense over from end to end, as pretty as you please. If he missed a trick, I haven't found it from reviewing the movies."

Felix McKnight's story in the *Dallas Morning News* gave the accolades to two Sooner defensive standouts. "The Cotton Bowl never knew a greater linebacker and defensive giant than Myrle Greathouse, a 6-foot, 184-pound ex-marine from Amarillo whose 44 jersey bobbed in and out of every Texas offensive effort," wrote McKnight. "The man just couldn't be handled. And if he wasn't handy, an amazing little fellow of 152 pounds, Wilbur Jones, was there to make tackle after tackle."

The longest segment of the season, the Big Seven Conference derby (Colorado was now in the league although not on the Sooner schedule until 1950), lay ahead. Don Faurot's Missouri Tigers had upset Southern Methodist's two-year record of no defeats. Kansas, under new coach Jules Sykes, had a fine team rising on the Kaw. And Kansas State, the next Sooner opponent, had broken its long losing string by upsetting Arkansas State 37-6.

Trouble didn't surface in the Kansas State game, but something else did, a terrific north wind that noisily rippled the pennants atop the Sooner stadium. Once when umpire Mutt Volz threw down his weighted red hand-kerchief while calling a penalty, the wind blew the hanky half the length of the field, and time had to be called until Volz could run back and re-trieve it.

With only a minute left in the first quarter came the game's most dramatic play. Jack Mitchell plucked a long punt out of the windy sky on his 4-yard line. He handed off to Royal, who, flanked by a wall of blockers, flitted 96 yards down the east sideline to a touchdown. Oklahoma blocked every State man off his feet, Ken Tipps expunging the last one as Royal romped untouched to score.

At the Monday noon meeting of the Oklahoma City Quarterback Club, Wilkinson recounted the play in a different light. "I had told the boys never to catch a punt inside the 10-yard line," he said. "When Mitchell caught the ball around the 4, I ran down the sideline yelling, 'Don't catch it! Don't catch it!' Then Darrell took the ball from Mitchell on the crisscross, and suddenly he was open for a touchdown. I ran up the sideline with him, yelling, 'Way to go! Way to go!' I guess that's what you call being an adaptable coach!"

Oklahoma won 42-0, sweeping their bench clean of everybody but the injured, an imposing list that included such regulars as Walker, Tillman, Greathouse, and Brewer.

Royal's feats of scoring two touchdowns, one a 96-yard school punt-runback record, throwing two touchdown passes, and booting all seven of his punts out of bounds gave the opponents a zero in runback yardage and caused the Associated Press to name him National Back of the Week.

Next opponent was Texas Christian, coached by Leo ("Dutch") Meyer, the Southwest's outstanding architect of the upset. Surprising Oklahoma with a 4-4 defense from which they cross-charged and shot the gap, the Froggies had won 20-7 at Norman the previous year.

The 1948 contest was played on Texas Christian's home turf. Texas Christian's record was 4-1, Oklahoma's 3-1. It was Oklahoma's only night game of the season. The battle was tremendously hard-fought with physical punishment being fiercely dealt and taken. The lead changed hands six times.

TCU led 2-0 when Royal dropped back to punt, but a low center snap struck the goalpost and bounded into the end zone for a safety. Then occurred the zigzagging in the score. With 1,500 Oklahoma supporters cheering them on, the Sooners ripped and slanted 89 yards to a touchdown in 17 ground plays, regaining the lead at 7-2.

Wilkinson was ready for Meyer's 4-4 defense. He forced the Dutchman out of it by posting Heath, his fullback, outside the end as a flanker, giving Oklahoma the outside blocking angle for sweeps. And when Meyer, in the second quarter, began moving his outside linebacker outside Heath, Wilkinson's inside game had the green light.

TCU led 9-7 at the half after Archer reversed for 29 yards with blockers all around him. Oklahoma regained the lead at 14-9 by driving from kickoff to a second touchdown, Pearson bursting off tackle to cross the goal. Meyer's Frogs surged back in a fighting rage, Lindy Berry shooting off tackle for 69 yards and a touchdown and moving so fast that the Sooner secondary lost him under the lights. Now TCU led 16-14, and the third quarter was nearly over.

Doggedly the Sooners bowed their necks and went to work. A fumble, one of five the Sooners lost that night, blunted their offense. But the Sooner defense, led by Buddy Burris, who was jumping over the Frog center to wreck plays, kept holding the enemy for downs and forcing punts.

Just before the fourth period started, Mitchell slipped the running attack into gear, and Oklahoma rolled 76 yards in seven plays. Pearson got the touchdown on a 38-yard cutback over the middle, stiff-arming the safety to cross the goal standing. Ming kicked goal. Now Oklahoma led 21-16.

TCU wasn't licked. The action ebbed and flowed. Unable to gain against OU's aroused defense, the Frogs surprised everyone by punting out on the Oklahoma 10. Joslin toed that kick. Only a minute and a half was left to play, and the Sooners' backs were to the wall. It was fourth down, 2 to go, from the Sooner 11.

On the sideline OU line coach Gomer Jones suggested to Wilkinson, "Let's take a safety. Give it to 'em. We've got a punter who can put the ball in the other end of the field."

The Sooners nearly gave their fans apoplexy when they came out for the fourth down without going into punt formation. And when Mitchell, with the ball, retreated into the end zone, dodging and doubling ahead of the pack, nearly everybody thought he had gone berserk.

Texas Christian finally caught and tackled him for the safety. That left the score 21-18, Oklahoma. Officials brought the ball back to the Sooner 20. Royal punted the free kick, and George Thomas ran down and leveled the TCU receiver on their 34. Berry threw a long pass to Archer, but the game ended before they could run another play.

Meyer sportingly gave Wilkinson, his young coaching antagonist, full credit for the maneuver that forced TCU out of the 4-4 defense. Wilkinson lauded assistants Bill Jennings and Walter Hargesheimer for their scouting chore on TCU. But the Sooner coach best told the story of the game in his alumni letter when he wrote, "We won . . . because of the superior punch of our line. Two big TCU lines were fine, too, but when the chips were down in the fourth quarter, our line outlasted theirs and beat them down."

Iowa State, the first conference opponent, was next. The Sooners finally wore them down 33-6 with superior manpower. Pearson whipped across the goal for the first Sooner touchdown, but Burris scored it when he alertly covered the halfback's fumble in the end zone. Ming kicked goal.

A few minutes later Sutherland, the Cyclones' fine punter, who had booted out of bounds three straight times to avoid the dangerous Sooner runbacking, made his first miscue, toeing a short kick straight down the middle. Mitchell fielded it on the run and found himself surrounded. He retreated wide to his left, backtracking in a great half circle toward his own goal then completing the arc down the right sideline, where there were blockers galore. Running out of the hands of the last tackler, he scored. The touchdown officially measured 55 yards, but the quarterback actually ran twice that.

Frankie Anderson, right end from Oklahoma City Northeast, became the symbol of Oklahoma's destructive line play in the third quarter by single-handedly throwing Iowa State backs for 50 yards in losses, all of it on four savage rushes in 14 minutes' time.

The Sooners lost a 5-yard touchdown run by Tommy Gray, the dash champ from Seminole, on an offside penalty. But Gray wasn't through. He suddenly scooped up a slowly rolling punt about to die at his feet and dashed back 35 yards to set up the final Sooner touchdown, a pass that lanky Claude Arnold rifled to Ed Lisak in the end zone.

In the opinion of Rod Rust, Iowa State center, Sooner guard Stan West had a fine game. West played over Rust in the battle. "After the game was

43

over, I didn't have a bruise or a sore place on my body but he still made every tackle that came through," Rust later told Pop Ivy, Sooner assistant coach. "I couldn't block him enough to even bruise myself. He could play so soft and maneuver so well without getting involved in body contact."

Wilkinson's team was attracting so much national attention that even their fifth-string center, 152-pound Boyd ("Bronco") McGugan, a geology major from Holdenville, became a national figure. McGugan symbolized the All-American substitute, the guy who never missed a practice or got to make a trip with his team. Sooner fandom, ever alert to reward stouthearted grit by a player of any weight, got busy in McGugan's behalf. A McGugan Marching and Chowder Society was organized by P. A. Sugg, Oklahoma City broadcasting executive. McGugan was made an official member of Governor Roy J. Turner's staff, and at a Monday meeting of the Oklahoma City Quarterback Club he wore his old black helmet while Sugg read the governor's citation praising him.

Time magazine gave the Sooners' All-American Sub a spread and used his picture. They summed up McGugan as follows: "Too small for the big time . . . typifies the unsung, inglorious, eternal scrub . . . . In Oklahoma City last week the Quarterback Club felt the least they could do was to buy fifth-stringer McGugan a shiny new helmet (a white varsity model), and they collected $75.25, enough to buy him four."

The Missouri-Oklahoma game at Norman was a match between two winning clubs. Each had won five straight. Missouri's 20-14 upset of a Doak Walker–directed Southern Methodist outfit was the Mustangs' first defeat in 16 straight games and vaulted Missouri into the Associated Press's ninth spot nationally. Oklahoma's feat of having conquered three formidable Southwest conference opponents was also impressive.

Bill Stern, NBC's ace sportscaster who broadcast the game coast-to-coast, irritated the Sooners with his Friday night show. Stern was a fearless soul who liked to pick the winners in advance. "Homer Paine and I were rooming together at the Skirvin in Oklahoma City and heard Stern say over the air that Oklahoma had no business on the same field with Missouri," Burris said later. "Our whole squad heard him say it."

Pop Boone, *Fort Worth* (Texas) *Press* columnist, wrote, "In their skin-tight golden britches and white jersies the Tigers were as fine a looking batch of stalwarts as ever made a coach's eye glitter." And right from the start they carried it to the Sooners. Braznell bucked for a touchdown and Dawson, their conversion specialist, who kicked in shorts and knee pads, came in to hit his twentieth straight conversion. Missouri 7, Oklahoma 0.

Late in the first quarter Oklahoma's linemen began to hit their blocks and tackles. Slowly but surely they moved Oklahoma 55 yards to the tying

44

touchdown, a strong-side buck by George Thomas hitting over Walker and Goad. Ming kicked goal, and at the half the two teams were deadlocked 7-7.

Then the incident occurred that decided the combat. On the fifth play of the third quarter Royal lofted a punt that soared along the sky. Ghnouly, Missouri safety, moved easily, gracefully under it but did not signal for a fair catch. Goad, Sooner right end playing with a bruised shoulder, struck him there.

"It was a clean, wipe-out tackle," wrote Bill Connors of the *Tulsa World.* Goad not only drove the pigskin out of Ghnouly's hand but recovered it on the Tiger 35. This was opportunity, and the Sooners lost no time seizing it.

On the first play Mitchell scored on a quarterback spinner Wilkinson had designed exclusively for Missouri. "There was no trap-blocking in the split-T," Mitchell remembers, "so Bud surprised everybody by putting one in. We faked the handoff to Thomas. Tillman and Mayes double-teamed the nose guard. Burris trap-blocked the left tackle. After the fake I was supposed to keep the ball, spin completely around, and run down the middle.

"We thought it was a silly play," Mitchell went on. "I never thought Bud would call it. But after Goad got that fumble for us, Bud sent word in from the bench to run the spinner. Lordy! Missouri took the fake completely, and when I finished spinning and began to run I couldn't see anything but green grass." Oklahoma led 14-7.

Three minutes later Homer Paine blocked Robinson's punt, the ball bounding out on the Tiger 16. Again the Sooners smelled a touchdown and got it. Thomas slanted across the goal after Mitchell, on fourth down, powered to the Tiger 4. Ming converted. Score, 21-7.

Three minutes later it was 28-7. The Sooners were steamed high. Myrle Greathouse threw Stephens for a 10-yard loss. Anderson trapped Braznell for a minus 9 yards. Robinson punted. Mitchell fielded it deep and, faking the handoff to Royal, hid the ball on his hip. The play seemed doomed. A Tiger end zeroed in.

"Few people at the game saw Myrle Greathouse throw the saving block," says Mitchell today. "All the newspapers missed it. The Missouri end had us cold right at the handoff spot. If Greathouse hadn't rolled him, he would have ruined the play."

Coming up the west boundary behind a wave of blockers, Mitchell ran within 6 feet of the overflow crowd sitting six deep along the sideline. Then daylight showed. Escaping a tackler on the outside, Mitchell cut back inside, burst into the open, and ran off from two pursuers to go 70 yards and score. Ming kicked goal.

Royal's 25-yard run off the double safety set up the fifth touchdown, a weak-side sweep by Heath. Later Heath ran 25 yards to another touchdown on the same play. The OU pass defense held Missouri to 111 yards in 30 throws. Joe Cunningham, Lisak, and Buddy Jones each scored interceptions. Truman Wright, senior right tackle from Houston, Texas, who spelled the injured Walker, also played well. In his alumni letter Wilkinson saluted him and also 17 others of his linemen. "It was their game," Bud said.

Sheehan, the big Tiger end, who was later voted to Oklahoma's all-opponents' team, was talking to Sooner players after the game. "I was sure glad," he said, "When you got that first team out of there, but say! Who in the heck was that big, rough son-of-a-gun who came in at left tackle on your second team?" Willie Manley was his name, Sheehan was told.

Although the Sooners played raggedly at times against Nebraska, yielding five fumbles and 150 yards in penalties, they fired up in the middle of the game, scoring six touchdowns in eighteen and a half minutes, and won 41-14. With Stan West, Enid guard, blocking two punts, the Sooner defense shone. It gave the Cornhuskers only 82 total yards.

"We checked lots to send our plays away from Tom Novak, Nebraska's great linebacker," Mitchell recalls. "He was tough." The Sooners were able to isolate Samuelson, the powerful tackle, with wide splits, keeping him off balance, but they could never entirely subdue him.

However, the Scarlet team continued to hex Mitchell. Not only did the quarterback lose a 70-yard touchdown punt runback because of a clipping penalty, but on the same run he took a blow on his right thigh that caused him to crouch on that limb thereafter each time he called a signal in the huddle so the muscle wouldn't knot. A charley horse might bench him five or six weeks.

"Joe Glander, our trainer, did a great job on it," Mitchell recalls. "At the half he put ice on it and also applied an ace pressure bandage to it. I kept the leg up until Monday. Then Joe put a light cast on it, and I wore that the whole game against Kansas."

Kansas had sold out the Oklahoma game at Lawrence, and no wonder. The Jayhawkers had won seven straight. The contest carried with it bragging rights for the Big Seven Conference championship, since only the Sooners and Jays were all-victorious in conference play. They were like two guys riding the same motorcycle.

Oklahoma combed Kansas 60 to 7. It was the Sooners' first win from the Jayhawks in three years. Dropping no fumbles, the Sooners played an almost perfect game mechanically despite the fact that they used 35 of their 36-man traveling squad. They rushed 346 net yards, passed 152, and ran back punts an additional 166. They had a big advantage in manpower and reserves.

Greathouse and Royal of the Sooners roomed together at Lawrence. After they retired the night before the game, a long distance telephone call notified Greathouse that his mother in Amarillo had died of a heart ailment. Myrle's mother had been an enthusiastic football fan. She had seen him play all his games at Amarillo High School and also several of his Oklahoma games.

"Myrle sobbed half the night," Royal remembers, "and I was upset too. I told Coach Wilkinson." Bud offered to fly the linebacker home to Amarillo, but Greathouse decided to play the game, then go.

"Mother was a great fan. I'm sure this is what she would have wanted me to do," he said. So he played.

His pass interception set up one Sooner touchdown. Later Simons, the Kansas punter, kicked deep. Royal fielded it, faked the handoff to Mitchell, kept, and cutting back inside three tacklers ran 73 yards to a touchdown. Simons, still shooting for out of bounds, later laced another long kick.

Wearing the light cast on his right thigh, Mitchell fielded this one on the bounce, almost on the sideline. There wasn't time for a double safety hand-off, but Mitchell ran in the right places and using a block by Tillman went the route, 67 yards. Tommy Gray buzzed 81 yards for a tenth touchdown but lost it on an offside penalty.

At the Monday noon press luncheon at Oklahoma City before the final game, Oklahoma versus Oklahoma A&M at Stillwater, Aggie sports publicist Otis Wile held up a *Daily Oklahoman* picture showing Royal's 73-yard run. So well had the Sooner linemen blocked for him that no Jayhawkers were visible in the picture. "No wonder Oklahoma beat 'em so bad," deadpanned Wile. "Kansas didn't even show up."

Reversing the usual procedure, the Sooner defense won the final contest from the hard-fighting, highly keyed Oklahoma Aggies, earning for Oklahoma a Sugar Bowl bid against North Carolina at New Orleans January 1. But Wilkinson's 1948 Sooners had to make three goal-line stands in the rain and give the Farmers a purposeful safety to save the victory. It was a battle between the Big Seven champions and Coach Jim Lookabaugh's Missouri Valley Conference kings.

With the Sooners leading 19 to 13 the Orange and Black opened drives deep into Sooner territory. Royal ended one with an interception on the 15. He derailed another by belting a wet-ball punt a tremendous 81 yards just before the fourth period began. But Oklahoma kept sloughing the ball to the Aggies on fumbles, yielding a record total of seven and ruining their own attack while immensely aiding that of their opponents. Once they fumbled to the Aggies on the Sooner 2, but Jim Owens threw Hartman for a 6-yard loss, and the Sooners broke up three passes and took the ball on downs.

It rained harder. Royal punted into the cold wind. "It wasn't long, but a nice tight spiral," he recalls. "The ball was slick." The Aggies drew an offside penalty on the play, which meant that the Sooners could punt again from 5 yards farther up the field. Homer Paine, Sooner captain, was going to take it.

Royal ran up to him. "Leave that thing where it is and let's play some defense," he said "I can't kick it any better than that in this soup." And that's what they did.

Oklahoma repelled two more stormings of their goal, their white jersies muddied by their defensive exertions. With the game almost over, the Sooners had the ball on their 3. It was growing darker. Wilkinson sent in the crippled Mitchell to direct the same delaying tactics that had thwarted Texas Christian, and the quarterback coolly did his job. Oklahoma won 19-15 and obtained the Sugar Bowl bid.

"I think we got a little cocky after the Missouri game," Mitchell said. "But the Aggies shook us up. They put us in a good frame of mind for North Carolina in the Sugar Bowl."

In New Orleans the populace was caught up in football fervor and activity. Ray Parr, *Daily Oklahoman* columnist, wrote: "The town's been a carnival of football madness all day. All windows are full of elaborate football displays. The blue of North Carolina and the red of Oklahoma blend in a blaze of colors. Banners fly in the wind and giant footballs dangle from wires strung across Canal Street."

The game matched Carl Snavely, who had been a coach for twenty-two years, with Wilkinson, a rookie mentor in only his second season. It was the class bowl game of the season, North Carolina having finished third in the final AP poll, Oklahoma fifth. Only common foe of the two clubs was Texas. The Sooners, 9-1, had shaded the Horns 20-14. The Tar Heels had flogged them 34-7.

The decisive question seemed to be whether any of Oklahoma's backs belonged in the same roundhouse with Charley ("Choo Choo") Justice, North Carolina's 167-pound All-American tailback. All fall, Justice's superb triple threating had been getting the highball sign in the national media. Running like the late Casey Jones's four-wheel flyer, he ranked second in the nation in total offense and led the nation in punting. In Art Weiner, their tall 212-pound end, Carolina had a pass receiver who had fielded 31 passes for 481 yards and 6 touchdowns.

Justice proved his class by playing the full game despite an illness that had left him weak. Owing to the power of the rival defenses, the game was low score. With Justice passing and running cleverly, Carolina returned the opening kickoff to its 37, then advanced 48 yards to the Oklahoma 15. It was here that Justice shot a pass into the right flat.

Greathouse, bandy-legged Sooner linebacker, intercepted it and scuttled for the Tar Heel goal. "My only thought," says Greathouse today, "was that it is a long way to the goal, and this ball is sure getting heavy." He slowed a minute so that Owens and Paine could catch up and block the last man in front of him, but Eddie Knox of the Tar Heels caught him from behind on the Carolina 13.

Now it was the Sooners' turn to be surprised. It took Oklahoma eight running plays to traverse that 13 yards and score.

"This was the only team I ever played against that stayed in their basic defense, and our split-T couldn't wipe them out," says Mitchell. "We'd never met a team so physically strong. They were well coached, too. They'd scouted us good and read us perfectly. Their linebackers were sticking their noses into our handoff holes. We had trouble moving the ball."

Mitchell carried the first four times, all strong-side keepers or sneaks, and got the first down by inches on the 3. Oklahoma was penalized for backfield in motion, but George Thomas ripped 5 and 2 on handoffs, and on fourth down the ball lay inches from the goal.

Mitchell faked the handoff, ran right, planted his heel, and cut back inside the defensive end for an easy touchdown. Ming kicked goal, and the Sooners led 7-0.

Bobby Goad says, "We were most afraid of their great forward passing battery, Justice to Weiner. Stopping that was big in Bud's game plan. If Weiner played tight, Wade and I would double-team him back on Justice. On the first play we did that, and Owens tackled their fullback for a 7-yard loss. After that, they split Weiner out 15 yards from their tackle. This hurt their running game. And when they tried to hit him with a pass, Royal ate his lunch in the secondary."

"Weiner was good," insists Willie Manley, Sooner tackle. "Best end I ever faced."

With Royal, only 5-10 and 158 pounds, retreating swiftly, right or left, Weiner caught only three passes for 35 yards in the game. Of that Royal says, "This sounds like false modesty, but I had a good day because our line put a very hard rush on Justice. He didn't have much time to throw. On Greathouse's interception our line put a great rush on Justice too."

The Sooners dropped a fumble on their 30 late in the first quarter. It was the only lost fumble of the day by either team. Five plays later Hosea Rodgers, Tar Heel fullback, bored 2 yards off tackle for the touchdown.

49

But Cox's conversion was wide. Oklahoma 7, North Carolina 6. The Sooners still had trouble moving the ball.

"An inebriated spectator wandered down on the field," Mitchell remembers. "He kept calling out, 'Wilkerson. Wilkerson. Wheresh Wilkerson?' Bud and I were standing on the sideline with the phone, wondering why our check plays weren't working. They were stopping us in spite of the fact that we were up for the game."

Bud paid no attention to the drunken fan, but Mitchell looked around at him. "Gol dern it, , Wilkerson," the alcoholized gentleman hiccuped as the police led him from the field, "jump up in the air and throw a little short pass."

To himself Mitchell said, "He's right! The linebackers have got their heads stuck in our handoff holes. So why don't we fake Thomas into the hole, then I'll jump up and throw our 22 pass, the little dump toss to Goad."

Mitchell turned to Wilkinson. "Coach, you know our 22 pass might be a hell of a play."

"That's what I've been telling you the whole game," Wilkinson replied. But Mitchell still doesn't remember it.

Upon reentering the game, Mitchell lost no time calling the play. His short flip was incomplete, brushing the tops of Goad's fingers. But the Tar Heel linebackers reacted instantly. Thereafter they kept their distance, and the Sooner rushing game began to roll.

Midway in the third quarter the last touchdown of the game occurred. "In special situations," recalls Darrell Royal, "Mitchell and I would exchange positions. Against North Carolina I was quarterback for one down. I threw a long pass to Frankie Anderson."

It was the only pass Oklahoma completed in the game. The Sooners threw only three. Anderson was covered every foot of his route by a Tar Heel back, but with his gift for relaxation he coolly leaped and took the ball away from the Carolinian, running to the Tar Heel 10. Two plays later Pearson gushed 8 yards over weak-side blocks by Manley and McNabb to score. The conversion snapback was low and a little to the side, but Royal alertly grabbed it and socked it onto the turf. Ming plunked it between the posts. Oklahoma won 14-6.

Mitchell, the Oklahoma quarterback playing his final college game, was voted the Warren V. Miller Memorial Trophy as the outstanding player of the contest. "Mitchell was the quarterback supreme, a peppery general who kept the opposition guessing," wrote Tom Siler, sports editor of the *Knoxville* (Tennessee) *Sentinel.* "Greathouse was no less a standout."

Royal punted very accurately. All six of his boots soared over either the sideline or the goal line. None was run back. Tackle Homer Paine was a standout in the raging Sooner line. Paine could tell where the play was going from the pressure of the blocks, and he would try to get the jump on it, fight right into it.

"The best-prepared, best-drilled team we ever met was North Carolina," says Bobby Goad, later the Kansas assistant coach. "They were also the best-mannered. They were such gentlemen, both after the game and at the player party that night. They were a credit to Snavely, a medical doctor who had never practiced. When we visited with them at the player party, we found them well educated, intelligent guys, very interested in getting their degrees."

Total game receipts were $103,081.48, of which Oklahoma retained half. The Sooners then were not compelled to divide their share with the conference. That would come later. Meanwhile the regents approved a $1 million expansion of Owen Field that increased the seating capacity from 30,000 to 55,000 and provided a new three-deck press box with an elevator. The cinder track around the football field was moved east behind the stadium across Jenkins Street so that the gridiron could be lowered six feet, thus providing thousands of ringside seats nearer the action.

Oklahoma in 1948 set two national records. The Sooners ran back punts 963 yards for an average of 22.4 yards each runback. The old record was 22 yards set in 1944 by New York University. They also lost 35 fumbles. The old record was 30 made by UCLA in 1946. The Sooners finished fifth nationally in rushing, seventh in total offense. Burris and Mitchell made first All-American teams.

State pride in the Sooners burgeoned. Jenkin Lloyd Jones, editor of the *Tulsa Tribune*, wrote, "Times change. Today Oklahomans forget to cringe at the sound of 'Okie.' The Wilkinson teams helped dispel this delusion."

The 1948 Sooners celebrate after defeating Texas for the first time in nine years.

Buddy Burris and wife, Betty, at the Sugar Bowl party after Oklahoma defeated North Carolina. Photo by Leon Trice Picture Service, New Orleans, La.

Myrle Greathouse holds the Sugar Bowl trophy after Sooners defeated North Carolina.

1948 SENIORS TODAY

Paul ("Buddy") Burris is contract negotiator for Tinker Air Force Base, Oklahoma City. He also owns and operates Burris Services, a landscaping and tree surgery firm in Norman.

Myrle Greathouse is president of the WES-TEX Drilling Company, of Abilene, Texas. He is also president of the Teltek Drilling Company, of Denver, Colorado, and of the TEX-MEX Drilling Company, of Roswell, New Mexico.

Jack Mitchell is president and chairman of the board of Mitchell Publications, Inc., a firm involving newspapers, cable TV, printing, insurance, oil investments, and drilling rigs. He also breeds, trains, and drives in competition his own harness horses in county-fair racing circuits in Iowa, Missouri, Kansas, and Illinois.

Homer Paine is manager of the Johnston Grain Company terminal elevator at Enid, Oklahoma.

Pete Tillman is director of personnel at Grants Municipal School, Grants, New Mexico.

4. THE STUMP HARVESTERS

After the quake of graduation five fissures appeared in the 1949 Sooner firmament. Gone was the left side of the starting line—tackle Homer Paine, guard Buddy Burris, and center Pete Tillman. Gone also were the 1948 team's natural leaders, quarterback Jack Mitchell and linebacker Myrle Greathouse. But there was still a great deal of talent left.

Willie Manley, who "hit like a big spring," as his teammate Jim Weatherall put it, moved to starting left tackle. Norman McNabb took over the left guard spot as if he owned it. Behind him came Dee Andros, "the only man on the squad who could double-team you all by himself," the Sooners satirized the Greek kid's girth.

Clair Mayes, the only sophomore to crash the starting line the year before, was back. Also Stan West, one of the cocaptains who at 236 pounds was the biggest and hungriest man on the squad. All four ends returned from 1948, Jim Owens and Ken Tipps on the left side, Bobby Goad and Frankie Anderson on the right.

At 6 foot 3 and 195 pounds Owens could do it all. "A smart young man with a fine attitude," Pop Ivy, the end coach, described him. As a freshman on Tatum's team, Owens had fielded five forward passes against Texas, one for a touchdown. "He was a big old steady guy," remembers Stan West. "Today he would make a great tight end." Of Bobby Goad, Willie Manley said, "Goad was a bony little guy. He was like a knife. You hit him and he'd cut you."

Charley Dowell, of Tulsa, who later became a minister, rated a thin edge at center over Harry Moore with Bob Bodenhamer of Waurika available for the long snap on punts and for hustling down and nailing the enemy safety.

"Enthusiasm was Dowell's strong point," Ivy remembers. "He was even enthusiastic about practice. He left the huddle fast and got up over the ball fast. He enjoyed playing, practicing, and being there."

Dowell's father, H. E. Dowell, a Tulsa oilman, made all the games and always took the coaching staff to dinner the night before. "I always got beat out on Friday night," Moore laughs about his and the younger Dowell's close rivalry.

It was Wade Walker's final season at right tackle. Quick and knowledge-

54

able, he knew everybody's assignment on every play. J. W. Cole, Hollis junior, played behind Walker. So did Dean Smith, an aggressive junior from Tulsa. The pass defense looked sharp as a locust thorn with Royal and Ed Lisak at the halves, Buddy Jones at safety, and Norman sophomore Jack Lockett coming on.

It was in 1949 that Bud and Gomer devised the Oklahoma Defense, a 5-4 that was a completely new concept. "It has since been used extensively in professional football, and still is today," says Pop Ivy. "We had been in the Eagle Defense, named for the Philadelphia Eagles. In it the linebackers played on the offensive ends. But it was Bud's idea that, since linebackers, playing on tight ends, can't see what's going on, no key is given. 'Let's move our linebackers in on the offensive guards and move our defensive tackles on the outside shoulder of the offensive tackles and key on the offensive guards,' Bud proposed. 'The guard will pull, or double-team, or do something to tell us what the play will be.' As soon as the offensive guard moved, we knew what to do."

Heath's fullbacking speed became a legend. Wilkinson developed speed by closing every workout with a series of wind sprints. The finale was a 50-yard dash in which ends ran in one group, tackles in another, guards in a third, and on through all the positions. There was a lot of rivalry in these races. Not only did the players sharpen their speed, they learned to run fast while fatigued.

Heath says, "Wilkinson had sold me on the fact that I had to have speed to make his team. Although I gained a little weight every year I played at OU, I picked up a little more speed each year too. For example, I was faster in 1949 than in 1948. My legs never got tired in a game."

George Thomas, Pearson, and Heath were fixtures in the backfield, but quarterback was another story. Mitchell, the departed, had played 80 percent of the time.

Royal, the cool little senior veteran, got the call. At Hollis High School he had chirped the signals and barked the snap count from double-wing tailback, and his team won the state championship. He was more studious about football than anybody else on the squad. Resolved to be a coach, he spent hour after hour in the coaching offices, asking questions and studying films. He visited with Gomer Jones to learn line play. "I was studying for my profession," he says today.

Royal was in his fourth year of Wilkinson's quarterback meetings and esteemed them very highly. "The reason Coach Wilkinson[1] was a great

---

[1] When I interviewed Royal at Austin in 1981, I showed him this statement which he had given me in 1963. He asked me to change the word "Bud" to "Coach Wilkin-

football coach was because of his ability to teach," said Royal. "He expressed everything in such clear, simple terms that players always understood him. He spent a lot of time with us quarterbacks. When I graduated from Oklahoma, I felt I had a good understanding of our offense.

"I could even talk intelligently about it to coaches. It wasn't any special gift I had. It was because Coach Wilkinson had taught me so well that there was nothing complicated or mysterious about it. Other Oklahoma players I've talked to have been able to do this too, but not players from other schools. When I talked to them, they usually didn't know why they were doing anything."

Ivy said: "Before the 1949 season we coaches got to looking at films of our '48 games. We asked ourselves, What kind of coaches are we not to play Willie Manley more? The films told the story. He wore out everybody around him on both sides. He ran over his teammates trying to get to the opposition. If he was playing on offense, he would block his man so far downfield that he'd cut off our offside blocking shield too. 'One-Round Manley,' Sarge Dempsey, the equipment man, called him. If he had polled the players, he'd have started as a sophomore. They were aware of him because every day in practice he knocked their heads off. He didn't know what dummy practice was."

"That's right," broke in George Brewer. "One day we had dummy scrimmage late in the week. Just bump and step. I was holding a dummy and gazing off south at that big old cottonwood tree. Willie hit me and that dummy both and knocked us for a double somersault.

"I got up screaming. 'This is a dummy, a half-speed drill!' I yelped. And he didn't even know what I was talking about."

Manley was the most underrated man on the squad. "He was the strongest physically and had the greatest tolerance against pain," says Norman McNabb, who roomed with him on trips. "He was also the most moral and ethical guy on the squad," McNabb added. "On trips he carried a little black leather Bible with him, and he read it every night."

Upon his discharge from the navy Manley married his high-school sweetheart, Johnnie Boggs. Johnnie was a quiet, reserved farm girl. Her parents owned a cotton farm twelve miles north of Hollis. Willie brought her to Norman with him. Since she was only seventeen, he enrolled her at Norman High School.

Manley's speed was incredible. The only man on the squad who could

_____

son." He still respected his former mentor so highly he was unwilling to take liberties with his nickname.

56

beat him at 100 yards was Tommy Gray, the dash champ from Seminole. "I was blessed," Manley quietly explains the speed.

Manley went around the campus on a motor bike, remembers Jim Keith, the student wrestling manager. "His brown hair would be flying and his shirt fastened by only one button," says Keith. "He'd be riding that thing in the dead of winter, without a coat on."

An amusing incident grew up around that motor bike. The old players still like to recount it. In summer each day after his construction work, Willie would run a mile getting in shape for football. His wife, Johnnie, wanted to go too. "You might as well follow me on the motor bike," Willie told her. He taught her how to drive it.

One night she was chugging along behind him. It was growing dark. The narrow road had a deep ditch on one side and a barbed wire fence on the other. Johnnie was falling behind, her headlight bobbing faintly.

"Come on!" yelled Willie. "Catch up!"

Johnnie opened the throttle a little until she got closer. Then she reached for the hand brake but got the throttle instead.

"I can't stop it!" she wailed. The bike gained momentum. "I could see her going into that barbed wire," says Willie.

Like a bullfighter, he jumped out into the path of the runaway vehicle. He grabbed the handlebars. There was a collision and a pileup. Johnnie flew over Willie's right shoulder. The bike lay on its side, the motor still growling. Willie had stopped it dead in its track. He reached around and turned off the motor. He looked at it. The handlebars were jammed together where Willie had crushed them. He looked at Johnnie, who was getting to her feet. She had a strawberry on one knee.

"Johnnie, you tore up my bike," said Willie.

The girl stood, brushing herself. She looked provoked. "You don't care anything about me," she said. "All you're concerned about is your bike!"

Willie stood the vehicle up. Straddling the front wheel, he grasped a handlebar in each hand and, flexing his muscles, bent them back almost to normal. But they always stayed a little crooked.

Wilkinson's name began to be coupled with coaching vacancies. Oklahoma had lost no time rewarding him generously. President Cross told him before the team enplaned from New Orleans that the regents had verbally agreed to raise his salary to $15,000 a year and give him a new five-year contract. That was $1,000 more than the president himself was paid.

Wilkinson assured the president that he was happy at OU and had no intention of leaving. But a few days later he visited with University of Wisconsin officials, and the Milwaukee newspapers announced that he would be given the Badger coaching job at $12,000 per year. Upon his return to Norman, Wilkinson denied that he had been offered a job and said that he had made only a courtesy visit and had taken part only in a general discussion of the Wisconsin coaching problems. On January 15 he agreed to sign the new contract with Oklahoma at $15,000 a year as football coach, athletic director, and professor of physical education.

For years this would be the general pattern of Wilkinson's negotiations with outside schools. He always seemed willing to talk with them, but Oklahomans soon learned to regard this less nervously because the University always kept on the front burner the matter of rewarding him liberally salarywise, and also because Wilkinson himself did not believe in breaking his contract. This was a day in which college coaches jumped their contracts like grasshoppers jumping over pea vines.

Recruiting became more vital than ever in 1949, the last year Oklahoma would have her war veterans. Being able to judge the relative potential of an athlete when he matured was the most valuable attribute a recruiting coach could possess. This was illustrated in the case of John Reddell, skinny Oklahoma City Classen High School standout in football, baseball, and basketball, who stood 6-1 and weighed 165 pounds.

Reddell was invited to visit OU and watch a Sooner football game. Afterwards, Wilkinson, Gomer Jones, and Ivy took him to dinner. "Gomer and Pop had to leave," Reddell remembers, "but Bud stayed. Bud could tell you exactly what you wanted to hear. 'You're the type we'd like to have,' he told me. 'You're going to grow some. Most important of all, we think you're a winner.'

"That's all it took," Reddell laughs today. "I just melted. At Classen, I was kind of a poor boy in a rich school anyhow. To me, this coach had everything. He was physically imposing, superintelligent, nationally successful. He had it all up one tree. I loved him. I was at an impressionable age anyhow."

When recruiting, Wilkinson looked for high school boys with character, as well as speed and scholastic aptitude. "Remember," he said, "The majority of players on a football squad are dissatisfied. Of your 55 men, only 22 get to play much and only eleven are completely happy. They're the starters. The rest aren't playing enough to suit themselves, their families, their girl friends, their fraternity brothers or their high school coaches. So we feel it's awfully important to get boys who are healthy both mentally and physically."

George Cornelius, son of a butcher at Cherokee, wanted to come to Oklahoma to play football and also for something else. "My mother died when I was eleven years old, and they didn't know what was wrong. I wanted to become a doctor," he says. Tryouts were legal then, and Cornelius joined two hundred others at Norman. "When Pop Ivy took me to the bus station that night, he offered me a scholarship. I grabbed it."

A fine freshman crop was harvested that fall, lads like Eddie Crowder, Buck McPhail, Chet Bynum, Bob Gaut, Ed Rowland, and Jack Santee. Jim Davis, a tackle from McAlester, followed his brother to West Point but was rejected for health reasons. He came to Oklahoma and became an excellent blocker. Tom Catlin, of Ponca City, joined the frosh. "Catlin breezed through his chemistry classes," remembers Cornelius. "I tried to get him to study medicine."

Meanwhile, word had come to Oklahoma's coaches of a well-nigh incredible feat by a high-school back at Cleveland, Oklahoma, a thickset speedster with a craggy face and a body set in lines of stone. In a game against Fairfax he had carried the ball only five times yet had peeled off touchdown runs of 97, 93, 90, 76, and 3 yards. Moreover, he did it with his right wrist in a cast. He had broken it in a previous game. His name was Billy Vessels.

"Gomer Jones recruited me," Vessels says. "He drove up twice. On the Sunday after Oklahoma beat Missouri in football in 1948, I visited Bud in the fieldhouse. He showed me movies of the game and tried to sell me on the split-T formation. But mainly I was sold on Bud. His style and approach were so soft. He was a new type of coach for that day. You knew he was a winner."

The opening game with Boston College was scheduled for Friday night, September 23, at Braves Field, in Boston. But the game wasn't played that night. A rain drenched the gridiron, the crowd stayed home, and Wilkinson persuaded Denny Myers, the Boston coach, to reschedule the game the following night.

"Those Boston baseball people knew how to deal with rain," recalled Clee Fitzgerald, Oklahoma's new ticket manager. "They stamped the football tickets of those who came Friday with baseball rainchecks and began working on the field. Next day the gridiron was fast for the game."

The East's cocksureness astonished the Sooners. Accustomed to Wilkinson's careful pessimism, they could hardly believe what they read in the August issue of *Illustrated Football Annual.* George Trevor, a respected eastern football observer, wrote: "Denny Myers, the coach who believes in his boys and dares to admit it, . . . has them big and he has them plenty up on Chestnut Hill, and the Irish cod-connoisseurs are proclaiming the greatest Eagle array since all-winning 1940, the swan song of Frank Leahy's consulship."

It was Royal's first game as Oklahoma's quarterback, and he naturally felt some tension. Line coach Gomer Jones helped him conquer it. As the Sooners ran out of their dressing room door on their way to the gridiron to play, Jones slapped Royal on the back and growled, "Stay loose, kid."

"He knew I'd been worrying about running the option play," Royal laughs today. "He wanted me to stay in the right mental attitude. He did this before every game we played that season. And if he hadn't been standing at the locker room door as we ran down the chute, I'd have gone back looking for him."

On the Sooner sideline Wilkinson summoned his three right halves, George ("Junior") Thomas, George Brewer, and Tommy Gray. "I may have to flip a coin to see who starts today," he told them. His choice was Thomas. On the morning of the game the Sooners had visited Bunker Hill, where, back in 1775, William Prescott had told the American minutemen, "Don't fire until you see the whites of their eyes." The Sooners forgot all about Prescott's advice. On the opening kickoff they opened the firing from long range by blocking Thomas down the right sideline for 95 yards and a touchdown.

Says George Brewer, "That ended all speculation about who was the starting right half. But that was no problem. We were all fiercely proud of the guys playing ahead of us. Junior and I roomed together on the road. We were fine friends."

West, the big Sooner middle guard, soundly whipped the Boston center and had Ed Songin, Boston's fine forward passer, on his back much of the night. His style was to pursue along the line of scrimmage, shedding blockers with every step, maneuvering outside to meet the play. "West looked like a grizzly bear on roller skates," one Boston writer painted him. The Sooners were excellently prepared.

When Songin faded back and began raising the ball in his hand as if to pass, they looked for the fullback draw. If he faded and didn't raise his arm, he was going to throw. He threw well, at that, completing 22 of 46 aerials for 154 yards. But Oklahoma won 49-0.

Oklahoma's offense against Boston College was pure split-T. "Even if we flanked the fullback out as a tight wing, we thought we had really opened up," Royal remembers. "We just lined up and went north and south."

In their second tiff the Sooners overpowered Texas A&M 33-13. Left end Jim Owens's downfield blocking, when he picked up in motion ahead of the Sooner sweeps, was devastating.

But Oklahoma's casualties had grown alarmingly. The most uncommon injury had occurred in the Boston College game, when Frank Silva broke both jaws. That posed a special problem. The sophomore quarterback couldn't open his mouth wide enough to eat or to call the snap signal. The food problem was solved by feeding Silva canned infant food every two hours, but nobody could figure a way to help him call signals. Silva began wearing a protective mask.

Oklahoma went into the Texas fray protecting a winning streak of 12 straight victories. Texas wasn't intimidated. Coach Blair Cherry's Orange Bowl champions stood 3-0, having leveled Texas Tech 43-0, Temple 54-0, and Idaho 52-7. A crowd of 75,347 partisans of Texas's fiery Orange and Oklahoma's flaming Crimson thronged the Dallas Cotton Bowl to get the answer. Could Wilkinson's red remuda turn the fiery Texas stampede into a circle of exhaustion?

Clouds darkened the sky, thunder pealed in the distance, and there was a scent of rain in the air. Ignoring the elements, Cherry's Longhorns attacked hotly. They drove to the Sooner 6, only to have center Charley Dowell intercept Paul Campbell's pass. They moved to the Sooner 23, only to have tackle Willie Manley wreck two plays, tossing fullback Ray Borneman for a 14-yard loss on the second. But on their third sortie the Longhorns drove 46 yards to score, Randall Clay twisting across for the touchdown.

It was a bad time for Oklahoma, the crossroads to a good or bad season. The Sooners hadn't made a single first down. Tackle Wade Walker, the best blocker in the line, was knocked out on his feet and, straying into the Texas huddle, had to be led to the Sooner bench. The Texas team was aroused to a fighting frenzy by its early success in the game.

Then the Sooners began to block and tackle fiercely. They drove 66 yards to a touchdown in six plays from kickoff. Royal, gaining poise and cunning with each game, directed the awesome Sooner power. From the Steer 40 he handed off to George Thomas and watched the halfback run. West, Dean Smith, and Goad broke Thomas through the line. He tore away from a linebacker and cut straight for the goal with a pursuing Texan hot on his heels. Thomas hip-feinted to the left, then cut diagonally to the right, gaining so much ground by the maneuver that his pursuer gave up the chase. It was a run of 40 yards.

Ken Tipps kicked goal, but it was disallowed because the referee hadn't yet whistled the ball in play. The Sooners were so fired up they hadn't waited for the signal. This put a lot of pressure on Tipps. Oklahoma trailed 6-7 and might need that conversion badly. Again Tipps thumped the ball through the uprights. The score was tied.

Then came the rain. The big crowd, most of it totally unprepared, adjusted to the downpour as best it could. So did the two teams on the field.

The rain stopped in the last half, but the Sooners didn't. Their attitude was reflected by Pearson, who ran the opening kickoff back 40 yards almost to midfield. From there the Sooners drove 50 yards to a touchdown in five plays with Jim Owens, Manley, Andros, Dowell, West, Dean Smith, and Goad throwing some walloping blocks as they moved the attack down the drizzle-freshened play yard. On the Orange 11, Royal laid the handoff on Pearson's meaty hip, and the Capital Hill youth smashed with bruising power, carrying tackler after tackler as he scored. Tipps kicked goal. Oklahoma led 14-7.

Texas recovered and battled hard all through the third quarter. Once Jim Weatherall, sophomore tackle, surged upon Borneman, knocking the ball loose from him and raking it beneath his own muddied red jersey. Another time, Sooner hearts flew up in Sooner throats when Texas threw a long forward pass off their Statue of Liberty sequence, Campbell pegging 50 yards and laying the wet ball squarely in the hands of Ben Proctor, their finest receiver, as Proctor raced ahead of all pursuit into the end zone. But Proctor dropped the ball!

Later Royal faked a handoff and spiraled the ball to Jimmy Owens, rangy Sooner end, who had gotten behind the Texas defense. Touchdown! Tipps missed goal. Score 20-7. Texas scored in the last 29 seconds on a draw by fullback Lewis Levine.

In the center of the field Wilkinson told Cherry, "We were very fortunate. You have a great team. That long pass that your boy dropped in the end zone might have changed the game." As Cherry walked amid his weary players to the dressing room, he said, "West, their guard, and the entire Oklahoma backfield were terrific. That end, Owens, was also great."

It was a big day for three unheralded Sooner squadmen who had to spell injured Sooner regulars. They were Delton Marcum, guard from Ada; J. W. Cole, tackle from Hollis; and Art Janes, guard from Holdenville. The Sooners got the job done as a squad, not as a starting eleven.

In the Big Seven Conference inaugural at Norman the following week, Oklahoma thrashed Kansas 48 to 26. The Sooners did many things well. They intercepted six Kansas passes (Lisak two, Royal, Ken Parker, Dowell, Bert Clark), blocked three Kansas kicks (Manley, Owens, Jack Lockett) and scored seven touchdowns (Thomas four, Heath, Royal, Pearson). Yet Wilkinson censured them in his letter to the alumni. It always seemed to me that instead of writing that letter to the paid members of the OU Alumni Association, the coach addressed it straight to his players, all of whom read it first thing Monday morning.

He pointed out that the team hadn't yet learned to be ready to play mentally as well as physically. They hadn't worked in practice as a good football team should. Their chance to defeat Nebraska in the next game depended greatly upon how hard they practiced all week ahead of the game. Then he went on; "A great football team is one that can soundly defeat an opponent, once it dazes him. Too many of our antagonists are jumping off the floor and felling us with a retaliatory punch."

Wilkinson spotlighted the game's Dad's Day motif by inviting the fathers of the Sooner players to sit on a sideline bench next to the Oklahoma players' bench. Each dad wore a white placard on his back showing the jersey number of his son on the field. After the game they visited with their sons in the dressing room, then went to the Union for coffee.

Nebraska needed coffee after the next game as Oklahoma rolled 48-0 at Lincoln to win their fifteenth encounter in succession. This time there was no lethargy in any department of play. And Wilkinson praised his squad afterward in his alumni letter.

As usual, he applauded the opponent too. "I thought Nebraska was as well coached and smartly handled as any club we have met all season," he said. "Our advantages in speed and manpower, and our depth, were too great for them to overcome in spite of their spirit and courage." "It had snowed at Lincoln, and we had to go by railroad train," recalls Willie Manley.

Some odd things happened in the game. A Nebraska back fumbled the ball into the air, and it plopped into the hands of Ed Lisak, who ran 68 yards down the sideline to set up a touchdown. Ken Tipps booted an extra point with only ten Sooners on the field. Later Tipps kicked off short and low, the ball striking Tom Novak, Cornhusker center, in the chest and bounding back into the arm of Dean Smith. It looked as if Halloween had come a week early.

Delton Marcum, Ada senior used at middle guard in that game, had a great day against Novak, Nebraska's standout center. Fast at coming off the ball, Marcum was lining up, with his chin a few inches off the turf, and storming in so fiercely that he made it difficult for the Cornhusker pivot to pass the ball and block too.

The Sooners respected Novak. "A fine player and a good guy," "did it all well," "knocked the fire out of people," and "had a great nose for the ball" were some of the encomiums they heaped upon him.

With Royal, West, and Lisak out of action with injuries, Oklahoma next entertained Iowa State at Norman and, as usual, found Coach Abe Stuber's team in a hostile mood.

It took a lineman to turn the game around. Willie Manley, who always covered fast on punts, sprinted down under Dick Heatly's long kick. Don Ferguson, the Cyclone safety, fielded it and danced back up the field. Manley struck him like a landslide and tore the ball loose. Jim Owens, who also liked to beat the ball to the safety, swept it up. Thomas scored on the handoff just 6:19 before the first half ended. It had taken the Sooners 24 minutes to put a 6 on the new electric scoreboard.

That whiff of the goal stimulated Sooner taste buds, and they quickly ran off four more touchdowns. The most spectacular by far came with the final seconds of the first half ticking away and the crowd filing down the stadium aisles toward the soft-drink stands. But Buddy Jones, Sooner safety, brought them up sharply.

Dana Omer, Cyclone kicker, punted away from Jones. The ball bounced leisurely toward the east sideline. Jones suddenly snatched it up and darted down the boundary. Quickly, Oklahoma's blockers formed to protect him, Goad delivering one especially timely block. George Thomas was cruising at Jones's side. As Chauncey, Cyclone fullback and last defender, veered in their path, Jones slowed and feinted inside. It was a touchdown feint. Chauncey gave ground to adjust, giving Thomas the blocking angle. Thomas flattened Chauncey, and Jones dashed down the sideline to score. It was an 83-yard runback. Oklahoma won 34-7.

The forward passing was good on both sides. Claude Arnold, in for Royal, was perfect, completing four of four. Billy Weeks, sprightly Cardinal and Gold quarterback, threw neatly and well despite the fierce Sooner rush, completing 18 of 27 for 281 yards and hitting Jim Doran with an 87-yard touchdown throw. Doran's 203 yards in catches and the 87-yarder pegged by Weeks are still all-time bests against Oklahoma.

Against Kansas State at Manhattan, which was playing without their best hand, fullback Gerald Hackney, who had lamed a knee, Oklahoma quickly established control. They had Royal back at quarterback and West at guard. They led 33-0 at the half and won 39-0, playing their entire traveling squad.

Missouri had won five straight and stood just two missed conversion kicks from an all-victorious season. The Tigers had lost 34-35 to an Ohio State powerhouse at Columbus that would later win the Rose Bowl. At Dallas they fell 27-28 to Southern Methodist and its star, Doak Walker. But they had won all the others. The Tigers came into the contest on the heels of a gigantic student pep demonstration.

The Sooners had their own demonstration before they left Norman. Their team plane waited an hour at Max Westheimer Field for guard Norman McNabb to rush by automobile from the Norman Municipal Hospital where his wife was giving birth to a baby. When McNabb raced up the boarding ramp and into the plane, the squad gave him a rousing cheer.

"I hadn't slept for two days nor attended any squad meetings," McNabb remembers. "On the plane Gomer kept me awake with hot coffee and taught me all the techniques we were using for Missouri. As soon as we landed at Jefferson City, I went to bed. I felt great on Saturday. I felt so good that on the second-half kickoff I ran down and tackled the ballcarrier, and for the first time in my life, I got knocked out."

Right from the start Oklahoma demonstrated that defense and ball control are hard to beat. On their third possession the Sooners wheeled 52 yards in seven plays to a touchdown. Heath hit over Owens, Manley, and Andros for the score. Tipps kicked goal. From the middle of the field Missouri scored in six plays.

With the game tied and the Missouri crowd roaring for another touchdown, the Sooners began to take charge. Without giving up the ball, the Oklahomans swung 70 yards down the damp turf to a touchdown. Pearson ripped 3 yards off left tackle for the score. Tipps kicked goal, and the Sooners led 14-7 at the half.

That second touchdown was the game's pivotal point. "We've got 'em! We've got 'em!" the Sooner players told their coaches in the dressing room at halftime. "The coaches thought they were crazy," recalls assistant mentor Pop Ivy. But when the two teams stood toe-to-toe in the third quarter and began slugging it out, Oklahoma's blows were the heavier. And the crack began to widen.

Heatly punted. Braznell caught it and faked a handoff, but Bob Bodenhamer, Sooner center, raced down and dropped Braznell. From the Tiger 36, Klein faded to throw, but McNabb, the new father, felled him for a 9-yard loss. Then Missouri fumbled, and Ken Parker topped the ball on the Tiger 27. The Sooners scored in five plays, Pearson passing 6 yards to Frankie Anderson off a reverse.

Late in the third period Glorioso tried a running pass, but Royal picked it off, hit the ground running, and put 45 yards behind him before the Tigers hauled him down on their 16. Missouri dug in valiantly, but Royal called on Heath, and the junior fullback left a trail of wreckage as he thundered across the goal. Oklahoma won, 27-7. Jim Owens, Sooner left end, threw a vital block on each of Oklahoma's four touchdowns.

"They'll never fill it," many had predicted, when President Cross originated and pushed to completion plans to almost double the seating capacity of Oklahoma's stadium to 55,000. Yet in the Santa Clara game on November 19 at Norman, the new facility was stuffed with an all-time record throng of 61,353, showing the clutch the Sooners had on their enthusiasts. Hundreds more were turned away.

The game had something of an all-Oklahoma motif. Hall Haynes, crack Santa Clara back, had been born in Duncan, Oklahoma. "I felt that I was partly responsible for that crowd," Haynes laughs today, "because I think about half of them were my relatives."

"Mercy," Stan West, Oklahoma's cocaptain and guard, says now of Haynes, "he was a fine player. And their big blond guard, John something-or-other, was too."

Darrell Royal recalls watching Haynes kick in practice before the game. "He was a talented punter," says Royal today. "He and Carl Knox of TCU were the best I ever saw. I watched them kicking into our wind. They were hitting the ball with controlled pure spirals. They knew how to play the wind."

Santa Clara, coached by Len Casanova, was a class opponent. Five weeks later they defeated Coach Paul ("Bear") Bryant's Kentucky Wildcats in the Orange Bowl.

In the middle of the first quarter Haynes, back to punt, fumbled. Grabbing up the ball, he circled end for 12 yards, but Oklahoma took over on downs on the Bronco 27. The Sooners scored seven plays later, Thomas ripping 2 yards over Mayes, Dean Smith, and Anderson. Tipps kicked goal.

Then came Santa Clara's first show of offensive strength, the Broncs traveling 67 yards to score on a pass, quarterback Len Napolitano to end Monty Osborn. However, Stan West, Sooner guard, blocked Joe Vargas's conversion.

"I lined up head-on with their guard, like I was going to slant outside," West recalls the play. "He stepped out to get me, and I went in and blocked it."

On the second play after the following kickoff Heath, Oklahoma's junior fullback from Hollis, whipped through a gaping hole for 81 yards and a touchdown. Tipps goaled. Oklahoma led 14-6. Clair Mayes and Dean Smith of the alternate line blocked strongly to release Heath into the secondary. Harry Moore and Dee Andros contributed downfielders.

Safety Buddy Jones's 33-yard punt runback introduced Oklahoma's next touchdown, a 24-yard cruise by George Thomas. Wade Walker threw the most telling block with Dowell, West, and Andros giving assistance. Tipps kicked goal, and the Sooners led commandingly 21-6.

Trailing by 15 points, Santa Clara could have said, "Oh, what's the use?" and stopped trying so hard. Instead, they battled the Sooners all over the field. Haynes kicked a towering punt, and when Royal was trapped in the end zone for a safety, the Sooner lead was reduced to 21-8. Recovering a Sooner fumble, Santa Clara scored on a forward pass, John Pasco to Dick Wilborn. Again Stan West, Oklahoma's burly senior guard, blocked Vargas's extra point to keep the Sooner lead at seven points, 21-14.

"I lined up head on with their guard again," West says. "I knew that guy wasn't gonna do the same thing twice. But again he took the outside charge."

The Sooners followed Tipps's second-half kickoff down hard, knocking

Leon Heath running 81 yards to Oklahoma's second touchdown as the Sooners defeated Santa Clara 28-21 at Norman in 1949. Photo by Oklahoma Publishing Co.

Tackle Wade Walker (70) and guard Stan West (64), Oklahoma linemen of 1949. The three Sooner All-American forwards that season were Walker, West, and Owens. Photo by Sports Information Department, University of Oklahoma.

End Jim Owens catching Claude Arnold's pass for 24 yards against Iowa State in 1949. Photo by Oklahoma Publishing Co.

the ball loose from Abe Dung, Walker recovering on the Santa Clara 15. On the first play Thomas darted through them for a touchdown with Walker making the key block, aided by Dowell and Andros. Tipps kicked goal, and Oklahoma led 28-14.

The Sooners kept attacking. They marched 48 yards to the Bronco 37, but Haynes intercepted Pearson's pass. They drove 41 yards to the Bronco 6 when Royal arched a 34-yard pass to Owens but lost the touchdown chance when Thomas fumbled on the goal, Santa Clara recovering.

Two minutes later the Sooners broke Lindell Pearson through the line on an inside pitch, and Pearson ran 65 yards down the sideline to a touchdown. But the Sooners were penalized for holding and lost that touchdown too. Instead of leading by four touchdowns, they led by only two.

In the fourth quarter Santa Clara scored when Del Rasmussen, their nineteen-year-old sophomore from Sacramento, ran 58 yards on a pitchout. Several times the Sooners seemed to have him trapped, but like a speedster avoiding the cops he escaped to the goal without drawing an arresting summons. This time the Broncs held West out, and Vargas got his kick away. It was good. Oklahoma led 28-21.

Haynes had one more bolt left in his arsenal. With three and a half minutes left, he kicked a 56-yard punt into the crosswind, the ball rolling out of bounds on the Sooner 4. Oklahoma was virtually a prisoner on its own goal, where a mistake of any kind might mean a tie.

The Sooners called on their rushing game, which totaled 295 yards. Choosing only inside plays, Royal drove them out of the hole and up the shadow-striped rectangle. Ten plays he called, six of them sneaks by himself over the middle. The ninth play was a 3-yard dive by Thomas that fetched a first down on the Sooner 40. The game ended with the Sooners still dreadnaughting their way forward.

They kept going forward the following week too, defeating Oklahoma A&M 41-0 at Norman and accepting an invitation to met Louisiana State at New Orleans on New Year's afternoon in the Sugar Bowl.

"I have never seen a team that played the game with such furious enjoyment," Wilkinson wrote of his 1949 club in his final alumni letter. He also pointed out that all nineteen seniors would graduate that school year with solid majors running chiefly to geology, engineering, and business.

It was Jim Lookabaugh's last game as coach of the Oklahoma Aggies, and when in the fourth quarter Bruce Drake, Sooner public-address announcer, paid him tribute while Lookabaugh stood in front of the A&M bench, the Sooner crowd of 47,937 gave the Aggie coach a tremendous ovation.

The spy incident that occurred during Oklahoma's Sugar Bowl workouts at Biloxi, Mississippi, added a bizarre touch to the game. After the Sooner practice Friday, December 30, Wilkinson received a telephone call from Clarence Johnson, of Biloxi, informing him that Oklahoma's last two workouts had been scouted by three men hiding under a tarpaulin on the roof of a garage overlooking the Biloxi gridiron.

"That was the only time I ever saw Bud real angry," recalls Pop Ivy, Sooner assistant. "His face was white."

Willie Manley adds: "At practice next day Bud told us that spies were watching us and not to let on that we knew. We got a little worried. We'd been practicing a new series where we used two quarterbacks under the center for this game only. We all craned our necks, looking around. It was a new experience."

Wilkinson quickly organized a counterexpedition involving Dr. C. B. McDonald, Oklahoma City dentist; Ned Hockman, University photographer; John Askin, Jr., a Biloxi policeman; John Scafidi, a professional player who had formerly played at Tulane; and Bill Dennis, a Biloxi photographer.

Next day at practice they moved in on the garage, and during a scuffle Dennis snapped a picture of the spy, which the Associated Press distributed nationwide.

When Darrell Royal, Sooner quarterback, saw the picture the next morning in a New Orleans newspaper, he said, "That's Piggy Barnes." Barnes, a former Louisiana State player, had played for the Third Air Force team at Tampa, Florida. Royal had met him in 1945 and recognized him.

T. P. Heard, LSU athletic director, denied that his coach or his school was implicated. Heard accused Wilkinson of using the incident to fire up his team for the game. "It didn't fire us up," maintains Stan West, Sooner cocaptain. "We were ready to play anyhow. We always lined up and played on Saturday."

Wilkinson publicly challenged Barnes and Elbert Manuel, his accomplice, who was also a former LSU player, to present themselves for identification by the three neutral witnesses who had accompanied the expedition that had discovered them. Neither appeared.

On the morning of the game the Sooner squad had eaten its pregame meal and was sitting around waiting for the stadium bus. A bevy of pretty girl cheerleaders, clad in lavender, came into the lobby. Their voices were trilling happily, and the aura of their perfume was in the air.

Leon Heath, Oklahoma's fullback, sat slouched in a chair. Head down, he was thinking about the impending combat. Several of the girls brushed against him. "But Heath didn't even look up," Pop Ivy laughs. "He was concentrating on the game."

At the Sugar Bowl, 82,289 jammed the double-decked steel stadium. The Sooners were 8-point favorites, but Louisiana State had the home crowd.

Denny Myers, the Boston College coach, picked Oklahoma to win. "I believe they are the best-coached football team in the United States," he was quoted. "This team doesn't try to fool you. They have a full knowledge of the basis of all football, and that's blocking and tackling. From a technical standpoint, this is the most amazingly interesting team I have seen in the last ten years. LSU will have its troubles."

But the first quarter was played mostly on Oklahoma terrain. Royal broke up two Pevey passes on the goal. Then Royal punted 50 yards out on the LSU 14, and Oklahoma got in gear. Pearson fired a long halfback pass to George Thomas for 34 yards and a touchdown. Tipps kicked goal. LSU fumbled the following kickoff, and Oklahoma drove 38 yards to score again, this time on a 5-yard handoff by Thomas. Tipps kicked goal. LSU launched another drive, but Gene Heape stormed in to throw Baggett for a 7-yard loss.

In the last half the great crowd marveled at the ferocity of the Sooner play. On the fifth snap of the ball the battle's most dramatic episode occurred. Leon Heath galloped 86 yards to a touchdown from scrimmage, a new Sugar Bowl record. The run was spectacular proof of how meticulously line coach Gomer Jones had taught his speedy Sooner forwards to think in action.

"Louisiana State was using a seven-and-a-diamond defense," recalls Heath. "They had their guard and middle linebacker cross-charging over center. We knew from watching their movies that they sometimes did this, so our line was ready for it. On the play I hit between center and right guard. Dee Andros, our guard, and Charley Dowell, our center, were supposed to double-team the man over our center. That was their orthodox assignment. But if LSU cross-charged, we were ready with something else.

"Sure enough, they cross-charged. Our line quickly adjusted. When the LSU man playing over center cross-charged to Dowell's right, Dowell drove him past the hole. Andros saw Dowell needed no help, so he turned the LSU linebacker in the other direction.

"Wade Walker, our right tackle, who was supposed to block the linebacker, saw that Andros had him wrapped up, so Walker ran down and blocked out the safety. I was scarcely touched as I ran straight down the middle. And in the secondary Lindell Pearson, our left half, came up fast to block out the nearest LSU man chasing me." Tipps kicked goal. Oklahoma led 21-0.

When Bert Clark, dimpled, tumultuous Wichita Falls, Texas, sophomore, knocked the ball loose from Mel Lyle, LSU end, running an end around, Buddy Jones recovered on the Tiger 13. Four plays later Royal sneaked 5 yards, and the score rose to 28-0.

Then it ascended to 35-0 when Clark intercepted an LSU pass and returned 8 yards to the LSU 30. On the second play thereafter Heath, on an inside pitchout, ran 34 yards over right tackle to score standing. Tipps booted both goals.

Walter Stewart, sports editor of the *Memphis* (Tennessee) *Commercial-Appeal,* best caught the slam-bang motif of the struggle when he wrote: "Operating with all the delicate artistry of an engineer battalion harvesting stumps with a bulldozer, Oklahoma's football field forces uprooted Louisiana State. . . . the tackling of Tiger and Sooner was strictly for blood. On the first play of the fourth quarter, Mel Lyle ran an end around for LSU, and we have never seen it run more ferociously. A shoe-top tackle lifted Lyle into the air where he was almost torn in two by a following thunderbolt. He lost the ball but was fortunate in retaining his head. Yet the game was played with exceptional cleanliness. It was simply man-sized!"

Heath rushed 170 net yards in the game, averaging 11.3 yards, more than a first down every time he unloosed himself on the velvety Tulane turf. No wonder the 200 covering sportswriters voted him the Warren V. Miller Memorial Trophy as the contest's outstanding player.

More than three decades later Heath's teammates were still high on him. "He was an old plugger," said Stan West, "an under-sized ground-pounder. He had more speed than anybody I ever saw to be as flat-footed as he was." "You couldn't arm-tackle him," said Harry Moore. "Good pass receiver," Norman McNabb added. Pop Ivy said, "Mule Train was a perfect nickname for him. He was always so dependable. Never had a bad game nor a bad play." Dobby Goad recalled, "Anybody who met Heath in the hole got a hell of a jolt."

At the close of the regular season Oklahoma had the number two ranking in the nation, behind Notre Dame, in both the AP and UPI polls. But if the polls had been voted after the bowl games, as they are today, Oklahoma might well have been number one. The Sooners led the nation in defense against rushing, yielding 55.6 yards a game. George Thomas led the nation in scoring with 117 points, 27 more than his nearest opponent. Oklahoma finished second in team rushing, third in total offense, fourth in penalties, sixth in fumbles lost, sixth in total defense, and ninth in punting.

Although Oklahoma in 1949 was the most passed-on team in the nation (opponents fired 290 aerials at the Sooners in the ten regular season games), only five touchdown passes went through. Safety Buddy Jones and halfbacks Lisak, Royal, and Lockett all had a hand in this. Five members of the team were named to first All-American elevens—Wade Walker, Jim Owens, Stan

Wade Walker (70) and Homer Paine (71), Sooner captains, watching the coin flip at the 1949 Sugar Bowl. Photo by Leon Trice Picture Service.

Jack Mitchell, Sooner quarterback, receiving the outstanding player award of the 1949 Sugar Bowl game. Photo by Leon Trice Picture Service.

Darrell Royal, whose precise punting and pass defense was excellent in both the 1949 and 1950 Sugar Bowl games. Photo by Sports Information Department, University of Oklahoma.

Leon Heath, Sooner fullback, receiving the outstanding player award of the 1950 Sugar Bowl game. Photo by Leon Trice Picture Service.

Stanley West (64) and Jim Owens (81) calling the toss against Louisiana State in 1950 Sugar Bowl game. Photo by Leon Trice Picture Service.

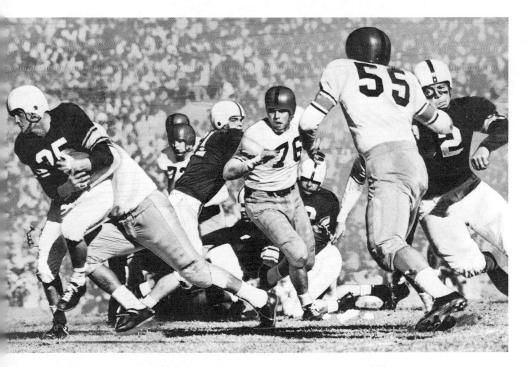

George Thomas running against Oklahoma State in 1949.

Buddy Jones returning a Missouri punt 50 yards to a touchdown in 1950.

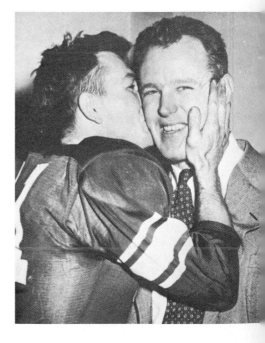

Quarterback Darrell Royal jubilantly kisses the cheek of Bud Wilkinson after the Sooners' 35-0 victory over Louisiana State in 1950 Sugar Bowl. Photo by Sports Information Department, University of Oklahoma.

West, Darrell Royal, and George Thomas. Wilkinson was voted Coach of the Year by the National Football Coaches Association.

Oklahoma fandom was fiercely proud of this team, and still is. Once after an AP sportswriter in New York carelessly referred to the Oklahoma team as "Okies," Ted Smits, national AP sports editor, received a postcard with the clipping pasted on it and the word "Okies" circled. The offended fan wrote, "Dear sir: You sonofabitch."

And thus passed the Sooners of 1949. "The best college team of all time," Billy Vessels still rated them in 1981. An Orange Bowl scout, Vessels has seen most of the great teams in the nation for two decades. "In 1949 we each were given a gold ring with a small diamond in it," says Jim Weatherall. "We still wear those rings and stay close together."

Ken Tipps said, "I wonder what that bunch would have been like if put on a weight program?" Then he added, "I loved that bunch. After four years of military service, it was refreshing to be irresponsible. Bud had the responsibility, and we had the fun."

1949 SENIORS TODAY

Dee Andros is athletic director at Oregon State University.

George Brewer is vice-president of Moore Energy Corporation, an Oklahoma City uranium firm.

The Reverend Charles K. Dowell is pastor of the Presbyterian Church at Junction, Texas.

Gene Heape is president of Heape Developments, Inc., and also of Heape Energy, Inc., both in Dallas, Texas.

Jim Owens is vice-president of the West Coast and Alaska divisions of Rowan Companies, contract drillers of oil and gas. Before that he coached the University of Washington football teams that won Rose Bowl championships in 1960 and 1961.

Darrell Royal coached the Texas teams of 1963 and 1969 to national championships and also served as Texas athletic director. Today he is assistant to the president of the University of Texas.

George Thomas is an independent oil-and-gas operator and owner of Thomas Drilling Mud Service of Liberal, Kansas.

Kenneth Tipps is an independent oil producer at Denver, Colorado.

Wade Walker is athletic director at the University of Oklahoma.

5. THE FIGHTING FOOLS OF '50

Oklahoma had had its "Beautiful Morning." Could the 1950 Sooners, drawing heavily on sophomores and squad men, keep everything going their way in the Big Seven Conference race?

The plain truth was that Wilkinson and his assistants—Gomer Jones, Frank Ivy, Bill Jennings, and George Lynn—were face to face with the crisis of their short coaching careers. Not only had the Sooners lost ten of their eleven offensive starters, including every one of the five All-Americans, but the parting, none of it sweet sorrow, also included seven valuable reserves. And Oklahoma was protecting a winning spree of 21 straight games.

Just before fall practice the Korean War broke out, and five additional Sooner players were called to active duty with the 45th Division, the Oklahoma National Guard. It didn't look as if the Sooners had even a slight chance of winning another Big Seven championship.

However, the Sooner sophomores had been a robust freshman aggregation. In their two jousts against outside opposition they drubbed Tulsa University 40-0 and Oklahoma A&M 40-20. With Wilkinson committed to using two teams, they were destined to see a lot of varsity action.

Billy Vessels thought that he was earmarked for defense at OU. "In high school I was a linebacker in our six-two defense," Vessels says. "I liked defense best. That's where all the action was." But when Tom Carroll was called to duty in the Korean War, Wilkinson switched Vessels to offense.

"In fall practice I weighed 235," recalls George Cornelius. "I had two pretty fair scrimmages. Bud told me, 'We can use you if you'll take off some of that weight.' I took off eighteen pounds in twelve days. I cut out bread, potatoes, and malts. I ate only meat and vegetables."

In the spring of 1950, John Reddell, the Classen boy, became the catcher on the Oklahoma baseball team coached by Jack Baer that won the National Collegiate tournament at Omaha without losing a game. "But when football started in the fall," Reddell says, "I was down on the fifth team because I'd played baseball and missed spring practice."

At 160 pounds, Reddell was pretty frail for blocking duty. Ivy, the end coach, said later, "We'd accuse Reddell of using an 'eye block.' He'd stand and glare at his opponent, and because of the power of that stare the guy wouldn't know what to do. Actually, Reddell was a little better blocker than he let on. He never did knock anybody down but he got pretty good at occupying them. He was a finesse blocker."

"I could catch the ball," Reddell sums up all the kidding. "They didn't throw it much, but when they did they liked to have it caught."

A week before the first game, Boston College at Norman, two eighteen-year-old sophomores, Kay Keller, end, and Vessels, left half, had fought their way to the first team. Weatherall was the left tackle, but Art Janes, a squad man and excellent blocker from Holdenville, played much of the offense.

Cocaptain McNabb, a seasoned 195-pounder with exceptional lateral quickness, and Bert Clark, a tough head-on tackler, played left guard. Clark was also used some at linebacker. Cocaptain Harry Moore, a good blocker, fine leader, and oldest man on the squad at 27, was the center. Behind him played a potential standout, sophomore Tom Catlin of Ponca City.

Clair Mayes, a nifty offensive blocker, and Joe Horkey, senior squad man from Tulsa, were at right guard. At right tackle were Dean Smith, also a senior from Tulsa, and J. W. Cole, the Hollis senior of whom the other players said, "When he comes across that scrimmage line he looks like a mowing machine."

Frankie Anderson, the former guard who had been transformed into an end, not only was a fine defensive player but he could catch the ball when a catch was sorely needed. Reddell supported him at right end. Dick Heatly, Mangum junior who had played behind Lindell Pearson in 1949 and while Royal's foot was crippled did much of the punting, was the right half. He was backed by Tommy Gray.

Pearson, the left half who had played only two seasons of varsity football, was lost for all time when the Big Seven Conference took away what would have been his senior season of 1950. During his short tenure at Arkansas, Pearson had played three games with the Arkansas freshman team, upon which varsity B-team players also competed in accordance with a Southwest Conference rule. However, Big Seven rules counted B-team competition equal to varsity competition.

Of Buddy Jones, senior safety, cocaptain Harry Moore said, "He could close faster than anybody I ever saw. Once they showed run, he was on 'em." Another crack defensive back was Ed Lisak, Kalamazoo, Michigan, senior, a corking pass defender with eleven interceptions for 200 yards the previous two seasons. He came up fast to meet the ballcarrier too. Lisak enjoyed the sub rosa give-and-take beyond football that players locked in combat sometimes indulged in. While held tightly in the grasp of an opponent he had just punched, Lisak would decorously raise both arms as he untangled himself and climbed to his feet, like a boxer breaking from a clinch.

High-school athletes who came to Oklahoma to play football responded to all sorts of recruiting stimuli. One of the most unusual cases was that of Darlon ("Doc") Hearon, Putnam City tackle and light-heavyweight wrestler. Hearon was a blond, combative 200-pounder who was always having to give weight to some superopponent and whose disposition, because of it, tended toward bellicosity. Hearon was recruited for OU by Casey Mills, an Oklahoma City police detective, who, doubling as a football referee, had just ejected Hearon from a high-school game for fighting.

"In spite of that fight, he took me down to OU twice," Hearon laughs today. "Charley Sarratt, the OU halfback of 1947, helped. But there was another reason—a big one—that made me decide not to go to OU. He was Gene Nicks."

Nicks, a 245-pound high-school wrestler from Ponca City, would later win two national collegiate heavyweight championships. He and Hearon had clashed six times on the mat in high school. Nicks won all six. When Hearon heard that Nicks had signed a wrestling scholarship with OU, he decided to go someplace else. He was tired of being torso-twisted by somebody 50 pounds heavier. So Hearon went to Oklahoma A&M.

"One day at Stillwater I walked into a cafeteria and bumped into Gene Nicks," says Hearon. "'What are you doin' here?' I asked. 'I've changed my mind,' said Nicks. 'I've decided to come to Oklahoma A&M.'" "That night I went back to Norman," Hearon concludes the incident.

At Norman, Hearon's freshman football coach was Port Robertson, also Oklahoma's head wrestling mentor. "My first run-in with Port was over my language in football practice," Hearon laughs today. "Port told me, 'You know more four-letter cusswords than any freshman I ever saw. Now, instead of saying those words you're so fond of, why not use a little class—like me—and say Pea-Head or Cotton-Picker?' So I cleaned up my language. I never swore again around Port."

Arnold, the quarterback from Okmulgee, had waited six years to play for the Sooners, eight to become the starting quarterback. In 1942, Myrle Greathouse had helped recruit him for Coach Dewey ("Snorter") Luster's Oklahoma freshman squad. Then came the interruptions. In 1946, soon after Arnold was discharged from service, Jim Tatum called on him in

Okmulgee, where Arnold was recovering from an appendectomy. Offering him a scholarship, Tatum persuaded him to come to Norman for Oklahoma's summer practice with the unhappy result that Arnold pulled muscles in both legs.

Also Arnold quickly saw that under Tatum Oklahoma threw "only one spot pass per game to an end going down," as he described it. "I was sorry I came to Norman," Arnold says.

But he stayed. Giving up his scholarship, he enrolled in industrial psychology, his parents helping with his expenses. But football flowed warmly in his bloodstream. In 1947 he coached and played intramural football for Delta Tau Delta, his fraternity. With Arnold's forward passes hitting a wide circle of hands, the Delts made a shambles of their league.

Wilkinson was aware of Arnold and his talent. In 1948 he talked the Delt Dazzler into reporting for Oklahoma's spring practice and gave him a scholarship. Arnold played quarterback behind Jack Mitchell most of that year and behind Darrell Royal in 1949. He took pride in avoiding errors and practiced hard.

His fellow players say that he was the "Mr. Clean" type who washed his hands a lot and kept his clothes immaculate and his hair groomed so neatly that his teammates would occasionally walk up and make a great show of parting it with their hands. Arnold tolerated this nonsense in the locker room, but on the football field he was all business. "Harry Moore and I were the captains, but Claude ran the team," says Norman McNabb. "If another player came up to him in the huddle and told him that a certain play would work, Arnold would turn away. 'I'll call the plays,' he would say quietly."

Eddie Crowder, the eighteen-year-old sophomore who played behind him, had captained, quarterbacked, and passed Muskogee High School to the state championship in 1948. An excellent ball handler and thinker, he would be heard from later.

Ten days before the Boston College inaugural, Wilkinson told the press, "Our new kids are working harder than either our 1948 or 1949 squads did. They have tremendous hustle. But they aren't the same boys who won them all for us last season. Can we keep them up after we get clipped this fall?"

The Sooners did the clipping in the first game, defeating Boston College 28-0. Weatherall kicked all four goals. Denny Myers, forthright Eagle coach, told reporters after the game, "The Oklahoma team this year definitely falls below their club of last year."

Wilkinson's comment was more encouraging. "I thought our new Oklahoma squad played a fine team game," he said. "We didn't make any bad mistakes. Trying and improving as we go along, we should slowly and steadily grow better."

In what is widely conceded to be the most thrilling football game ever played in Norman, the Sooners nipped Texas A&M 34-28 on October 7 at Owen Field. With only 3:36 left to play, the Sooners were beaten 28-27, and Texas A&M possessed the football. Vessels had fielded a forward pass from Arnold and scored the tying touchdown, but Weatherall, Oklahoma's kicking tackle, tragically missed the conversion boot that would have tied the score.

"I guess I hooked it a little," the tackle says today. It was Weatherall's first miss of the season. The Cadets led 28-27, and Oklahoma had to kick off to them. Alas for Oklahoma's string of twenty-two consecutive victories!

As he trotted off the gridiron to the Sooner bench in what must have been the longest trip of his life, Weatherall cried unashamedly before his home crowd. Then a wonderful thing happened—a fine, generous thing. The Oklahoma crowd of 36,586 rose to its feet and cheered the sobbing tackle to the echo. Although it looked as if the Sooners were beaten, that grand gesture by the Oklahoma spectators was something nobody ever wanted to forget.

"I was proud of our crowd then, very proud," said Wilkinson.

Behind one point, Oklahoma had to kick off to the Cadets. "When our offensive platoon came off the field," recalls John Reddell, "Bert Clark told us as he passed with the defensive unit going on, 'Don't worry! We'll get the ball right back for you!' I saw that all our juniors and seniors seemed to feel the same way. That gave me goose bumps. I'd just about given up. I was only a sophomore. I'd never seen a miracle before."

"You guys gotta stop 'em!" George Cornelius says Wilkinson told the defensive team going out. "You can't let 'em make a single first down! If you make 'em punt, we'll win this game yet."

Cornelius also remembers Gomer Jones huddling the offensive platoon. "Cheer up!" Jones growled. "You're goin' right back in there! You can't miss a single block. You gotta block perfect on every play."

It was then that the 1950 Sooners showed everybody that, while they lacked the manpower and experience of the 1948 and 1949 clubs, they had the hearts of champions. They dug in. On third down and 2, they stopped Bob Smith, the Cadets' fine fullback, for no gain. Yale Lary punted out of bounds on the Sooner 31. There was only 1 minute 46 seconds left to play.

"We've got 'em, coach! We've got 'em!" Arnold told Wilkinson as the offensive unit ran onto the field. "I thought he was crazy," Wilkinson said later.

It was then that Arnold came into his own as a cool, resourceful quarterback. With a final spate of forward passing, he directed his team 69 yards to a touchdown. Every play he chose was just right. With the scoreboard clock ticking away the final precious seconds, his fakes, pitchouts, and forward passes in the high wind were perfect at a time when any kind of slip might have been fatal.

First, Arnold pegged into the left flat to Vessels for 30 yards and a first down on the Cadet 39 with Keller, the sophomore, throwing the key block. He hit Leon Heath in the right flat, but because of the sun's glare Heath never saw the ball. Then he shot a down-and-out pass to Tommy Gray for 11. Each time, the receiver raced across the sideline to stall the clock.

"Arnold's passes were soft to catch even though he lined 'em with a lot of zip," recalls Gray. The quarterback whipped a throw to Heath for 14 more and again to Gray for 10, Gray running to the Cadet 4 and almost scoring.

There were 44 seconds left to play, and the crowd was tumultuous. Arnold took the offense out of the air and onto the ground. He faked a handoff inside, then scooped a long pitchout to Heath speeding wide around his left flank. Heath ran around one tackler then hurled himself across the goal in the northwest corner of the field.

This time Weatherall booted the conversion. Three Cadet passes were stifled just before time ran out. When the scoreboard siren signified the end of the game, the crowd tossed red, orange, and blue seat cushions high into the sky and breaking out on the field engulfed the Sooners. Earl Wells, Henryetta coal operator sitting in the stadium, noticed that Mrs. Wells was gone from her seat beside him. Then he saw her down on the sideline beating a stranger over the head with her purse. In Oklahoma football was no plaything. It was as serious as your life.

"I gained lots of confidence in that game," Billy Vessels reveals. "After that, I knew I could play. It was so exciting for a new team to come from behind like that. Before that game Claude Arnold was almost unknown to me. We were young and new and just didn't know. But he would bring us from behind like that all year."

Oklahoma's ribbon of 23 consecutive victories was now the only unbroken string in the nation. Notre Dame, which had played 39 straight without defeat although yielding two ties, had been upset by Purdue two weeks earlier, and Texas had just beaten Purdue, scoring five touchdowns on them. And now the youthful Sooners were facing Texas at Dallas.

Gomer Jones, coach of Oklahoma's line and also of its defense, faced a formidable challenge. With his entire starting line, both linebackers, and Darrell Royal, his gifted punter and pass defender, gone from 1949, Gomer's new defense had yielded four touchdowns and 271 net yards rushing to Texas A&M. Jones had far too much pride to accept any part of that.

With only four practice days available, he went to work on it. Much of Jones's coaching success was due not only to his ability to teach line techniques but also to the fact that his players liked him warmly and sincerely. "He was jovial, pleasant, easygoing—the daddy image," says Darrell Royal. "He was a good teacher and always had time to sit down and explain."

"A dear guy," Eddie Crowder later painted him. "He had a charm that everybody felt." "He touched the lives of hundreds of boys," says Harry Moore, "but I never heard anybody make a detrimental remark about him." "Gomer was the soothsayer," John Reddell sketches him today. "No matter how low, upset, or disappointed you might be, he'd stroke you. He'd give you those warm fuzzies."

There were 75,000 fans sitting in the sweltry heat of the Cotton Bowl when the game began. Could Oklahoma's young cubs play with Coach Blair Cherry's Steers?

Oklahoma landed the first scoring punch with a 58-yard drive. Two long runs galvanized Sooner fans. Vessels squirted 19 yards on a pitchout. On the counterplay Heath shot down the middle for 29 yards to the Orange 2. On the handoff Vessels rooted straight ahead to score. Weatherall kicked goal.

Texas dominated play the rest of the half. Oklahoma's youthful defense was under constant assault. Jack Lockett stopped a Texas drive with a pass interception on the 5. Three plays later Arnold was hit hard and fumbled, Texas recovering on the Sooner 12.

But Jones's reorganized defense tightened. On a Texas pitchout Tommy Gray threw Byron Townsend for an 8-yard loss. Dean Smith stopped Levine for no gain. Ben Tompkins, trying to pass, was trapped by Frankie Anderson for a 10-yard loss. Texas punted. However, early in the second quarter Townsend, on a trap, ran 15 yards and crossed the goal. Bill Porter kicked the extra point. Score 7-7.

Both teams were beginning to sag in the fierce heat. "The hardest I was ever hit in my life," says Billy Vessels, "was in this game. On an end sweep I was tippy-toeing down the sideline with the ball. Dan Menasco, Texas linebacker, put a tackle on me. It hurt. It kinda rung my bell."

Texas took a 13-7 lead early in the fourth period when Bobby Dillon, their fine defensive back, intercepted Heatly's halfback pass with a spraddle-legged leap and ran it back 45 yards down the sideline for a touchdown. Porter missed goal. When Buddy Jones was pinned back on his 15 after a long punt by Porter, the Sooners were bogged deeply, and time was fleeting.

The Sooners met the tough situation with poise. Heatly, kicking beautifully in the boisterous breeze, curled one out of bounds on the Texas 23. There was 6:17 left to play.

Here Jones's Sooner defense became savage. They stopped Townsend twice, Jim Davis and Dean Smith tackling. They rolled Raley for a 9-yard loss, back to the Orange 21. Texas called a punt, but the snapback was too low, and Oklahoma's charging forwards buried Bill Porter back on his 11 before he could swing his leg. It was Oklahoma's ball there with 4:45 to play.

On the second play Vessels took a pitchout reverse from Arnold and bowled over two Texas tacklers to score. "It was a new play, a reverse trap," Vessels says today. "Bud sent the play in from the sideline, but Claude already had it called. Moore threw a great block." Cornelius threw one too. Score 13-13.

Jim Weatherall walked back for the conversion try. Raising his arms to silence the crowd, the tackle belted the ball high and far against the wind, almost pumping it out of the stadium. "The goal posts looked small," Weatherall says today. "I concentrated hard. Boy! If I'd have missed that one, I would have kept right on going up that south ramp." But the kick sailed true.

Defense won the game, Wilkinson said in his alumni letter. Texas's net rushing total was only 80 yards and their passing netted 118. The Sooners trapped them for 77 yards in losses. "Every one of the 26 players we used played his heart out," Wilkinson wrote. "Buddy Jones, our 157-pound senior safety, came up to make half a dozen slashing tackles, and his pass defense was superb.

"Bert Clark led the tackling table with ten unassisted stops and did a great job calling defensive signals," Bud added. The coach also applauded Gray, Lockett, and Lisak, the defensive backs and also Dean Smith and co-captain Norman McNabb. "It was plainly a day for our defense," he concluded, "and much of this was due to the excellent scouting done on Texas by Bill Jennings, our freshman coach, and Orville Tuttle, our varsity assistant coach.

"Blair Cherry, the Texas coach, was most gracious after the game," Wilkinson said. "I only hope that when it becomes our time to lose, I can be as generous and poised in defeat as was he."

At Owen Field the following Saturday a Homecoming crowd of 38,546 saw Oklahoma trim Kansas State 58 to 0. The Sooners achieved this in spite of losing five fumbles, of injuries that benched Leon Heath, Buddy Jones, George Cornelius, and J. W. Cole, and despite the fact that Wilkinson sent a total of 55 players into the game. The game was historically remarkable in that Hoyt Givens and Harold Robinson of Kansas State were the first blacks ever to play at Owen Field.

The Sooners got a laugh when they looked at the game film. Harry Moore, Sooner cocaptain and center, played with a dental bridge in the front of his mouth. There were no face masks in those days, and Moore's Kansas State opponent had forearmed him across the mouth, knocking out his false teeth. The film showed the Sooner captain on hands and knees in the grass searching for his lost bridgework.

Oklahoma's 20-7 triumph over Iowa State at Ames was another plum for the defense. "It was wonderful to have Buddy Jones back at safety," said Wilkinson. Out of the Kansas State fracas with a knee bruise, Jones directed the Sooner pass defense that shut down Billy Weeks, Iowa State quarterback and the nation's leading forward passer. Weeks completed only 9 of 19 for 121 yards. Jones and Clark of Oklahoma each bagged interceptions. Generally overlooked was the fact that Claude Arnold, Oklahoma's senior quarterback, himself had thrown 59 forward passes that season without yielding a single interception. "I think interception on every throw," Arnold said, "When I go back to throw I tell myself 'I'll go down with it or throw it away before I throw an interception.'"

Oklahoma unloosed its defensive fury against Weeks as impetus to its first touchdown. Weeks had passed the Iowans to the Sooner 22. Then Frankie Anderson ran over Weeks's protection shield to throw the Cardinal and Gold marksman for a loss of 15. On the next play Jim Weatherall overpowered the other side of the Cyclone line to trap Weeks for a 17-yard loss. Thus the Cyclones lost almost a third of the field in two plays. They punted from their 46.

Wilkinson's most difficult coaching opponent in the Big Seven year after year was his closest friend in the league—the late Dal Ward of Colorado. When Wilkinson quarterbacked Minnesota to the national championship in 1936, Ward was the Gopher freshman coach. "We were good friends," Ward said later. "We talked football a lot, and other things too. In fact, Bud was an usher at my wedding."

At Colorado, the newest member of the conference, Ward became a master craftsman of the single-wingback offense. "It's main advantage," he said, "was that the opponent saw it but once a year and had only one week to prepare for it." When Ward joined Bierman's staff at Minneapolis, he learned even more about it. "Bierman relied a lot on power," said

Ward, "but I couldn't help adding a few wrinkles. We saved our surprises for Oklahoma."[1]

When Ken Tipps, Sooner end the preceding year who was then in business at Denver, went to the Denver airport Thursday to welcome the Sooners flying in, he saw that every Oklahoma player wore his fighting face. "They all got off the plane looking as if the Russians had just bombed Washington and they were moving into the trenches," Tipps recalls. "I knew that Wilkinson had been talking seriously to them about Colorado."

"How beautiful the game day was," remembers Billy Vessels. "It was the first time I'd ever seen the mountains."

Once the game started, Billy forgot all about the mountains. Colorado was big, rough, and determined. Their best play all day was their fullback spinner with Merwin Hodel bucking up the middle after first faking the ball to the blocking back who in turn faked a pitchout. Their line trap-blocked to open the hole. Soon Oklahoma began conceding this play to Colorado to prevent their going wide around each flank on tailback Zack Jordan's sweeps or the wingback reverses.

Colorado scored the first touchdown when on fourth down the 210-pound Hodel blasted over from the 2. But Bert Clark broke through to block Lee Venske's conversion, and the score stayed 6-0.

Oklahoma retaliated early in the second quarter when Arnold called the strong-side pitchout to Vessels. With Heath, Dean Smith, and Reddell each dominoeing opponents, the sophomore ran 46 yards to score, making a clever cut to clear the last tackler. Weatherall kicked goal. Oklahoma led 7-6.

The Sooners built it to 13-6 before the half ended, when Vessels took another pitch, swung wide to his right as if to run, then pulled up and forward passed to halfback Dick Heatly in the end zone for a touchdown. Weatherall missed goal. Score 13-6.

In the last half Colorado, knowing that Arnold seldom ran with the ball and in fact didn't like to, began giving Arnold his keeper play and sending their end out to cover Vessels. That put it up to Arnold. His seasonal running average was only 1.3 net yards a carry. Also, he was a devoted team man. He was afraid that if he called his own play too much he would lose the squad's good will. But he had no choice. So he began to run with the football.

And how he ran! He kept the ball five times in a row to score a touchdown on the last five yards of a 75-yard drive. Later he kept it eight times in a nine-play drive, stumbling across the goal on his darning-needle legs

[1] Dal Ward to author, July 10, 1980.

to score the clinching touchdown. He carried the ball 24 times, gained 132 yards, and never fumbled. Oklahoma won 27-18. On the team plane going home, the quarterback apologized profusely to his teammates for having monopolized the spotlight.

A bitterly cold day greeted the Kansas and Oklahoma teams when they squared off at Lawrence the following week. Drawing on his experience while he was a player at Minnesota, Wilkinson had straw strewed a foot deep all around the Sooner bench so that his gladiators could thrust their feet into it and stay warm. That worked fine.

But something else didn't. The Sooners also used chemically treated pocket hand warmers that trainer Joe Glander had found in a Kansas City sporting-goods store. Designed for duck hunters, they kept the Sooners' hands warm but didn't prevent them from losing seven of nine fumbles to the Jayhawkers. Playing without straw or hand warmers, Kansas, coached by Jules Sykes, handled the ball perfectly, making no fumbles.

Oklahoma gained 305 net yards rushing, 200 passing, 49 in pass interceptions, and 82 in punt runbacks, and Gomer Jones's defense intercepted two passes and threw the Jayhawks for 68 yards in losses. Yet early in the third quarter Kansas led 13-0, scoring on a long forward pass and on a 71-yard run by Wade Stinson. What would be the Sooner attitude after that? the coaches wondered.

The first play provided the answer. A team that has won 27 in a row doesn't duck its duty. The Sooner line charged tremendously and the low-running Heath powered through the Jayhawkers for 21 yards, almost getting away. It was a walloping carry that made the Kansas crowd gasp.

Oklahoma kept passing the chalk lines. When they reached the Kansas 22, Arnold faked the handoff and, retreating a step, zipped a forward pass to Kay Keller for a touchdown. Weatherall kicked goal. Kansas led, 13-7.

Then Arnold, Oklahoma's clearheaded senior quarterback, began to riddle the Jayhawk secondary with forward passes. Throwing with the decimal-point precision that characterized his style, Arnold hit Jack Lockett for 32 yards and a touchdown, hit Vessels for 50 yards and a touchdown, and hit John Reddell for 11 and another score. Meanwhile, Tom Catlin picked off an interception and ran 19 yards for a fifth touchdown. Oklahoma won 33 to 13.

Heath was the contest's top rusher with 140 net yards in 25 carries. In those days a singer named Frankie Laine was popularizing a song titled "Mule Train." Every jukebox in the country was playing it. Heath's powers of propulsion were so great that when he kept dragging tacklers long after they met him, one was reminded of Frankie Laine's song. Thus Heath's nickname "Mule Train" was born.

With the conference season nearing its mid-November climax, Oklahoma had won 28 straight and stood high in both national polls. Against Missouri at Norman, Wilkinson's charges gave their finest performance of the season, winning 41-7 in spite of the fact the starting backfield did not play in the last half.

Although Wilkinson thought that Claude Arnold's signal checking and play selection was his best of the season, the quarterback had the bad luck to suffer his only pass interception of the year. Arnold pegged a long one to Jack Lockett. Two Tigers shadowed Lockett closely. Harold Carter, Missouri safety, leaped to intercept the ball deep in the end zone.

"Well," Arnold remembers muttering to himself, "that takes care of that." However, the quarterback had achieved something that he didn't realize at the time. Yielding no more interceptions that year, he set a new all-time national collegiate record for interception avoidance of 0.9 percent, giving only one interception in 114 throws. That broke the old mark of 2.4 percent on four interceptions in 167 tosses by Davey O'Brien of Texas Christian in 1939. And it's still an all-time NCAA record.

Frankie Anderson, famous for his ferocious rushing of enemy passers, his deceiving speed, his deadpan nonchalance in the heat of battle, his "rassle" walk, his shoulder wiggle to adjust his pads, and his custom of relaxing on one knee to store up energy between plays, had a good day. Four times Anderson threw Missouri backs for losses. Twice he caught sweeps from behind. Once he cut clear across the field, from right to left, to tackle the receiver of a screen pass.

Before a crowd of 53,066 that John Bentley, Cornhusker sports publicist, called "a full barn," once-beaten Nebraska, old-time football scourge of the prairies, and Oklahoma, seeking its thirtieth consecutive triumph, clashed at Norman for the Big Seven championship. Five thousand red-garbed Nebraska fans made the long trek south for the game.

For the Sooners it was their first game since being voted number one in the nation by the Associated Press poll, a distinction that had already boomeranged disastrously that year against Notre Dame, Southern Methodist, and Ohio State.

Nebraska, possessing the nation's most voracious rushing attack, was led by the most talked-about player in the conference, Bobby Reynolds, sophomore halfback from Grand Island, Nebraska. Reynolds had sprinted to 19 touchdowns and 1,260 net yards rushing and had scored 134 points in his first eight games that year. Besides, he had fielded nine forward passes and had done most of his team's passing, all of its conversion kicking, and all of its punting.

The Sooners began hostilities by driving 86 and 67 yards to touchdowns the first two times they possessed the ball. Claude Arnold scored the first on a 16-yard keeper. Then he whipped a pass to Heath, and the fullback cut neatly behind a block by Jack Lockett to count the second. Weatherall twice kicked goal. Oklahoma led 14-0.

"I was so keyed up!" recalls Norman McNabb, Sooner cocaptain. "Reynolds slipped returning a punt, and I overreacted. I hit him while he was down and got a 15-yard penalty. I apologized to him. He smiled and thanked me. "'Don't worry,' he said. 'That's all right.'"

Oklahoma was definitely controlling the game. The Sooners smothered Bobby on Nebraska's first series. Buddy Jones rocketed in to nail him for no gain. He made 3 yards, Jones and Clair Mayes tackling. Then Norman McNabb trapped him for a 10-yard loss. Nebraska had to punt.

"None of us was worried," says McNabb. "All we had to do was control Reynolds. Then suddenly that turned into a hell of a chore."

Vessels fumbled, and Nebraska recovered on the Sooner 20. And here came the Cornhuskers. On their first play their excellent offensive line broke Reynolds free down the middle, and he scooted 20 yards to a touchdown, slipping the Sooner tacklers as if he were greased.

Midway in the second quarter Nebraska drove 64 yards in five plays. Hitting very fast and faking and squirming cleverly while running at full speed, Reynolds scored on a 14-yard sweep. The Sooners made another disastrous fumble, Goeglein recovering for Nebraska on the Sooner 16. On the first play Reynolds whipped around Oklahoma's left flank for a third touchdown without going off his feet.

Reynolds kicked all three goals. With only 3:03 left in the first half, Nebraska led 21-14, dazing the Sooner crowd.

Wanting none of the disaster that had befallen the other three poll-leading powerhouses—Notre Dame, Southern Methodist, and Ohio State—the Sooners reached down into their socks for poise and fighting spirit. Arnold laid a short pass on Heath's hands, and picking up a key block by the hustling Lockett, the fullback galloped 59 yards before safety Ron Clark felled him on the 10. Two plays later Vessels spurted 7 yards off tackle to the tying touchdown. Weatherall booted the extra point. The score stood 21-21 as both teams went in for halftime.

The Sooners obviously needed cheering and counseling with respect to the nimble visitor. Harry Moore, Sooner cocaptain, says, "I remember at the half Bud and Gomer telling us, 'Quit going for his fakes. He's too fancy-footed. Hit him higher and hit him quicker. Don't look at his belt buckle; look at his shoulders.'"

Billy Vessels says, "We'd never seen anybody as exciting as Bobby. He was probably as talented a player as ever played the game. Of course, after Gomer made some adjustments at the half, it was much harder for him."

Oklahoma played a furious third quarter, bagging three touchdowns to double the score, 42-21. First they drove 75 yards in eight plays to a touchdown from the second-half kickoff, most of it smashes by Vessels and Merrill Green. A minute later Reynolds tried to skirt his right end but Keller knocked him loose from the ball, Catlin recovering on the Cornhusker 9. It was Nebraska's first error in the game. Vessels shot off tackle for the touchdown.

Then Lisak intercepted a long pass by Nagle, and Oklahoma had the ball on its 17. Green smote off left guard for 14 and a first down on the Sooner 31, and the stage was set for the longest run of the game.

Vessels took a pitchout from Arnold and started a sweep to his right. The Nebraska end covered it, whereupon Billy turned around, changing direction completely, and sprinted the field's entire width to gain the opposite sideline. While the Oklahomans were cutting down the Cornhuskers with downfield blocks, Vessels swerved around a block by Lockett and crossed the goal. It was an electrifying 69-yard run that plunged the Sooner crowd into pandemonium. During pileups, a Sooner player kept punching Reynolds in the short ribs. Reynolds just jumped up grinning. Wilkinson benched the offending Sooner. "You sit down there!" Bud told him, pointing to the bench, "and don't you get up anymore today."

Nebraska countered with a 70-yard drive that saw Nagle, their fine quarterback, sneaking over from one foot out, but the Sooners retaliated midway of the fourth quarter when Vessels shot off guard for 30 then ran wide with a pitchout and pegged a running pass to John Reddell whose baseball hands welcomed it in the end zone. Oklahoma led 49-28.

Then Reynolds made a phenomenal play. On fourth down he dropped back to punt but the Sooner defense closed so fast that he didn't have time. Instead, he ran wide to the right and surprised every fan in the stadium by suddenly punting the ball while on the run. It was a 54-yard boot down to the Sooner 22.

That set up Nebraska's final touchdown. The Scarlet marched 68 yards. With 53 seconds left, Nagle passed 6 yards to end Gerald Ferguson for the score. When Reynolds kicked his fifth conversion, he had logged 23 points against the Sooners, an all-time record by an opposition back. Oklahoma won 49-35.

Oklahoma paid dearly for the win. Buddy Jones reinjured his knee in the third quarter and was out of the bowl game with Kentucky. Tommy Gray, starting defensive right half, also came out with an injury.

After the game, Bobby Reynolds came into the Sooner dressing room.

Bud Wilkinson, Sooner coach (center), congratulating Bobby Reynolds (left), Nebraska's All-American back, following Oklahoma's 49-35 victory at Norman in 1950. Bert Clark (right) rugged Sooner linebacker, regards Reynolds with awe.

Oklahoma's captains, Norman McNabb (65) and Harry Moore (55), run on to the field for the coin flip before the 1951 Sugar Bowl game with Kentucky. Photo by Leon Price Picture Service.

Claude Arnold, Oklahoma quarterback, in the Sooner dressing room after he led Oklahoma to a 14-13 victory over Texas in 1950.

"Where's Buddy Jones?" he asked. "I want to shake hands with him. He was wonderful." Wilkinson thought that Bobby himself was pretty wonderful too and told him so.

All Oklahoma had to do to win its first national championship was defeat Oklahoma A&M handily in the last game. The polls took their final vote after the regular season ended.

Dead in earnest, the Sooners started fast. Although a cold northwest wind swept Lewis Field, Arnold pitched four touchdown passes in the first half, 26 yards to John Reddell, 10 yards to Jack Lockett, 29 yards to Lockett, and 15 yards to Lockett. Heath counted the final touchdown when he zoomed across the goal through a rent in the Orange and Black line opened by Clair Mayes and Melvin Brown, seventeen-year-old sophomore tackle from Denison, Texas.

Bud's final statement summed up the 1950 team very well. "Our squad was thinner and greener than ever before," he said, "but they improved steadily and despite their physical imperfections proved time and time again that in the qualities of courage, spirit, and poise they need bow to no other football team anywhere."

They had more offensive balance than any of Wilkinson's other teams at Norman to that date. They rushed 2,931 net yards and forward-passed 1,223. Arnold took pride in avoiding any kind of ball-handling errors. No one can recall that he made a single bad pitchout all season.

Four 1950 players were selected on first All-American teams—Weatherall, Anderson, Heath, and Buddy Jones. In the national statistics the Sooners were first in interception avoidance (2.1 percent), tied for second in fumbles lost (27), seventh in total offense (415.4), and ninth in rushing offense (293.1). The high quality of Wilkinson's planning was plain to everybody, and the popular lament for a coach of Tatum's stature was stilled forever.

Kentucky, the Southeastern Conference champion, had finished 10-1, losing 0-7 to Tennessee in their last regular season game. Defense was Coach Paul ("Bear") Bryant's dish. His Wildcats had blanked five opponents, given only one touchdown to each of four others, and yielded an average of only 5.6 points per game.

"Bob Gain and Walter Yowarski were a great pair of tackles," recalls Norman McNabb. Incidentally, it was McNabb's fourth bowl game, probably a record. He had also played in the 1946 squad's Gator Bowl, and the 1948 and 1949 squads' Sugar Bowls. A knee operation benched him in 1947.

"Kentucky was very tough, experienced, and physically strong," recalls Billy Vessels. "They stunted lots with their linemen going one way, their linebackers another. With Buddy Jones out with a knee injury, I had to play defense, too, totaling about 59 minutes.

Claude Arnold says, "On our first play of the game one of their tackles came through without being touched. I had my hand stretched out to give the ball to a halfback, and there he was, right in the middle of our handoff."

Recovering the rolling ball on the Sooner 21, Kentucky scored in one play. Their passer, Vito ("Babe") Parilli, hurled a high lob into the Sooner end zone. Wilbur Jameson, the receiver, leaped to make a fantastic catch. In the second quarter Parilli lofted a 46-yarder that Al Bruno leaped to field over Sooner hands. Gain kicked the first conversion, missed the second. Kentucky led 13-0.

After Fucci punted 60 yards dead on the Oklahoma 8, the Sooner line began asserting itself. Heath bucked for a first down. Gray reversed for another, this one on the Sooner 34. Then Arnold pitched to Vessels, who, running with savagery and speed, dashed 51 yards to the Kentucky 14, only to have the play recalled by a holding penalty.

"The official was right," Vessels says today. "We were guilty."

Oklahoma threatened again on the next series when Heath ripped 28 yards to midfield and Arnold passed to Vessels for 18 more to the Kentucky 31, but the blue-clad Kentuckians stopped them.

Seeing their 31-game winning streak going up in smoke, the Sooners came out fighting in the last half. On fourth down from the Sooner 40, Arnold gambled on the dive tackle, and Tommy Gray got it by inches. Heath bucked for 10, carrying tacklers in true "Mule Train" fashion, and Oklahoma was on the Wildcat 4. Heath hit for 2. Vessels tried left tackle, but Gain jammed it for zero yardage. On a pitchout to the right, an Oklahoma lineman blocked the wrong opponent, and Yowarski dived and ticked Vessels's heel, tripping him back on the 8.

On fourth down Arnold led Frankie Anderson with a pass in the end zone. Anderson's fingertips brushed the ball, but he didn't have enough flesh on it. Kentucky took over.

In the fourth period the Sooners marched 80 yards to a touchdown. Arnold began calling pitchouts. Vessels rounded right end for 20. He repeated for 12 and a first down on Kentucky's 46. On a fourth-down gamble Arnold called Heath, and "Mule Train" rambled 6 to the Wildcat 33. On another fourth and 1 situation Heath smashed for 6 more and a first down on Kentucky's 17. Then Arnold called the halfback pass, Vessels pegging into the end zone to Merrill Green for a touchdown. Weatherall kicked goal. There was 7:02 to play, but Kentucky stood the Sooners off until the end.

"I really think we were a better football team than Oklahoma had anticipated or had been playing against," Bryant commented.[2] "The thing I remember most about the game was the fact that Parilli completed nearly all his passes the first half, and we led by 13. In the second half, since I was a coward, I didn't let him pass any, and I well remember Vessels's run that was called back and Green's touchdown pass that made the score 13-7 . . . . I really wanted to cut my throat, but the good Lord was with us and we controlled the ball until the end of the game."

John Reddell, Sooner end, says, "In our dressing room the tears flowed freely. Bud came in and told us how great it was to establish a record of 31 straight. That losing was nothing to be ashamed of. How every man gave everything he had. How proud he was of us. After that, the guys really did cry. Guys cry with guys, not with girls."

The Sooners outrushed Kentucky 189 to 84 net yards. Heath, with 112 yards, outrushed the whole Kentucky team. Oklahoma led in first downs, 18-7. Kentucky led in passing, 105-38. Kentucky played errorlessly. Its aggressive defense forced Oklahoma into seven fumbles, five of them lost. Kentucky lost no fumbles.

"Kentucky had great people," Norman McNabb and Harry Moore summed it up. "At the party that night, we enjoyed seeing them. Bryant was tremendous too."

[2]Letter, Paul Bryant to author, January 23, 1981.

1950 SENIORS TODAY

Claude Arnold is sole owner of Arnold Petroleum, Inc., of Oklahoma City.

Tommy Gray is an independent oil producer in Oklahoma City.

Heath is senior sales representative for N. L. Baroid, an Oklahoma City oil-well-services company.

Norman McNabb later became president of Oscar Rose Junior College of Poteau, Oklahoma. Today he is senior marketing executive of the Noble Drilling Corporation, of Tulsa, Oklahoma.

After starting in oil production, Harry Moore became interested in uranium and founded his own company, Moore Energy, of Oklahoma City.

94

6. THE WILKINSON WAY

There were all kinds of problems to vex the 1951 team. Because of the war in Korea nearly all the players were in the university's Army, Navy, or Air Force Reserve Officers Training Corps. Seven starters had graduated, plus the whole of the secondary defense, Tommy Gray, Ed Lisak, and Buddy Jones.

The 1950 freshman team was good. It had lost 9-10 to Tulsa but spanked Oklahoma A&M 55-13. However, the varsity defense needed strengthening. It had yielded three touchdowns to Colorado, four to Texas A&M, and five to Nebraska. The alternate team needed rebuilding. A crippling succession of injuries, perhaps the worst of Wilkinson's career, added an additional plague.

A further disaster surfaced in early March, when Wilkinson informed President Cross that he had decided to resign his coaching position to accept a job in public relations with an oil company headed by Eddie Chiles, of Fort Worth, Texas. Seeking Wilkinson's advice at finding a successor, President Cross and his wife, Cleo, invited Bud and Mary Wilkinson to dinner.

As the two men talked in a small library, the president sensed that the coach was mildly reluctant to leave the university. Desiring very much to keep him, Cross turned on all his powers of persuasion. He talked about the impact the coach had on the personal development of his players and the great respect of the faculty for the integrity of his program.

"I asked him whether after his years of working with young athletes in such significant ways he could find fulfillment as an employee of a business where his sole responsibility would be improving profits for the corporation,"[1] the president wrote. Wilkinson changed his mind, deciding to stay.

Spring practice was enlivened by the visit of Roberto Mendez, football coach of the National University of Mexico. "In 1951 I write in Spanish to Bud Weelkinson asking if I can come spring training to Norman," Roberto told me when I interviewed him for a news story. "He reply I could. He

[1] George Lynn Cross, *Presidents Can't Punt* (Norman: University of Oklahoma Press, 1977), pp. 152-54.

95

reply me in English. I have a almost as much trouble decipher his English as he my Spanish. I can read a few words English if I have a dictionary on my side." Smiling brightly, Roberto paused to regroup.

"So I come in 1951 and I like a many theengs here in Oklahoma. The first theeng is the friendship I find here in all the people. And the second is the good organization they have here—his meetings, his practice, everything. I have a thees idea on my mind. If you no have good organization, you no have good football. You have lost."

Roberto's admiration for Wilkinson's organization is shared by Frank ("Pop") Ivy, Sooner assistant coach of 1948-54. "Bud is the best coach I've ever been around," says Ivy. At the time he made the remark, June 18, 1980, Ivy had been for ten years a head coach of professional football. He started, 1954-57, with the Edmonton Eskimos of the Canadian Football League, who won the Grey Cup three of his four seasons there. He was later head coach of the Chicago Cardinals, 1958-59, and of the St. Louis Cardinals, 1960-61. In 1962-63 he coached the Houston Oilers, who lost the 1962 championship game after a six-quarter sudden-death overtime. For the past two decades Ivy has been an assistant coach and personnel scout for the New York Giants. But he got his start with Wilkinson at Oklahoma.

"When I started on Bud's staff at Oklahoma I didn't know anything about coaching," Ivy says. "And not until I left OU did I find out how far ahead of other coaches Bud was. Years later I realized how fortunate I'd been being with him. It doesn't happen to many people."

Ivy went on: "After I left Oklahoma and got into pro football, I saw a lot of coaches. Organization was where Bud had all the others beat. He tried to teach people how to play on the football field. He would tell a player, 'This is what we're going to try to do. This is the way we're going to try to do it. This will help us win because we're going to try to do it this way.' He wasn't the type who walked in on game day and tried to motivate the squad with a lot of oratory. Bud started on Monday.

"Bud worked hardest against the weaker opponents. If you watched OU practice the week of the Kansas State game, you'd think we were playing Notre Dame. By the time we got ready to play, I'd be scared to death that Kansas State was going to beat the hell out of us. I could see that Bud himself sincerely believed it. He psyched himself into believing it.

"When he had a real hard game coming up, a shoot-out with somebody, he would reduce to a bare minimum the number of plays we would use— offense, defense, and kicking—so our players wouldn't make mistakes. He knew that in a big game, the winner is usually the team that makes the fewest mistakes. Players do familiar things best.

96

"On Sunday afternoon we'd go to the fieldhouse and look at films of the game we'd just played. Then we'd go over the scouting report of the upcoming opponent with our scout present. The players would come in to see the previous game film. Meanwhile the coaches had graded the film and given each player a graded report on his own performance in that game, another place where Bud was years ahead of other coaches. On Monday we saw our players for the first time and talked about our plan for the next game. On Monday, Tuesday, and Wednesday nights we would all study the game films of our next opponent.

"After Thursday's practice, we felt there wasn't much else to do. We'd all go to Bud's house to have a cocktail and relax. Our wives would be there. Bud was always interested in political issues and talked lots about them. He was well posted. Bud believed in keeping his coaches and their wives together like a family. His wife, Mary, was very hospitable and helped him very much in this."

Mary was everybody's favorite. Of her, trainer Ken Rawlinson said later, "Few people realize the contributions she made to Bud's life and career. Nothing was ever overlooked in her mind that would make things better or easier for him to relax. She created an atmosphere that was conducive to bringing out the very best in him. She sublimated her entire existence to this purpose."

"Bud disciplined his players with the depth chart," Ivy remembers. "We'd have a coaches' meeting each day, and the first thing we discussed was, 'Does any player need moving up or down on the depth chart?' He'd pump us hard about that. He always wanted us to play our best football players. Bud never yelled or cursed or berated a player. Even if they got out of line in some activity off the field, he'd move them up and down for that too. He knew that players always rush to the training room on Tuesday to see where they were in the newly posted lineups."

Making All-American was no guarantee that a player stayed high on the depth chart, as Jim Weatherall found out in the fall of 1951, his senior season. "In fall practice one afternoon I found myself bumped down to the fifth team," Weatherall remembers. "I was holding dummies. I began to work my tail off. I was scared I wouldn't make the club. I finally had a good day blocking and was promoted to the third team. Bud's strategy worked. I still don't know why I was demoted. I was too proud to talk to them about it."

Ivy says that Wilkinson was extremely cool during a game. "He never got rattled or lost his presence of mind," says Ivy. "I was always upstairs on the phone in the press box. When things go wrong on the field, most coaches phone the press box and say, 'What the hell's going on?' He didn't do that. If you had something specific you wanted to give him, he'd listen."

Jack Mitchell, Oklahoma's 1946-48 quarterback and later the Kansas coach, says that Wilkinson had a nightmarish horror of some opposition coach springing a new special defense that would stop the Sooner offense flat. "He'd worry about it all week," Mitchell remembers. "'What if their defense does something we haven't seen or practiced against?' he'd ask us in quarterback meetings. It was as if he were playing against himself.

"But we never got surprised like that. The other coach always chose to go with what he was familiar with, what he did best.

"If Bud had a weakness," concluded Mitchell, "it was that he was always outthinking himself. 'He'd give the opposition coach credit for a move that the other guy would never have thought of making because he didn't have Bud's football mind. Thus Bud would sometimes spend valuable time on things that would never happen. Of course, if they had happened, we'd have been ready."

Two new assistant coaches joined the staff that year. Pete Elliott, who had quarterbacked the all-victorious Michigan team to a 49-0 annihilation of Southern California in the Rose Bowl game of 1948, came on as assistant coach and scout. Dee Andros, blocking guard of Oklahoma's two Sugar Bowl championship teams, became assistant line coach to Jones.

The Sooners' new line was as green as custodian Jim Houston's lush Owen Field turf. With so many new men contending for status, some savage battles occurred in spring practice. One of the best involved Jim Weatherall and Darlon ("Doc") Hearon, the Midwest City High School sophomore-to-be who had been recruited by police detective Casey Mills.

"One day in spring practice I made up my mind to make the OU team," Hearon recalls. "I was serious about it. I had a wife and a little girl, and I was ambitious to make something of myself. My opponent that day in scrimmage was Weatherall [21, 6-4, 230, senior, All-American]. I thought I was having a real good day on him.

"Suddenly big Jim whip-blocked me and I found myself sitting on the ground holding my aching shins. 'After practice is over I'm going to whip your big tail,' I told him. He just grinned.

"Later, I was taking off my gear in the dressing room. Weatherall came through the door, darkening everything. He walked up to me. He grabbed me by the back of the head and pulled my face up tight against his stomach. "'Me an' you ain't never gonna fight,' he said.

"We hugged each other. We both cried a little. I was sure relieved."

One of the best new fighters was Dick Bowman, guard from Ponca City. "Everybody hated to block against his bony elbows," remembers Hearon. "One day we were running half-speed drills rushing the passer. I was on defense, he on offense. It was the only time I was ever kayoed on the field. He hit me on the chin with an elbow. I came to on the ground. I looked up.

"Bowman and Gomer Jones bent over me, looking very concerned. I looked at Bowman, 'Which SOB hit me?' I asked.

"Bowman said, 'It was me but I've already told Gomer I'm sorry.'

"He never did tell *me* he was sorry," laughs Hearon. "Not to this day, he hasn't."

With the William and Mary opener fast approaching, the Sooners were scrimmaging savagely, and it had been costly. Kay Keller, starting left end, was lost for the season with a shoulder separation. That left cocaptain Weatherall the only returning starter in the line.

Eddie Crowder, Muskogee junior who had played some at quarterback behind Claude Arnold the year before but not very much because of a kidney bruise, looked fine while coxswaining the new team at quarterback, and he could do far more than just sit in the shell and vocally direct the bark. He was becoming an interesting ballhandler and forward passer and gave the team a little more running zip off the split-T. He could also play defensive safety.

The players say that Wilkinson had the gift of keeping them happy. When George Cornelius became discouraged at his lack of progress, the coach called him into his office and put his arm around him. "He showed me my goof-ups in the game films," Cornelius remembers today, "and he'd say 'This fellow is doing it a little bit better than you right now, but you're coming along. You're going to get better. You're very much in our plans.'"

Doc Hearon remembers that he wasn't playing very well one day in practice. Wilkinson walked up, put his arm around him, and led him away from the group. "What's the matter, Doc?" Wilkinson inquired solicitously. "Don't you feel well? Anything wrong at school, or at home?"

"Although he seemed sincerely concerned," says Hearon, "I saw that I wasn't doing what he wanted me to in practice. I went back and busted my butt for him."

Freshmen were eligible that year because of the Korean War. Although none of them had participated in spring practice, some would play anyhow. Most of them were Oklahomans. One of the fastest learners was Carl Allison, who had played fullback at McAlester High School. "Carl is a good athlete," Wilkinson told the press after the fall workouts began. "He's not the fastest boy in the world, but he's intelligent. You just have to tell him once. Also, he's a good competitor and he likes to win."

Another was Gene Calame, quarterback from Sulphur. Calame's father, Guy, coached the Oklahoma School for the Deaf at Sulphur and was himself deaf. He had played football at the Gallaudet School for the Deaf, a college in Washington, D.C. Gene's mother was also deaf.

Another freshman was Pat O'Neal, smallish hard-twisted lad from Ada who as an eighth-grader began playing yard football. "The older kids ran the game," says Pat, "and if you wanted to play you had to knock the heck out of somebody in scrimmage." Pat was a walk-on at Norman. The coaches welcomed him, but he got no scholarship. "At OU I was always mad because they played me at safety on the kickoffs, and I didn't get to run down-field and hit somebody."

Another freshman that season was Don K. Brown, of Kermit, Texas, a deeply dimpled tackle whose measurements were only 5-9 and 184. Only seventeen years old, Brown looked totally unfit to be playing tackle on a college football team. In West Texas he was famous as a French horn tooter in the Kermit High School band. As a sophomore he made third chair in the state band clinic at Galveston. As a junior he followed the clinic to Mineral Wells and made first chair. That meant he was the best in the state. As a senior he again made first chair. Nearly every college and university in Texas offered him a band scholarship.

Only Oklahoma and Texas Christian tendered him football scholarships. Myrle Greathouse, former Sooner linebacker then living in Odessa, had seen Brown play and recommended him highly to Wilkinson and his staff.

When Brown came to Oklahoma, he had a tough decision. He had to decide between football and blowing his beloved French horn. For a week he tried both, making both the B football squad and Leonard Haug's concert band. But in college there wasn't time for both. So Brown sold his French horn and concentrated on football.

Another freshman was John ("Buddy") Leake, a polite, soft-spoken back from Memphis, Tennessee. Oklahoma didn't know about him and hadn't sought him. But Dr. Phil White of Oklahoma City, Oklahoma's All-American halfback of 1920, had studied medicine at the University of Tennessee School of Medicine at Memphis and while playing on their football team once threw a 62-yard forward pass to an end named John Leake. The elder Leake, father of Buddy, became a Memphis lawyer. And Dr. White, after seeing Buddy play football with Christian Brothers High School, lost no time recommending him to Oklahoma.

Buddy had been invited to play in the All-American high-school game in Memphis. Bill Jennings, Sooner assistant, went to look at him. Young Leake played quarterback and halfback. Later he was switched to defensive halfback and ran back a pass interception 65 yards to a touchdown. "That was good enough for me," laughs Jennings today. "When it began raining, I left at the half."

Leake came to Oklahoma on a football scholarhsip. "And when on the first day of practice," says Gene Calame, "we all watched him kick, run, and throw, I concluded I'd never play a down for Oklahoma."

William and Mary was just starting the split-T formation. On their first play Gene Ball, Sooner end from Muskogee, raked the ball out of their quarterback's hands. Billy Bookout recovered. Frank Silva scored. Then the Indian center wild-pitched the snap over his punter's head on fourth down, and Silva skirted end for another touchdown.

"I jumped offside three times in that game," remembers guard J. D. Roberts, Dallas sophomore. "It was a great thrill just to start. It was all I could think about. You never knew until Bud gave out the lineups in the dressing room."

Buck McPhail, the sophomore fullback from Oklahoma City, learned a great truth in that game. In blocking practice he had been missing his man. He had watched Leon Heath run and block pulverizingly and wondered if he'd ever learn the trick.

"Keep your chin up," advised Heath. "The reason you miss so many blocks in practice is because these guys know our plays. It's twice as easy to block strangers in a real game."

That's what happened against William and Mary. On his first carry Buck broke 57 yards to a touchdown. He kept hitting the target with his blocks. "That gave me confidence," said McPhail later. "It was easier to block strangers. Also, I learned that the more a fellow gets to play, the better he should play."

An unfortunate injury occurred in that game. On a Sooner pass Billy Vessels was trying to block the receiver across the goal. He overshot Pat Reeves, the safety, then swung back to block him high. Reeves suffered a broken nose and was taken to the hospital. "Jim Weatherall, our captain, chewed me out for that," Vessels recalls. "We drew a penalty for unnecessary roughness." Reeves stayed behind his team in the hospital at Norman. Wilkinson and Vessels visited him daily.

In the second game, a night affair with Texas A&M, the Sooners played at College Station for the first time since 1907. Coached by Ray George, their new mentor, the Cadets had beaten UCLA 20-13 at Los Angeles and defeated Texas Tech 20-7. They retained one-half the line and their entire backfield from 1950.

The weather was nasty. A cold north wind laced with sifting rain blew, but the thick turf held well. A crowd of 30,000 filled the horseshoe-type stadium at Kyle Field. The entire Cadet student body, 7,000 men in uniform, stayed on their feet roaring every minute of the game. Their cheering rose and fell in shrill peals and never entirely subsided.

101

George's big team punished the rebuilt Sooner defense, leading 7-0. Ten seconds before the half ended, from the Oklahoma 26-yard line, the Sooners put on a perfect play. "It was a great call by Eddie," remembers Billy Vessels. "Everybody, even their crowd, was looking for the pass." Quarterback Eddie Crowder pivoted and made a little fake, while Vessels, the left half, stayed in place. Then Crowder retreated, as if he were going to throw a forward pass. Instead he made a low underhand shovel toss to Vessels, then continued to retreat, still faking the forward pass.

Fooled, the Texas Aggies began backing up. Meanwhile left end Jack Lockett trap-blocked a Cadet lineman. Weatherall and Roger Nelson, Wynnewood sophomore, pinched out another, and with J. D. Roberts screening a linebacker, Vessels spilled through the rent and, cutting left and right behind a downfielder by Reddell, rocketed 74 yards to a touchdown. The half ended as Billy crossed the 30, but the play had to go on to completion, and the touchdown counted. Weatherall kicked goal, and the score was tied 7-7.

In the fourth period the Cadets moved 68 yards in 15 plays to the winning touchdown, Lippman bucking over and Hooper kicking goal. Final score, 14-7. "We lost to a better team," Wilkinson acknowledged, "but I promise you that we'll keep battling and learning."

Texas, the next opponent, had beaten Bear Bryant's Kentucky Wildcats 7-6, Purdue 14-0, and North Carolina 45-20. Ed Price, their coach, had switched to split-T, and his boys ran it more soundly every week.

Back at Norman, freshman Buddy Leake was depressed. "Like all freshmen I was homesick," Leake says today. "Carolyn, my girl, who is now my wife, was coming with my parents to see the Texas game, but on Thursday I got a letter from her saying that her father didn't want her to come. That really deflated me. I was running third-string offense and second-team defense.

"I went to see Bill Jennings. 'Can I ride back to Memphis with my folks after the game?' I asked him. 'If you can get back here in time for the Sunday night meeting,' he said. 'Fine!' I said. 'I can do that.'

"On Friday noon before the team left for Fort Worth, Bud called a squad meeting in Jeff House," Leake continues. "This was very unusual. He said, 'Too many of you are worrying about what you're going to do after the game. Let's keep our minds on the game.' I knew he was talking straight to me."

Leake went on, "I went back to my room. I remembered John Hofer, my high-school coach, once telling me, 'Always be ready when you get your chance. You might not get a second one.' My bag was all packed for the long trip home. I left it lying in the middle of the floor."

Against Texas the young Sooners lost 9-7 and also lost Billy Vessels, their cyclonic left half, for the remainder of the season with a knee injury. "Eddie threw a screen pass to me in the right flat," Vessels recalls. "I got tackled, planted my foot, got hit, tore the ligaments in my knee. Harley Sewell, their guard, hit me. He was a clean player and a good one."

Wilkinson said after the game, "I'm as proud of the way our team fought against Texas in defeat as I've ever been when we won the last three years."

Early in the second quarter, Oklahoma was on the verge of taking a decisive beating. Texas led 9-0 and had a first down 4 yards from the Oklahoma goal. But the Sooners made a spirited goal line stand. Then came Oklahoma's retaliatory drive for 94 yards and the lone Sooner touchdown. McPhail started it with a 12-yard surge. Crowder swung around tackle for the touchdown. Neither team could score in the last half. The rival defenses ran the show.

On the Oklahoma bench the eighteen-year-old Leake saw Vessels carried off the field on a stretcher. Wilkinson came over to Leake. He put his arm around the freshman's shoulders. "Buddy," he said, "next time we get the ball I'm going to put you in. Now don't get nervous."

"Fine, coach," said Leake. He was ready to go.

After an exchange of punts Leake went in. The ball was on the Sooner 6. "On the first play," recalls Leake, "I faked to the right. On the second play I faked into the line. On the third play, Eddie called my number. When we broke the huddle, I looked across the line and saw all those orange shirts. I told myself, 'I'm gonna hit it as hard as I can.'

"The line opened, and I popped through. I saw only one defensive halfback and all that green grass. My mind began spinning about what I was going to do with the situation. I tried giving him a leg and taking it away, but he tackled me. But we got 11 yards. Our line made a hell of a hole." Freshman Leake had made the team.

Wilkinson lengthened the practices the week of the Kansas game and piled on the work. The squad started in the afternoon and finished under the stadium lights. The coach was so intent upon improvement that he even raised his voice twice in practice.

In a midweek drill McPhail fumbled. "McPhail," yelled Wilkinson, "get out of here until you learn to hold onto the ball!" Buck blinked, then jogged obediently to an adjacent practice field.

"Three plays later I dropped a forward pass that was right in my hands," remembers John Reddell. "Coach Wilkinson yelled, 'Reddell, get the hell out of here and go to the other field until you learn how to catch the damn ball!'

"I was shocked," Reddell says today. "So was everybody else. I'd never heard him raise his voice before, let alone say 'hell' or 'damn,' and here he'd done all three. I felt like the world had ended. I felt wiped out."

When practice was over, on the way to the locker room, Wilkinson found Reddell, patted him on the rump, and grinned. "It'll get better tomorrow, John."

"I think he had a blowup coming," concludes Reddell today. "After all, he'd just lost two in a row for the first time in his life."

Oklahoma's casualties had reached the saturation point. Loss from injuries of Vessels, right end Kay Keller, right half Merrill Green, and also right guard Melvin Brown left Jim Weatherall the only returning starter from the previous year. "Melvin Brown never missed a blocking assignment," recalls Doc Hearon. "That's why he was on the first team."

Kansas, coached by Jules Sykes, finished the year at 8-2. A crowd of 44,462 saw the game at Owen Field. Late in the third quarter Sykes' slashers from the Sunflower state drove 80 yards to a touchdown on ground plays. Chet Strehlow rammed over and John Konek kicked goal. Now Kansas led, 21 to 20.

The fourth quarter had started. Crowder, Sooner quarterback, coolly brought Oklahoma up the field. He mixed up the running game, shooting handoffs to Leake, Heatly, and McPhail all along the scrimmage front. He snapped three short passes to Heatly. From the Kansas 6, Oklahoma's offensive line—Hugh Ballard, Weatherall, Bowman, Catlin, Roberts, Janes, and Reddell—dug them out, and Heatly scooted across the goal. Weatherall booted the extra point. Oklahoma led 27-21. Later Larry Grigg intercepted a long pass. Hit by tackler after tackler, Grigg ran it all the way back to the Kansas 43.

That play spawned another Oklahoma touchdown. Again Crowder began his patient probing of the Kansas defense. On the tenth running play Leake, freshman left half, twisted across the goal. Weatherall missed the conversion. That left it 33-21, Oklahoma. Later Grigg pulled down another Kansas pass, and the game ended.

Wilkinson was pleased with the poise and fight of the Sooners when the chips were on the green felt. He said, "All day our offense had the continuity coaches hope to see. Five times in the game we drove inside the Kansas 40 with the ball. Each time we scored."

Sykes praised the Oklahoma power. The Sooners rushed 425 net yards for an average of almost 7 yards a play. McPhail spurted through the Crimson and Blue for 215 net yards, a new OU modern school record. He averaged slightly over 10 yards a carry.

Few realized that Tom Catlin's explosive blocking was a terrific factor in McPhail's running until Wilkinson himself disclosed it at the next ses-

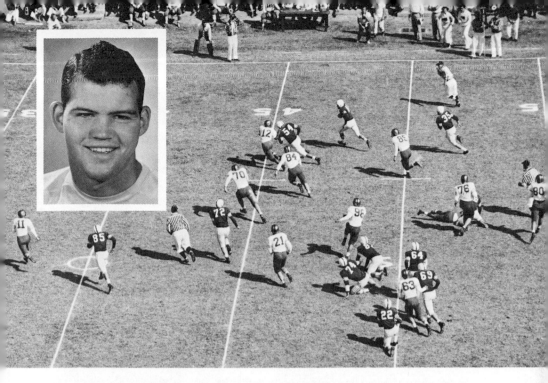

Tom Catlin, Sooner center (54), blocks Henry Ford, Pittsburgh safety, to free Buck McPhail, Sooner fullback (41), 37 yards down the sidelines as Oklahoma defeated Pitt 49-20 at Norman in 1952. Photo by Oklahoma Publishing Co.

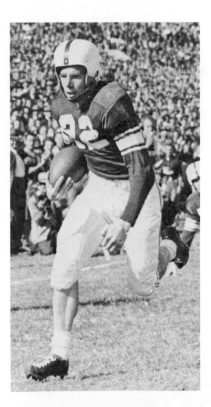

Jim Weatherall, Oklahoma's All-American tackle of 1950 and 1951, first Sooner lineman to win the Outland Trophy.

John ("Buddy") Leake, Oklahoma's 18-year old freshman halfback, scoring one of his three touchdowns against Kansas in 1951.

sion of the Oklahoma City Quarterback Club. McPhail knew it. Every time Buck drove down the middle for yardage he jumped up and patted Catlin on the seat of Tom's white satin playing pants.

Freshman Leake scored three touchdowns. Later reporters cornered him. "I felt great," Leake told them, "but I know Billy [Vessels] would have done better."

All week Vessels had worn a cast and used crutches. He was delighted with the Sooner victory and with Leake's play. "You can always be replaced," he said, "even by a freshman. Of course, Buddy is a very talented freshman."

Remembering the close game at Boulder the year before, 46,686 fans, the biggest crowd of the season at Owen Field, defied sweeping rains Friday night and Saturday morning to see the second clash between Dal Ward- and Bud Wilkinson-coached Colorado and Oklahoma teams. Both were all-victorious in the Big Seven.

The turf had been protected for two days by the Sooner field tarp, and the footing was fine. It was a frosty day, 46 degrees, with a cold north wind blowing. The rains held off, and the crowd enjoyed the action. Especially did they relish the disclosure of a new facet of the Oklahoma offense in which the ball was hidden from the view of everybody—players, spectators, officials, hot food salesmen, the press—then suddenly revealed as a forward pass so unexpected that it often resulted in an Oklahoma touchdown. The "counter option pass" the Sooners called it.

The key finessers in the maneuver were a pair of juniors, Eddie Crowder, the quarterback, and Buck McPhail, the fullback. Crowder first faked the handoff to his right halfback and then spun with his back to the play and as the fullback came by pretended to hand off to him. The key to the play was for Crowder to let the defense see the ball go into McPhail's stomach but not to let them see Crowder take it out again and, while holding it out of sight in his left hand, conceal it in his crotch.

As McPhail went past, Crowder let his right hand flare forward naturally as it would during the normal exchange. Meanwhile, the quarterback was careful to watch the play intently over his right shoulder. Then he dropped back and looked for the safety. If he came up, Crowder threw to the tight end deep. If the safety stayed back, Crowder hit the halfback in the flat, right or left.

"My sensation," says Crowder today, "was a sort of cowardly one, like a guy going into combat. 'If I just play dead, maybe they won't shoot me again,' I'd tell myself. Usually they smacked old Bucko. He was a master at pretending that he had the ball. There was lots of sacrifice by him. Buck knew that the better he faked the harder he was going to be hit. But Buck had such a good attitude that he did it with delight. He never complained, never joked about it. He took it seriously. He was a devoted team man."

The new sequence was Wilkinson's idea. "He had a real sense of brilliancy about those things," remembers Crowder. "The subtleties made it successful."

But first the Oklahoma coaches were concerned about the single-wing-back reverses run to the weak side by Woody Shelton, Colorado's shifty little wingback. Pop Ivy remembers that Wilkinson decided that what was needed was a smallish, aggressive, sure-tackling end. "We settled on Gene Calame, our freshman quarterback from Sulphur," remembers Ivy. "We pulled him out of a hat. Gene did such a great job that we made him a starter."

But Calame remembers something else about that game, the opening kick-off. "I was knocked out running down on it," he says today. "I made the tackle on about their 20. The guy I tackled was the Big Seven's leading tailback, Carroll Hardy. They carried me off on a stretcher. I woke up later on the sideline." But he went back in.

Meanwhile the Sooners began to unveil their chicanery. With McPhail beautifully faking his buck and the Buffalo secondary rushing up to stop him, Crowder had only to step back, select an open receiver, and hit him with the pass. The Sooner aerial play, with Crowder pegging five of five completions for 167 yards and four touchdowns in the first seventeen and a half minutes of play, completely broke down the Buffalo defense.

First he tossed a 27-yard touchdown pass to Dick Heatly, Mangum senior who was standing in virtual isolation near the goal. Then he threw to John Reddell for 67 yards and a second score. "When I retreated and turned around, Tom Brookshier, Colorado's fine safety, was tackling McPhail," remembers Crowder. "Reddell was all alone. I was so surprised that I under threw the ball. He had to come back and get it. He still had plenty of time to turn around and score."

When Reddell returned to the Sooner extra point huddle he said, "Crowder, with your rag arm you just threw the deepest hook pass in the history of American football."

Then Crowder hit Leake for 38 yards and a touchdown with only five seconds left in the first quarter. He hit Lockett for 28 yards and a fourth touchdown with 12:44 left in the second quarter. Meanwhile, Leake had scored on a line buck between the second and third aerial touchdowns. Weatherall kicked four of the five conversions, and the score, 34-0 with the second quarter only 2:16 old, seemed all out of reason. So did the final score, 55-14. Wilkinson swept his bench clean, using every man of the forty-six he had suited.

Crowder's most baffling fake of the season in the opinion of Weatherall occurred in this game. The Buffalo nose guard broke through and wrapped his arms completely around Crowder, then released him to chase McPhail into the secondary. The Sooners would make no wholesale revealment of the play, saving it for strategic situations.

On the Sooner sideline Wilkinson was notified by press-box phone that Crowder was close to the national record of five touchdown passes in one game held by Parilli of Kentucky. However, the Sooner coach withdrew Crowder to give quarterbacking experience to others.

Later Dal Ward told Wilkinson that it was Catlin's ability to handle the Colorado middle guard by himself, thus releasing the Sooner guard next to him for downfield blocking duty, that most complicated Colorado's defensive problem. "Catlin is one of the truly great centers in football, offensively as well as defensively," the Colorado coach declared.

Oklahoma's twenty-fourth consecutive conference victory was 33-0 over Kansas State at Manhattan. The fracas was played in a strong north wind with the mercury standing at 40. The 11,000 fans saw Coach Bill Meek's purple-shirted gladiators fight the Sooners all over the field. Led by Veryl Switzer, their black safety, whom Meek called "the finest old-time tackler I've ever seen," the Purple knocked the ball loose from Sooner balltoters five times, blocked an extra point, and held Oklahoma for downs from the 1.

Although Oklahoma won, Wilkinson gently chided his charges in his alumni letter: "I hope our squad won't forget that football is still primarily a game of preparation and effort during the practice week." This would always be a Wilkinson shibboleth. You play exactly as well as you practice.

On defense Larry Grigg, Oklahoma's sophomore safety, seemed conscious of the great effort Switzer was expending at the other end of the field and himself had a super day. First he caught Dick Shockley, their freshman tailback, from behind after Shockley had got past the whole Sooner team for 41 yards. Later Kansas State hurled a deceptive double reverse around the Sooner left that seemed headed for a touchdown. But Grigg sprinted across the field, knifed through their blockers, and tackled the ballcarrier on the Sooner 14, and Oklahoma held for downs.

Buck McPhail set a school record in this game for the longest rush, breasting the north breeze to dash 96 yards to the Wildcat 2 before being pulled down from behind by Carvel Oldham, a small Wildcat speedster. Lockett authored the block that cut McPhail through the Purple's goal-line defense.

Thirteen inches of snow had fallen at Columbia two days before the Missouri-Oklahoma game. The snow was so deep that the Sooners had to go by railroad to Jefferson City, where they stayed Friday night.

John Reddell didn't accompany the team. His wife was about to give birth to a baby. Reddell was nervous. "What'll I do?" he asked Wilkinson.

"You can ride up tomorrow with Pete Elliott on the scout plane," Bud said.

At the Norman Municipal Hospital there were no chairs in the labor room. Reddell stood all night. The baby was born at 10:45 Friday morning. "I got a look at him and raced to the airport," Reddell remembers. When he walked in on the team at Jefferson City, they had just sat down to eat. Reddell ignored the food.

"See you later," he told them. He went upstairs and fell in bed. "In the game next day, I felt great."

Two surprises greeted the Oklahomans when they arrived at Columbia on game day. The field was dry and the footing fast. After waiting until the snow started melting, Missouri's freshman football players had rolled off every flake into the largest snowballs the Sooners had ever seen. The snow was piled nearly waist-deep all around the field.

All through the game Missouri fans showered snowballs on the Sooner bench. "We all got hit," recalls George Cornelius. Tiring of the punishment, J. D. Roberts and Doc Hearon each fired one back into the crowd, whereupon Dee Andros, Sooner assistant line coach, reproved them. Then a snowball struck Andros.

"The back of Dee's head was flat as a board," recalls Doc Hearon, "and that's where this snowball hit him. And it was thrown hard. Dee picked up a folding chair and started up into the stadium after them, but the other coaches persuaded him to sit down. The restrainer had to be restrained."

The other surprise was a mortal Missouri forward-passing attack delivered off a "shotgun spread." Tony Scardino, Coach Don Faurot's 165-pound freshman from Kansas City, threw on nearly every down, completing 23 of 42 for 365 yards and two touchdowns. Hurt late in the game, he was replaced. All Tiger passers together shelled Oklahoma for 406 yards that day, an all-time record for the conference. Oklahoma intercepted five, one of them by tackle Ed Rowland, who ran 15 yards to a touchdown. Oklahoma won 34-20.

Against Iowa State, Buck McPhail jerked away from a tackler in the secondary and ran 51 yards to the first Sooner touchdown. Later the Sooners thrust 52 yards to a second touchdown. Tackled by the Cyclone safety, Heatly, while spinning, had the quick wit to lateral to Crowder following the play. Crowder needed one sharp downfield block to go the route, and he got it from dependable Jack Lockett. Later Heatly slanted off guard for two more touchdowns.

Reddell scored the finale with an incredible catch. Reddell was covered tightly in the end zone by a Cyclone between him and the ball. Leake, the passer, fired. It looked like a Cyclone interception. But the Cyclone's hands only deflected the ball, and Reddell, close behind him, somehow fielded the deflection for a touchdown as he might have gloved a foul tip in baseball. Oklahoma won 35 to 6.

That catch illustrated Reddell's chief talent, going for a thrown football as if it were a high foul twisting in the wind. He had little speed, size, or power. His gaunt legs looked like soda straws. He rarely ran over anybody. He had been caught from behind more than anyone else on the team, but in spite of all this, he remained the team's blithest spirit and one of its toughest fighters.

Reddell's hands seemed magnetized. An example of that was his second catch against Texas. Reddell did a split in midair to clutch the football one-handed with a Texan hanging onto him. A *Daily Oklahoman* photographer caught that catch neatly. His Sunday picture prominently displayed Reddell's reed-thin legs, much to the merriment of the other Sooner players.

They borrowed a pair of scissors and clipped Reddell's head and torso off the top of the picture, leaving only those bony legs showing. They stuck it up in the dressing room with adhesive tape. Under it they lettered in the caption: "Guess who?"

Reddell got his biggest kick out of jockeying somebody else with emaciated underpinning. When the Nebraska baseball team played at Norman in 1950, their first base coach was a tall lad with pipestem legs. "Hey, Mike," Reddell rode him, "do your legs swell up like that every spring?"

In the Nebraska game a week later Oklahoma completed a string of consecutive conference victories as long as the alphabet, 26 in a row. Each team was crippled by the loss of a stellar back. Vessels of Oklahoma had gone down with a knee injury. Bobby Reynolds of Nebraska was benched with a shoulder separation.

In the Sooner huddle Crowder liked to challenge his teammates, promote competition among them. He knew he'd get a better block. "It was one of his finest traits," says J. D. Roberts. "I played right guard. Dick Bowman played left guard. It was third down and one. Nebraska had called time. We were using the open huddle. Crowder was facing us."

"Jesse Dog," said Crowder, using his nickname for Roberts. "What do you think? Can we make it over you?"

"We can make it with 22, Eddie," answered Roberts, using the number of the handoff over his space.

"Naw!" said Bowman. "Let's call 23." That was the number of the handoff over his position.

110

Crowder called it over Roberts. "It was close," Roberts remembers. "The officials were measuring it."

"You shoulda called 23," Bowman growled, "then they wouldn't be measuring it."

"We had made it by inches," Roberts laughs, but Oklahoma won by four touchdowns, 27-0.

Closing out their season at 8-2, the Sooners defeated Oklahoma A&M 41-6 at Norman in the final game. Oklahoma was voted tenth nationally in the Associated Press poll. The victory also gave Wilkinson's newly crowned Big Seven Conference champions possession for another year of the game's prize, the historic bell clapper that in 1930 was stolen by Sooner students from the belfry of Old Central Hall, on the Aggie campus. Later both schools agreed that the clapper would go annually to the winner of the game.

The 1951 team showed a world of squad spirit. Wilkinson pointed to fullback Buck McPhail, whose faking was neat, his blocking crisp, his attitude superb. "Buck's sacrifice was typical of what has made us go this year—squad spirit," said Wilkinson. And then he added, "All year we've had spirit like that from boys like Sam Allen, Larry Grigg, Billy Bookout, and Carl Allison, all of whom were offensive standouts in high school but who loyally play mostly on defense for us. Also, Tom Catlin, our center, whose fine blocking has been little noticed by the spectators."

All seven Sooner seniors graduated, five in June, 1952, two the following January. Moreover, in accordance with Wilkinson's urging, they graduated in responsible fields, cocaptain Bert Clark in geology, cocaptain Jim Weatherall in business administration, Dick Heatly in business management, Jack Lockett in business, Fred Smith in physical education and coaching, Frank Silva in industrial engineering, and Art Janes in geology.

In national team statistics, Oklahoma ranked fourth in the nation in rushing with 316 yards a game, sixth in scoring with 32.1, sixth in total offense with 406.2 net yards, sixth in rushing defense with 104.9 yards, and eighth in total defense with its yield of 221.5 net yards a contest.

In individual stats Weatherall ranked second in the nation in percentage of extra points made, 83 percent. He also was voted the Outland Award that goes to the outstanding guard-tackle in the nation. Oklahomans selected on first All-American teams were Weatherall and center Tom Catlin. Although he played in only seven full games his freshman season, Leake led the Big Seven in scoring with 13 touchdowns and 78 points.

On December 12, 1951, the Big Seven Conference adopted and announced shocking new measures banning all postseason athletic events including football bowls and NCAA tournaments. They sharply restricted recruiting practices. Coaches, staffers, and alumni were no longer to visit high-school athletes off campus, nor could they pay travel and other expenses to bring these lads to their own campuses. Spring football practice was reduced to twenty sessions, and redshirting was outlawed.

Wilkinson was disturbed because the nearby Southwest Conference with whom Oklahoma competed for high-school athletes was not bound by the new canons. Meanwhile, Oklahoma's 1952 spring practice was approaching.

1951 SENIORS TODAY

Bert Clark is a stockbroker with Shearson–American Express, of Dallas, Texas.

Dick Heatley and his wife own Mountaineers Ltd., a janitorial contract services and supply firm in Spartanburg, South Carolina.

Art Janes, a geologist for Humble Oil Company, was killed June 1, 1966, in a tractor accident.

Jim Weatherall is sales manager of Mid-Continent Mud Sales, Inc., an oil-field drilling-mud service company of Oklahoma City.

7. THE FINESSERS

With each of the first four foes highly rated and Notre Dame to be met at South Bend in November, Oklahoma's coaches and players attacked the new season with eagerness and zest. The hardest-working man on the squad seems to have been the recuperating left halfback, Billy Vessels.

Soon after his injury, Vessels began soaking the knee daily in the hot whirlpool bath and running distances with the Sooner cross-country team. In the spring he joined the Sooner track squad. On May 10 he entered the University intramural meet, winning the 100- and 220-yard dashes and anchoring a relay.

In the 1952 spring football practice Vessels put his knee through all the rigors. He played in five spring games and several scrimmages. In the varsity-alumni game, which the old grads won 27-20, he ran back the opening kickoff 85 yards to a touchdown, squirming out of the arms of four different tacklers in four different parts of the field. He was never hurt.

When summer arrived, he kicked off his shoes and ran barefoot in the sand of the Arkansas River near his hometown, Cleveland, Oklahoma. "By August the sand was hot and dry, and it was difficult to navigate but great for my knee," he says. When fall practice started, Vessels was ready.

The spring of '52 was remarkable for two things. Tackle George Cornelius logged an A in organic chemistry despite his heavy football duties. Guard J. D. Roberts reduced his weight from 240 to 200 pounds. "There wasn't anything I didn't like to eat," Roberts remembers, "but Gomer took me into the film room and showed me in movies of our 1951 games that in my lateral pursuit I was often just one step from tackling the ballcarrier. After that I ran and played handball and was careful about what I ate."

Eating wasn't the only thing Roberts liked to do. During the 1952 two-a-days, Roberts "got mixed up in a fight," as he puts it, and was called before President Cross. Wilkinson went with him. The president listened patiently to the details.

"In the future, J. D., if you even see a fight on the campus, I want you to go two blocks around it," the president said. "We really don't have any name for probation. But whatever the name is, you're now on it."

When Roberts became a senior, President Cross sent him a letter. "You're off probation," the letter said. "You've been a good boy." He had also become a very good football player. More about that later.

Two sophomore fullbacks, Carl Allison of McAlester and Max Boydston, were converted into ends that fall. Frank Ivy, Sooner end coach, himself a converted high-school fullback, quickly taught them the rudiments of the position that Wilkinson considered the most difficult of all to play.

Colorado, the first opponent, was hard to beat at Boulder. Pete Elliott, the Sooner scout who put the glass on the Buffs in their victorious opener against San Jose, was optimistic. "If we'll hit it out with them, I think we'll win," said Elliott. "But we haven't been hit since last year."

Colorado quickly corrected that. With only 7:15 left to play and Colorado leading 21-14, the Oklahoma offense finally began to move, and the Sooners convoyed the ball 78 yards to score the tying touchdown, Vessels diving across the locked lines with only 1:51 remaining. But Oklahoma still had to kick the goal. And Buddy Leake, kicking the first crucial conversion of his short college career, dropped back to boot it.

Dal Ward shrewdly decided to let the Memphis sophomore think about it. Ward called time-out. The crowd was roaring for the Buffaloes to block the kick.

"Eddie Crowder, our holder, and I were standing by ourselves back by the kicking tee trying to relax each other," Leake recalls today. "But all I could think about was that if I missed the conversion Oklahoma's record of never having lost a conference game under Bud Wilkinson would go up in smoke.

"'You just hold it, and I'll kick it,' I told Eddie, trying to be calm." Tom Catlin eased the pressure on everybody when his center snap shot back perfectly. Crowder set the ball up nicely. Leake drilled it dead center. Final score, 21-21.

"Catlin was a strong, quiet, intelligent guy," remembers Eddie Crowder. "Bud had always told the team not to come into the huddle and say, 'Run this' or 'Run that.' 'Let the quarterback call them,' he told everybody.

"We were trotting back to our huddle against Colorado," Crowder continued. "Catlin intercepted me before we got to the huddle. He said, 'Eddie, I'm sure I can block my man on the fullback counter."

Crowder called the play. With Catlin obliterating his opponent, the Sooners gained 15 yards. Crowder hustled back into the huddle and lined up in the center position, his rump to the ball.

"Tom," said the quarterback. "You can call the plays better than I can. You're our quarterback now." The Sooners chuckled. Catlin grinned.

"You bet I was just joking," Crowder laughs today. "I wanted to keep my little body in a safer position."

With Oklahoma ahead 14-7, Zack Jordan quick-kicked 77 yards, and Vessels lost a fumble on the Sooner 22. Three plays later Jordan ran his own left end for 6 yards and the tying touchdown. "I'll always have to live with that fumble," Vessels says today. "It hurt us bad."

Six minutes later the Buffaloes went ahead 21-14 with a clever passing offensive, Lee Venske hitting Jordan for 16 yards and the touchdown. Williams kicked goal. It had grown cloudy and colder, and the frenzied cheering of the Colorado crowd seemed to echo off the nearby mountains.

"We had the left end and the tailback out on the same side," Dal Ward recalled the touchdown play.[1] "If the OU halfback came up, we'd throw over him to the left end. If the halfback stayed back, we'd pass to our tailback in the left flat, always to Jordan because he had running skills. The Oklahoma game was the first in which we'd ever used it."

The blazing Sooner effort in that closing surge that brought the 21-21 tie was epitomized by Jack Ging, black-haired Alvan. A great little fighter, Ging was all heart and hustle. With 1:51 to play, he ran down on the Sooner kickoff and on the 17 tackled the Colorado ballcarrier, who was thirty pounds heavier. Then the Colorado crowd gasped and laughed. Ging not only tackled his man but tried to pick him up bodily and throw him out of bounds to stop the clock. It looked like an ant wrestling with the carcass of a beetle. Oklahoma wanted that ball.

Wilkinson gave Ward and Colorado full credit. "I thought Zack Jordan's quick-kicking was the best I'd ever seen," he said. "Even when we were expecting them, he was deadly, booting low driving punts away from our safety."

Pittsburgh, a dominant eastern colossus coached that year by Lowell "Red" Dawson, former head mentor of the Buffalo Bills professional club, was next on the Sooner slate. The sprightly Panthers had stopped Iowa of the Big Nine 26-14 the previous week. After their Oklahoma game Pittsburgh defeated Notre Dame 22-19.

The Pitt-Oklahoma game illustrated with ominous clarity the Sooners' chief problem in 1952. The Sooner offense was slick and poised. Not only did it click off seven touchdowns against the Panthers, but it drove 76 and 78 yards to touchdowns from kickoff at the start of each half. The Sooner defense was thin and vulnerable. Pitt drove 63, 45, and 52 yards to touchdowns against it, each a long, sustained march.

Yet the game broke on three rugged Oklahoma defensive plays, each of which led to touchdowns. On the first of these Ed Rowland, senior tackle from Odessa, Texas, recovered the ball after Doc Hearon, with one tigerish

---

[1] Dal Ward to author, July 10, 1980.

charge, had slapped it out of the hands of quarterback Rudy Mattioli. The second was Tom Catlin's interception of Mattioli's forward pass. The third was Rowland's feat of bursting through and blocking Zombek's punt high into the air. Left end Dick Ellis fielded the ball and, following a bevy of blockers down the west sideline, ran 45 yards to score. Oklahoma won 49-20. Jack Ging ran up Rowland's back to block the only missed conversion of the game.

Texas, a proud team that later finished the season 8-2, won the Southwest Conference championship, and combed Tennessee 16-0 in the Gator Bowl, came next on the Sooner slate before 75,504 at Dallas.

Defeated 14-3 by Notre Dame the week before, Coach Ed Price's Steers came into the game in their usual sod-pawing, horn-tossing mood. The Oklahoma disposition was more restrained. The Sooners had just lost by injury their other big tackle, Roger Nelson, a 220-pound All-Big Eight choice. With Nelson's elbow in a cast, Wilkinson and Gomer Jones moved Don Brown, the stubby little sophomore French hornist, into Nelson's position.

At the Worth Hotel in Fort Worth, the Sooners were having breakfast the morning of the game. Wilkinson told Crowder, the Sooner quarterback, "Ed, come by my room thirty minutes before we catch the bus to the stadium." "He was packing his suitcase," Crowder remembers, "putting his clothing and shaving kit into it." "'Ed,' he said, 'I have a premonition that if we use the counter option pass today, as we did against Colorado last year, we'll have the same success.'"

Billy Vessels says that Wilkinson also put in a new variety of pass cuts for the Texas game. "We'd been sending the halfback out flat and the end deep," he remembers, "but against Texas the halfback faked toward the sideline and went deep while the end went into the right flat and made a sideline cut. Every guy on our squad did his job perfectly. It was like running a diagrammed play in practice."

When Oklahoma's deceptive attack ripped through a fine Texas team for four touchdowns after only 10 minutes and 50 seconds of the first quarter, the crowd sat limp with astonishment. Oklahoma led 28-0. The Sooners actually scored a fifth touchdown during this interval on a pass, Crowder to Boydston, but lost it on a holding penalty.

Gene Calame, Crowder's substitute at quarterback, remembers that "Crowder and McPhail fooled not only the cameramen but the referees as well. The officials would blow the ball dead, and Crowder would rise up in another part of the field and throw a forward pass."

Crowder gives McPhail full credit. "It always made me kinda ill to look over my shoulder and watch poor old Buck get clobbered, yet it was a

116

revelation to see how well he ran without the ball, dodging and twisting and leaping over people while pretending to cradle it with both hands."

Off the football field McPhail was the most gregarious man on the squad. He liked everybody. He greeted everybody. Even if you met him on the campus six times the same day, he'd stop and grin and shake hands and mean it each time too. "The way he played against Texas, he should have shaken hands with himself after every play," said Pop Ivy.

With Jim Davis and Dick Bowman levering their opponents back on straight-ahead blocks, Vessels scored the first touchdown on the handoff. Three minutes later, from the Sooner 35, Crowder resorted for the first time to the Sooner legerdemain, concealing the football.

While Texas was looking for it, "Heady Eddie," as the quarterback had been nicknamed by the press, retreated, saw Leake was open, and fired to him. Cutting behind a decisive downfield block by John Reddell, Leake dashed 65 yards to a touchdown and booted his own goal. Score, 14-0.

Three plays later the Texas kickoff receiver was gang-tackled and relinquished the ball to Calame on the Steer 29. Again Oklahoma tried the hocus-pocus, and while the Orange Shirts were frisking McPhail near the scrimmage line, Crowder sprang from hiding and forward-passed to Max Boydston for another touchdown. But Oklahoma lost that one because of a holding penalty.

Undismayed, Vessels reversed left end for 29 yards to the Steer 12. Then he bored off tackle, was stopped, and while falling pitched a lateral to McPhail who ran for a touchdown. Score, 21-0.

The Sooners yoked two fine plays together for their fourth touchdown. Grigg slithered back 34 yards with a punt. Don Brown, the Kermit French-hornist, set it up by decking two Orange tacklers with a running body block. Then Crowder again turned to his aerial wizardry. Emerging from a tangle of bodies, the quarterback spied Reddell waving an uplifted arm in the secondary. Crowder lined the ball to him for 29 yards. Touchdown! With the scoreboard clock still showing 4.10 left to play in the first quarter, Oklahoma led 28-0. And could have led 35-0.

"It was a classic example of what finesse can do in football," said Pop Ivy later. "It didn't fool 'em once. It fooled 'em four times."

What was the secret of Crowder's deceptive faking and ball handling, I once asked him. "Trying to look real relaxed," the quarterback replied. "When you give the ball away on a handoff, you naturally look relaxed. So when you fake to give it but secretly keep it, you try to look and act exactly the same way. I practice this by making a mental picture of how I think I look when handing off."

After each Sooner touchdown, Oklahoma's Ruf-Neks, student rooters

In this revealment of Oklahoma's counter option pass, Eddie Crowder, Sooner quarterback, retreats, hiding the ball in his crotch after faking a handoff to fullback Buck McPhail (41) in center of picture.

Then Crowder hurls a long touchdown forward pass to end John Reddell, wide open in the Texas secondary.

clad in red flannel shirts and white trousers, celebrated by firing double-barreled shotguns loaded with blanks from near the Texas bench. "Boom! Boom! Boom!" the crescendo broke out. Harley Sewell, Texas guard, who was in for a rest, had recently returned from service in the Korean War. "Harley," called Coach Price of Texas, "are you rested? Wanta go back in?"

"Yeah, coach," said Sewell, "but this is worse than Korea!"

Nobody ever saw a Texas team quit. This one didn't either. Trailing by four touchdowns, the Longhorns carried it to Oklahoma all through the second quarter, driving 74 yards to their first touchdown. And they would have had a second if Tom Catlin had not come in hard on fourth down to make a vital stop one yard from the goal. In his alumni letter Wilkinson called this "the most decisive play in the game."

In the fourth quarter the spectators were treated to five touchdowns by both teams, illustrating the offensive class of each. After Leake scored on a buck, Texas drove and scored from kickoff. Oklahoma scored from kickoff. Texas scored from kickoff. Oklahoma scored from kickoff when Vessels, while falling in the grasp of a Texas halfback, lifted a lateral to McPhail, who ran 60 yards to the goal. And the shotguns boomed, and the spectators roared.

The press comment was a tribute to McPhail's histrionics. Clark Nealon, of the *Houston Post,* wrote: "McPhail barged up the middle, bulled through the line, quivered but held his feet and came again after dropping his shoulder into the linebacker. Big Buck was still battling with the closing-in Longhorns when, out of the corner of our eye, we caught Crowder draw back his arm and hum one up the field. There stood Buddy Leake, all by himself. . . . It seemed unjust that McPhail couldn't get at least a percentage of the ground he gained while only faking that he had the ball."

Texas tricaptain Jack Barton said in the *Dallas Morning News,* "They're the best I've ever seen. They're the hardest playing, yet clean, ball club I've ever played against."

Marching to the fourth showdown battle of the season and the third off its home field, Oklahoma went north to face Kansas, winner of nine straight. The crowd of 37,946 at Lawrence had been sold out for a month.

Despite its fourth straight yield of three touchdowns and 205 yards of Kansas forward passes thrown by Jerry Robertson, the Sooner secondary defended staunchly. Larry Grigg, Carl Allison, and Sam Allen each intercepted Kansas passes, and two of those led directly to Oklahoma touchdowns. Grigg, Sooner safety, was kept very busy. He made three touchdown-saving stops of hard-running Kansas backs in the open.

Kansas scored first when Charley Hoag, their fine halfback, dove across the goal. Two minutes later the Jayhawkers fumbled, and Rowland recovered on the Kansas 16. From there Leake skipped across the goal in three plays, and the score was tied 7-7. "Crowder, a skinny six-footer with a thin disdainful face, ran the offense with the deft aplomb of a blue-sky stock salesman," wrote Robert Phipps, football writer for the *Omaha* (Nebraska) *World Herald.*

Then Larry Grigg made a leaping, clutching pass interception, and the Sooners scored in one play, hoodwinking the Crimson and Blue with the counter option pass. Crowder faked to McPhail, and Buck himself faked so realistically that he drew the Jayhawk line and linebackers to him. Crowder fired the ball long and true to Boydston, the fastest man on the Oklahoma squad. Boydston outran everybody down the sideline on a 58-yard touchdown play.

A moment later Allison intercepted a Robertson pass, and Oklahoma moved 64 yards to its third touchdown, McPhail, Bowman, and Davis blocking Vessels over. The Sooners lost Leake, their halfback, during this drive. "A Kansas tackler hit me," Leake recalls today. "My cleats must have hung in the grass after I threw a pass. I heard something pop and felt a pain in my ankle." When the lead was 21-7, it looked like the Sooners were in command.

But the third Sooner touchdown seemed to infuriate Kansas. Ablaze with fighting spirit, the Jayhawks marched 61 yards to a touchdown from kickoff on quarterback Jerry Robertson's forward passing. Later Brandenberry bucked across another touchdown. Instead of leading comfortably, the Sooner margin was trimmed to one point, 21-20, and they were battling for their lives.

Then Konek of Kansas made a sensational diving interception of a deflected pass and with the roar of their crowd rebounding off the bluffs of Mt. Oread, Kansas drove to the Sooner 6. There Catlin made two great plays to save Oklahoma.

First he shot through a hole left by a Kansas guard pulling and caught Robertson's ankles for a 5-yard loss. On fourth down Robertson fired a pass, but Catlin sprinted to break it up. "No matter what developed, Catlin seemed privy to the secrets of the Kansas huddle," wrote Phipps.

That heroic stand encouraged Oklahoma tremendously. The next three times they got the ball, the Sooners drove 90, 73, and 55 yards to touchdowns. On the first, J. D. Roberts and Melvin Brown blocked Green over. On the second, Jim Davis and Boydston blocked Vessels over. On the third, Boydston, Davis, and McPhail blocked Green over.

Kansas spectators in the stadium frequently called out, "He's still got it!" as a warning to the Kansas players that Crowder actually had not handed the ball off to McPhail. "Hope sprang again in the hearts of the

Kansans. Crowder killed it with surgical neatness," Phipps reported. With Leake out, McPhail kicked the last four goals. Final score: Oklahoma 42, Kansas 20.

Dick Cullum, sports columnist of the *Minneapolis Tribune,* was perhaps the most knowledgeable football writer in the Big Ten area. He went to Lawrence to see the Sooners against the Kansans. After the hostilities Cullum wrote that if the Sooners went undefeated they would deserve full consideration for the national championship.

"Oklahoma has this in its favor," he continued. "It plays by far the toughest schedule of any of the highly rated teams except, possibly, the team that finishes in the lead in California."

Cullum was enamoured with "the most interesting of Oklahoma's stars —slim, scholarly Eddie Crowder, the quarterback. This man must surely be the season's best. . . . Most of the national experts picked John Scarbath, Maryland quarterback, as their back-of-the-year on a preseason basis. As long as Maryland wins, they will stay with Scarbath.

"However, having seen both men this season, I have to cast a most emphatic vote for Crowder. Scarbath is famed as a tricky ballhandler. Crowder could give him lessons all day long," Cullum concluded.

Wilkinson's modesty when importuned by the press to comment on this new deviltry he had contrived is understandable. Finally a writer named George Bugbee "wrung a few purple syllables from this strong silent man," as he put it. "Bud explained it simply when he said, 'They make their faking work because of their poise. With lots of people after you it's hard to look lackadaisical, especially when some of them are 220-pounders.'"

Otis Wile, the sage from Stillwater who directed Oklahoma A&M's sports-information program, had his own interpretation of the Sooner deception and with characteristic drollery expressed it in one of his "Dear John" letters to John Cronley, sports editor of the *Daily Oklahoman.* On the following Saturday, Kansas State played at Norman and Detroit at Stillwater.

"So this week," Wile began, "one envisions the distraught fan pondering the question, which game to see. Dear Hearts and Gentle People, when you go to a football game, what is it you watch? What is it you go to see? You watch that football and the bird carrying it. You betcha.

"Go on down there to Norman Saturday, chump. Shuck off your dough and play that shell game. Guess with the man. . . . Or be sharp, be smart. You come on up to Aggieland Saturday and watch that football shuttle around. When you yell, 'Go, go Bennett' or 'Drive, Halcomb,' you know you are yelling for the right guy."

Kansas State, 1-4, used their best player in the key role of defense in the next game. He was Veryl Switzer, 180-pound black safety who had been picked on the Associated Press's second All-American defensive team the year before. His teammates called him Joe.

Coach Bill Meek's Wildcats gave the Sooners trouble all through the first quarter with their 5-2 diamond defense, which featured the tackling of Switzer, used as a roving middle linebacker. Switzer logged 18 unassisted tackles in the game.

Doc Hearon, Sooner guard, said, "I blocked Switzer off his feet twice, but the third time he stood his ground. Knocked me down. Jammed my neck. If he hadn't been colored, I'd never have got up."

Just before the first period ended occurred the contest's most dramatic and amusing play. From the Wildcat 1-yard line Crowder called the Vessels sweep to the right. Switzer swooped in to make the tackle. McPhail flattened him with a rolling block. Vessels scored standing.

In the grass behind, Switzer and McPhail, both on their hands and knees, faced each other. True to his personality, McPhail delighted the crowd with a gesture of sportsmanship. Grinning broadly, Buck thrust out his right hand. Switzer, also grinning, grasped it, and they shook hands warmly. The crowd roared with laughter and applause.

Oklahoma intercepted seven passes, one by Lester Lane, basketball player from Purcell, and won 49-6. Wilkinson used 52 men. With the Notre Dame game coming up in two weeks, Wilkinson looked anxiously at his wounded, tackle Roger Nelson, end Carl Allison, and right half Buddy Leake.

Only one of them, Nelson, played at Iowa State as the Sooners, cruising at their national high of 42 points a game, lacked one point of equaling it against the Cyclones, who were beaten 41-0.

Leake did, however, continue booting extra points, and after hitting 28 in a row he missed his fourth at Ames. It was a difficult shot. A cross wind of almost galelike proportions was blowing, and the ball slanted a yard outside the left post.

Jim Davis, the senior left tackle from McAlester, who threw the decisive block on Vessels's 50-yard touchdown run against the Cyclones, was a smart, loyal player who knew not only his assignments but also those of his teammates. He was usually the most scratched-up player in every game. "Shuffles" the Sooners called him, or "the Mentholatum Kid."

"You can't have a steady girl when your face is all scratched up," Jim once told me. "They all feel sorry for you, but none of them want to be seen in public with you," he laughed. "They always want to go to some dark place and dance. That doesn't fool me. I know I'm no Gene Kelly.

I know they know it too. Besides, after a game I'm too tired to dance anyhow."

Davis blocked for Vessels on the latter's handoff play. "Curly's my favorite player," said Davis. "If you make a hole for him, he pats you on the back. 'Good hole that time,' he says. If I don't make a hole I feel awfully low."

Everybody teased Davis about his scratches. Dr. Howard Larsh, who taught Jim's class in bacteriology at the University, always peered curiously at Davis's scars on the Monday morning after a Sooner game.

"Did you win or lose?" the professor would ask the tackle.

"Won," grinned Jim, painfully.

Larsh snorted. "Huh," he said, "you don't look like it."

Billy Vessels says, "I just loved Jim Davis. On the split-T handoff you depend on the man in front of you. You have to cut off his blocks. Like Wade Walker, Jim Davis had lots of blocking finesse. He helped me like Wade used to help Junior Thomas."

The Oklahoma-Notre Dame game at South Bend, Indiana, was a prestige struggle. Notre Dame teams, coached by Jack Marks, Jess Harper, Knute Rockne, and Frank Leahy, had been the monarchs of American football since 1912. Oklahoma, tutored by Bud Wilkinson, had the highest winning percentage of the past five years. Could the new kings dethrone the old?

Dick Cullum, the football pundit from Minneapolis, warned the Sooners in a column on the morning of the game. "This one," wrote Cullum, "is the big one the Irish want. They are getting ready for it with all the tested measures which have made Notre Dame the greatest of all known odds-spillers when the great day comes on Notre Dame's home field.

"It starts back on the newsstands of Chicago. There a press which is sympathetic to the Irish begins the process of preparing the visitor for his doom. The visitor is told he is invincible. He is told Notre Dame is no longer the power of yore. One who has traveled across this strip of Indiana with other great and confident powers could tell these Oklahomans, who are making their first visit, that, win or lose, they are going to be wiser people on the way home.

"Next stage," Cullum continued, "is the student rally. Once each season, at the most critical point, the (Notre Dame) students take over the football team. They conduct a week of emotional preparation which could not be duplicated on any other campus. It is climaxed by a gathering on the eve of the game where the Notre Dame spirit comes out in pure and irresistible essence."

Leahy's Irish had won 74, lost 10, tied 8 for .880 percent. Wilkinson's Sooners had won 50, lost 6 and tied 2 for .909 percent. A crowd of

57,446, 9,000 of whom were Oklahomans, had been sold out for weeks. Oklahomans descended upon the Indiana football capital by plane, automobile, and in 13 special trains containing 104 filled Pullman coaches. Mel Allen's coast-to-coast telecast, heard by more than 20 million people, was declared the heaviest-drawing broadcast of all time.

Tickets were impossible to come by. B. S. ("Cheebie") Graham, a friend of Wilkinson's, needed two tickets and asked Wilkinson to help him. Wilkinson advised him to phone Leahy and tell him that Bud had asked him to call. Graham did.

"I honestly can't help," replied Leahy.

Graham pleaded, "Well, then, Mr. Leahy, can you make a suggestion that might help me?"

"Well," replied Leahy. "You might phone the Pope. Maybe he'd be willing to ask a couple of the brothers to stay home."

Buddy Leake's ankle seemed fully healed. "It was in great shape," says Leake. However, when Wilkinson sent him into the final Sooner scrimmage two days before the game, he was tackled, and while he was lying on the turf, somebody fell across his ankle, injuring it again.

The Sooners scored first. After Bob Ewbanks blasted a long punt out of bounds on the Irish 10 and Notre Dame kicked back short, Oklahoma had the ball on the Irish 27.

Here the Sooners went early to their counter option pass and put on a perfect play. Crowder faked to McPhail and hid the ball in his crotch. McPhail faked so well that he was hit by several Notre Dame tacklers. Even Johnny Lattner, the Irish All-American safety, came up to support. Then Crowder stepped back from his handoff spot and passed to Vessels, all alone in the left flat. Touchdown! Leake kicked goal, and Oklahoma led 7-0.

Midway in the second quarter, Crowder fumbled and lost a handoff on the Notre Dame 40. The Irish advanced 60 yards in nine plays, Ralph Guglielmi passing to Joe Heap for the tying touchdown. The Sooners got it back two minutes later. On a handoff over left tackle, Jim Davis took his man in. Max Boydston blocked his man out. Dick Bowman cut down the linebacker. Billy Vessels shot through the hole, took a fast outside cut, and ran 62 yards to a touchdown. Leake kicked goal. Oklahoma led 14-7 at the half.

Meanwhile, an unfortunate incident had occurred. J. D. Roberts, Oklahoma's guard, was sent from the game. "They were hitting me from behind and trying to hold me," Roberts recalls. "Finally I was hit in the middle of the back and knocked across the sideline." Instinctively, Roberts turned to defend himself. "I swung on him and hit him—not hard—trying to pull the punch."

As is so often the case, the official didn't see the original provocation and expelled Roberts. It was his first penalty all season. After the game, on his own initiative, Roberts went to the Notre Dame dressing room and apologized to Coach Leahy and also to the Notre Dame player for losing his head.

The Sooners missed him in the last half, and also Ed Rowland, the right tackle, who had lamed his knee and was finished for the season. Hearon sprained an ankle, lost maneuverability, but stayed in. Says Eddie Crowder, "After that, Notre Dame started ripping us with inside plays with Lattner cutting back down our middle."

The Irish pass defense was excellent. Lattner's interception and 23-yard runback to the Sooner 7 led to their second touchdown. Fullback Neil Worden scored it. Arrix kicked goal, tying the score 14-14.

Again Oklahoma met the challenge with a furious onslaught. On the third play after the Sooners received the short Irish kickoff, Crowder saw that the Irish were in an eight-man line. At the line of scrimmage Crowder changed from a Vessels handoff straight ahead to a Vessels pitchout around Oklahoma's right flank. Instead of tipping off the Irish by checking the signal, Crowder said "Gap!" a concealed check Wilkinson had told him to use. The Irish stayed in their 8-3.

The Sooners blocked like mechanical doom. McPhail rolled the Irish end. Spurting fast down the sideline, Vessels cut back inside another great downfield block by Merrill Green and sped 44 yards to a touchdown. Leake kicked goal, and Oklahoma led 21-14.

Notre Dame received the kickoff and in 13 bruising plays scored on a 79-yard drive. Arrix's conversion tied the count at 21-21. The fourth quarter had begun.

Then came two climactic plays. On the Irish kickoff Dan Shannon, one of their boys, followed the ball down fast. "He made a 30-yard dash and never slowed down," recalled Pop Ivy. Larry Grigg, the Sooner receiver, was struck with such shattering impact that he turned a half flip in the air and lost the ball. Kohanowich recovered on the Sooner 25. Shannon was hurt and was through for the day. But Grigg stayed in to make a notable play of his own.

Notre Dame scored after four plays on a 1-yard sneak by Tom Carey. Then came Grigg's climactic effort. Still a bit dazed from Shannon's tooth-jarring tackle, Grigg tore through the Irish defense to block Arrix's kick. Notre Dame led by six, 27-21.

125

"To me, that was one of the great plays of a great game," Wilkinson said later, "and exemplified the spirit with which our team played for sixty minutes." That play nearly won the game for Oklahoma. If the Sooners could have scored another touchdown—and twice they came close—and Leake had kicked goal, which he had done 32 of 33 times that year, Grigg's blocked kick would have won the game 28-27 for Oklahoma, and he would have emerged as a hero of the contest.

Meanwhile, there was controversy on the field about how Notre Dame had advanced from the Sooner 8 to the Sooner 3. The Irish lined up in T formation then shifted suddenly into another formation as if the play had already started.

"It looked to us like their blockers were moving," says Billy Vessels. But Oklahoma was penalized to its 3-yard line. "Notre Dame picked up five of the toughest yards on the gridiron," reported the *Associated Press*, "and then scored the winning touchdown." Oklahoma's protests on the field were unavailing. Wilkinson never protested publicly.

Previously, in the third quarter, Oklahoma had been assessed a similar offside penalty that moved the ball from the Sooner 6 to the 1. Notre Dame's third touchdown followed.

"I would have screamed about that one too," said Jim Tatum, the Maryland coach, who saw the game. "Wilkinson didn't, but I guess he's a nicer fellow than I am. Notre Dame shifted from the T to the box and drew Oklahoma offside. There's a rule in the book covering that kind of stuff and it puts the guilt on the team with the ball."

Notre Dame still had the Oklahoma offense to contend with. "As a team we hadn't played very well before then," Eddie Crowder says. "Notre Dame had played awfully well. But our team still thought it could win."

Again Notre Dame kicked off. Vessels fielded it, then slipped and fell on the Sooner 7 with nobody close to him. "When I put my foot down, there wasn't any ground there," Vessels explained later. "I was so fired up and eager to get started down the field that my feet began running before I fielded the ball. We all wanted to win so badly."

Pouring out their energy, the Sooners drove with stubborn determination 66 yards up the field before Notre Dame stopped them on the Irish 27. Notre Dame made one first down then punted to Jack Ging who fair-caught on the Sooner 34.

Again Oklahoma attacked hotly. Vessels ripped off tackle and lateraled to McPhail. With Dick Bowman cutting off the Irish linebacker, McPhail ran 30 yards. Then Vessels hit the handoff for 9 and again for 7 to the Notre Dame 20 but had the bad luck to fumble there, Lattner recovering. "Some fellow grabbed my arm," says Vessels today.

Frank Leahy (left), Notre Dame coach, visits with Gomer Jones and Bud Wilkinson of Oklahoma before the Irish-Sooner battle of 1952. Photo by Oklahoma Publishing Co.

"The only satisfaction I got out of the game came in the fourth quarter," says Buck McPhail. "We drove from our 7 to their 20. The only thing that stopped us was a fumble. They were the guys hanging on the ropes at the end."

Says Crowder, "On that last drive I kept looking into our huddle to see who was tiredest. Buck and Billy were both fagged out. Larry Grigg was still glassy-eyed from his collision with Shannon. My problem on each play was choosing whether I would go with a tired back or one who was slightly groggy."

With two minutes to play, the Sooners were on their own 45. Vessels bucked 4 yards. Larry Grigg, on an end around, ran 11 to the Irish 40. On

127

Billy Vessels, Sooner halfback, running 62 yards to the second touchdown against Notre Dame at South Bend in 1952. In this game Vessels scored three touchdowns and rushed 195 net yards, averaging 11.4 yards a carry. This feat won for him and Oklahoma the 1952 Heisman Award. Photo by Wide World Photos.

a later fourth down, Grigg ran 11 more yards to the Irish 25. Only seconds were left to play.

"We tried our 26-screen pass to Max Boydston," says Crowder. "The Notre Dame crowd was roaring and Max didn't hear me say 'screen.' He ran the 26-pass route and I had nobody to throw to."

McPhail's face softens as his mind goes back. "I remember Jack Alessandro, their captain, coming to our dressing room after the game to speak to us," he said. "He was a fine fellow."

Vessels scored three touchdowns and rushed 195 net yards to average 11.4 a carry. He won the Heisman Trophy on that feat, won it in a game his team lost. The Sooners rushed 313 net yards to achieve their highest average of the season, 7.4 net yards a carry. In the fourth quarter alone, the spunked-up Sooners rushed 142 net yards—nearly a length and a half of the gridiron—while making their final desperate effort to come from behind and win.

In his alumni letter Wilkinson congratulated Leahy and his staff for preparing their team so well technically and emotionally. "I believe the story of the contest is wrapped up in the physical element," Bud wrote. "Football is a hard, tough, driving game. Notre Dame was able to play tougher physically. They beat us with their superiority in this phase of the game. Only one of our fumbles was mechanical. On the others Notre Dame just knocked us loose from the ball. A lot of people criticize that kind of football, but they aren't justified in doing so. The willingness to hit harder than the other fellow, to go all out for something you want and believe in, is one of the great lessons of the game."

Later, when he wrote his memoirs for *Look* magazine, Leahy said, ". . . the best team our lads ever faced—I did not see the powerful Army aggregations of '44 and '45 because I was in service—was Oklahoma of '52. Upsetting them was my greatest coaching thrill."

The whole team was so battered from the Notre Dame ordeal that Wilkinson gave them a complete holiday from practice Monday and Tuesday before the Missouri game.

It was good medicine too, for Oklahoma won 47-7. Sam Allen blocked a punt. Don Brown snatched it up and ran to the Tiger 5. Eddie Crowder punched it over. Later safety Jack Ging pulled a Tiger punt out of the sky and returned it 65 yards to score.

In the last half Gomer Jones adjusted Oklahoma's defense against Tony Scardino's passing off the Tiger spread, and the Sooners intercepted seven passes. Catlin got two, Vessels two, and Jerry Ingram, Kurt Burris, and Lester Lane one each. Green, in for Leake, scored three touchdowns.

Buddy Leake, his ankle operated and his leg in a cast, remembers watching the Nebraska game, which Oklahoma won 34-13, from the stadium. He wanted to study the Crowder-McPhail exchange as a spectator. "I went with Buck every time," Leake laughs today. "They both faked perfectly." That they could bamboozle one of their own backs looking down on them from the stadium seems the best proof of all of their incomparable technique.

129

With J. D. Roberts and Dick Bowman, those twins of mayhem, obliterating the end and the halfback, the final Sooner touchdown came on a 29-yard power plunge by Vessels. He flat ran over both the Nebraska halfback and safety.

"Billy was a superb competitor," Crowder says. "He made the supreme effort as a normal thing."

In the final game of the season, Oklahoma A&M at Stillwater, the field was soft from a previous rain. Bill Bredde, a part-Pawnee Indian halfback wearing Aggie silks, quickly proved that the Aggie field was fast enough. In returning the opening kickoff 98 yards to a touchdown, he ran all over it. Bobby Green kicked goal, and the Aggies led 7-0.

A few minutes later the Sooners found that they too could run on the Aggie rectangle. Doc Hearon partly blocked Kenneth McCullough's punt, and starting from the Aggie 21, Oklahoma scored in three plays, Vessels hammering off tackle then lateraling to McPhail as he fell. The Heisman Trophy winner tossed four laterals in that game, his last for the Sooners. Three went to McPhail, one to Crowder. This generosity was typical of the senior left half.

Later, Crowder twice saw that the Aggies were overshifted on the weak side. Twice he checked the signal, sending Green wide around end. Twice Green scored. In the third quarter with Crowder directing the spoof, the Sooners went to the counter option pass. The quarterback hid the ball, watched with cool detachment McPhail buck off Catlin's hip, then produced the ball and whipped a forward pass to Boydston, who made a fast inside dart, shook off one tackler, outran another, and scored on a 48-yard play.

An earlier Reddell catch was notable in that it permitted the senior end to set a new career seasonal school record for the most yards received in forward passes. The old record was held by Bill Jennings, former Sooner wingback and later Oklahoma coach.

The next time the Sooners went to the bench, Jennings, scouting in the press box, phoned down to the Sooner bench, asking for Reddell. He said, "John, you just broke my record. Hey, I'm proud of you. Congratulations!"

In the fourth quarter Roger Nelson, senior tackle, scored the first touchdown of his life when he somehow intercepted an Aggie pass thrown down his throat and ran 20 yards. Final score: 54 to 7.

The game was rough. "They had a linebacker," recalls Reddell, "who liked to bat me around. Every time I'd go downfield he'd fist me in the eye. In those days there weren't any masks or bars on helmets. He was marking me up pretty good. I didn't retaliate because I knew Bud didn't like penalties." Finally Reddell decided that he had to protect himself.

The Wilkinson family at home. From left to right: Bud, Pat, Jay, and Mary.

"The next play," he recalls, "went to the opposite side. I cocked my bony elbow, took a nice little jab step and caught him across the chops, falling on top of him. My elbow went numb. It felt paralyzed. 'You finally did something dirty and broke your damned arm,' I told myself. They worked on it a little, and it felt better. I went back in for the extra point.

131

The 1952 backfield, from left to right: Buddy Leake, Billy Vessels, Eddie Crowder, and Buck McPhail.

"'There he is!' I heard one of the Aggies say. For a while I was very busy. I would have liked a little more friendliness in my last game." On the final play, and the last of his life as a Sooner, Billy Vessels tackled Bredde for a 7-yard loss.

It was axiomatic that Oklahoma would be invited to play in an attractive bowl despite the defeat to Notre Dame and the tie with Colorado. But the Big Seven had just passed a rule barring all bowl play. The Big Seven was the only conference in the nation with a rule so drastic.

Displeased by the conference regulation, the University regents decided that if the team and coaches wanted to play in a bowl they should be allowed to do so. The regents left it up to a vote of "Coach Wilkinson and his staff, and the boys." President Cross warned them that such action would result in Oklahoma's being expelled from the conference. The regents remained defiant.

President Cross asked Wilkinson to poll the squad. Wilkinson did. Football captains Tom Catlin and Eddie Crowder discussed it with the players. Although they wanted very much to go, the players voted against an action so arbitrary, declaring sensibly that "we don't think it proper for our group to make an important decision like this that involves policy making of the university." The regents talked it over and backed down.

Later Wilkinson discussed with President Cross the possibility of the athletic department sending the football squad to the Orange Bowl as spectators.[2] Cross replied that such a trip would violate conference regulations. Wilkinson did not agree and asked Cross to ask the regents for an increase in the athletic department travel budget to finance the trip. The president presented the matter to the regents but warned them that it would defy conference regulations. The regents did not agree with him about that either.

The president decided not to punt. He telephoned the six other presidents of the Big Seven schools and discussed the matter frankly. All predicted that Oklahoma would receive severe disciplinary punishment if such a course was pursued. Meanwhile the state's press had learned about the matter, and its ridicule seemed more influential than anything else. Another meeting of the regents was called. The president detailed for them all the new developments. Regent Joe McBride moved that the president's advice be upheld and the matter dropped. His motion passed 6-1.

Regent Quintin Little still wanted Oklahoma to explore the possibility of joining the Southwest Conference. At his insistence Oklahoma sent Walter Kraft, its faculty representative, as an emissary to a December meeting of the Southwest league. Kraft was treated courteously, but it was explained to him that admission to that conference was by invitation only and that the Southwest Conference was already heavily involved with pressure from two nearby Texas schools, the University of Houston and Texas Tech.

Oklahoma's showing in the NCAA's 1952 national statistics illustrated Wilkinson's genius for developing many phases of the game. The Sooners led the nation in scoring with 40.7 points a contest, ranked second in rushing with 303.6 net yards a game, second in defense against opponents' punt returns with 5.2 yards yielded, third in punt returns with 16.9 yards a runback, fourth in interceptions with 26 in 191 enemy throws for 13.6

[2] George Lynn Cross, *Presidents Can't Punt* (Norman: University of Oklahoma Press, 1977), p. 190.

percent, and fifth in total offense with 425.5 net yards a game. Oklahoma placed fourth in both the Associated Press and United Press polls.

Vessels scored the most touchdowns of any back in the country, 18. Leake had the highest percentage of extra points kicked, booting 32 of 33 for 97 percent. Eddie Crowder's average of 13.5 yards for each forward pass attempted, regardless of whether it was completed, set a new national record. The Oklahoma team's similar average of 10.9 yards each time a Sooner passer swung his arm set another national record. The football principle Wilkinson was developing so successfully was that of designating every phase of the Sooner offense, running and passing, so that it reacted to the movement and charge of the defense after the ball was snapped. Vessels's winning of the Heisman Trophy was the top individual honor. Of him Wilkinson said, "Vessels was the first player I ever saw who was both the fastest and the toughest man on the field." Catlin, Crowder, Vessels, and McPhail were selected on first All-American teams.

Dick Cullum, the Big Ten Conference football writer from Minneapolis, summed up the season with a final column. He had personally watched five of the six top-ranked teams in both the AP and the UP polls. Four of the five he had seen twice.

"Beyond a doubt, Oklahoma has the best offensive platoon of the season and, so far as I know, the best ever," Cullum wrote. "When Buddy Leake, the right halfback, was well, the Oklahoma backfield of Eddie Crowder, Billy Vessels, Leake, and Buck McPhail was the best balanced, most versatile backfield I have ever seen. Every one of them was at the All-American level. So were Tom Catlin at offensive center and Ed Rowland at offensive tackle.

"Yes, this was a ground-gaining machine probably unsurpassed in football history and it was all brought up to the peak of excellence by the superb generalship and ball-handling of Crowder.

"For sheer class, I do feel that Oklahoma, going into any single game without injuries and having no bad luck as to injuries in the course of the game would win that game from any other team on the list. However, that may be setting up conditions not in accord with the normal fortune of football."

1952 SENIORS TODAY

Tom Catlin is defensive coordinator for the Seattle Seahawks, professional team of the American Football Conference of the National Football League.

Dr. George Cornelius is an ophthalmologist in Oklahoma City.

Eddie Crowder, athletic director of the University of Colorado, previously coached the 1971 Colorado football team that finished third in the Associated Press poll.

Buck McPhail is account sales manager for the jeansware division of the Levi Strauss Company of Los Angeles.

John Reddell is football coach at Trinity High School, Euless, Texas.

Ed Rowland owns a garage-door repair firm at Longmont, Colorado, and teaches shop at Longmont Junior High School.

Billy Vessels is assistant to the president of Deltona Corporation, a real-estate development firm in Miami, Florida.

8. THE START OF THE LONG STRING

Port Robertson's main job in the Athletic Department was varsity wrestling coach. He was the best in the nation. His Sooner wrestling teams of 1950 and 1951 had just won national collegiate team championships. As a student at Oklahoma, Robertson himself had been a skilled wrestler. In World War II he handled men so well that he rose to the rank of captain in the field artillery and was decorated for gallantry in action during the Normandy invasion. He was also awarded the Purple Heart.

It was also Robertson's task to supervise the study hall for freshman athletes. Organizing and enforcing discipline was his specialty. Nobody else in the department could do it as well.

The punishment that he dealt out was running the stadium steps, which in those days soared 62 rows high. The number of "laps," as the athletes called them, varied with the severity of the infraction. At six o'clock in the morning Robertson, carrying a stopwatch, would meet the sleepy sinners at the stadium and time the run before breakfast. The early hour did not deter the coach in the least. A onetime farm boy from Edmond, he arose before dawn every morning anyhow.

"I was scared to death of Port," confesses Tommy McDonald, also a freshman that season. "He was the best thing that ever happened to OU football. He could make the players keep their noses in their books. We all really respected him."

"Peahead" was Robertson's favorite appellation for a freshman in disfavor. "Delivered with scorn, it applied to anybody who needed to shape up, become wiser," recalls Calvin Woodworth, varsity tackle from Minco, "but after he had scorched a boy and the lad had left, the coach would say, 'That's one fine boy. One of the finest we've got here.'"

Billy Pricer, Perry High School's crack quarterback, was recruited that fall by Pop Ivy. As a freshman at Oklahoma, Pricer was the object of a lot of raillery. He had surgery on both knees that year, whereupon his teammates stole his crutches. Unperturbed, Pricer crawled downstairs to the dining hall.

Bruce Drake, Oklahoma's basketball coach, returned from a coaching clinic at Albuquerque, New Mexico. "Check up on that McDonald kid from

136

Albuquerque Highlands," he admonished Oklahoma's football coaches. "I heard some awfully good things about him."

Although Wilkinson didn't recruit much then outside Oklahoma and nearby Texas points, he sent Pop Ivy to Albuquerque. Hugh Hackett, the Highlands High School coach, met Ivy at the airport. With him were two of his players, one of them Tommy McDonald, a small, friendly, blond youngster who looked about as combative as a choirboy.

At the coach's home, the film of a Highlands game went into a projector. "McDonald ran inside and he ran outside," Ivy remembers. "He had wonderful speed. He threw the ball and hit the target. He caught the ball all over the field. He intercepted a pass. He made tackles everywhere. He dominated the game."

Enthusiasm seemed the lad's greatest attribute. It wasn't something you could pour out of a bottle into a spoon. It was born in him. Ivy returned to Norman and reported. Bud said, "Offer him a scholarship." The boy's mother had written to Notre Dame and mailed the Irish a scrapbook filled with stories about his feats. The Irish had replied that they were afraid he was too small and would sit on the bench too much. "We think it best that he go to a smaller college so he can get more playing time," they said.

Meanwhile Oklahoma alumni living in North Texas had been praising a 6-foot, 1-inch boy from Terrell, Texas, who had played single-wing tailback and safety for Terrell's class AA state champions. Jimmy Harris was his name. In track he ran the 220-yard dash and was a jumper. Bill Jennings of the Sooner staff had visited him twice, and Harris had come to Norman for a visit.

In the spring Roy Guffey, an Oklahoma graduate who had played guard on Coach Bennie Owen's Sooner team of 1920, Missouri Valley Conference champions, brought Wilkinson to Terrell to meet Harris. "I was highly impressed with Bud," says Harris today. "My mother liked him too. My dad had died. Bud didn't make any big promises. He told me that if I came to Oklahoma and started, I'd be nationally recognized, and even if I just made the third team I'd still be playing with the best. I decided to go to Oklahoma."

Another who decided to go to Oklahoma but couldn't get the Sooners to take him was Delbert Long, of Ponca City. Like most other backs, he was weak defensively. The coaches tried to drop him. He wouldn't let them. He told them he was going to make the OU team if it was the last thing he did.

Quarterback Jay O'Neal of Ada, who had begun playing flag football in the fifth grade, also signed that year. Unknown to Port Robertson, O'Neal had been salutatorian of his high-school graduation class. O'Neal and an

137

Ada classmate came to Norman to take the University placement tests. On the mathematics examination O'Neal correctly answered 38 of 40 questions, and his companion answered 36. "We'd had a good high-school math teacher at Ada," O'Neal explains.

Glenn Couch, dean of the University College, could hardly believe his eyes when he saw O'Neal's high score. A football fan, he phoned his friend Coach Robertson. "Port," he said, "I can't accuse these young men of cheating, but they can't be making scores this high."

Robertson sent for them. "You peaheads get in here. Slam that door. They can't accuse you of cheating, but I can."

O'Neal's eyes widened incredulously. "Boy," he told himself in awe, "this college sure is tough."

He turned to Robertson. "You mean you think we cheated?" he asked.

Robertson replied grimly, "I'm going to put you in a calculus class because of your high scores." Calculus, a five-hour course, was a formidable mathematics subject for upperclassmen. O'Neal knew that if he flunked it he would be ineligible for football. He also knew that he wasn't going to flunk it.

O'Neal made an A in calculus. Thereafter, whenever he met Robertson on the campus, the coach would stop him and grin, "Remember the time I accused you of cheating, and you clipped off that A in calculus?" he would start, and they'd enjoy a laugh together.

"Bud was always on us to graduate in a field in which we could make a good living after graduation," says O'Neal. "He talked constantly about that to the whole squad. Port pushed us hard in that direction too." Nearly one-fourth of the 1953 squad was enrolled in either geology or petroleum engineering, reflecting the squad's interest in the Southwest's sprawling oil industry.

Two more Burrises became regulars in 1953. Kurt was a rough-hewn junior center, Bob a sophomore fullback. Both grew up on their father's farm one mile west of Muskogee. "There were eleven kids in the family," says Kurt Burris, "six boys and five girls. We had to live in the country so we could raise enough food to feed thirteen people. We couldn't afford to live in town.

"One day about twenty of us kids got caught swimming in a stock pond," Kurt Burris adds. "The farmer made us tear down the raft we had built out of his lumber and carry it back where we'd got it. I was surprised to see one rugged little kid carrying a railroad tie all by himself, and he wasn't even straining. That was the first time I ever saw Bo Bolinger. His daddy was an ironworker."

Although line coach Gomer Jones ran his practices very seriously, he

138

would tolerate a little clowning upon occasion. The player with whom he especially seemed to enjoy this relationship was Doc Hearon.

One day in practice Gomer stopped the scrimmage to talk about technique. Doc Hearon became bored. The tackle had his own way of showing his disenchantment upon these occasions. He turned his helmet around on his head, back part in front, and pretended to be paying rapt attention.

"Knock off that bull, Doc!" Gomer bellowed hoarsely. "Where'd you get that goofy-looking headgear? You're not even smart enough to know how to wear it." Hearon grinned and readjusted the helmet.

Of Gomer, Hearon said, "You played hard for Gomer because you loved the guy. You wanted to make Gomer look good."

Jerry Tubbs, center on Breckenridge, Texas, High's split-T operators, was recruited by Bill Jennings with help from Wilkinson and Eddie Chiles, the Texas oil executive and OU graduate of 1934.

"I worked for Eddie one summer, but I always got my own summer jobs at Breckenridge while I was attending OU," says Tubbs. "This wasn't hard. I knew everybody in town."

With the abolition that season of the free-substitution rule and platoons, Wilkinson selected his starting and relieving elevens for their defensive ability then fitted them into whatever segment of offense they could best be utilized. Thus he hoped to have a sound defensive player in each position.

Of the 1953 season, guard J. D. Roberts said, "It was totally different. I thought Bud, Gomer, and the staff did the finest coaching job of all time that year. We didn't have a lot of great talent. Bud did a super job keeping the team's confidence up."

Notre Dame, everybody's favorite to win the 1953 national championship, was first on an ominous early schedule. Never in his seventeen-season career as Sooner head mentor was Wilkinson so badly outmatched on paper in a single game. Bud and his staff toiled busily to replace 1952's staggering losses of backs Crowder, Vessels, and McPhail, and linemen Catlin, Rowland, Reddell, Jim Davis, and linebacker Sam Allen.

"I've never been around a football squad that reported so trim on opening day," declared Ken Rawlinson, who was starting his first year as Sooner trainer. It was also the first year for Dr. Donald Robinson, the new team physician, though Dr. Mike Willard still made the trips.

Buddy Leake, who was being groomed for quarterback, had injured a shoulder in spring practice and sat out most of it, a bad break for the team.

Gene Calame, Eddie Crowder's first alternate of the previous season, was also being considered. "It was pure pleasure, playing for Bud," says Calame today. "He spent long hours with his quarterbacks and constantly encouraged us. He'd give you the game plan we were to use that week and lay out the

139

defense the opponent would use. Then he'd confront you with the different situations you'd encounter, along with the down and yardage situation. Working up and down a miniature gridiron, he would teach you to make the appropriate call.

"'Okay,' he'd say, 'you made a yard. It's second and nine. What would you call?' We were simply an extension of how he would have called the game had he been the quarterback."

Pat O'Neal, then a junior, attended those 1953 quarterback sessions. "Bud was one of the most highly organized, intelligent people I've ever been around," he says today. "At one time I actually thought he could predict the future. He would tell us before a game that certain things would happen. 'How does he know that?' I'd ask myself. But sure enough, those things would happen just like he'd said. I held him in complete awe. He was truly unique."

The youthful Sooners began the Notre Dame game by moving the ball all over the premises. After J. D. Roberts stacked two Irish plays and Bo Bolinger one, fullback Neil Worden of the Irish fumbled, Bowman recovering on the Notre Dame 23. Oklahoma scored in eight plays. Leake flipped an inside pitchout back to Larry Grigg, and when Allison took Notre Dame's cornerman in, Grigg cut inside for the first touchdown. Leake kicked goal.

Five minutes later the Irish got it back, Ralph Guglielmi hitting Heap in the end zone with a short forward pass. Guard Menil Mavraides kicked goal. Score, 7-7.

Oklahoma began the second quarter with savage defensive play. Notre Dame had the ball back on their 23. Lattner tried to pass, but Hearon felled him for an 11-yard loss. Guglielmi faded to pass, and Bolinger, the sophomore guard, pulled him down for a 10-yard deficit. Notre Dame tried a trap play, but Tom Carroll, Sooner linebacker, rocketed in to meet Johnny Lattner solidly and hurl him back. They punted out.

Five minutes later the Sooners were back on their 20. On the counter option pass, Buddy Leake, the new quarterback, faked to fullback Boydston, hid the ball in his crotch, and when the Irish halfback came up to stop Boydston's buck, Allison cut into the vacated territory, and Leake hit him with a long pass for 62 yards to the Irish 18. The Sooners scored four plays later, Ging weaving between Allison and Bowman and shooting across the goal. Leake converted. Oklahoma led 14-7.

Of Ging's touchdown carom, Art Gleason, broadcasting the tilt coast to coast for Mutual, told his radio audience, "If the south stands hadn't been there, that little guy would have been in Pauls Valley by now."

With only 3:13 left in the half, Don Penza, Notre Dame's captain and end, not only blocked Boydston's punt but recovered the bounding ball on

140

the Sooner 9. Oklahoma defended furiously, but Notre Dame scored on fourth down when Guglielmi faked a pitch, kept the ball, and ducked inside. Mavraides kicked goal, and the score was tied 14-14 at the half.

"He blocked that punt right over me," says Doc Hearon. "J. D. and I both took the guard and let the linebacker come through." Wilkinson said, "The blocked punt was the changing point in the game."

Notre Dame played a strong third quarter, counting two touchdowns. Leading 28-14, it looked as if Leahy's team was routing the Sooners.

"That was the longest afternoon I ever spent," recalls Doc Hearon. "Most of our games seemed too short, like we were out there only a few minutes. Time was flying, our adrenalin was flowing, and we were usually kicking the whey out of them. But Notre Dame was tough. We kept losing the ball on mistakes. Most of us were young and trying too hard."

The Sooners were still in no mood to be routed. Once Lattner, the Irish ace, ran Oklahoma's left end. J. D. Roberts, Sooner right guard, broke through from the right side, gave chase and tackled Lattner from behind on the opposite sideline.

It was here that Merrill Green, Chickasha senior, came into the game at right half when Larry Grigg twisted an ankle. President of Oklahoma's Varsity O Club, the breezy, rollicking Green presided with class over the football game's fourth quarter too.

First he ran the Sooners out of a hole by darting 34 yards on a Statue of Liberty play behind a block by Milton Simmons, El Dorado, Arkansas, junior. Later Lattner tried a pitchout, but Green tossed him for a loss. Lattner punted, the ball spiraling far up the field.

Eyes glued to the sky, Green caught it on the Sooner 40. Cutting cleverly and using every ounce of his fresh speed, Green kept dodging tacklers one by one. Thirty yards from the goal he was helped when Jack Ging picked off Notre Dame's right linebacker with a side-body block. Other downfielders sprouted in his path until down on the Irish 10 Green came face to face with the last Notre Dame tackler, the kicker of the punt, Lattner. Green fooled Lattner with a hip feint and ran across the goal while the crowd roared. Leake kicked goal, and the Irish lead was cut to 28-21.

With 3:08 left in the game Green leaped to intercept a pass on the Sooner 40. The Sooners narrowly missed scoring the tying touchdown on the next play. Leake gave ground before a wave of Irish rushers, then flipped a screen pass to Allison on the east sideline. Carl had two blockers shielding him. Only one Irish player was in his path. But he was Lattner. Filtering between the Sooner blockers, he tackled Allison after a 17-yard gain. The game ended soon afterward.

Although the Sooners were ragged mechanically, permitting the Irish eight turnovers—five lost fumbles, two interceptions, one blocked punt—they had held the nation's number one team to 120 net yards rushing and 104 passing and had tossed the gifted Irish backs for 64 yards in losses. After the game Coach Leahy of the Irish wrote to J. D. Roberts, Sooner guard, congratulating him on his fine play. Nobody tried to take that letter away from J. D.

The faculty liked Wilkinson's program and seemed proud to be a part of it. Some faculty members even collected tickets at the stadium gates during Norman games. One of these was W. E. Livezey. In the fall of 1953 Livezey came to Ken Farris, Sooner athletic business manager, and told him that he no longer would have time to serve. Farris asked why, and if there was any problem. The professor answered, "I have just been named Dean of the College of Arts and Sciences."

Pittsburgh, the second opponent, defensed the Sooners so savagely that they held Oklahoma to 63 net yards rushing, the all-time low for a Wilkinson-tutored Oklahoma team. They handcuffed the Sooners with only one first down in the last half, forcing them to punt eight times and make four goal line stands.

The Sooners scored their lone touchdown with startling suddenness in the second quarter. Quarterback Buddy Leake hid the ball in his crotch, faded, and passed to cocaptain Larry Grigg, who was all alone trodding the right sideline. Helped by a block by Kay Keller, Grigg outran a pursuing Panther halfback. The play went 80 yards. Leake kicked goal. After that the Sooner offense got nowhere. The game ended in a 7-7 tie.

The symbol of the Sooner spirit and dash had been Jack Ging, 157-pound senior left half. In the second quarter against Pitt, Ging suffered a shoulder separation when he was trapped while trying to forward-pass. It was feared he was out for the year. Since Ging was a senior, that meant that he had probably played the last football of his life.

I sat next to Ging in the plane bringing the Sooners home from Pittsburgh. His right arm was taped tightly to his body. There were hurt and shame and utter desolation in his face, a man's face on the body of a boy.

"I feel embarrassed," he said. "This is the first time in my life I ever got hurt playing football. I don't like to get hurt. It shows weakness in a person."

He stared hard at the gray upholstered seat in front of him. "What makes me so mad is that everybody will say that I got hurt because I'm little."

All his life Ging had had to struggle against that handicap. "Only I never felt handicapped," he said. "I've always felt that I'm as good as the big boys. It always irritates me to hear that a guy is great because he's got a big body. I always thought it more important to be a man no matter how big or little a body you have."

A twinge of pain swept him, stemming from his shoulder, but he stifled it. "I love football," he said simply. "It's the best game of them all. But all my life they've tried to discourage me from playing. I've always had to prove myself to everybody. They never wanted me until they saw me play."

Ging set his jaws with determination, his splendid faith as bright as ever. "I'll be back out there in three weeks," he said. "You just watch. I heal fast. I know my shoulder's going to be all right."

Wilkinson made several adjustments before the Texas game. Into Ging's spot at left half went Tom Carroll, of Okemah who, back from the Korean War, where he'd been a communications sergeant and had ridden everywhere in a jeep, had lost all his fine speed. All through January and February, 1953, Carroll had reported to track coach John Jacobs who outfitted him in shorts and spiked shoes and poured him over the hurdles and down the dash lanes. He ran all summer.

Max Boydston, who started at fullback against Notre Dame, was moved back to right end. Gene Calame, 165-pound Sulphur junior, was shifted to quarterback. Pop Ivy, the end coach, didn't like that and said so.

"They took a pretty fair defensive end and ruined him by making a quarterback out of him," Ivy complained, tongue in cheek.

With cocaptain Roger Nelson ready to resume play after a long layoff because of a rib injury, he was moved to right tackle ahead of Hearon who was dropped to the alternate team. This ruffled Hearon who had played the best game of his life against Notre Dame. Taking J. D. Roberts with him, he went to see line coach Gomer Jones.

"You said I played well against Notre Dame and Pittsburgh, and here I am down on the second team," he charged.

Gomer put both hands on Hearon's shoulders. "Now, Doc," he soothed, "you know we don't have a second team. We have two first teams."

"Gomer," said Hearon, "if it's all right with you, I'd like to be on that other first team." Both Jones and Roberts burst out laughing, but Hearon was dead serious. He was a fine player. So was Nelson, who was twenty pounds heavier. Don Brown and Melvin Brown received promotions to the starting line. Bob Burris, Muskogee sophomore, was switched to fullback.

In the Texas game Oklahoma swirled into a 19-0 lead, had a fourth touchdown called back, and marched 77 yards to within 3 yards of a fifth. Carroll, the Korean War veteran starting his first college game in three years, emerged as the contest's top rusher. He ran as if he were still wearing John Jacobs's spiked track shoes.

Carroll made the first Sooner touchdown possible with an alert defensive play midway through the first quarter. Smelling a Texas pitchout, Tom swept in fast from his halfback position and with one hand intercepted Cameron's lateral to Billy Quinn. A Texan struck Carroll's arm, knocking the ball loose, but Carroll dived and covered it on the Texas 25. Roger Nelson and J. D. Roberts blocked Larry Grigg across the goal on a handoff. Calame missed the extra point but the Sooners led 6-0.

Midway in the second quarter, Oklahoma scored on an 80-yard punt runback by Merrill Green. Wray Littlejohn, junior fullback from El Reno, gave him early running room by erasing two Texans with a block that left both sprawling. J. D. Roberts hung a rattling downfielder on another tackler. Dick Bowman whiplashed a third.

"Get out the kickin' tee!" shouted the effervescent Green as he swept past the Sooner bench.

The Sooners kept hitting and hustling. Early in the fourth quarter, Calame faked a handoff feed, kept the ball, came around his own right side, and pitched out to Tom Carroll. With Don Brown taking out the last Texas tackler, Carroll ran 48 yards to a touchdown. Green kicked goal, and Oklahoma had the Texans reeling at 19-0.

Texas retaliated typically, fighting 78 yards to a touchdown from kickoff. With Oklahoma leading 19-7 on fourth down from their 1, the Sooners decided to give Texas a safety, making the score 19-9, then safely execute a long free kick. Calame was the carrier. The game was nearly over.

"I was running around in the end zone trying to kill time and forgot where I was," Calame describes the incident today. "I was close to the goal when a Texas player hit me, knocking me back on the field. Texas tackled me there. It was their ball."

Texas cashed the point-blank touchdown and the final score was 19-14. Carl Allison, Sooner left end, played the full 60 minutes in the 91-degree heat without relief despite the fact he had bruised his ribs eight minutes after the opening kickoff.

The next week against Kansas at Norman, the Sooners did something Wilkinson had always advocated but seldom saw happen—they went all out every minute of the game. "Pressure relentlessly applied through the full sixty minutes" was the way Bud phrased it in his alumni letter. Oklahoma rushed to a new school record of 537 yards, averaging 8.3 net yards a carry. Although Wilkinson used all 45 players he suited and substituted liberally, the final score was 45-0. But Oklahoma lost Tom Carroll from a knee injury.

At the Sunday player meeting the Sooners talked about a brilliant defensive play by Don Brown. The dimpled little French-hornist flashed in and hit the Kansas end, then tackled the fullback coming through, released him when he saw he didn't have the ball, and his stubby legs blurring like an eggbeater, chased the halfback going wide and tackled him over the sideline after a 1-yard gain. All this on one play.

Early in the fourth quarter the Sooner alternates were on the field. The ball lay on the Kansas 2. As the Sooners gathered in a frown-faced huddle, tackle Don Brown turned to quarterback Gene Calame.

"Call 23, Gene," he suggested.

Calame called it. Brown and Allison fired out hard. Calame slipped the leather to Bob Herndon, Medford junior. Herndon shot through the gap to score the first college touchdown of his life. Brown, who had asked Calame to call the play, was Herndon's roommate. He knew that Mr. and Mrs. F. L. Herndon, the halfback's parents, had driven 150 miles from far-off Grant County to see him play.

On the following Monday Dee Andros, Kansas's massive assistant coach and former Sooner guard, stopped at a Lawrence cleaning shop to pick up some clothing. At home later he discovered that a pair of pants was missing. He went back to the cleaning shop. As he walked in, the proprietor, who hadn't been there on the first visit, saw Andros and spoke first.

"How come you guys keep fumbling that ball all the time and losing it?" he razzed, probing a KU sore spot.

"How come you keep losing my pants?" Andros shot back. "They're a darned sight bigger than that football."

Dal Ward, Colorado's coach, had given Oklahoma two dogfights in the three years he had faced them. "Our kids looked forward to playing Oklahoma," Ward said. "I never had to pep 'em up. They did it themselves. I just let 'em go."

He did indeed. With only 44 seconds left to play in the 1953 game, the score stood 20-20. Apparently Ward had done it again. Oklahoma's starting line was very tired. Wilkinson had substituted his alternate line of Joe Mobra, Dick Bowman, Bo Bolinger, Gene Mears, Cecil Morris, Doc Hearon, and Kay Keller. Calame was at quarterback with Leake and Herndon at the halves and Littlejohn at fullback. The Sooner crowd of 40,000 stood and resignedly reached for their wraps. Suddenly the Sooners gave them something to talk about all the way home.

The play was a rollout trap. Keller trap-blocked the man over center. Morris and Hearon double-teamed the tackle. Bolinger picked up the middle linebacker. Green scooted through the hole and cut outside. Here he got his first downfielder, Don Brown wiping out another linebacker. Allison hooked the safety and Green threw a hip feint on the final tackler and then outran him. Leake kicked goal. Final score, 27-20. As Gomer Jones earlier

145

had told Doc Hearon, Oklahoma indeed had two first teams.

The most rejuvenated football team in the country, Kansas State, awaited Oklahoma's invasion at Manhattan, Kansas. "We are going to try hard to get out of the cellar," Coach Bill Meek had said in summer. In 1952 the Purple and White had been the Big Seven's basement club with a 1-9 record. Now Meek's Cats led the conference at 3-0 and stood 5-1 on the year.

The Sooners had a surprise at left half on the alternate team—Jack Ging. Ging had haunted the Sooners' new training room, baking the shoulder red with diathermy. Every day he exercised it. Every day he sprinted and jumped dummies. Two weeks after he was hurt, he began wearing his full uniform each day in practice.

On Monday, three weeks and two days after his injury, he scrimmaged and got by creditably. Thus the bantam from Woods County made good his statement on the plane coming back from Pittsburgh, "I'll be back in three weeks."

Before an all-time record Manhattan crowd of 22,500, Oklahoma won 34-0. Jack Ging scored from 9 yards out on a pitch from Calame. Ging also played some defense.

In his abridgment of the game in the alumni letter, Wilkinson portrayed the 1953 team accurately. He said, "Our team has to get its victories the hard way. We don't throw outstandingly, we haven't had many breakaway runs, and our overall finesse isn't too good. But we blocked and tackled with great determination at Manhattan. A team that plays like that is hard to defeat."

Later Meek did escape from the Big Seven cellar. In fact, he did much better than that, Kansas State finishing 6-3-1 and zooming to a second place tie with Missouri.

Missouri, coached by Don Faurot, was always a class opponent. The Tigers had played a hardening nonconference schedule, losing 6-20 to Maryland, 7-20 to Southern Methodist, defeating Indiana 14-7 and Purdue's Big Ten cochampions 14-7.

After playing six games, Wilkinson's Sooners had completed only ten forward passes all season. They were winning on the ground. Gomer Jones's two fast lines were blocking so awesomely that after their statistical mishandling by Pittsburgh they had zoomed from eightieth place to fourth in the national rushing tables.

Turning point of the Missouri game came in the fourth period. With the score tied 7-7, Missouri was on Oklahoma's 17, third down, 10 to go. Vic Eaton lined a perfect forward pass over the goal to Harold Burnine, Tiger end. It looked like a certain touchdown. Burnine was open. But before Burnine could catch the ball, a figure in Oklahoma white raced to the spot, leaped, stretched, and by the width of an outthrust hand slapped the ball away. It was Larry Grigg, Sooner cocaptain. If ever a player rescued his team from a precarious situation, it was Grigg on that occasion.

In his alumni letter Wilkinson praised the Sooner reaction drills given the squad day after day in practice, drills that seemed like drudgery but sharpened Sooner reflexes and paid off at crucial moments. "Because of Larry's continued all-out effort in practice, he was able to make the great play when the occasion demanded," Bud wrote.

Missouri still had one down left. They tried and missed a field goal. It was Oklahoma's ball on their own 20, but the Missouri goal was so far away that the distant posts looked like crossed matchsticks. On the first play Bob Burris swung around right tackle for 12 yards. The sure-handed Calame quarterbacked them up the field, the blockers cleaning out heroically ahead. "No better competitor ever played at OU than Calame," J. D. Roberts said later. "He was a Bobby Goad guy."

Bob Burris took the ball across the 50. The Missouri stadium buzzed with alarm. This Sooner drive had the same fateful continuity of so many other Oklahoma marches they had seen on this same field. Ging ran five yards to a first down on the Tiger 3. Here Faurot's fighters made a valiant stand, throwing back three Sooner rushes. It was fourth and 1 from the Mizzou 1. Calame saw that the Missouri defense was tightly compressed to stop the handoff.

Checking the signal at the line of scrimmage, he called a sweep to the left, faked neatly to draw the Tiger end in, then pitched out to Grigg, who scored easily around the Old Gold and Black's right flank. Leake kicked goal. Oklahoma won 14-7.

All four of Oklahoma's fullbacks were disabled as the Sooners headed into their Band Day game with Iowa State. "When those fullbacks fall, they fall in windrows," quipped Ted Owen, the veteran trainer.

Wilkinson used 47 players against the Cyclones, and Oklahoma won 47-0. As they did so often, Oklahoma marched from the opening kickoff, Calame scoring on a five-yard keeper. It was his first touchdown of the year. The Sulphur boy had always been reluctant to call himself once the touchdown range was reached. Although Oklahoma had scored 32 touchdowns that season, the quarterback had almost blanked himself in this department.

Early in the fourth quarter the Sooner crowd saw what it came to see. Hank Philmon, Iowa State's halfback, kicked a line-drive punt that Buddy Leake fielded and while crossing the field laterally slipped to Merrill Green. Green was in his element. On the Sooner 32 he wrenched away from one tackler, cut behind a red wall of blockers, and was on his way with the

147

Left, J. D. Roberts, unanimous All-American guard 1953, selected Lineman of the Year by AP, UP, Fox Movietone, and Philadelphia sportswriters. He also won the Outland Award. Right, Kurt Burris, unanimous All-American center 1954, selected Lineman of the Year by the Philadelphia sportswriters. He was runner-up for the Heisman Trophy with 838 points, highest total ever received by a lineman.

Robert Burris bucking for the second touchdown against Kansas.

Merrill Green running 51 yards for the winning touchdown in the last 36 seconds of the Colorado game.

With Oklahoma trailing No[Dame 14-28 at Norman in 195 Wilkinson looks a little low. F new team rallied to pull up 21-28.

crowd in pandemonium. Philmon cut across to head him off near the goal, but Calvin Woodworth, Minco sophomore, sprinted down and bumped him just enough to let Green slip around them to score.

In a game remembered for its punting gymnastics and for a stellar defensive save by Calame, Oklahoma bested Nebraska 30-7 at Lincoln, bolting down a sixth-straight Big Seven championship.

All the punting singularities happened to Ray Novak, Cornhusker fullback. In the first quarter Novak was back on his goal to punt. The Scarlet center wild-pitched the ball far over Novak's head into the snow behind the end zone for an automatic safety. After another exchange of punts Novak showed what he could do, kicking out of bounds on the Sooner 7.

In the last half occurred the play for which the game is hallowed. Novak again backed up almost on his goal to punt. Again his center pegged the ball over Novak's head into the end zone. Novak whirled and pursued it with J. D. Roberts, Sooner guard, on his heels.

Then the fast-thinking Nebraska fullback made an unusual play. Scooping up the ball on the hop deep in his end zone with his back to the gridiron, he punted it back over his head into the field of play. The ball rolled out of bounds on the Nebraska 9. Moreover, the Cornhuskers dug in and held the Sooners for downs.

Then came Calame's defensive gem as the fourth quarter began. On a counterplay Bob Burris went through so fast that Calame couldn't quite get the ball to him. It squirted into the air, and Ted Connor, Nebraska's left tackle, caught it and ran down the east sideline with four blockers fronting for him. Only Calame was between them and the touchdown.

Hand-fighting the Nebraska blockers, Calame hurdled the last one and made the tackle, felling Connor over the sideline on the Sooner 13 and preventing the touchdown. Fullback Jerry Donaghey's rushing that frigid afternoon totaled 153 yards.

The victory let Oklahoma keep its number four position in the Associated Press poll. Also, it earned the Sooners a crack at the national champions. Coach Jim Tatum's Maryland Terrapins, in the Orange Bowl. Fast-moving friends, Tatum and Wilkinson were dueling for the first time. The Big Seven had rescinded its unpopular rule barring bowl play.

But there was still one game left on the regular slate, Oklahoma A&M at Norman. On a crisp, sunny afternoon both student bodies were home for the Thanksgiving holidays, but 50,524 fans came, a new all-time attendance record for an Aggie-Sooner battle. Coach J. B. ("Ears") Whitworth's Aggies stood 7-2, Wilkinson's Sooners 8-1-1.

Just before the first quarter ended, the Sooner crowd was treated to another thrilling touchdown punt runback by Green. But that time it wasn't the Sooners' Green. Bobby Green, Aggie quarterback, was the culprit. Fielding Buddy Leake's punt, he ran 57 yards to score. As soon as he caught his breath, he kicked his own goal.

But the rest of the game belonged to Oklahoma. Ging scored on a pitch from Calame. Calame scored on a keeper when the Aggies went for his faked pitch. Melvin Brown blocked Bredde's punt and Leake fired to Mobra in the end zone. When the Aggies went for Grigg on a pitch, Calame kept and darted inside for six. Boydston purloined a wild Aggie handoff and sprinted 43 yards to the goal. Jack Van Pool scored on a keeper. Grigg lost another touchdown because of a holding penalty. Final score, 42-7.

Oklahoma showed well in the national statistics released December 14 by the NCAA. The Sooners led the nation in rushing offense, ranked fourth in punt returns, fifth in kickoff returns, and ninth in total offense. Larry Grigg scored the touchdown at Stillwater that would have made him the nation's leading scorer, but the play was recalled by penalty. He finished in a two-way national tie for third.

Merrill Green topped the nation in most yards gained for each punt runback with his average of 45. Buddy Leake had the highest conversion point percentage in the country, 17 of 18 for 94.4 percent.

J. D. Roberts, All-American right guard, swept all the awards a lineman could get in college football. He won the Outland Trophy. He was voted AP Lineman of the Year, UP Lineman of the Year, and Fox Movietone Lineman of the Year. He won them all decisively. The Notre Dame squad voted Oklahoma the outstanding team it met in 1953 and selected end Carl Allison, guard J. D. Roberts, and halfback Jack Ging on their all-opponents' team.

Maryland's national champions, coached by Jim Tatum, Sooner coach of 1946, had finished 10-0 with no close games. They had blanked six opponents and held three others to a single touchdown. Their defense against rushing was so good that they led the nation widely with their yield of only 83.9 yards per contest. "This is the greatest team I ever coached," Tatum told the press at Norman, when he came personally to scout the Sooner-Aggie finale.

The contest was remarkable for its quarterback casualties. Bernie Faloney, Maryland's excellent signal caller, was injured in midseason and played only a little at the end. Pat O'Neal, Oklahoma's number two quarterback, separated his sternum during a drill at Miami and was out of the game. Oklahoma also lost Calame, its number one quarterback, just before the first half ended.

All the battle's drama came in the first and second quarters. The high wind seemed to give all the advantage to the team at whose backs it blew.

In the first quarter that was Maryland. When Bill Walker of the Terrapins kicked a magnificent punt out on the Oklahoma 1-foot line, the Sooners were hanging on by their eyelashes. Calame sneaked twice to gain a little room, then Leake stroked a punt out on the Sooner 37. And here came the national champions.

Boxold, the quarterback, shot a pass to Nolan for 9. Nolan bucked for a first down. Then Hanulak hit, then Nolan again, and Pelton bucked to another first down, this one on the Sooner 4.

With their cleated toes planted just inside the goal line, Oklahoma dug in. Boydston held Hanulak to 2. Nolan went wide to the left, but Grigg came up fast to nail him for no gain. Hanulak tried again and got only 1. From the 1-yard mark, the Terps called on Pelton, their fullback, but the Sooners smothered him 6 inches short.

"Who stopped him?" the press asked J. D. Roberts later in the Oklahoma locker room. "Nobody," replied Roberts without blinking. "It was a stack job."

The raging wind again gave Maryland the ball close to the Oklahoma goal, but Oklahoma's battling alternate line came in and refused to yield a foot. Even when the Sooners fumbled to the Terps on the Oklahoma 20, the Sooners threw them back. The quarter ended, and the antagonists changed goals. From the Sooner 20, Maryland tried another field goal, but against the gale the ball twisted wide to the right. It was Oklahoma's ball on its 20. Now the Sooners could run their offense with the wind.

"The hardest thing about quarterbacking," Gene Calame once said, "is trying to keep your offense balanced by running wide enough, inside enough, and passing enough." Oklahoma's ensuing 80-yard advance was a striking illustration of how to mix all three.

Oklahoma's starting team was in. Ging snapped a short forward pass off the pitchout to Boydston for 5 yards. Ging hit off his left tackle for 3 yards behind blocks by Allison, Don Brown, and Melvin Brown. Calame pitched to Grigg, who ran wide to his left for 12 and a first down on the Sooner 40. Calame forward passed to Bob Burris for 6. Grigg faked a pass and reversed around right end for 12. With a first down on the Terp 39, the Sooners were delighting their partisans with the momentum of their advance.

Maryland's massive line smeared two bucks, but Calame forward-passed to fullback Bob Burris for a first down on the Maryland 28. Bob Burris cracked off tackle for 3 more, and now the Sooner advance had reached Maryland's 25. Maryland called time-out.

Calame called the pitch to Grigg around the left flank. "It was third and 1," he says. "I thought they expected us to go inside."

151

The play developed fast to the left. First Calame faked the handoff to Ging going straight ahead, then he swung around the left side. Bob Burris blocked out the halfback, wrapping him up cleanly. J. D. Roberts rolled the Maryland cornerback. Calame feinted inside, flashed out again, pitched to Grigg, and staying in motion ran down and threw a key block to free Grigg on the goal.

Grigg scored almost in the corner, dragging a Maryland tackler over with him. The play went 25 yards. Leake kicked goal. Oklahoma 7, Maryland 0. "Maryland had the best physical defense we ever encountered," says Calame. "Their only weakness was wide."

That was the game's only scoring. The rival defenses warred fiercely. Joe Mobra threw Boxold for a loss of 11 yards. Once Don K. Brown, Sooner left tackle, sent Stan ("the Man") Jones, Maryland's 250-pound All-American guard, sprawling with a savage forearm shiver and vaulting the giant's prostrate form, trapped Boxold for a 5-yard loss.

Just before the half ended, Calame left the game with a separation of his collarbone. With both Calame and Pat O'Neal, Oklahoma's top quarterbacks, injured, Wilkinson had only one quarterback left, Jack Van Pool, who was number three. Van Pool hadn't even lettered as a junior, playing very little. But he had been in scores of Wilkinson's quarterback meetings.

"What shall I call this half?" Van Pool asked Wilkinson between periods.

"It's your ball game," Wilkinson answered. "You call it."

"That shocked the pants off me," Van Pool says today. "The ball game was still close, and we were playing the national champions."

On the fifth play of the last half Walker of Maryland dropped back to punt. Again Don Brown, Oklahoma's left tackle, broke past Stan ("the Man") Jones and hurled himself upon Walker so fast that the Terp punter wisely refused to kick and tried to run. Brown pinned him for a 12-yard loss. Once Leake punted to Hanulak, and the Maryland safety returned it so brilliantly that only Leake, the last man between him and the goal, felled him.

The combatants moved into the fourth quarter. The crowd of 70,000 was roaring. "As Capitol Hill's quarterback, I was used to big crowds," says Van Pool. "I didn't know that Orange Bowl crowd was there. All I wanted was to do my part, keep the drive going, because the other guys had done their part all season long."

"Although Jack Van Pool hadn't even made some of our trips, he was an example of our squad's great attitude," says J. D. Roberts. "Van Pool didn't make a single error. He played super."

When Grigg intercepted Boxold's long pass in the end zone and crouched there with the ball, earning free access to Oklahoma's 20, there were four

152

Larry Grigg scoring the winning touchdown of 1954 Orange Bowl game against Maryland's national champions. Bob Burris, on the turf, has just flattened the halfback, sprawling at Burris's feet. J. D. Roberts (64) cuts back to roll the cornerback who was chasing the play. Gene Calame, ahead of Grigg, later threw a key block.

Jack Ging (left), Carl Allison, and Calvin Woodworth with the 1954 Orange Bowl trophy. Photo by Oklahoma Publishing Co.

minutes left to play. Employing line plays, Van Pool moved the Sooners 41 yards to three first downs, all of them by Ging, and reached the Maryland 39. The Sooners were still going forward at the gun.

Afterwards Wilkinson smilingly refused to claim the national championship. "It was a helluva ball game," was Bud's first comment in the Sooner dressing room. "Desire, spirit, effort—anything you want to call it—won for us today."

The Sooners were happily pummeling Van Pool on the back. "The best thing old Jack did was hold onto that melon," they declared. Pete ("Sarge") Dempsey, the Sooners' sixty-seven-year-old equipment man, didn't see the game. He stayed in the dressing room and got it by relay. He'd had a heart attack the preceding summer, and the boys were taking care of him.

Bob Addie, sports columnist for the Washington (D.C.) *Times-Herald,* praised "the fine conduct of the Oklahoma players when Faloney (Bernie Faloney, Maryland's crippled quarterback) was in the game. Not an Oklahoma player laid a hand on Bernie, scotching the insidious rumor that the Sooners were going to 'rack him up.'" It was the first shutout Maryland had suffered in 51 games—since 1948. And it was the eighty-fifth straight game in which Oklahoma had scored.

Tatum took the loss sportingly. "Bud outcoached me," he said simply at the Orange Bowl party that night for the players of both teams.

Stanley Woodward, prominent eastern critic, wrote that Grigg of Oklahoma was the best player he had seen in the last five seasons. "When the Sooners stopped Maryland on the goal line in the first period, he was in on every tackle," Woodward wrote. "He knocked down or intercepted all the dangerous passes from his position as safetyman. He recovered a Maryland fumble. He blocked like fury, gained the most ground, scored the touchdown."

Not all the Sooner players were happy and joyful. The seniors were particularly melancholy. "That was the saddest moment of my life," said tackle Doc Hearon. "We'd played our last game for our school. We felt sorry for OU the next two years because the kids playing behind us—the freshmen—would have to carry the load. I felt sorry for little old Ed Gray."

"In 1955 and 1956 those 'little old kids' won two national championships," Hearon laughs today.

1953 SENIORS TODAY

Dick Bowman, vice-president of sales, Monument Well Servicing Company of Oklahoma City, died there on April 2, 1983.

Melvin Brown is a salesman for Mutual Supply and Rental, Inc., an oil-field-equipment firm in Houston, Texas.

Jack Ging is a character actor in television and motion pictures and also sells real estate in Malibu Beach, California.

Merrill Green is athletic director and head football coach at Bryan (Texas) High School. Before that he was assistant coach at Wichita State, Missouri, Arkansas, and Texas Tech.

Darlon ("Doc") Hearon owns and operates Hearon Steel, a steel fabricating plant in Muskogee, Oklahoma.

Kay Keller owns Keller Sports, Inc., a sporting goods store in Oklahoma City, Oklahoma.

Roger Nelson is vice-president and general manager, Durkee Drilling Company, Denver, Colorado.

J. D. Roberts is manager of customer relations of Superior Casing Crews, Inc., New Orleans, Louisiana.

Col. Jack Van Pool, U.S. Army, is stationed at Fort Sill, Lawton, Oklahoma.

9. BONER AT BOULDER

California's Golden Bears, coached by an old Sooner nemesis, Lynn ("Pappy") Waldorf, against whom Oklahoma had won only one game of seven while Waldorf coached at Oklahoma A&M, Kansas State, and Northwestern, were the opening opponents in 1954 at Berkeley.

Frank Leahy, Notre Dame's retired coach, told Jack McDonald, sports editor of the *San Francisco Call-Bulletin* in April: "The Sooners are sluggish starters. Pappy is lucky to catch them early before their split-T really gets to rolling."

The 1954 Sooners bade farewell that season to two highly regarded assistant coaches, Bill Jennings and Frank ("Pop") Ivy. Jennings joined the Noble Drilling Company's Fort Worth office. Ivy became head coach of the Edmonton, Canada, Eskimos, a professional aggregation. Ray Nagel, former UCLA quarterback and Chicago Cardinal scout, succeeded Jennings. Melvin ("Sam") Lyle, Georgia Tech end coach who had played at Louisiana State, replaced Ivy.

Like all of Wilkinson's other Sooner squads of the period, the 1954 team was recruited primarily from the state of Oklahoma. Of the top twenty-two players, seventeen were Oklahomans. They were also good students. Oklahoma lettermen of the Wilkinson era were graduating at a 93.1 percent clip. The record slanted upward in 1954, when several ungraduate players then in professional football returned to get their degrees. Among these were Leon ("Mule Train") Heath, 1950 team, B.S.; Bert Clark, 1951, B.S.; and six from the 1952 aggregation: Sam Allen, B.B.A.; Tom Catlin, B.S.; Jim Davis, B.S.; Ray Powell, B.S.; Ed Rowland, B.S.; and Billy Vessels, B.S. Of the thirty-nine lettermen on Bud's first three teams, thirty-six received degrees.

The Sooners took pride in their behavior. One of the freshmen that year, Doyle Jennings, of Lawton, was by his own admission "pretty wild and rowdy." He adds, "Billy Vessels, back to play in the Varsity-Alumni game, cornered me once after practice. He told me that I ought to tone it down, get hold of who I was and where I was at. Bud called me in and talked to me frankly. 'I don't want you to bring any reproach on the team,' he said. So we had a good understanding from then on."

With only two and a half weeks of practice available before the California game, the Sooners worked like stevedores in a shipyard. Three captains were chosen that season, center Gene Mears, quarterback Gene Calame, and end Carl Allison. Only one sophomore made the starting eleven, Edmon Gray of Odessa, Texas.

At Odessa, Gray had his football start on the eighth-grade team when the boy playing ahead of him was kicked off the squad for going to a Boy Scout camp instead of spring football practice. At Norman, Gray always played with a skinned nose and a crick in his neck. The crick came from butting his opponent in the tummy when he blocked him. And when Gray got bopped on top of his head, his helmet always slipped down, peeling his nose. The Sooners called him "Beaky Buzzard."

Tropical fish were Gray's hobby. When Gray cleaned his fishbowls, he plugged the shower drain in Jefferson House where the Sooner pigskinners lived, turned on the tap and emptied the fish on the tile floor. When other players came in to bathe, they were startled to see fish swimming about.

Billy Pricer, Perry sophomore, had been Perry High School's freshman quarterback and safety until Perry met Blackwell, coached by Jack Mitchell. On the first play Blackwell faked a fullback counter up the middle. "I came up and popped him on the line of scrimmage, only he didn't have the ball," Pricer remembers. "Their quarterback threw it to an end crossing over, and they scored a touchdown through my position. A few minutes later they did the same thing."

Hump Daniels, Perry's coach, called time. He made Pricer and the Perry fullback change positions. "For the rest of my life I was a fullback and a linebacker," Pricer chuckles, "and that was fine with me. I loved it up there."

Gomer Jones taught Pricer the niceties of linebacking. "He'd stand behind me with one hand holding my belt at the small of my back," Pricer remembers. "The minute he saw the guard pull, he'd push me in the way I was supposed to run." Pricer rates Wilkinson "by far the best head coach I ever saw, college or pro, and I later played five years with Baltimore, which twice won the world championship."

Buddy Oujesky, a Fort Worth boy who played guard, chose Oklahoma that year over Texas A&M. "If you go to Oklahoma you can never come back to Texas to work," some Texas people warned him, and they still use that on recruits today, says Oujesky. Oujesky came to Norman anyhow because "I figured if I could make the team at Oklahoma, I'd have reached the pinnacle as a player." His real name was Joseph Buddy Oujesky with no quotation marks around the Buddy. "My dad had a good friend named Joseph Buddy so he called me that too," he explains.

157

California had two big lines and Paul Larson, a talented quarterback who had led the nation in total offense in 1953 and was destined to top it in forward passing in 1954. Jim Hanifan, their left end, led the country that season in received forward passes.

Oklahoma had a gifted quarterback too, one who didn't mind playing when he was hurt. At Wilkinson's insistence Gene Calame's tender ribs were given a careful sheathing before the California game. The attending physician, interviewed later by Art Rosenbaum, a San Francisco sportswriter, said, "His 11th and 12th ribs were loose, sort of bouncing together like two xylophone boards. We put plenty of nonflexible tape directly on the affected area, and flexible tape around his body. Then we waited for him to wince. He didn't. He's quite a boy, isn't he?"

Pricer kicked off for the Sooners. "It was the first kickoff of my career," Pricer remembers. "I was so scared that I belted the ball into the lower seats."

The theme of the grueling game, California fumbling to Oklahoma deep in California territory, Oklahoma cashing both fumbles for touchdowns, became apparent midway of the third quarter when the two teams, practically tied in the score, struggled for the mastery.

Oklahoma led 7-6, but California's big team, with Larson forward passing beautifully, had driven to a first down on the Sooner 8-yard line and with their crowd of 58,000 shouting encouragement, was threatening to score the go-ahead touchdown.

But Gomer Jones's Sooner forwards planted themselves in the turf like so many cedar corral posts, resisting furiously. Cecil Morris and Bo Bolinger, junior guards, blunted the first play for a 1-yard loss. Linebacker Kurt Burris stacked the next one for a 3-yard deficit. On the third, California tried a long pitchout, but Allison and Kurt Burris struck the runner hard, knocking the ball loose. Don K. Brown, Sooner left tackle, pounced on the fumble like a chicken on a bug. The Sooners had possession on their 8.

Three plays later Calame made a fine call. As the Sooners came to the line of scrimmage, Calame noticed that the California left linebacker had slipped up into the line as a crashing end, leaving the flank behind him wide open. Calame checked the signal and called a forward pass off a pitchout. Buddy Leake laid the ball on Max Boydston's eager fingers.

Muskogee Max lit out for the distant California hinterlands. He was closely pursued by two Bear backs, Paul Larson and Sam Williams. For 25 yards they ran it out with everything in their legs. Larson dived at Max's flying heels but missed. Williams chased Boydston on into Bear territory, but he couldn't close the gap either. Twenty yards from the goal

Boydston began to cut and weave, watching his opponent warily over his shoulder until he crossed the goal after an 87-yard run.

Two plays later Ted Granger, California fullback, tried a sweep, but Bob Loughridge, Oklahoma's junior tackle from Poteau, raked the ball out of his hands, and Gene Mears recovered it on the Bear 25. Allison, Don K. Brown, and Bolinger fired steamy straight-ahead blocks to break Leake cleanly across the goal. Leake toed the conversion. The Sooners won 27-13, as each team scored once more.

Oklahoma tried to jump the second barrier of a formidable early schedule when it moved against Texas Christian at Norman. All sorts of hardships bedeviled the Sooners in that game. They fumbled ten times, losing five. They even fumbled once while crossing the goal for a touchdown, TCU recovering for a touchback. Worst of all, they lost Calame, their senior quarterback. Hurt just before the half, Calame had a bone chip off his right shoulder removed by surgery Sunday morning and was to be out for an indefinite period.

Into Calame's place Wilkinson sent Jimmy Harris, 170-pound Terrell, Texas, sophomore. Harris had just lost both upper front teeth during a squad scrimmage. "With my teeth out, I couldn't make the team understhand—I mean understand—me in the huddle," Harris lisped next morning as he stirred his breakfast cornflakes vigorously. "When I tried to call a play off our fifty series, I kept saying 'thifty.' I had to repeat it two or three times. The crowd noith—I mean noise—was terrible."

Jimmy's flying feet didn't lisp when he scored two of Oklahoma's three touchdowns in the last half, one of them a 69-yard punt runback that plunged the lively Sooner crowd of 50,878 into an excited frenzy. The slender sophomore picked his path meticulously around shattering blocks thrown by Allison, Boydston, and Brown. That moved Oklahoma ahead 7-2, the Frogs having scored a safety in the second quarter because of a low Sooner center snap.

Then occurred a gesture of sportsmanship that was rare in football. TCU appeared to have scored on a long pass into the end zone, but Johnny Crouch, their captain and right end, told field judge Don Rossi who had signaled the touchdown that the ball was trapped by the TCU receiver, an opinion sustained by the head linesman, who was closely following the play.

Coach Abe Martin's Frogs moved 81 yards to score in ten running plays with quarterback Chuck Harris sweeping the Sooners off the spread. Accepting the challenge, Oklahoma drove back 56 yards in ten plays before Herndon fumbled a handoff into the end zone, center Hugh Pitts of TCU recovering for a touchback.

At this misfortune the Sooners became discouraged, while TCU's morale soared. They launched another touchdown drive, this one going 80 yards. Now the Frogs led 16-7 and apparently had put the game away. The fourth quarter had begun. Oklahoma had lost Calame, its quarterback. But the Oklahoma crowd of 50,878, rallied by its cheerleaders on the sidelines, began to roar encouragement to the Oklahoma squad. That helped tremendously.

With Jimmy Harris at the controls Oklahoma marched 75 yards from kickoff to score. Bob Herndon slanted 21 for a first down on the Frog 7. Harris scored standing on a keeper behind blocks by Northcutt, Boydston, and Gray. Leake kicked goal. Now TCU led 16-14. And when Ben Taylor, TCU right half, booted a 47-yard punt down the field there were six minutes left to play.

Buddy Leake fielded the punt 15 yards ahead of the TCU coverage and cut sharply to the right sideline toward the Sooner bench. Bob Herndon rode out the TCU end. Jimmy Harris hurled himself across the legs of another opponent. Sensing that it might be a long return, the crowd stood, bellowing.

The thunder of its cheering seemed to blow Buddy goalward. Hemmed in along the sideline, he cut suddenly to his left and, choosing his openings skillfully, brought the kick back 50 yards to the TCU 10 before Crouch, their last tackler, felled him. The crowd's glad roar rang off the stadium walls.

Oklahoma scored on its first play, Herndon hitting hard and twisting out of the grasp of two tacklers. Leake kicked goal. Oklahoma led 21-16.

The Frogs were always great fighters against Oklahoma. In the final moments they rallied, completing three forward passes, all caught by Crouch, before Kurt Burris nailed Clinkscale cleanly on the 7 on the battle's final play.

Concerned about Sooner casualties, Wilkinson reorganized his lineups for the clash against Texas, always a major hazard on the schedule.

Jerry Tubbs went to first team fullback. On the alternate eleven were tackle Tom Emerson of Wilson, right end John Bell of Enid, and fullback Billy Pricer of Perry. It looked as if Coach Ed Price's Longhorns had the Sooners in an ideal spot for an upset. The Sooners had been elevated to number one in the national polls the same week they had lost Calame, their starting quarterback.

Calame's protégé, Jimmy Harris, with whom Calame continued to work daily, was starting at quarterback against Texas, lisp and all. Except this time Harris had to lisp his signals above the roar of a crowd of 76,204.

160

"When he gets his new store teeth the week of the Kansas game, watch out!" his teammates said.

Pat O'Neal, senior quarterback reserve from Ada, went to see Wilkinson. "Is there something I need to do to improve?" he asked the coach. "I want to play. We've had two games, and I haven't been on the field."

"Don't worry," Bud told him. "You'll play against Texas." In practice O'Neal ran with the alternates. At Dallas, just before the kickoff, he realized his greatest thrill. "Just standing on the floor of the Cotton Bowl before 70,000 people was it," he says.

Texas won the toss, took the wind, and kicked off. Oklahoma fumbled, and Brewer, the Texas quarterback, recovered on the Sooner 29. Texas hurled seven running plays at the Sooners. Don K. Brown, Oklahoma's fast-reacting French-hornist, helped stop three of them. Then Brown suffered the misfortune of breaking a small bone in his ankle. Carried wet-eyed from the field by two of his teammates, he was out of football for the rest of his life in only the third game of his senior season.

It was a tragic happening. Brown was the best-liked man on Wilkinson's squad. The other players called him "Gabby" because he rarely opened his mouth. They wrote "Asst. Coach" across the back of his sweat shirt. They all applauded noisily when they could get him to sing "Do You Need Any Help?" or, wearing cowboy boots and accompanied by a guitar, he went into a fast, plank-spanking clog dance as the players forsook study hall to enjoy what they called a "session" in Jefferson House, where they lived.

Now Brown was through for keeps, cut off in his prime from the thing he loved to do best, play football. And his going severed a tradition for Oklahoma fandom too. Sooner crowds always enjoyed seeing Brown fell some enemy ballcarrier like a cut tree, then, with a slightly swaggering swing of his toy shoulders, trot with satisfaction back to his position on legs so bowed you could have shot arrows through them.

Calvin Woodworth, a sandy-haired Korean War veteran from Minco, was moved from right end to left tackle. Woodworth's weight was 195 pounds. "Our tackles are lighter than our fullbacks," lamented line coach Gomer Jones.

Although his wife worked as a secretary, Woodworth had learned that the life of a married football player wasn't easy. His jobs the last four summers had been varied. He had worked all night at a Norman service station, had been the shovel man on a ditch-digging crew, had labored as a roustabout in an Oklahoma City pipe yard, and had done electrical and plumbing duty at his father's big store in Minco.

"I wish somebody had led me to some of this subsidization all college football players are supposed to get," snorts Woodworth today. "I've never seen any."

After Texas took a 7-0 lead, Oklahoma began a long drive. Texas resisted hard. It was fourth down, 1 yard to go at the Sooner 36. Harris gambled and handed off to Herndon, who bucked 14.

The Sooners were rolling. On a pitchout around right end, the ball sailed wild and bounced off the turf, but Leake, like an infielder in baseball, scooped it up and ran to the Texas 1-yard mark for a first down. That was the big play. Harris handed off to Leake, who broke fast off blocks by Allison, Woodworth, and Bolinger to score. Leake kicked goal. Score, 7-7.

It was hot down in the Cotton Bowl. The starting team was tired. On the sideline Pat O'Neal wiped his hand across his mouth. "I was always confident of my ability," he says. "That doesn't mean that I didn't occasionally get frustrated or fail. But I felt I could get the job done. I had confidence in myself. If I could just get on that field."

And then Bud put him on it. On the last play of the first quarter Wilkinson substituted his entire alternate team with Pat at quarterback. Six of them were sophomores who had played very little.

Pat O'Neal shot a forward pass to John Bell, who raced 40 yards to a first down on the Texas 15. Having just been switched from guard, Bell ran the wrong route on the play but hustled so hard that he made the catch anyhow. That was the play that won the game. Wilkinson sent in the starters. They got the touchdown in five plays with Harris keeping from 1 yard out. Score, 14-7.

At this point of the season Oklahoma stood 3-0 and was ranked number one nationally in both polls. Texas sportswriters covering the Dallas game —and there were always some sharp ones there—had their own explanation for this. Blackie Sherrod, of the *Fort Worth Press*, wrote, "You hear vocalisms about this being Oklahoma's greatest team in years. This is so much ripe balderdash. . . . the acid test of a good football team is whether it can conquer its own mistakes. Oklahoma has managed to do just that." Tom Davison, of the *Houston Post*, called the Sooners "sometimes sloppy but always superior."

Don Pierce, Kansas sports publicist who had played football for Kansas and later for the professionals, wrote a cogent description of Wilkinson's 1954 club before its Kansas game.

"Bud Wilkinson's savage gentlemen come into this one as the nation's No. 1 team and with good reason," wrote Pierce. "Oklahoma . . . faster and quicker than ever on the dive tackle, keeper and pitchout. Oklahoma, who can gang the middle and still react so swiftly that it holds the fleetest backs to short yardage on the wide stuff. Oklahoma, ever alert for the game-winning extras of pass interception and punt return. Oklahoma, who shatters granite defenses with its turf-searing rushing, then kills them with a sudden scoring pass.

"These are the modern Sooners, resourceful and eager. And, if skillful execution isn't enough, they simply pull back the throttle to the last ounce of playing passion."

All the Sooners, clear down through the fourth eleven, loved to play. On the week of the Kansas game the Oklahoma squad was eating lunch at Jefferson dining room. Jay O'Neal, then the fourth-string quarterback, hustled the fourth team out of the dining room onto the grass outside.

"Come on! Let's practice!" he challenged them. "We might get to play Saturday." Disregarding the fact that they wore their street clothing and were full of food, they joined him, and he put them through their paces.

With only four minutes remaining in the half, the Sooners led Kansas 14-0 but were pinned back on their own 9-yard line. Jimmy Harris, the sophomore quarterback who in this game began calling signals with all his teeth in place, saw that the Jayhawker guards were split exceptionally wide. He audibled to a quarterback sneak and whooshed down the middle as if pulled by a powerful suction. Although he was tagged several times by Kansas tacklers, Harris stayed catlike on his feet and ran 91 yards to a touchdown.

The Sooner third team played nearly all the last half. Delbert Long, Ponca City sophomore, scored two touchdowns and rushed 87 yards. Ed Gray blocked a punt. Pat O'Neal wriggled over for two touchdowns, and his younger brother Jay also scored. The final count was 65-0.

"My team was on the field, and Bud called me over to the bench," Jay O'Neal remembers. "'Don't run wide and don't pass,' he told me, not wishing to embarrass Kansas further. That left us with only two plays, the handoff to the halfback and the fullback counter. We scored twice more anyhow. We were eager to play, I assure you."

Kansas State, 4-0, was next. Since it was Band Day with 6,811 gaily caparisoned high-school boy and girl musicians at Norman for the annual event, I chatted with Leonard Haug, "coach" of Oklahoma's red-jacketed marching band.

He had started 93 freshmen in his "first game." Was he pleased with his 1954 outfit? "The potential is there," Haug declared. "We've lost a lot in marching skill, but we've gained in musical ability. How well we improve depends upon the band's attitude and desire."

Desire? That was the quality Bud Wilkinson valued so highly in football. How could a bandsman show desire? "By accepting our rugged rehearsal sessions, by being willing to adopt our style of marching and playing, and by being willing to march with a thirty-inch stride instead of the twenty-two-and-a-half-inch step they used back in high school," Coach Haug replied.

What were the advantages of marching with a 30-inch stride? Haug looked thoughtful behind his amber-colored horn-rims. "There's a certain dignity about it. It covers ground. You go someplace. There's movement. It becomes most apparent when we do our 'three-company front' maneuver —you know—the three long marching lines stretching from sideline to sideline."

How did the band do at Dallas? "Pretty well. However, our movies showed that we made lots of little mistakes that the public didn't notice. We weren't always hitting the yard lines with the arches of our feet. We have a new freshman drum major this year."

A new band quarterback? Who was the band's new Jimmy Harris? "George Ingels. Last year he was Norman High's drum major. He's doing very well. Lots of poise. Pretty sharp. We expect great things of him."

Were the alumni ever critical of the band? Haug smiled faintly and uttered an explosive "Hah!" Then he added, "I'll say. We get a lot of comment pro and con. Like 'Why don't you play the Alma Mater before the game starts?' But we appreciate all suggestions. We know that the people who make them are out there watching and listening."

There were 48,000 watching and listening when Kansas State invaded. They saw Oklahoma win the game 21-0 but fail to score in the last half. "We weren't playing under wraps, either," Wilkinson said in his alumni letter. "We were trying hard. The reason we didn't score in the second half was because we weren't quite good enough to score. Kansas State didn't fold. With their backs to the wall they fought back wonderfully well and, in so doing, proved they are a fine football team."

Pat O'Neal, the number three quarterback, liked his football rough, and it nearly cost the Sooners a severance of their long string of 40 straight conference victories.

Colorado was the foe at Boulder and Oklahoma's red-shirted Ruf-Neks, white-togged cheerleaders, and 3,400 fans were doing their best to show as much spirit as Colorado's Silver and Gold horde of 32,000, with the snow-frocked Rockies looking down upon the scene.

Pat loved to hit and mix it up in a football game. While that's useful in all positions, it probably should not be the dominant trait of quarterbacking temperament. However, with Pat it was an obsession and therein hangs an extraordinary aspect of this game.

"The most fun I ever had was when Elvan George, my Ada High School coach, played me at defensive guard my junior year," Pat once said. "I weighed only 150 but that made it all the more fun. The hitting was pure pleasure. In those days, if I didn't get to play defense and bust people, I didn't think I was in the game."

In the second quarter of that Colorado game Pat chose hitting over thinking. For the first time in his life he was quarterbacking the Oklahoma first team, and that made it his biggest game ever. "I guess I was drunk with power," he says today. Although Pat was a senior, he was only third string. But Gene Calame, the starter, was still slowed by his shoulder injury. Jimmy Harris was weak from influenza and had come out for a rest. Everybody needed lots of rest when the opponent was Colorado at Boulder.

The score was tied 0-0. The situation involved a mishmash of fours. The Sooners had the ball on their own 44, fourth down and 4 to go. Then suddenly they didn't have it.

A punt was obviously in order. On the sideline Wilkinson and Gomer Jones hoped that the line would hold so that punter Max Boydston could belt the ball clear to the Wyoming line.

But out on the gridiron Irish Pat didn't order the kick. His combative urge blazed so brightly that he decided to run for the yardage, a risky business under the circumstances. Moreover, he didn't burden anybody else with the ball-carrying responsibility. He called himself on a strong-side run. "Nobody questioned it," O'Neal says, "and we had a captain on the field."

On the sideline Wilkinson was shocked. He had to do something quickly. He grabbed Calame by the shoulders.

"Quick! Go in for Pat. Stop the play!" Bud shouted, pushing Calame onto the field. He hoped the officials would see Calame in time to nullify the play and give Oklahoma a five-yard penalty so the Sooners would still have a fourth down in which to punt. But he was too late.

Jay O'Neal, Pat's sophomore brother sitting on the bench, knew better than anybody about Pat's aggressive attitude. "Pat was coming," Jay remembers. "Bud was screaming. I pulled my heavy sideline coat down over my head. 'Oh, Lord,' I said to myself."

Out on the field Pat paid no attention to Calame. "I could have pitched to Buddy Leake, our left half, but I didn't. I wanted to hit somebody. As a kid I'd learned that the fastest way to get to play was to hit somebody hard. Then they'd find you a place."

Later, coming home on the team plane, Pat grinned. "When I saw Calame coming, I decided he was coming out to slug me for calling that dumb play." But dumb or not, the play had started and Pat had to make it go, if he could.

He didn't. Colorado's gold-shirted operatives paid no heed to Calame either. They concentrated on Pat, piling him up two yards short of the first down. The crowd roared with elation. It was Colorado's ball. The Buffaloes ran to position. They were eager to smash that seven-year tradition.

Pat felt miserable and dejected. "When I came off the field, I told myself, 'Boy, you've played your last down for Oklahoma. You go out there and fight your guts out and all it gets you is the opportunity to foul up.'"

Bud met him at the sideline. "Don't you know we kick on fourth down?"

"Yes, sir," said Pat. End of conversation.

Starting from the Sooner 46, Ward's Buffaloes drove commandingly to a touchdown, scoring it on a screen pass, Carroll Hardy to Frank Bernardi. Gene Mears blocked the try for point, but Colorado led 6-0.

"At the half," Pat O'Neal remembers, "we walked across the field to their old gym and sat on bales of hay."

Wilkinson said to Pat, "I'll bet you thought it was third down." It would have been a good excuse for Pat had he cared to give it. Bud would have accepted it.

"No, sir," Pat replied. "It was fourth down. I knew exactly what down it was. I made a mistake. I'm sorry. I thought we could make the yardage."

That answer impressed Wilkinson. He liked the way Pat took it. The coach knew that mistakes in football hurt the fellow who makes them far more than anybody else.

Not only did O'Neal's error give Colorado the lead, it fired them so terrifically that they came out twice as tough in the second half, grinding out a 67-yard advance to the Oklahoma 13 before the Sooners stopped them. The third quarter was nearly over. It was Oklahoma's ball but the Sooners were reeling. They still trailed 0-6. Calame, who hadn't played in a month, was taking a pounding. Harris was weak from flu. The Colorado goal was 87 yards away. Who would Wilkinson send in at quarterback?

"I decided that Pat O'Neal deserved another chance," Wilkinson said later. "Our first team was battered from the pounding it had taken. I sent Pat out with our second team, which was fresh."

Licking his fingers, Pat buckled on his white helmet and went to work. Wilkinson's relieving elevens were always faunching to go into action anyhow. "Run the fullback off tackle on the first play but don't give it to him. Keep it yourself," Bud told Pat. Pat did, and the first play gained 7 yards. Now there was more room.

In ten plays Pat moved Oklahoma out of the hole, up the field, past the midstripe, and down to the Colorado 26, calling the right plays, handling the ball coolly and errorlessly. In those days the quarterback, not the coach, chose the plays. "Bud had instructed us so diligently that we knew what to do with no word from him," Pat says.

The play that took them into Buffalo territory was a pass, Pat O'Neal to Robert Burris. When the drive totaled 61 yards and reached Colorado's 26, Wilkinson sent in the first team. It scored in four plays, the fourth a pitch, Calame to Leake. Leake kicked goal. Now Oklahoma led, 7-6.

Colorado came back hard, but Leake intercepted a long pass by Hardy. Boydston quick-kicked 59 yards, stranding them on their 15. Kurt Burris stopped Bernardi and battered Hardy for a loss of 6, and when Tommy McDonald ran back their punt to the Sooner 48, the Oklahomans were on the march.

Again Wilkinson sent in Pat O'Neal and the feisty alternate eleven. In six plays Pat moved them 52 yards to the insurance touchdown. Pat scored it himself on a sneak off left guard with only 4:06 left to play. Pricer missed goal but Oklahoma won 13-6.

"I've never seen a finer comeback in football," Wilkinson said later. Pat was undoubtedly the game's hero. No wonder the Oklahoma players—first, second, and third teams indiscriminately—mobbed him when the thrilling battle ended.

The low-score wins over Kansas State and Colorado, 21-0 and 13-6, caused the Sooners to be dropped to number three nationally in the AP poll. Iowa State was the seventh opponent. Oklahoma won 40 to 0 in the game played at Clyde Williams Field at Ames, Iowa. Calame was back in action, and he played superbly, moving the Sooners 75 yards to a touchdown from the opening kickoff, handing off to Leake for the touchdown. And when Iowa State, on their first play of the last half, tried a pass by Breckenridge, Calame came in fast to pick it off and cut to the right. The Sooners' white-shirted blockers walled him off neatly, and he ran 48 yards to cross the goal standing. Wray Littlejohn, El Reno senior, set up the final touchdown with an interception of Finley's pass on the Sooner 22.

The Missouri game the following week, played at Norman before 54,173, third-largest OU crowd of all time, saw Wilkinson's team competing so intensely that it earned 22 first downs to Missouri's 1. But once the Sooners neared Missouri's goal, they met with all sorts of frustration, fumbling once at the Tiger 8 and twice being held for downs. With only two minutes left to play in the first half, the game was scoreless.

Suddenly the Sooners scored two touchdowns within 25 seconds of each other. Pat O'Neal, in at quarterback, engineered both. "Every week we'd been practicing a rollout series with a flanker out, but hadn't used it in a game," O'Neal remembers. He spun out from behind center and threw to Bob Herndon in the left flat for a 14-yard touchdown.

On the following kickoff, Bill Rice, Missouri back, was struck head-on by Jerry Tubbs, the ball flying loose from him. Bo Bolinger recovered it on the Tiger 16. "There was still another play off this rollout series we hadn't used, a pass to the fullback," O'Neal remembers. "Pricer broke into the open, I dumped him the ball, and he ran for another touchdown." The Sooners led 14-0 at the half.

Calame danced around the left side for the third touchdown. He was aided by Leake's fine handoff fake, which drew many of the Tiger linemen. "Buddy Leake played his best game," Wilkinson wrote in the alumni letter. "He drove for yards better than ever, getting us several key first downs with his strong running and his great effort."

Oklahoma's coaches also liked the play of Cecil Morris, junior guard from Lawton. Of him Wilkinson said, "Cecil not only blocked and tackled well but he played heads up football besides, recovering a Tiger fumble, fielding a short Missouri kickoff perfectly, and reacting beautifully to make a spectacular shoestring interception of a Tiger forward pass that set up our fifth touchdown." Oklahoma won 34-13.

The Nebraska-Oklahoma game at Norman, which would decide the Big Seven championship, was touted as the most physical battle of the year in the league. Nebraska's muscular rushing attack, which had gained 311 yards over Colorado, 383 against Iowa State, 331 against Missouri, and 416 over Kansas, collided with the aggressive Sooner rushing defense that had just stopped Missouri's split-T with 7 net yards and one first down.

Wilkinson's Sooners overran the Cornhuskers 55-7 to win the championship before a Homecoming Day crowd of 55,172. Wilkinson used 42 players in the game. Nebraska later went to the Orange Bowl and lost to Duke.

"The score was misleading," Bud pointed out in his alumni letter. "Nebraska had the misfortune to lose both Ron Clark and Willie Greenlaw, its starting halfbacks, early in the game." From the Nebraska dressing room Coach Bill Glassford told the press, "They're a great football team but we're not that bad."

One game remained, Oklahoma A&M at Stillwater. Lewis Field was bone dry, the sun shone warmly, and the wind blew gently from the south. Oklahoma won the game 14-0, but in the last half Coach J. B. ("Ears") Whitworth's Aggies carried the fight to the Sooners. In the dressing room afterwards, the Sooners walked around looking as gloomy as if they had lost. They didn't like to be out-hit.

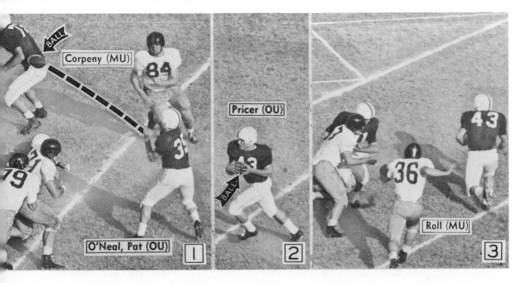

Pat O'Neal fires a pass to Billy Pricer, who cuts behind Max Boydston's block to score against Missouri at Norman in 1954.

ackle Don Brown after breaking s leg in the Texas game.

Max Boydston leaps to palm Gene Calame's long pass against Nebraska at Norman in 1954. Photo by Lee Randall.

Gene Calame, Oklahoma's injured quarterback, mans the sideline phone to help his team against Texas.

With only 1:57 left in the half, the Sooners were on the Aggie 37. A touchdown seemed unlikely. In went the first team. Calame faked a pass and ran down the sideline for 17. The Aggies braced and began to hold the Sooners for short gains. Time was running out. The pressure was on Calame.

Fitting all the plays within the allotted time was Gene's genius. When Leake hit off tackle for 2 to the Aggie 1, only seconds remained. But on the next play Calame hurried the Sooners into position, took the snap, ran to his left, danced momentarily before the Aggie end, then ducked inside him for the touchdown.

In his final alumni letter Wilkinson lauded three underpublicized men on his squad. Wray Littlejohn, he wrote, was "a fine football player, a great team man and one of the finest boys we've ever coached." George Nelson, the reserve center, Wilkinson said, "exemplified everything that college football should be. He's a B student in engineering. He has had no scholarship assistance of any kind. And yet he likes football and its competitive challenge and during his four years with us he contributed greatly to our team."

Of Carl Allison he wrote, "I never hope to coach a finer football player. Carl started every game we have played the last four years. He was never late to practice, never hurt, never sick. He was a fine captain. He is a straight B student. In reliability and character he stands at the very top of our squad. We could always depend upon him to do his job well. I don't mean to take anything away from our other more-publicized boys but I've never seen a better all-around football player, nor a more reliable one, than Carl Allison."

Meanwhile it was time to select the winner of the Heisman Award, which went annually to the outstanding college football player in the United States. This prize was mistitled. It should have been called the "Heisman Award for Backs" because the voters, the nation's well-meaning sports press, had usually cast their ballots for a back. No interior lineman—center, guard, or tackle—had ever won it or come close.

After Oklahoma's seventh game Wilkinson pointed out to me that Kurt Burris, our center, was having a phenomenal year and was probably more deserving of the Heisman than any other man in the nation in any position. We both knew that the sports press had always ignored interior linemen and that Burris, a center, was as interior as one could get. But we decided to try anyhow and strike a blow not only for Burris but for all deserving interior linemen of the future.

We decided to write a short personal letter of only three paragraphs to every sports editor in the nation—approximately 3,500 of whom were listed

170

in *Editor and Publisher Yearbook* with names and addresses—pointing out the unfairness of this and detailing the 1954 feats of Burris. But we had only three or four days.

I explained the problem to my friend Raymond White, chairman of the university's Department of Office Administration. He called in two classes of his students training to be secretaries. There were 100 typewriters in two large rooms. White explained the problem. The students were enthusiastic. They had seen Burris play. They typed the 3,500 personal letters, I signed them, and they were dispatched by first-class mail at the post office on Gray street.

What happened? As usual, a back from the populous Big Ten Conference area won it. He was a fine fullback, Alan Ameche of Wisconsin. He gathered 1,058 votes. But Burris was a strong second with 838, distancing such fine backs as Howard ("Hop-along") Casady, of Ohio State; Ralph Guglielmi, of Notre Dame; Paul Larson, of California; and Dick Moegle, of Rice.

Harry H. Kennedy, chairman of the Heisman Trophy executive committee, wrote that Burris finished the highest of any interior lineman in the history of the trophy. The previous high was 336 votes for Chuck Bednarik, Pennsylvania center of 1948.

Ameche and Burris collided head-on in the North-South game Christmas Day at Miami, Florida. Burris's South team triumphed 20-17. The AP story said, "Kurt Burris, Oklahoma's All-American center and runner-up to Ameche for the Heisman Award, was a defensive standout. He halted one North thrust in the first half by intercepting a pass from Helinski and in the third quarter with the North at the South's 10-yard line, he played a big part in halting the drive by tossing Ameche for a loss."

Wilkinson's 1954 team was preeminent in more defensive departments than those of any other club he ever coached. It allowed an average of 6.2 points a game, yielded only three pass interceptions for 15 total yards all season, and gave only 69 total yards in punt runbacks. Gomer Jones's Sooner lines barred the door to opposition rushing attacks after the third game against Texas, permitting no opponent to score on the ground in the last seven contests.

In national statistics Oklahoma placed second in rushing defense, second in pass interception avoidance, fourth in defense against scoring, fourth in rushing offense, fifth in total defense, seventh in total offense, eighth in scoring, ninth in punt return defense, and tenth in punting. Buddy Leake finished second nationally in scoring with 79 and second in points after touchdown with 25.

Oklahoma finished third in the AP poll, placing in the top ten for the seventh year in succession. Kurt Burris and Boydston made first All-American teams. The 1954 Sooners punted only 31 times, the record low during Bud's period. Bud's teams had won 19 straight games.

Wilkinson received a fine compliment when Jess Harper, 71-year-old Sitka, Kansas, ranchman who in 1917 resigned as Notre Dame coach with a five-year record of 32-5-1, refused to rate Knute Rockne over Wilkinson in coaching ability. Harper had coached with Rockne.

Dick Snider, sports editor of the *Topeka Daily Capital,* asked Harper if he nominated Knute Rockne of Notre Dame as the greatest football coach of all time.

"You've asked me something there that I can't answer," Harper replied. "There have been a lot of great coaches. There's a fellow down at Oklahoma right now who's a pretty fair coach. I'm a great admirer of Bud Wilkinson and have great respect for him. I saw the Notre Dame game at Oklahoma in 1953 and I thought Notre Dame's manpower was far superior. I liked the way Oklahoma played 'em. I've also seen Oklahoma a few times on television and I've been impressed."

The most dramatic event of Sooner football in 1954? Pat O'Neal's comeback in the last half of the Colorado game and also in later contests that year. And it all started that tragic afternoon when, after he had committed that horrendous boner at Boulder and Wilkinson questioned him about it between halves, Pat came clean instead of alibiing.

"No, sir," he had said. "It was fourth down. I knew exactly what down it was. I made a mistake. I'm sorry. I thought we could make the yardage."

1954 SENIORS TODAY

Carl Allison is director of the White's Ferry Road School of Biblical Studies, West Monroe, Louisiana.

Max Boydston is football coach at Piner Middle School, Sherman, Texas. He also owns and directs a computerized football scouting program at Sherman.

Don K. Brown teaches business courses at Granbury (Texas) High School. Before that he was for many years a football coach at Granbury and Kermit, Texas, high schools.

Kurt Burris is president and owner of the Burris Drilling Company, Denver, Colorado.

Gene Calame is executive vice-president, secretary, and general counsel for the Globe Life and Accident Insurance Company, Oklahoma City, Oklahoma.

John ("Buddy") Leake is a chartered life underwriter representing the Massachusetts Mutual Life Insurance Company in Oklahoma City, Oklahoma.

Pat O'Neal is head football coach at East Central State University, Ada, Oklahoma.

10. RUN, TOMMY, RUN!

"Our 1955 team will be so new that our own fans won't recognize it," Wilkinson told the press that spring.

The squad was strong from tackle to tackle and no place else. Three-fourths of them were native Oklahomans and most of the rest came from nearby Texas towns. Line coach Gomer Jones strongly endorsed southwestern boys. "We get a different type of kid from most eastern coaches," he said. "This is a young country, where boys grow up with ambition and pride, so that to help them all you have to do is emphasize self-improvement. Boys from the Southwest grow tall and rangy. They are mainly quick and tough. The older boys start the newer players right. If one is down hurt, the others are apt to tell him, 'Hey! You might as well do a few push-ups while you're resting!'"

The coaches spent eight hours a day just planning two hours of practice. John Cronley, veteran sports editor of the *Daily Oklahoman,* found it almost impossible to reach one of them on the telephone. "What a bunch of monks!" Cronley would mutter, slamming down the phone in disgust.

Clendon Thomas, gangling sophomore halfback from Oklahoma City Southeast, a new high school, was recruited by a newspaperman, not a coach. Hal Mix, of the *Daily Oklahoman and Times* (Oklahoma City), saw him play and told Pop Ivy about him.

Enrolling at OU, Thomas found himself on the fifth and last freshman team. There were only eight or nine boys on it. They called themselves the "A.O.'s" ("All Others"). Adam Esslinger, former Oklahoma A&M player who owned a dairy store near the stadium, was their coach.

"I guess they didn't really want me an awful lot," Thomas grins today, "because at Southeast High we had won only two games in the three years I played. They didn't realize it, but there was no way they were going to run me off at OU."

Thomas in football togs ran with surging speed despite his 6-2 height and 185-pound weight. There was no track at Southeast, but the football coaches hand-timed their athletes over the chalked yard lines of the football field. Wearing baseball shoes, Thomas once ran 220 yards in 21.3 seconds in an all-school meet.

In spring practice Thomas made the Sooner varsity. However, in the fall

Wilkinson asked him to accept a demotion to the alternates. "You've earned the right to start," Bud told him, "but I want you to play with the alternates and give them balance." That was fine with Thomas. A powerful alternate team was blossoming at Oklahoma that fall. "We knew we were going to play half the game time anyhow, so why sweat it?" philosophized quarterback Jay O'Neal.

Small-town boys also found a world of opportunity at Oklahoma. One of the best was Ross Coyle, of Marlow. His father, Edwin Coyle, was the town postmaster. An all-state end, Coyle visited several schools, among them Alabama, Vanderbilt, Notre Dame, and Oklahoma A&M. But Assistant Coach Sam Lyle signed him for the Sooners. Why did he choose Oklahoma?

"There's more romance to the game at Oklahoma," Coyle said. "It's not so commercial there. It's the only place to play."

In spring Wilkinson invited each freshman on his squad to his office for a private visit. "He always took a keen interest in each of us," remembers Buddy Oujesky. "This was when he urged us to get our degree in a major that would bring a good living after graduation. I was always amazed in these sessions to discover that he seemed to know more about me than I did."

A starter at left end that season was 205-pound Joe Mobra, from Wyandotte. A right-handed baseball pitcher who had just shut out Missouri's defending NCAA champions that spring, Mobra announced his arrival at football practice each day by giving his coon-dog yell. There was also a new coach. Ted Youngling, a thirty-year-old New Yorker, had joined the staff in February.

Billy Pricer, the new fullback, was once demoted five teams during a two-a-day practice that fall. "I was using my old high-school habit of walking back to the huddle," he recalls. Pricer asked freshman coach Port Robertson why he was dropped so low. Robertson stuck his finger in Pricer's face. "Because you weren't hustling, you little peahead," he said. In two days Pricer was back at starting fullback.

"Pricer was probably the most underpublicized but truly excellent player we had," says Jimmy Harris. "Pricer blocked down so many opponents ahead of our halfbacks that they should have taken him out to dinner every Sunday," said Buddy Oujesky.

Tommy McDonald recalls a similar demotion. In spring practice he was dropped to the second team. He went to Gene Calame. Calame told him that he was blocking the defensive man low instead of high, as Wilkinson had taught him. "You're going to have to start working on that block," Calame advised.

"That turned me on," McDonald remembers. "I tore everybody up with that high block. If a pole moved, I hit it. Next day I was back with the starters. That was Bud. If you did something opposite from the way he'd shown you, he'd drop you a team or two to let you think about it."

Ed Gray, the happy-go-lucky tackle from Odessa, Texas, "kept everybody loose," remembers Buddy Oujesky. "He could get by with things the rest of us were afraid to try. He was the only player on the squad who called Coach Wilkinson 'Bud.'"

Jerry Tubbs, moved back that year to his natural position, center, was "a whale of a team player, a leader who led by example," says Calvin Woodworth. "After every meal he brushed his teeth carefully and combed his hair, which he didn't have much of."

"Tubbs was a low-key person," remembers Buddy Oujesky. "I doubt if he liked practice. He lived for game day."

"Who did like practice?" Tommy McDonald burst out. "Anybody who liked practice should have gone to see a psychiatrist. But we all had to do it."

A new end who was coming on strong was Don Stiller, of Shawnee, who answered to the nickname "Tab" because he looked like the movie actor Tab Hunter. Stiller, a sophomore in 1955, was a good receiver and an able blocker. "He stepped on my hand once during an extra-point try," laughs Calvin Woodworth. "I still don't know what my hand was doing on the ground."

Oklahoma's freshman team, the Boomers, was permitted by the conference to play only two games. One of them was with the new Air Force Academy, in Denver, Colorado. Norman McNabb, who assisted Port Robertson with the coaching, took the Boomers to Denver in a bus. Both teams dined together at the academy, and the Boomers stayed that night at the base. The propriety of the plebes astonished the Boomers, remembers Joe Rector, Boomer end.

The plebes jogged in formation to the dining hall, carrying hats and books. They held their forks at right angles while eating. "Sir, pass the potatoes, please," they'd say politely when they wanted food. After the meal they grabbed their hats and jogged back to their study hall.

"We killed them in the football game, but we sure lost the decorum deal," Rector laughs today.

"Port Robertson had an arm lock that could get you in the study hall when you hadn't planned to go," remembers Ross Coyle. "He'd come in your room, fasten that awful thing on you, grin, and lead you out the door. He had you tiptoeing, I guarantee you. Yet he kept scores of kids of various egos and personalities in school. Nobody ever said anything derogatory about Port. He was highly respected."

In the spring of 1954, President Cross had received a letter from Walter Byers, executive director of the NCAA, inquiring about Oklahoma's recruiting. No accusations were made, but the NCAA wanted to know what were the University's athletic policies, who was responsible for their enforcement, and whether funds outside the University were made available to the athletes.

Legislation and enforcement of college athletics had begun seriously in 1951, when the NCAA office was moved from Chicago to Kansas City, and Byers, a newspaper man who had been Midwest sports editor and foreign sports editor of United Press, was named executive director.

"Before World War II recruiting matters were handled chiefly by the different athletic conferences," Byers recalls today, "but they had different rules and interpretations, and without strong national control the situation had become unbalanced and unsatisfactory."[1]

After the war Oklahoma operated loosely, as did many other schools. Well-meaning alumni and friends were behind much of this, and most coaches rarely learned of it until they heard an alumnus boasting about how much he had done for the program.

In the early 1950s, Big Seven Conference rules forbade the financing of visits of high-school athletes by schools that were trying to recruit them. However, this was legal in the nearby Southwest Conference. To stay abreast of Texas schools, Bill Jennings, the Oklahoma coach who headed Sooner recruiting, circumvented the Big Seven Conference rule (which was soon abolished) by going to Arthur Wood, Oklahoma City accountant and Oklahoma graduate, and soliciting funds for visitation transportation of the high-school athletes to Norman. Wood provided funds for this and also for other minor essentials.

On April 26, 1955, after a careful scrutiny of Oklahoma athletics during which twenty-six Sooner players were personally questioned, the NCAA found Oklahoma guilty of (1) offering high-school athletes cost-free education beyond their normal period of eligibility, (2) paying emergency medical expenses for wives and children of athletes, and (3) permitting "university patrons" to provide some Oklahoma athletes "fringe benefits . . . of relatively nominal value."

The Sooners were placed on probation for two years beginning April 26, 1955, and ending April 26, 1957. No ban was placed on bowl games. Most

[1] Walter Byers to author, June 20, 1980.

Oklahoma followers thought the punishment too stiff in view of the minor nature of the findings. Many believed that the NCAA went after only schools prominent in sports and also that no school investigated had much chance to beat the charges.

They were mistaken on both counts. Under Byers's leadership, the NCAA investigated and punished 17 schools before it investigated Oklahoma, among them Kentucky (whose basketball program was disbanded for one year), Arizona State, Michigan State, Notre Dame, Texas Tech, and Arizona. Kansas State, of the Big Seven Conference, was charged on May 7, 1954, almost a full year before the Sooners were.[2] Moreover, 95 other colleges and universities against whom charges were brought were, after an official inquiry, absolved of the charges.

The opening game against North Carolina at Chapel Hill was the most physically demanding of any Oklahoma ever played under Wilkinson. It was the Sooners' first dip into Dixie, and the humidity was between 90 and 95 percent. Without their alternate team the Sooners could not have survived against a big, high-keyed Carolina outfit that was geared for an all-out effort before its home crowd. The Sooners used 2,200 pounds of pressure from trainer Ken Rawlinson's oxygen tank, an all-time high for an Oklahoma team. "Although the sun was shining brightly, it was raining," Rawlinson recalled the scene.

Oklahoma, a team with a new backfield and new ends, came into possession thirteen times in the game. They fumbled to the Tar Heels three times, Carolina recovering one for a touchdown. They fumbled once and lost the ball in the Carolina end zone when they were about to score. The battling Tar Heels held the Sooners for downs three times, on the 31-, 13-, and 1-yard lines. They stopped Oklahoma four times, compelling punts.

In the last half the Sooners steadied, making no more costly errors. Starting from their 26, they flitted over the yard lines. With Bill Krisher, Midwest City sophomore, and Gray cleaning out ahead, Robert Burris bucked 15 yards. John Bell threw a trap block and Robert Burris tunneled 25 yards down the middle. McDonald hit Bell with the running pass for 16 to the Carolina 8. Harris pitched out to Robert Burris, who skirted left end for the touchdown behind a smashing block by Billy Pricer. Harris kicked goal and Oklahoma led 7 to 6.

Thomas made the last touchdown possible with an unusual punt. Fielding a rolling center snap that was crawling along the ground like a snake, he kicked out on the Carolina 14, leaving them so deep that, when they punted back, Oklahoma had only 39 yards to traverse and drove it in in five plays,

---

[2] David Berst, NCAA Enforcement Officer, to author, June 18, 1980.

178

McDonald sweeping right end for the touchdown. The Sooners won 13-6. They outrushed Carolina 403 to 134 and outpassed them 80-11, but Carolina made no turnovers and had most of the end-zone luck.

On the night before the next game, Pittsburgh at Norman, the Sooners stayed at the Skirvin Hotel, in Oklahoma City. Next morning they were walking about the lobby, waiting for their bus. The hotel was filled with groups of Sooner fans who saw Jay O'Neal and mistook him for Tommy McDonald.

"Hey there, Tommy, come over here a minute," they called.

O'Neal, who was never tense on game day, sauntered over. "How you all doin'?" he inquired.

"How're we gonna do today, Tommy?" they asked eagerly.

"Oh," shrugged Jay "McDonald" modestly, "I think I'll score three or four."

He didn't miss it far, at that. The real McDonald averaged 11.2 net yards—more than a first down every time he carried the ball—and tallied two touchdowns, one of them a scintillating 43-yard reverse, with Bo Bolinger blocking the Pitt end and Calvin Woodworth throwing a cross-field fend on a linebacker to bring the crowd of 56,807 to its feet roaring.

Oklahoma whipped into a 19-0 lead and needed it. McDonald's 43-yard reverse fetched the first touchdown. Bob Burris stabbed powerfully across the goal for the second after Don Stiller picked off his second pass interception. With the alternates on the field Clendon Thomas scored the third on a 31-yard reverse with Wayne Greenlee blocking the end, and Delbert Long and Eldon Loughridge getting cross-fielders.

Coach Johnny Michelosen's Panthers rallied with last-half touchdown jaunts of 71 and 43 yards and booted both goals, trimming the score to 19-14. Oklahoma had won 20 straight, but Pitt wasn't taking anything off anybody.

Trailing by only 5 in the fourth period, Pitt started another drive. Alarmed, the Oklahoma crowd began to murmur anxiously. But John Bell fought through the Pitt blockers and wrecked one play. Bolinger and Woodworth smashed a crucial third-down effort. Pitt punted. There was 6:30 left to play.

Could the Sooners move the ball? They had to move it to keep it away from Pitt. Cool and sure-handed in the crisis, Jimmy Harris brought Oklahoma up the gridiron. From midfield Pricer barreled into the Panthers for 8 and 11 yards. Behind a block by Pricer, McDonald wriggled out of a tackler's grasp and sped 20 yards to the Pitt 9. On the weak-side handoff, Bolinger, Woodworth, and Stiller opened Pitt's defense, and McDonald was scarcely touched as he shot into the end zone. Harris kicked goal. The

179

Sooners won 26-14. "After that game we saw that we had a terrific team," says McDonald today.

Five pass interceptions, three by center Jerry Tubbs, and four booming quick kicks, three by fullback Billy Pricer, spelled the difference in the Texas game played before 75,504 at Dallas. Oklahoma won 20 to 0, registering its first shutout of the season. Wilkinson complimented Coach Sam Lyle for his sound scouting job. He also praised defensive coaches Gomer Jones, Pete Elliott, and Ted Youngling.

"Oklahoma's overpowering Sooners were as sure of themselves as the carnival barkers in checkered vests roaming the State Fair grounds outside," one Texas writer wrote, but the Sooners never could physically conquer the Longhorns. The Steers actually outfought Oklahoma late in the contest, and at the end it was the Sooners who looked tired and abashed when the two teams walked off the field.

"You all look like you'd lost the ball game," teased Willie Dean, wife of Calvin Woodworth, Sooner left tackle.

It was in the locker room before the game started that Wilkinson told the squad his story about "The Boy Who Took the Bird to the Wise Old Man." "Is it alive or dead?" the brash youth asked the old man, holding the sparrow in one hand with only its head showing. The old man knew the youth's intent. If he said "alive," the youth would squeeze the bird to death. If he said "dead," he would free the bird, and it would fly away. The boy wanted the old man to be wrong.

Realizing this, the old man said, "As you will, my son. As you will." Bud used the story to motivate the Sooners against Texas. If they willed it strongly enough, they could defeat the Longhorns seemed the point of the story.

They willed it right from the start. Joe Clements, big Texas sophomore, pegged a pass down the field. Tubbs, a long-winged Sooner hawk whose swoops menaced the Texas airways all day, picked it off, giving Oklahoma possession on the Texas 33. The Sooners scored six plays later using a fake trap play. Jimmy Harris called it, faking and handing off expertly. McDonald used all his speed and slipperiness during his 28-yard dash to a touchdown. A high snapback prevented the extra point.

The Texas sports press was enthralled with McDonald. "McDonald's fire and desire burned so intensely he once fell down running back to the huddle," wrote Jack Gallagher, of the *Houston Post.*

Of his own prowess McDonald said after the game, while chewing nervously on his fingers, "I wouldn't gain a foot if it wasn't for Billy Pricer's blocking and Robert Burris's great faking that holds the defense in, and

180

Jimmy Harris's slick ball-handling and accurate pitchouts. I could have ridden through the hole piggyback." Then he added, "With Buddy Leake gone, I try harder."

The Sooners had a good alternate team that year, perhaps Bud's best of all time. Jay O'Neal, the team's quarterback, said, "If we could get the opposition to substitute with us, our second team would usually kick the heck out of their second team. Or if they left their first team in, we'd stay with them too. And as the game wore on, their first team got awfully tired."

Then the game took on a Keystone Kops quality. The alternates were in. Jay O'Neal lateraled to Dennit Morris, who ran to the Texas 9 before he tumbled across the sideline amid players of both teams.

"The referee dropped his cap on the 9 and dove into the crowd to get the ball," recalls O'Neal. "While he was looking for it, one of our girl cheerleaders came up and stood by the cap. She looked mischievously over her right shoulder, then over her left. Then she kicked the referee's cap 5 yards down to the Texas 4. The ref finally surfaced, hesitated a minute, then marked the ball on the 4 where she'd kicked the cap. Bud put in the first team, but darned if Texas didn't hold them for downs."

McDonald rescued the situation by intercepting a pass and returning it to the Steer 7. "Then this 169-pound fireball literally exploded at right tackle and was in the end zone before the Texas defense could get him bore-sighted," wrote Blackie Sherrod, *Fort Worth Press* sports editor.

It took a former college coach, Homer Norton, of Texas A&M, writing for the *Houston Post,* to spot the newest feature of Wilkinson's offense. "Oklahoma ran its plays quicker than any college team I've seen in a number of years," he wrote. More about that later.

Fighting very hard, Kansas, coached by Chuck Mather, opened hostilities by driving 71 yards to a touchdown on eight crushing ground plays. The Sooner Homecoming audience of 39,789 sat stunned.

"We were always disappointed when we let anybody score," remembers Clendon Thomas. "We wanted to beat everybody 40 to zip." Tommy McDonald was so annoyed that he shot through the Jayhawk defense and blocked their extra point. But Kansas led 6 to 0.

Oklahoma retaliated with a two-team assault. Jimmy Harris drove the starters 67 yards to a touchdown, McDonald sidearming his halfback pass 33 yards to Bell, then scoring on a pitch from Harris. Then the alternates entered the game. Carl Dodd, Norman sophomore, scored around the weak side on a pitch from Jay O'Neal over a block by fullback Dennit Morris, Tulsa sophomore. Morris intercepted two passes, one for a touchdown.

Bill Sturm, a small preministry student from Muskogee, quarterbacked

181

the third team 56 yards to another touchdown, forward-passing to Robert Derrick, Woodward junior. Wilkinson used all 51 players on his squad. Final score, 44-6.

In his letter to the alumni Wilkinson wrote: "Late in the game I was much impressed with the way our alternate teams crouched along the sideline in front of our bench and rooted for our third and fourth elevens. This is the kind of morale and attitude that makes the difference in football. You need spirit and loyalty throughout the entire squad."

Colorado, a fast-forming front curling down from the Rockies, was the next to push across Oklahoma's weather map. It was in this game that the Sooners began unleashing the fast break, and the public began noticing it. Wilkinson preferred to call it the "Fast Recovery" because its success depended upon how speedily the Sooners raced back into the huddle after the preceding play. The Sooner intent was to launch their plays before the defense got settled and looked at Oklahoma's line splits.

Much of the credit for it belonged to Tommy McDonald, hurrying little junior halfback from Albuquerque. He practically had a patent on it, Bud told Dick Snider, sports editor of the *Topeka Daily Capital.*

"McDonald is a funny kid," Wilkinson said. "He figures any play that doesn't go for a touchdown is a failure. When he carries the ball and doesn't score, he gets mad and wants to hurry up and take another crack at it. Tommy jumps up and tears back to the huddle, running almost as hard as if he had the ball. It's nothing we taught him. It's something God gave him, or his parents, or somebody. We didn't do it.

"The other boys more or less picked it up from him and then we started working on it, seeing how fast we could go. It has to be used in the right situation to be effective. But the boys are sold on it and that's half the battle."

Coach Dal Ward's Buffaloes, who, like the Sooners, came into the game 4-0, set the early pace, recovering two Oklahoma fumbles and driving to a touchdown with each. Soon Colorado led 14-0. The Sooner crowd of 57,663 stood nervously on both sides of the stadium urging the Oklahomans to get with the situation.

Then Oklahoma began releasing its plays like arrows from a bow. Robert Burris, who Wilkinson said played the best game of his life, ran the kickoff back to the Buffalo 46. Burris scored on a handoff slant behind blocks by Cecil Morris, Ed Gray, and John Bell. Pricer kicked goal.

Oklahoma kicked off. Bolinger, Pricer, and Bobby Darnell, of Sherman, Texas, a senior spelling Tubbs, who had a disabled elbow, stopped the Buffs. They punted. Fielding it, McDonald wormed all the way back to Colorado's 27. On the handoff Burris took two terrific swipes at the tough

182

Buff line and careened into the end zone. Pricer converted, and the score was tied 14-14 with only 2:57 left in the half.

It didn't seem there was time to score again, but the Sooners shifted into their fifth speed. McDonald shot his halfback pass to Bell for 8 and to Mobra for 16. Robert Derrick gushed 34 yards on a handoff, moving the Sooners to the 2. McDonald jumped across the goal behind blocks by Bolinger, Woodworth, and Mobra. Pricer converted, and Oklahoma led 21-14 at the half.

Early in the third quarter Jenkins quick-kicked over the Sooner secondary, and the ball was rolling apparently dead in midfield. Then Robert Burris triggered a sensational play. Suddenly he blocked Colorado's oncoming end off his feet, spilling him roughly. The physical decisiveness of this block seemed suddenly to activate the Sooners. Quickly, McDonald snatched up the rolling punt and ran 37 yards down to their 13. Four plays later Burris hit powerfully on the handoff for the touchdown. Pricer's conversion moved Oklahoma in front 28-14, and the Sooners kept going.

"Oklahoma scored about every way except under water," wrote John Cronley, sports editor of the *Daily Oklahoman*.

Later, Oujesky covered a Buffalo fumble on the Colorado 20. The third Sooner team came in, quarterbacked by little Bill Sturm, the predivinity student. Sturm stayed cheerful despite three consecutive bad breaks, a holding penalty, a fumbled pitchout, and a penalty for illegal receiver downfield. He overreached them all by rainbowing a long forward pass to Duane Goff, Newkirk senior, for 35 yards and a touchdown. Then he pronounced the benediction by kicking the extra point. Final score, 56-21.

From the Colorado dressing room afterwards, Coach Dal Ward told reporters, "Without a doubt this Oklahoma team is the fastest I ever saw." End Lamar Meyer said, "No other team hustles like they do." In his alumni letter Wilkinson wrote: "There's nothing that gives a football team a greater feeling of unity than to rally strongly together and win after starting the game two touchdowns behind. A football team doesn't learn to know itself until it gets in trouble."

Cut to thirty-six men by conference rules, the Oklahoma squad flew Friday to Topeka, Kansas, worked out at the Washburn University field, and went by bus Saturday morning to Manhattan to meet Kansas State.

The drive on highway 24 along the Kansas River led through the autumnal-tinted Kansas countryside. On the bus the Oklahoma team sat somber and silent, as Wilkinson wished, thinking about their keys, their calls, their blocking assignments, and the game. Jay O'Neal, alternate team quarterback, was sitting with halfback Robert Derrick.

"We kept passing tall silos on the big Kansas farms," O'Neal remembers. "I quietly asked Robert if he'd heard about a farmer dying recently in one of those silos.

"'No,' replied Robert, wide-eyed. 'What happened?'

"He ran himself to death looking for a place to go to the bathroom," said O'Neal.

Derrick's booming laugh shattered the pregame quiet. Everybody on the bus jumped. Later, Gomer Jones asked O'Neal not to sit with Derrick any more.

"Why not?" asked O'Neal.

"Because he's interfering with your concentration," answered the coach. O'Neal grinned and told the line coach what had really happened. "But it didn't do any good," he laughs today. "I still didn't get to sit with Derrick the next week going to Missouri."

The Oklahoma starters drove 77 yards to a touchdown the second time they had the ball, quarterback Jimmy Harris slithering 7 yards around right end. Kansas State, from deep in her territory, tried a pitchout. The ball struck the shoulder pad of one of their players and bounded into the air. With his quick hands Calvin Woodworth, Oklahoma's senior tackle, plucked it out of the sky and streaked 24 yards to a touchdown. Later, Oklahoma was penalized back to its 2 for clipping. Bud sent the alternate team back into the game.

There was nothing wrong with quarterback O'Neal's concentration during this 98-yard advance. He pitched to Dennit Morris, who bowled down the sideline for 27 yards. O'Neal then faded and heaved a long pass that Bob Timberlake, running fast, pulled down for 51 yards. Thomas scored the touchdown on the handoff. Final score, 40-7.

Don Faurot, the long-time Missouri coach, was the only opponent Oklahoma met that year who fearlessly substituted an alternate eleven every time Oklahoma did. His Yannigans were good and went 0-0 against Oklahoma's.

But Wilkinson's starters managed three touchdowns, two in the first quarter, to win 20-0, and when the action ended, the white-garbed Sooners and the gold-shirted Tigers met in the center of the field and shook hands all around. Later Wilkinson said, "If the fans would pattern their sportsmanship after that of the players, the game would come much nearer fulfilling the purpose for which it was created."

Most of the scoring came in the first quarter. Quarterback Jimmy Harris's clever use of halfback passes featured the first drive. After Oklahoma passed midfield, McDonald ran to his right and flipped his running toss to Robert Burris for fourteen. Two plays later Burris ran to his left and pegged to

McDonald for twelve. Then McDonald set up the touchdown by passing to Burris again, Robert running to the Tiger 3. Burris hit hard over blocks by Cecil Morris, Ed Gray, and John Bell to go into the end zone. Pricer kicked goal.

The pace of Joe Mobra's long, windblown kickoffs was important. But the Sooners lost their kickoff ace in the last half when Mobra was knocked unconscious.

"He was knocked out standing up," grins Clendon Thomas. "He was standing glassy-eyed in our huddle. 'What's your name, Joe?' somebody asked him. He didn't know. The trainers came out and got him."

Jimmy Harris's deft work brought the final Oklahoma touchdown. From the Missouri 22, Harris faked the handoff, kept, and darted around his right flank. As he was tackled, he lateraled to McDonald, and Tommy waltzed into the end zone.

Voted number one in the nation in the AP poll, just 51 points ahead of Coach Jim Tatum's Maryland Terrapins, Oklahoma had an incentive to play well against Iowa State and did, calming the Cyclones 52-0.

The Sooners led 7-0 when Robert Burris broke off left tackle and scurried 34 yards to a touchdown. Then the Oklahoma crowd was thrilled to its toes. Ray Tweeten, the Cyclones' kicking tackle, booted a high punt that soared along the ceiling of the sky. Gauging it in the breeze, Tommy McDonald glided beneath it, fielded it on his 9 and, making liberal use of his speed and his broken-field choreography, returned it 91 yards through the whole Cyclone team to a touchdown.

The Sooner alternates put two more touchdowns in the hopper. Carl Dodd passed to Delbert Long for one. Clendon Thomas ripped off tackle for the other.

"Between halves, Bud had to have something to chew us about," recalls Billy Pricer, "so he got on us for not blocking anybody on our punt returns. 'You aren't hitting anybody,' he scolded. 'Go after 'em.'

"We kicked off and forced Iowa State to punt," remembers Pricer. "It was my job to knock down the end then fall back and get somebody else. Then—boom!—somebody wiped me out, cut me in two. I rolled over on my side so I could see who he was and pay him back later. Darned if it wasn't Ed Gray, our own right tackle! Fired by Bud's halftime talk, he had put a downfielder on me.

"'Hey, Ed, I'm on your side,' I told him.

"'Yeah,' grinned Gray, 'but Bud said to hit somebody. And you were the only one around.'"

Joe Mobra was back, belting his streaming kickoffs. Cecil Morris, 220-pound tackle, didn't enjoy running down under them.

"Kick the hell out of it," Morris would growl to Mobra, as the end teed up the ball. The farther Mobra shot his kickoffs, the less hard Morris would have to run.

"That's the way to boot that melon," Morris praised. Later Mobra's lined shot struck the ground on the Iowa State 8 but bounded into the end seats.

"Good 'un!" yelled Morris.

Mobra protested. "Gosh, Cece, it hit the ground inside the goal."

"Yeah, but it went on out of there," Morris insisted.

In the Iowa State dressing room after the game, end Mel Westoupal said, "OU ran more plays per minute than any team we ever played." Halfback Hank Philmon added, "They're so fast you don't get much chance to see who it is that hurt you."

From the Sooner locker room, end Bill Harris, Ardmore senior, said, "All the hard practice that all us subs go through is worth it. I wouldn't trade this for anything in the world. Just sitting on the bench inspires a guy to do great things." Harris played on the fifth team.

Both Oklahoma and Nebraska had 5-0 records as they squared off at Lincoln for the Big Seven championship. Disaster threatened Oklahoma on its first scrimmage play when quarterback Jimmy Harris dodged nimbly down the middle for thirteen yards, then suffered an injured shoulder when he was tackled. The injury forced him from the game. Wilkinson substituted Jay O'Neal, who bossed both the starters and the alternates for the rest of the contest and got a good workout directing all that fresh speed. O'Neal also saved a touchdown with a timely tackle of Willie Greenlaw, Scarlet ace, when Willie broke loose down the east sideline with O'Neal the only man between him and the goal.

O'Neal squirmed through the middle behind blocks by Northcutt, Oujesky, and Krisher for the first touchdown. Tubbs made a leaping interception of Greenlaw's pass to set up the second, a scoring clout by Bob Burris. Burris also smote for the third. McDonald dived across for the fourth. Clendon Thomas struck around right end with a pitchout to count the fifth. Dennit Morris intercepted a pass.

With 6:07 left to play, Wilkinson substituted his third team, quarterbacked by Bill Sturm. A clipping call against Oklahoma moved the ball back to the Sooner 42. Sturm's jinx had struck again.

But little Bill weathered this one too. Despite penalties and fumbles, the tiny theologian took his team 58 yards to a touchdown. Sturm kept for 11. Sturm passed to Fred Hood for 30 and a first down on the Nebraska 7. From there Oklahoma scored on fourth down, Sturm handing off to Robert Derrick. Hood, Ladd, and Kenneth Hallum, Seminole sophomore, blocked. Sturm booted the conversion and dismissed the congregation.

Back at Norman the Sooners received two pieces of good news. Jimmy Harris had only a sprained shoulder, no break. And Oklahoma had kept its number one rating in the AP poll.

The Sooners had too much at stake to take lightly their final regular season game, Oklahoma A&M at Norman. Bud's Sooners were playing for the national championship and needed a convincing triumph to achieve it. A win over the Aggies would assure Oklahoma its 29th straight victory and mark the 105th straight game in which the Sooners had scored.

In spite of his lame shoulder Jimmy Harris, Oklahoma's injured quarterback, started the game and scored the first touchdown, a quarterback sneak, with Bolinger, Tubbs, and Cecil Morris ramming the Aggies back. Pricer kicked goal.

Cliff Speegle, former Sooner center who was just starting as the Aggie coach, said afterwards that the game turned on Clendon Thomas's 65-yard punt runback, which brought the second touchdown. Thomas fielded Tom Pontius's punt and sailed down the east sideline, running south. So sharp was the Sooner blocking that he was scarcely tagged. Later Harris flicked a pass to Joe Mobra, who caught the ball on the 1 and stepped across. The final score of 53-0 meant that Gomer Jones's defense had blanked seven of its ten opponents that year.

With Wilkinson playing all 56 men he suited, the third team came in and with Sturm in the pulpit drove 25 yards to score. Robert Derrick popped through from 3 yards out. Sturm kicked goal.

From the Sooner dressing room Wilkinson told reporters, "The one big thing that caused all this was the over-all spirit of the squad. Everyone has worked hard and that includes the boys who were playing and those who knew they wouldn't play." From the Aggie locker room Coach Speegle told the press, "Their speed killed us. They are definitely the number one team."

The AP poll, which was determined in December and wasn't affected by later bowl play, awarded the national championship to Oklahoma with Michigan State second, Maryland third, and UCLA fourth. The Sooners placed two first-team All-Americans that year, guard Bo Bolinger and halfback McDonald. Bolinger was runner-up to Calvin Jones, of Iowa, for the Outland Trophy.

Wilkinson, in a *Saturday Evening Post* article, praised Gomer Jones, his line coach. "Gomer and I work as partners," said Bud. "There's no other term for our relationship. All we do at Oklahoma is as much Gomer's thinking as mine."

In the national statistics Oklahoma led the nation widely in total offense, amassing 410.7 net yards a game. The Sooners also spread-eagled the field in the rushing table with 328.9 net yards a contest. They rated sixth nationally in both total defense and rushing defense. They placed second nationally in interception avoidance and ninth in number of interceptions. They ranked sixth in punt-return yardage and tenth in kickoff-return defense and led the nation in penalty yardage with 86.2 yards a game.

In the Orange Bowl game against Maryland, Oklahoma was a shining target for these reasons: (1) Oklahoma had just won the national championship, and national champions have a difficult time in bowl games; (2) Oklahoma had upset Maryland's national champions 7-0 in the Orange Bowl two years before, and the Terps wanted revenge; and (3) Oklahoma had won 29 straight games, giving Maryland a further incentive.

Maryland's 7-0 defeat of UCLA, only loss in two years for the powerful Bruins, was the most impressive victory scored by either Orange Bowl team. In this game Tatum's craggy defense throttled UCLA's rushing, holding them to a minus 21 yards. Afterwards, Coach Henry R. ("Red") Sanders of UCLA described Maryland as "a majestic team, the greatest team of the era." Asked if he would be willing to renew the series with Maryland, which ended that fall, Sanders said, "I hope we never see them again." But the Sooners had to see them, and go against their power, before 76,561 in the Orange Bowl.

The first appearance of the Oklahoma alternates in the battle was nearly disastrous. On the first play from Maryland's 24, Ed Vereb, their ace back, started around the right side. "We were concerned about Vereb," remembers Jay O'Neal. "Bud and Gomer put in a secondary roll in which our left cornerback, Delbert Long, fiercely attacked the play, and we all rolled left to protect."

But Vereb braked himself and cut back so sharply to the inside that he eluded the Sooner deathwatch. Jay O'Neal, Oklahoma's deep defensive half, was the only Sooner close. "Jay was the slowest guy on our team yet he caught Vereb from behind," Tommy McDonald still marvels today. They ran it out down the sideline. O'Neal, diving, knocked Vereb out of bounds on the Sooner 10. The play gained 66 yards, but it didn't score. "O'Neal came as near playing to the full potential of his ability as anybody we've ever had," Wilkinson later told the Oklahoma City Quarterback Club. "He wasn't robust physically, but he always made the play."

Tamburello, of Maryland, hit off tackle for 5. Healy tried a buck, but Northcutt and Timberlake stopped the effort. Tamburello was hit hard by Carl Dodd and fumbled, Stiller recovering on the Sooner 10.

The hitting was resounding. McDonald hit Mobra with the halfback pass, but Maryland hit Mobra too. No completion. The Sooner starters reentered the fray, and Harris drove them 51 yards to the Terp 31, where Maryland stopped them. A Sooner holding penalty left Oklahoma dangerously deep

Sooners of 1955 fast-breaking to the scrimmage line against Colorado.

Jimmy Harris, Oklahoma quarterback, running behind center Jerry Tubbs in 1955 against North Carolina at Chapel Hill.

Beightol, Maryland passer, harassed by Sooner pass rush led by Wayne Greenlee (71), Tom Emerson (69), and Buddy Oujesky (68).

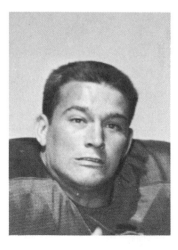

Bo Bolinger.

on its own 5. But Harris called the right play, a quick kick by Thomas. Nicz ran it back to the Sooner 39. Six minutes remained in the half.

The lone touchdown of the first half followed. Maryland got it in seven plays. The muscular Terps stayed on terra firma. The Sooner alternates made them go four downs for a first and ten that had to be measured. Bud sent in his starters. Tatum sent in his starters too. Vereb bucked off guard for 10, McDonald tackling. Vereb faded back to the right to pass. Oklahoma had his receivers covered. With his genius for running the wrong way for bucks in the bank, Vereb made a screeching U-turn and swung back left, sprinting to the touchdown.

Tubbs blocked Laughery's try for point, and Maryland led 6-0. The lanky Sooner center played the whole Orange Bowl game without having scrimmaged a minute all during the month of December. He had injured his knee in the finale against Oklahoma A&M, and during Oklahoma's bowl drills he could do nothing but stand and watch. In the bowl game he went in cold and played superbly, mostly on desire.

Maryland's touchdown was the first scored against Oklahoma in four games and 17 consecutive quarters. With 20 seconds left Jimmy Harris intercepted a Terp pass and then completed two of his own to advance the ball to the Terp 25, but the half ended. The Sooners trooped disconsolately to their locker room. Wilkinson came in. Calvin Woodworth, the left tackle, describes what followed.

"Sit down!" Bud ordered. "I've never seen anything like this in all my life. They're not doing one thing we haven't worked on. Our line isn't blocking. Our backs are running backwards. If you guys don't get busy and start playing football, you're going to get the hell beat out of you."

Flabbergasted at their coach's use of even mild profanity, the first they had ever heard from him, the Sooners blinked and sat up. "He was so disgusted," Woodworth says, "he left us sitting there. He just walked out. When the officials came in to tell us it was time to begin the second half, Bud walked in behind them. "Let's go out and play football," he said.

"In the last half the coach told Jimmy to start the 'go-go' offense, as we called it," recalls Tommy McDonald. "Jimmy told us that there would be no huddle, that every play was going to be called from the line of scrimmage. The second number he called was the number of the play."

"Oklahoma came out of its bathhouse as if catapulted," wrote Bob Considine. Mobra kicked off. Hamilton returned to the Terp 30, Bolinger tackling. Vereb reversed for a first down on the Maryland 41. That was the only first down Maryland made in the third quarter. Bolinger held Healy to 5. Vereb reversed again, but Tubbs tackled him for a loss. Vereb punted to McDonald, and the tough little Sooner swiftly turned on all the

191

juice to dash 32 yards down the sideline to the Maryland 46, a vital play.

Harris sent the Sooners into the go-go. Pricer hit over guard for 5, then over tackle for 4. The Sooners were sprinting to and from the scrimmage front, listening to Harris's verbal call of the signals on the run. Robert Burris bucked 8 to a first down on the Terp 28. Then Harris called McDonald on four consecutive plays.

Tommy reversed for 2. He passed to Burris for 19 to the Terp 7. He bucked over Mobra, Woodworth, and Bolinger to the 4. He took a pitch from Harris and sprang into the end zone as if shot from a toaster. Pricer kicked goal. Oklahoma led 7-6.

"We were running plays while Maryland was still getting up off the ground," McDonald remembers. "They were trying to hold us down between plays. They would lie on me, put their arm on my arm, entangle my leg with theirs. 'Keep him down! Keep him down!' they would talk among themselves. 'Lemme up! Lemme up! Lemme up!' I was shouting, as I tried to jerk loose." Clendon Thomas remembers that once Pellegrini, the Terp center, was hit in the back by a Sooner play while he called defensive signals. "That destroys a man," Thomas added. "They don't know what they're fighting."

Oklahoma's alternates kicked off. Emerson and Northcutt wrecked a play. Beightol hit a pass, but Stiller slapped it out of the receiver's hands. Beightol punted. Thomas ran it back to the OU 48. With Jay O'Neal accelerating them, the Sooner alternates turned it on too. It was an advance of 52 yards, and so fiercely did Maryland resist that Oklahoma needed 17 plays, with the Sooners twice making the yardage on fourth down. Once officials called for the chains to measure the distance.

"Jay called the signals fast," remembers fullback Dennit Morris. "Bob Timberlake, our end who had to run downfield to block the safety, was getting back to the huddle just in time to hear O'Neal say, 'Break!' Carl Dodd had to tell Bob the signal and the count."

The Terps were tired. Sandusky, a fine Maryland lineman who had got the first three tackles of the game, had his shirttail out, recalls Billy Pricer. "His high-top shoes had come unlaced, and the tongue was flopping." Once Sandusky was down on one knee, panting. Pellegrini tried to help him up. "Get out of the way!" Sandusky yelled. "Here they come again!"

But Oklahoma was weary too. "We were almost as tired as they, but they fagged out first," remembers Clendon Thomas.

O'Neal crossed the goal on a sneak from 1 yard out. Krisher, Northcutt, and Oujesky made room for him behind their charge. Pricer kicked goal, and Oklahoma led 14-6. In the last half they had sped to touchdowns the

Sooners of 1955 riding team bus to practice before the Sugar Bowl game in which Oklahoma defeated Maryland 20-6.

Jay O'Neal's diving tackle halts Vereb, Maryland ace, and prevents a touchdown after Vereb's 66-yard run in 1956 Orange Bowl. Associated Press Wirephoto.

Carl Dodd intercepting the Maryland pass which he returned 82 yards to a touchdown in the 1956 Orange Bowl. Associated Press Wirephoto.

first two times they got the ball. Then Robert Burris, the Sooner right half, went out with a knee injury.

Oklahoma scored again in the fourth quarter, when Carl Dodd intercepted Beightol's forward pass and ran 82 yards to a touchdown. Pricer missed goal. Oklahoma 20, Maryland 6. There were 5:02 left to play. In the closing moments Harris quarterbacked the Sooners 56 yards to the Maryland 7, only to have big Pellegrini, still a rough fighter, intercept McDonald's pass on the 10, two plays from the end. It was Oklahoma's thirtieth consecutive victory, tying the record set by Wilkinson's 1948-50 teams.

Wilkinson surprised the press after the game when he said, "I don't honestly think that we're superior to Maryland. Today we won. Tomorrow we might not. I'm awfully glad it was today."

Tatum was most gracious, as he had been in the 1954 Orange Bowl loss to Oklahoma. Standing outside the Terp dressing room, he wore a big white cowboy hat and had his hands jammed in his hip pockets. "Oklahoma is the best team in the country," he began. "They beat us in every department. They handled themselves better. They outhustled us. They had more speed."

Ray Parr, special writer for the *Daily Oklahoman,* typified the Sooner jubilation with the following verse:

> Squeeze me an orange and drink up a toast
> To the Terrible Terps of Tatum.
> The toughest critters on the coast
> But burp! We dern shore ate 'em!

1955 SENIORS TODAY

Bo Bolinger, of Tempe, Arizona, is a personnel scout for the St. Louis Cardinals professional football team.

Robert Burris is a salesman for Newpark Drilling Fluids, Inc., Oklahoma City, Oklahoma.

Joe Mobra, of Tulsa, Oklahoma sales representative for Rockwell International, died March 4, 1981.

Cecil Morris is head football coach at Cameron University, Lawton, Oklahoma.

Calvin Woodworth owns and operates Woodworth Hardware and Furniture, Minco, Oklahoma. He also services electrical, heating, and air-conditioning, plumbing and water pumps in the town. He is the Minco fire chief too.

11. A REMARKABLE TEAM

Slimmed by summer running and dieting, Oklahoma's defending national champions scrimmaged on the second morning of fall practice as they began drills for the opening game of 1956 against Coach Jim Tatum's North Carolina Tar Heels at Norman. Tatum had switched from Maryland back to Carolina, where he had coached in 1942.

Led by cocaptains Jerry Tubbs and Ed Gray, the Sooners reported for duty nearly six pounds lighter per man than they had been in spring practice. Oklahoma kept most of its 1955 talent and drew a fair number of sophomores besides.

"I hope everybody tries as hard this year as last," Wilkinson said. "Last year we had great effort. We went after everybody hard. However, very few people try as hard to stay good as they do to get good."

The Sooners assimilated that challenge just as they did their daily training routine. They were awakened in three waves, at 5:30, 5:40, and 5:50 A.M. Clad in pajamas and jeans and yawning, they walked across the street to the stadium and drank a juice consisting of two parts of frozen grape to one of lime. Trainer Ken Rawlinson said that concoction stayed down better than anything else.

Scheduled early to avoid the 90-degree heat, the morning workout lasted from 6:30 to 8:30, after which the Sooners showered and trooped back to Jeff dining room for breakfast, a two-hour nap, and group instruction meetings with various coaches in the fieldhouse. After lunch was served, with sherbet for dessert, came the afternoon nap, more meetings, and the afternoon workout from 4 to 6.

Midway in both morning and afternoon practices all activity was halted while student managers distributed cartons of frosted orange quarters that had lain all night in the deep freeze. The hot players went for those. There was no water on the field. If it was dusty, an astringent was brought out, and practice halted while the players gargled.

After dinner the men had free time. If the night was hot, they sometimes went to a movie theater and dozed in the air-conditioning. There was an inflexible rule that they must be in bed with the lights out at 10:30 P.M., but the coaches made no bed check. They didn't have to.

"We disciplined ourselves," says guard Buddy Oujesky. "A strong closeness existed among us."

Would Oklahoma fast-break again in 1956, the press asked Wilkinson. "Very probably," Bud replied. "It's a system that succeeds because it creates a tempo the defense isn't accustomed to. To combat it, the defense must learn to use fewer defenses and call them faster. Any time you can play a game at your own tempo, it's to your advantage."

As the Burris brothers had proved, farm work was excellent for developing football players. One of the sophomores that fall was Bob Harrison, of Stamford, Texas, whose father lived in town but farmed 1,000 acres, chiefly row crops like cotton and maize. Harrison drove a tractor, chopped cotton, and pulled bolls. Stamford always had a good team.

"During my last three years they finished 14-1, 12-1, and 9-1. After they got rid of me, they won 35 straight," Harrison chuckles.

The sophomore who got kidded the most was swarthy little Jefferson Davis Sandefer III, of Breckenridge, Texas. "Lots of yes, sirs, in a name like that," he remembers. "Always had a lot of nicknames," he went on. "Don't want to repeat some of them."

The Sooners called him Jakie. His dad was J. D. Sandefer, Jr., a wealthy Breckenridge oil operator. The only trouble with that was the Sooners never let Jakie forget it. The first thing he did as a sophomore was sprain his ankle. "They said I fell off my purse and hurt it," he recalls. They made a great show of urging him to persuade his father "to buy the university so we can all pass."

Young Sandefer took all the well-meant jesting in stride. Usually he just grinned and went along with the gag. Occasionally he would originate some of it. Like the recession. Everyone was talking about it. "If it doesn't slacken off, I'm gonna have to let my old man go," he told the team. He was highly respected by the Oklahoma players.

Brewster Hobby, a freshman from Midwest City, had his mind set on becoming a major-league baseball player. With his father he was planning a visit to a professional club when Wilkinson and Sam Lyle, Bud's assistant, showed up at the Hobby residence to have breakfast with the family.

"Bud sold me, strongly and sincerely, on the importance of getting a good education," Hobby recalls. "He said I could play baseball at OU, and I did."

Hobby recalls his first contact with Port Robertson. "When he walked up behind you and cleared his throat, a gentle little scratchy sound, you knew you were in trouble," says Hobby.

When Hobby missed a week of classes while recuperating in an Oklahoma City hospital after surgery for removal of a calcium deposit, he for-

196

got to get a dismissal slip from the surgeon. Robertson made him go back to Oklahoma City for the slip. When you missed a week of classes, you had to give Port a reason.

The 1956 backfield had one change. Robert Burris had graduated at right half. Clendon Thomas, who had played left half for the alternates, was moved into Burris's spot. "At first it was awkward trying to run and throw going to my left," Thomas says. "Also learning the corner position on defense. But it got a little easier with each game."

Thomas and Tommy McDonald made a great pair of halfbacks. Let's let quarterback Jimmy Harris describe each. "Clendon ran with a long stride. He'd be going full speed after the first two steps. He kept his head up and hit the open hole as well as anybody I ever saw. He was easy to hand off to. I always knew exactly where he'd be. He was a fine defensive back too.

"Tommy's strong point was enthusiasm. He had more desire than anybody I ever saw. He was a bit of a showman, and the people loved it. He could jump and catch the ball, and he could throw it. He was smart, and he could hit. He could have played defensive back with the pros. He was an excellent player."

After the Orange Bowl game Pricer again had surgery on both knees and then rejoined the team. He is believed to have submitted to more knee operations—seven—than any other Sooner player in history. His powers of recuperation were remarkable.

Joe Rector, a Muskogee sophomore, learned right off about Wilkinson's meticulous preparation for each game. "He was so organized," Rector remembers, "that we'd play the game back and forth ten times before the actual kickoff. Once it started, we could have played it blindfolded. This gave us lots of confidence. I always knew exactly what I was supposed to do on every situation. It was automatic."

The North Carolina opener was notable because the Sooners were aiming for a new record of thirty-one straight victories, tying that of Bud's 1948–50 teams. How many schools have had coaches who twice directed their teams to thirty-one-game winning skeins?

Oklahoma's problem was casualties at left halfback (McDonald, hyperextended knee; Jakie Sandefer, ankle twist). Otherwise the Sooners were ready. So was the 140-piece Oklahoma marching band. Bandmaster Leonard Haug seemed proudest of Mary Bettis, a home-economics major and tuba player from Amarillo, Texas, who was married and had two daughters.

Tatum's Tar Heels, like nearly every opponent Oklahoma met, came after the Sooners hard. But the Sooners quickly put the game away. Billy Pricer's 78-yard quick kick set up the first touchdown. Clendon Thomas's deft handling of an intercepted pass, which he lateraled to McDonald for 40 more yards, introduced the second. With only 44 seconds left in the first half, Jimmy Harris saw McDonald streaking for the end zone with Tar Heels in hot pursuit. Like a smooth roper whose hemp flows freely through the loop, Harris shot the pass in a long beeline, and McDonald snared it. Pricer kicked goal. Wilkinson used 59 players. Oklahoma won 36-0.

In the most unusual double injury in Sooner football history, both tackle Wayne Greenlee and guard Ken Northcutt broke small bones in their legs and were lost for the season. Both were hurt in the first half while playing side by side in the Sooner starting line. Each broke his leg about three inches above the ankle. They shared a room at the University infirmary. The scheduling of the operations put an end to the parallel. Both couldn't be operated on simultaneously. They tossed a coin. Northcutt won the flip. He decided to go second so that Doctors Don O'Donoghue, the surgeon, and Mike Willard, team physician, could "practice on Greenlee and be ready for me." That's the way it was done.

Wilkinson played his starters only eighteen minutes during the 66-0 romp over Kansas State at Norman, but the Sooner seconds and thirds performed so impressively that they got most of the praise dished out by the Wildcats when reporters interviewed them after the game. Center Kerry Clifford praised the Sooner middle guards, "especially that 70 [Dick Gwinn]." The entire Kansas State squad acclaimed the Sooner hustle.

A classic illustration of the burning Sooner hustle was contributed by Tommy McDonald while the starters were on the field. Once when McDonald was roughly upended across the sideline and lost his shoe, he left it lying on the turf and, hurrying back to the huddle, worked his fake into the line while wearing only the sock on his left foot.

The Texas-Oklahoma series had reached an odd milestone. Although Longhorn outfits had thrashed Sooner clubs thirty times while losing eighteen and tying two, Oklahoma teams coached by Wilkinson held a 7-2 margin over the Orange, and all Oklahoma gloried in it.

"When we flew into Fort Worth the day before the game," recalls Billy Pricer, Sooner fullback, "we were kidding and cutting up. Bud called off our Friday practice. Then he called a team meeting. To our surprise, he was quiet, subdued, resigned to defeat.

"You haven't practiced at all well this week," he said, "but then it's no disgrace to be beaten by a team as strong as Texas. Even when they beat you tomorrow, remember, you're still Oklahoma. So be sure to hold your heads up high."

"That got us to thinking," said Pricer. "We had a team meeting and voted not to go to the movie that night. Instead, we chose to stay in our hotel and study our game assignments. But at breakfast next morning, the coach was still gloomy. During our pregame meal he let us have it again. 'Keep your heads high,' he told us. 'It's no disgrace to get beat by as strong a team as Texas.' By that time we weren't about to let Texas beat us. We had too much pride, speed, and togetherness."

In the Sooner dressing room before the game, the Oklahoma squad was suited, ready to play. But Wilkinson hadn't come in to lead them out. It was almost kickoff time, and the tension was as thick as low country fog.

Ed Gray, lying on the floor, raised up on one elbow. "Wish the old man would come on in and tell us that bird story so we can go out and kick the hell out of 'em," he growled. The Sooners roared. That crack by their cocaptain loosened them up beautifully for the fray.

The Sooners showed their enthusiasm from the opening kickoff. Tommy McDonald ran it back 54 yards to the Texas 44. Oklahoma scored in seven plays. Clendon Thomas knifed across from 2 yards out, riding the shirttails of blockers John Bell, Emerson, Krisher, and Tubbs.

Coach Ed Price and his staff had Texas ready to play. Once Texas rushed so hard on a pass that Oklahoma lost 29 yards. Then Harris called a fooler. Pricer backed up a step, faking a quick kick. He swung his leg but instead of booting the ball handed it off behind him to Thomas on a Statue of Liberty play. Picking up downfield support by Tubbs and Oujesky, Thomas ran 44 yards to the Texas 20. Two minutes later McDonald zipped between two tacklers to score.

Just before the half Jimmy Harris rocked back on his heel and sent the ball winging on a long cross-country ride that suggested a squadron of wild geese cruising in regal splendor toward some distant feeding ground. Down on the Texas 20, McDonald leaped for it, speared it on his fingertips and, helped by Bell's block and also Oujesky's, raced across the goal with only 27 seconds left on the clock. Elated, McDonald turned around, ran back up the gridiron, and, grinning joyfully, jumped astride Harris, yoking his legs around the quarterback's middle and his arms around Harris's neck.

"McDonald's enthusiasm, . . . the obvious thrill he got out of doing something well, certainly was impressive," wrote Homer Norton, former Texas Aggie coach who covered the game for the *Houston Post.* Norton's 1939 Texas Aggies had won the national championship. Anything he wrote about football was read with attention.

Oklahoma's starters began the last half by driving 80 yards from kickoff to score. Thomas took it over with an 8-yard shot. McDonald helped with an incredible catch of a Harris pass while lying almost on his side.

199

Fullback Billy Pricer fakes a quick kick and hands off to Clendon Thomas, who ran 44 yards against Texas as the Sooners won 45-0.

Tommy McDonald flitting 45 yards to a touchdown against Texas.

Fullback Billy Pricer rolls 37 yards to the first touchdown in the 1956 Oklahoma A&M game.

Jimmy Harris pegs a long one to Don Stiller against Missouri in 1956.

Blackie Sherrod, *Fort Worth Press* sports editor, described the game as follows: "The rampaging citizens from up country did everything with a tremendous display of energy. They ran furiously, blocked and tackled like they were angry with the universe. They passed, and yes, even fumbled, in a high-handed manner."

Once in the last half the Sooners came out in a Swinging Gate formation, in which all their linemen were strung out fifteen yards to the right of Tubbs with Thomas stationed behind them. Tubbs, the center, got over the ball. Harris, Pricer, and McDonald lined up in tandem behind him. With Tubbs blocking, Harris ran down the left sideline to the Texas 39. There he lateraled to Pricer who ran 10 yards farther. The Sooners soon scored.

"They are an exceptionally interesting club to watch," Homer Norton wrote of this maneuver. "They used everything in the book. . . . I was impressed with their ability to come up with a surprise play when they needed big yardage for a first down. . . . Oklahoma has now put the pressure back on the defense. . . . Bud Wilkinson has done an outstanding job. I sincerely believe that he is the smoothest and cleverest coach in football today." Final score was 45-0.

In the Kansas game Oklahoma yielded two touchdowns while winning 34-12. Those Jayhawker touchdowns were the first scored against Gomer Jones's defense in eight straight regular season games.

The most astonished person in the stadium was probably Buddy Oujesky, Sooner guard. "Some Jayhawker 'chinned' me when I rushed through trying to block a punt," Oujesky remembers. "I was knocked colder than a wedge. When I came to on the bench and saw that '12' under 'Kansas' on the scoreboard, I couldn't understand it. I got scared. I jumped up and started to go back into the game, but Gomer wouldn't let me."

The Sooners started well. Clendon Thomas ran back the kickoff 40 yards and six plays later scored on the handoff. With McDonald holding, Harris kicked goal. Then the militant mood of the Jayhawkers asserted itself. Homer Floyd, their speedy fullback, ran the kickoff back 36 yards to McDonald, last Sooner tackler. Tommy nailed him, but Kansas drove 45 yards to score. Dennit Morris got a hand on their extra-point try. Oklahoma led 7-6.

Then the Sooners scored three times. McDonald used a block by Pricer to skirt the strong side for 12 yards and the first one. After Bob Harrison, Dennit Morris, and Doyle Jennings stopped Kansas runs, forcing a punt, the alternates trekked 61 yards to pay dirt, Bob Timberlake making a diving catch of David Baker's pass to score. Baker kicked goal.

The starters came in and scored on a dash by McDonald, and Oklahoma led 27-6 at the half and apparently was cruising. With the Notre Dame game next on the slate, there seemed no purpose in trying to annihilate one's northern neighbor. But Oklahoma won the last half only 7 to 6. Kansas fought magnificently.

"After the game," Tommy McDonald remembers, "the Kansas fans swarmed the field like they'd beaten us."

"We had our feelings hurt," remembers Pricer. "Bud and Gomer were busy cheering us up. We didn't think anybody could even score on us, let alone score 12."

Oklahoma destroyed Notre Dame 40-0 at South Bend, the first time the Irish had been shut out in forty-seven straight games going back to Michigan State in 1951. The Sooner defense held the Irish rushing to 1.9 net yards a play; intercepted four passes, two of them for touchdowns; blocked an Irish punt; and held Paul Hornung, the big Irish quarterback who later won the Heisman Trophy, to a total of 7 yards rushing in 13 carries, knocking the ball loose from him three times. The game was broadcast to millions on national television. The South Bend crowd of 60,128 constituted an all-time record.

"We were all emotional and tight," remembers quarterback Jimmy Harris. "We wore our game faces. Although they'd been beaten by Michigan State, all we heard was how tough Notre Dame would be at South Bend.

"Jay O'Neal and Dale Sherrod and I went into Bud's room for a quarterback meeting," Harris went on. "Bud had a funny little fighting grin on his face that we'd never seen before. 'Just relax,' he told us. 'We're going to kick the hell out of these guys.'" The quarterbacks stared at him in awe.

Harris remembers that against the Irish the Sooners used for the first time a new formation with the left end widened and the right half flankered. "This was new to Oklahoma," Harris points out. "We could option either way. This opened us up, got us out around the ends, gave us a lot of versatility for the type of team we were—lean, quick, superfast." In this game the Sooners abandoned their fast break, staying mainly with the double flankers, who needed time to return to the huddle after each play.

The Sooners came out first for their calisthenics. "Notre Dame's squad appeared, ran through the Sooner circle, then came back through it again, stopped, and started taking their calisthenics, growling like dogs," recalls Billy Pricer. Wilkinson moved the Sooners off a little and soon sent them to the dressing room. The afternoon was bright and sunny, 64 degrees at kickoff. A slight east wind was blowing.

The Sooners got off to a great start, marching 69 yards in ten plays to score. Oklahoma's blockers cut McDonald around right end for 18. Then they broke Thomas around the opposite flank for 9 more. Harris kept moving Oklahoma with ground plays until they reached the Irish 14. Then he rolled out to his right and hit John Bell with a running pass for the first touchdown. "Jimmy was a fine thrower," recalls Clendon Thomas. "He was more accurate than Billy Wade."[1]

On Notre Dame's first scrimmage play Hornung, 205-pound Notre Dame quarterback, swung the Sooner left flank at full speed. Jerry Tubbs, Sooner center, flashed in fast from his linebacker post and hit Hornung a solid crack, driving him back deep into his own backfield.

"Tubbs was the nicest guy in the world until he put on his helmet," remembers Clendon Thomas.

"We had an X-stunt on for the play," recalls Buddy Oujesky, Sooner guard. "I slanted to the inside. Notre Dame's right guard and right tackle both went for me. This left Tubbs an open avenue. I'd grown up wanting to go to Notre Dame. I'm sure my size didn't impress them, so I was delighted to be a small part of beating them." The only Catholic on the Oklahoma team, Oujesky would have no difficulty making the All-American Catholic team that year.

Wilkinson sent in the alternates. David Baker quick-kicked 60 yards to give Oklahoma field position. On fourth down from their 22, Notre Dame tried a punt by Dean Studor. A faulty snapback made him kick late. Steve Jennings blocked the ball. Bob Timberlake caught it in midair and ran to the Irish 3. Two plays later Jay O'Neal scored on a quarterback sneak behind blocks by Bob Harrison, Steve Jennings, and Doyle Jennings. Carl Dodd kicked goal. Oklahoma led 13-0 at the first quarter.

Early in the second quarter the Sooner starters entered and wheeled 64 yards to the end zone in eight plays. Jimmy Harris's 17-yard pass to McDonald to the Irish 18 was the long gainer. Thomas hit very fast on the handoff and was scarcely touched after his blockers burst the Irish line. Thomas still remembers Krisher's block. "As we ran up to the scrimmage line, Bill widened out to within a foot of Tom Emerson, our right tackle. His Notre Dame opponent widened out with him. When the ball was snapped, Bill drove straight through his man. The hole was so wide that after Tubbs came across to get their linebacker all I had to do was run."

Just before the half ended, Morse, of Notre Dame, tried a forward pass. Rushed by Pricer, he threw hurriedly. McDonald snatched the ball from an Irish receiver's hands and, using open field blocks by Pricer, Emerson, and Thomas, ran the interception back 55 yards to score. When Harris kicked goal, Oklahoma led 26-0 at intermission.

---

[1] Billy Wade, former Vanderbilt star, was a prime passer for the Chicago Bears and the Los Angeles Rams.

Boyd Gunning, OU alumni secretary, related an amusing sidelight to that play at a later alumni breakfast in Chicago. "A big Irish rooter, weighing about 260 pounds and wearing a little green derby over one eye, was making himself obnoxious in the stadium. When on an Irish punt McDonald signaled for a fair catch, this big guy stood and yelled, "Chicken! Chicken!"

Later, when little Tommy picked off Morris's pass and, hitting the ground in high leaps, ran 55 yards to a touchdown, an Oklahoma woman who was wearing a white dress, and sitting four rows down from Green Derby stood and faced him. "Sir," she said, "that's chicken, southern style!"

Notre Dame came back hard in the last half, driving from kickoff to the Sooner 35 before McDonald intercepted a Hornung pass. Here Oklahoma drove 83 yards to a touchdown. Tubbs, Krisher, and Oujesky blocked Harris over on a sneak.

Early in the fourth period Thomas intercepted Hornung's pass and ran down the right sideline 36 yards to another touchdown, with John Bell taking out the one tackler who might have stopped the play. Pricer remembers, "I hit Hornung just as he released the ball. I rolled over on one knee. I heard the crowd roaring and I thought Hornung had completed the pass. I looked up and here came a wave of green jerseys chasing Thomas, who had the ball."

Bell, who had fielded a pass to score Oklahoma's first touchdown and had thrown a smashing block to set up the last one, was living proof that you don't have to have exceptional ability to be a good football player. His hustle and aggressiveness were the talk of the Oklahoma squad. They called him everything from "Mad John" to "Herman the German." "He's the tiredest and hustlingest guy out there," said tackle Tom Emerson. "He and Tommy McDonald set the pace." "A full-speed guy. Can't do it any other way," laughed assistant coach Sam Lyle. "He hits like a horse and a half," said Tommy McDonald, who played behind Bell on defense.

A quiet, droll, mature fellow, Bell could sit down with you and talk about crops, farm parity, or politics. He subscribed to five magazines. He could sleep like a log with the radio or television turned on full blast. Although he was the most immaculate dresser on the squad, in a football game he tried to undress every opponent he tackled.

The Sooners were lighthearted, almost festive and gay, on the night before the Colorado game as they watched a Bud Wilkinson Quaker Oats commercial on national television while having dinner in a Denver hotel. In the commercial Wilkinson was holding a small boy on his lap.

"I don't like Quaker Oats. It's sissy food," fussed the boy. Bud said,

Coordinated charge of Oklahoma alternate line as it blocks quarterback Jay O'Neal to a touchdown against Notre Dame in 1956.

Line coach Gomer Jones and tackle Ed Gray embrace following the Sooners' 40-0 triumph over Notre Dame at South Bend in 1956.

John Bell, Sooner right end in 1955 and 1956.

"If it's sissy food, then I have sixty sissies who eat it every morning as part of their training schedule."

Next morning the Sooners were having their pregame breakfast. Harris, McDonald, and Pricer were sitting together. Wilkinson and Gomer Jones were dining at a small table in a corner. There was no oatmeal anywhere.

Harris asked the waitress to go to Wilkinson's table and ask "the white-haired gentleman" when his boys could have their oatmeal. She approached the two coaches just as Gomer was picking up his cup of hot coffee.

"Your boys want to know when they can have their oatmeal," the waitress told Bud.

Gomer, strangling with mirth, began spitting his coffee all over Wilkinson. "Bud always blamed me afterward, but I had nothing to do with it," Pricer insists. "I was too busy eating. When there's food around I don't talk. I eat."

That afternoon Oklahoma kicked off before a sellout crowd of 46,563 that packed Colorado's new stadium at mile-high Folsom Field. The mercury stood at 27 degrees, and it was tooth-chilling cold. Business manager Ken Farris remembers that he had purchased thirty-six sets of long underwear for the Sooners to wear beneath their uniforms. The sky was overcast. Although it had snowed five inches, the Colorado people had done a thorough job of cleaning the field. The footing was excellent, considering the circumstances.

After Ward Dowler, the Buff quarterback, punted out on the Oklahoma 10, the Sooners tried a quick kick, but Colorado was ready for it. John Wooten, their guard, blocked it, and John Bayuk, their fullback, had only to field the bounding ball in the end zone for a touchdown. The sellout crowd stood and roared its pleasure.

After the Sooner alternates came in and fought evenly with the Buffs, Wilkinson sent his starters back into the game, and they scored when quarterback Jimmy Harris drilled a forward pass down the middle to McDonald, who caught the ball on the run and sped across the goal. The 6,240 Oklahomans who had traveled nearly 700 miles, mostly by auto, part of it through a blizzard, cheered, but the Sooners missed the conversion. Colorado led 7-6.

Then came a tragic play. Late in the first quarter Colorado quick-kicked. McDonald ran back and swept up the ball. "I had a bad cold," McDonald says today, "but I didn't tell anybody because I wanted to play so badly. I kept asking Ken Rawlinson for throat lozenges to suck on. I looked around and saw that Colorado was all spread out. Picking a path, I ran the punt back 75 yards to a touchdown when Billy Pricer, our fullback, rolled the last Colorado tackler with a beautiful downfield block.

"In the end zone I turned around and saw a red flag lying on the grass back up the field. To myself I said, "Who in God's world could pull a red flag out of his pocket under circumstances like these? If he only knew how sore my throat was, how hard it had been to sprint 75 yards in that altitude, and how difficult it was for me to breathe, he would never have dropped that flag.'"

Colorado's ground game tore Oklahoma to shreds in the second quarter. Jimmy Harris postponed touchdowns by tackling Dove and later halfback Howard Cook in the Sooner secondary. Dove double-reversed for a touchdown. Later, on a pitchout off Coach Ward's T-formation, Stransky crossed the goal standing with only 36 seconds left in the half.

McDonald shot through to block Stransky's conversion. This proved to be an important play. However, the Sooners trailed 19-6 and appeared doomed to defeat.

In the Sooner dressing room at the half, Wilkinson hadn't come in. "Everybody was getting antsy," Joe Rector recalls. "Then Jerry Tubbs yelled 'Sit down!' and we all sat down. Nobody panicked. Finally Bud walked in. His face was white.

"'Men, take off those OU jerseys,' he told us. 'You don't deserve to wear the colors that the people who played ahead of you wore while building that fine Oklahoma tradition.' He'd warned us all week that we weren't practicing well after the Notre Dame victory."

President Cross, who frequently visited the Sooners' halftime sessions recalls that Wilkinson, gradually becoming calmer, told his team to put the first half out of their minds and start a new ball game when play resumed. They were not to try to catch up. The second half would be a new game that they were capable of winning by three touchdowns if they put their minds to it. He finished his commentary with the remark, "Here's one man who thinks you can still win."

"He left the dressing room to let us think about it," remembers Buddy Oujesky. "Our senior leaders took over." Tubbs and Ed Gray, the captains, arose. "Okay," they said, "let's go out and get it done."

"And when our guys decided they could do it, we went down on the field," Clendon Thomas remembers. "I don't mean to sound cocky, but we knew we could do anything we wanted to do. Nobody could beat us. Nobody could handle us. Get out of our way!"

The battle's turning point came on only the fourth play of the last half. Colorado had kicked off over the Oklahoma goal. Oklahoma had the ball on its own 28, fourth down, 2 to go. Quarterback Jimmy Harris decided to gamble, going for the first down. "Let's block," Harris warned his huddle. "This might be the ball game."

Clendon Thomas got it on a slashing 3-yard buck behind blockers Bill Krisher, Tom Emerson, and John Bell. "I knew that Clendon could hit the hole and cut fast," Harris explains his choice. "He was big and fast and easy to hand off to. He and Bob Herndon were the best I ever played with at taking a handoff at full speed."

With the line blocking magnificently, the Sooner drive lengthened. Mc-Donald's 11-yard burst with a pitchout put them over the center stripe. McDonald's 22-yard cutback earned a first down on the Colorado 15. Soon the Sooners were on the Buffalo 6, fourth down and 1 to go.

Tubbs, Sooner center, brought word back that Colorado was loaded in a goal-line defense. Harris called the option run or pass. McDonald threw to Thomas in the end zone for the touchdown.

"Jimmy pitched it to me," McDonald remembers. "The Colorado players were in my face. Clendon was so wide open. I said to myself, 'Okay, boys, come and get me. Here goes the ball.' I was elated. Nobody was within 3 yards of Clendon!" Harris kicked goal. Now the Buffalo lead had been cut to 19-13.

"I was never so tired in my life," remembers Jerry Tubbs. "A winning tradition gives you so much pride. You reach down and get a little bit more." Clendon Thomas added, "That pride was started by the guys 'way back. Then it rubbed off on us. We played to win. None of us wanted to be on the team that ended the long winning streak."

In the third period Harris skipped back 18 yards with Dowler's punt. The Sooner line began blocking with purpose and savagery. From the Buffalo 11, Harris pitched the ball to McDonald running wide to the right. Tommy faked a pass and with a surge of speed dove past a tackler into the end zone. That tied the game, 19-19.

On the extra point Tubbs snapped the ball perfectly to the kneeling McDonald. The Sooner line protected stoutly. Tommy fielded the ball and set it up. Harris booted it squarely between the posts to give Oklahoma a 20-19 lead.

Billy Pricer said, "Dennit Morris was hurt, and I had to play three quarters. And after our third touchdown I had to kick off. Bud had told me, 'If you're tired, tell us and we'll get somebody else in.' I walked to the sideline. 'Coach,' I said, 'I'm pooped.'

"Bud grinned. He reached over and patted me on the rump. 'Go ahead and kick off and go down and get the tackle,' he said. Damn! That pat on the rump lifted me sky-high. I did kick off and go down and get the tackle. I could have played another full quarter."

The fourth period began. Tubbs and Pricer contained the Buff attack with smashing linebacking. Harris rolled to his left and spied Thomas running laterally across the end zone. Harris hit Thomas in the corner with a perfect pass good for 16 yards and the game-clinching touchdown. Harris kicked goal. Oklahoma 27, Colorado 19.

"That Colorado crowd was a wild one," remembers Doyle Jennings. "They kept shelling us with snowballs and coke-bottle tops. We were glad we wore helmets. Colorado had cleaned the snow off the field good, but after the game the field was so snowy from those snowballs that it looked like fresh snow had fallen."

After the game Wilkinson had high praise for Ward's Coloradans. He said, "Their offense is by far the most potent we have encountered this season. They are a sound, poised, courageous team." The Buffaloes proved it that season by finishing 8-2 and defeating Clemson in the Orange Bowl.

At Ames, Iowa, the weather was good and the field dry, and the Sooners laced the Cardinal and Gold 44-0. Oklahoma started the fracas by twice crisscrossing its halfbacks with pleasing results. First Harris pitched to McDonald who ran wide to the right then handed off to Thomas coming back wide to the left to the Cyclone 22. Five plays later McDonald bucked it over.

Three minutes later Harris reversed the strategy. This time he pitched to Thomas going wide to his left. Thomas handed off to McDonald coming back wide to the right. Tom Emerson blocked the end, and Jerry Tubbs flattened the defensive halfback so neatly that Tommy ran the distance without being touched. Oklahoma led 13-0.

With only 28 seconds left in the half, the Sooner starters came into possession on the Iowa State 45. It didn't seem possible to score in such a short time. But Harris somehow fitted four plays into 26 seconds. On the first, his screen pass was slapped down by Chuck Latting of the Cyclones. Then Harris passed to Don Stiller for 14 yards and Stiller rolled across the sideline to stop the clock. Harris pitched to McDonald who skirted the Cyclone left flank for 15 more and was tackled out of bounds with only eight seconds left.

On the fourth and final play Harris flicked a pass to Stiller for 16 yards and a touchdown with McDonald blocking out an opponent on the goal.

Joe Rector, sophomore right end, was the surprised recipient of a battle-field promotion that left him unnerved. "I was playing behind John Bell and Timberlake," recalls the rookie from Muskogee, "It was my first road trip, and I thought I was going to sit on the bench and watch the whole ball game. But in the first three minutes Bell was ejected by the officials, and Timberlake sprained an ankle, and before I knew it I was in there, and I wasn't ready.

"I played lousy. Going down on a punt, I ran into Tubbs, fell, and lay there, resting. I thought of something Vince Lombardi once said, "Fatigue makes cowards of us all." It was a great lesson for me. After that I always heeded Bud's insistence that everybody should be ready mentally."

As the last half started, Tubbs made a play that sparkled like a new silver dollar. Iowa State had reached the Sooner 30 after completing a pass. Quarterback Charley Martin tried another. Tubbs intercepted it and headed up the field. He ran the first 15 yards like a fullback, bowling over two tacklers. Then he adopted the tactics of a halfback, outsprinting all his pursuers, cutting away from one tackler on the 10 and diving into the end zone to evade the last one. The play illustrated the great determination with which the rangy Sooner pivot played.

Stung by a curious AP poll that dropped them into second place in the nation, though they drew 92 first-place votes to 58 for top-rated Tennessee, the red-jerseyed Sooners were in an exasperated mood when they spread across the field to receive the opening kickoff against Missouri. It was the first time in six weeks that Oklahoma had been forted up at home.

Oklahoma promptly fumbled that opening kickoff back to the Tigers on the Sooner 30. However, Billy Pricer and Jerry Tubbs wrecked Tiger plays. Ed Gray rushed the passer so hard that he threw wildly. On fourth down Missouri went for it, but John Bell rocketed through and tackled quarterback Jimmy Hunter for a 13-yard loss, giving the Sooners possession on their own 43.

Then the game went down its logical groove. Wanting the victory badly and restoration of their leadership in the national polls, the Sooners struck off touchdown after touchdown. As so often happened, they did it largely with defense. Four times they intercepted Tiger forward passes (McDonald 2, Harris 1, Coyle 1), and each time these led to touchdowns.

Once Missouri came storming back with a 36-yard run by Hank Kuhlmann around the Sooner left flank. Kuhlmann seemed loose for a touchdown until McDonald sprinted across and knocked him over the sideline, turning him a complete flip. When only twelve seconds remained in the first half and the Sooners had the ball on the Missouri 41, Harris, as usual, laughed off the odds and spiraled a long touchdown pass to Don Stiller to beat the gun. At that point of the campaign Harris's seasonal record was 20 completions in 28 throws for .714 percent, though many of his pegs were running throws delivered while going to his left.

Early in the second half the stadium public-address man announced that, back East, Tennessee had beaten Mississippi 27-7. Goaded by the information, the Sooners turned it on and scored five more touchdowns, though Wilkinson used five full teams.

The final score, 67-14, distressed Wilkinson. "I've been thinking all night about the size of the score," he told me Sunday morning. "We were all fired up. You can't ask your boys to turn it off." An unusual coach, Wilkinson spent all day molding those slick Sooner powerhouses and then worried all night because they had done so brilliantly what he had taught them to do.

McDonald had another dashing day. Although he played less than half the battle, he rushed 136 net yards, averaging 12.3 a carry, and twice trod just inside the white chalk of the sideline for thrilling 58- and 23-yard touchdowns. He also pegged a touchdown pass to Thomas, intercepted two Missouri passes, and prevented a Tiger touchdown when he capsized Kuhlmann with the sideline tackle.

Concluding Wilkinson's first decade as head coach undefeated in conference play, the Sooners subdued Nebraska 54-6 at Norman, rushing 506 net yards and passing 150. With Tennessee extended a bit while conquering Kentucky 20-7, Oklahoma pulled further ahead in the AP and UP polls to determine the national champion.

With 1:43 left in the half Oklahoma fans had the thrilling situation they so enjoyed, Jimmy Harris versus the stadium time clock. Could Jimmy take the Sooners across the goal, 43 yards away, in 1:43? Jimmy did it so quickly that he punched out the stadium timepiece with one blow. Rocking back on his heel, he fired the ball down the fairway to McDonald who made a leaping grab and scored. Bud suited 55 men and played them all.

New goals awaited Oklahoma every week they played, yet the biggest of all confronted the Sooners at Stillwater. Gilmour Dobie, like Wilkinson a former Minnesota quarterback, had coached University of Washington teams that from 1908 through half of 1914 won 39 straight games, the all-time national record, Stone Age or modern, in college football. The Sooners had tied it with their Nebraska victory. Could they break it in the last game of the season?

Ineligible for bowl play, the Sooners closed their year against Oklahoma A&M at Stillwater. A few days before that game Vernon Snell, long-time sports editor of the *Oklahoma City Times,* asked Sooner seniors how they felt about their final tilt against the Aggies.

Pride came into Jerry Tubbs's face when the question came to him. "I only hope I'm able in life to be in an organization with as much unity and spirit as this team. I'm taking away so much more than I can ever repay," he said.

Byron Searcy, Oklahoma's rangy part-Indian tackle, who scaled a slim 203 and wore a burr haircut, likened the Oklahoma team's flaming spirit to a biblical passage in Matthew; "And whosoever shall compel thee to go

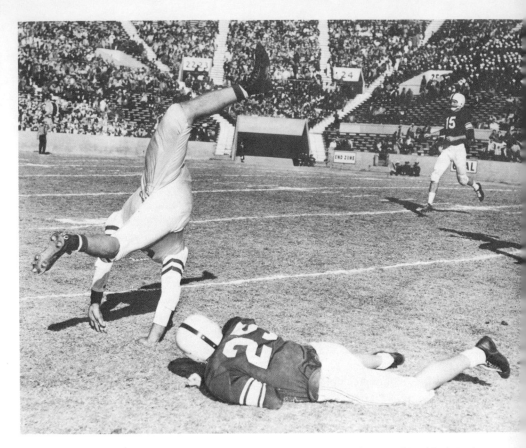

Tommy McDonald upends Nebraska end Clarence Cook with a smashing block in the 1956 game at Norman.

Tommy McDonald.

a mile, go with him twain." "It's that second effort you learn at Norman that's so important," he said. "In high school I think I made a real good first effort. But at Oklahoma it's the second effort they're most interested in. They go on the theory that everybody will make a good first effort."

Tom Emerson, the 6-foot, 4-inch tackle from Wilson, a serious, studious zoology major, grew taut for a moment when reminded that the Aggie game was the last of his life for the Sooners. "I truly hate to see it come," Emerson said slowly. "Somehow I foresee emptiness after it's over. These years have passed by so fast. It's a shame we couldn't bow out at home."

But the Sooners didn't bow out badly at Stillwater. They drove the opening kickoff back to a touchdown. Fullback Billy Pricer burst through, cut back, and ran 37 yards to score. The Aggies tried a pass, but Jay O'Neal leaped for it, scooped it off his shoestrings, and ran 63 yards down the sideline for another touchdown.

In the final moments Wilkinson inserted an all-senior team that marched 77 yards to the Aggie 2-yard mark. Ed Gray, the tackle and cocaptain, faced Harris in the huddle with a challenging grin. "I've never scored," he said. "It's my time."

Adjustments were made, and Harris called the play. Gray and Clendon Thomas traded positions, Gray going to right half and Thomas into the line. "If you think I didn't block for him after all those times he'd blocked for me, you're crazy," Thomas said later. McDonald leaped into one of the guard spots.

"On Gray's play, I was the center," says Billy Pricer. "The ball was snapped. Old Beaky came over the top. He was carrying the ball like a girl, with both points exposed, front to back. His whole arm was wrapped around the center of the ball. After he scored, he wouldn't give the ball to the referee. On the sideline Wilkinson was laughing his head off."

"You've been playing me at the wrong position for four years," Gray told Bud when the coach sent in another unit. The Sooner seniors wanted Bill Harris, senior end from Ardmore, to try the extra point, but somebody erred on the snap, and Bill didn't have a chance to get the ball off the ground. But he was in there with his group at the end. Final score, 53-0.

Thus the Sooners won their third national championship in six years under Wilkinson. They measured Tennessee 104 first-team votes to 48 in the AP poll and outdid the Vols 26-5 in firsts in the UP coaches poll. Wilkinson's career record with Oklahoma was ninety wins, seven defeats, and three ties in regular season play for .927 percent. His bowl record was 4-1.

Oklahoma's statistical feats in 1956 were almost endless. In offense, the Sooners led the country in total yards with 481.7 net a game, in rushing with 391 a game (national record), and in scoring with 46.6 points a game. They were second in kickoff returns with 24.5 yards' average per runback; second in own fumbles lost with 32; third in most yards penalized, 76.3 a game; and ninth in punt-return defense, holding opponents to 6 yards each runback. They averaged scoring seven touchdowns a game, garnering a total of seventy in the ten contests.

The Sooners submitted their finest national defensive showing of all time. They placed second in team defense with 193.8 yards a game yielded, second in pass interceptions with 26 or 423 yards, fourth in interception avoidance yielding only 5 interceptions in 100 throws, fifth in punting with 40.7 yards averaged, eighth in rushing defense with 138.3 yards yielded, and eleventh in pass defense with 55.5 yards yielded a game.

Clendon Thomas led the nation in scoring with 18 touchdowns and 108 points; McDonald was second with 17 and 102. McDonald placed fourth in interception returns with six for 136 yards. Pricer punted eleven times for an average of 48.6, but the Sooners didn't kick enough to qualify him for the national minimum. Only one other man in the country had a better average.

Oklahoma won the foremost-player prize of the times when the nation's coaches voted center Jerry Tubbs the Walter Camp Award as the outstanding player in the nation. No interior linesman had ever won it before. McDonald won the Robert W. Maxwell Memorial Award and also the *Sporting News* Award. McDonald and Tubbs knocked each other out of the balloting for the Heisman Trophy, Tommy finishing second, Tubbs fourth. Four Sooner players were selected on All-American first teams: Tubbs, Krisher, McDonald, and Gray.

McDonald's admiration for Tubbs still runs high today. "He was a coach's dream," the halfback praised, "smart, tough, great competitor, great attitude, great agility, excellent speed. He'd do anything the coaches asked. He was just plain old Jerry. He wasn't cocky. He was everything that typified an Oklahoma player—humble, compassionate, unselfish, ready to lay his life on the line for that football team. We all liked him so well that we wanted him to be our captain. Later he and I spent a week together with the College All-Stars and he was everybody's choice there for captain too."

Wilkinson's football lettermen were then graduating at a 90.6 percent pace, with his powerful 1949 team having graduated every one of its nineteen senior lettermen, his 1951 team having graduated all seven of its seniors, and his 1954 team having graduated twelve of thirteen. The thirteenth man on that squad, Tom Carroll, lifted his outfit to a perfect rating

214

Jerry Tubbs and Edmon Gray, co-captains of Oklahoma's 1956 national champions, receiving the Grantland Rice Award at Holmberg Hall, on the University campus. On their right are Wilkinson and Tim Cohane, sports editor of *Look* magazine.

three years later when he took two degrees simultaneously, one in petroleum engineering, the other in geological engineering.

Of his 1956 team Wilkinson said in his alumni letter, "I hope Gomer and I will be coaching for a fair number of years, but I doubt if we will ever be associated with a group of seniors, or a squad, with a finer balance of personalities or a more wholesome attitude towards the game than those who played for Oklahoma in 1956. These are the basic reasons why our team has played well."

215

1956 SENIORS TODAY

Tom Emerson is professor of zoology in Michigan State University, East Lansing, Michigan.

Ed Gray, owner of the Permian Pipe Company of Odessa, Texas, died in April, 1976.

Jimmy Harris is president of the Harris Oil and Land Company of Shreveport, Louisiana, and partner in the Midroc Operations Company of Shreveport.

Tommy McDonald is owner and president of McDonald Enterprises, which makes oil paintings of photos, and of Old McDonald Had a Firm, which makes plaques from photos, in King of Prussia, Pennsylvania.

Billy Pricer is vice-president and half owner of Neco Industries, an industrial supplying firm of Oklahoma City, Oklahoma.

Jerry Tubbs is linebacker coach of the Dallas Cowboys professional football team.

12. FORTY-SEVEN STRAIGHT

Prentice Gautt almost became a tuba player and a snare drummer instead of the first black football player ever to perform for the University of Oklahoma.

As a ninth grader at Oklahoma City Douglass Junior High School, Gautt had an idol: Frank Jones, quarterback of the Douglass High School football team. Jones was also a good musician. "I wanted to be just like him," Gautt recalls, "so I got in the Douglass Junior High band and played football too." They put him on the punt-return team.

"I lasted only two days," Gautt remembers. "Two Korean War veterans who came back to play for Douglass Senior High tried to run over me. They succeeded. They hit me just as I fielded a punt. Exit Prentice." Groggy and bruised, Gautt went back to the tuba and the drums.

Mose Miller, the Douglass coach, protested. "Hey," he told Gautt, "you'll never get a scholarship playing in the band. You're big and muscular. Come out for football and beat up on some of these people instead of on all those drums." Gautt returned to football.

In the summer, as a boy growing up, Prentice and his black companions would ride the interurban to Norman, walk to the OU stadium, climb over the seven-foot chain-wire fence, and run up and down the gridiron at Owen Field.

"Then we'd reclimb the fence and go back to the interurban station for the trip home,' he says. "Once we met a guy on the street at Norman. 'Better be out of town by six o'clock,'[1] he warned. We definitely beat the deadline.

Gautt wasn't the first black to try football with the Sooners. In 1954, two years earlier, three blacks from Oklahoma City Dunjee High School, Charles Parker, George Farmer, and Sylvester Norwood, had enrolled at OU and joined the freshman squad. Their coach at Dunjee was C. L. ("Curly") Sloss, who taught the split-T.

Norwood and Farmer commuted but, having no financial means, had to

---

[1] Norman's unwritten sundown law prohibited all blacks from living in Norman or inhabiting the streets after dark.

quit. Parker received a concussion when his head struck the steel frame of a blocking sled. He passed all 13 hours he carried but later transferred to Central State. [2]

"At Douglass they took winning for granted," Gautt says. "We traveled as widely as a college squad, meeting all the big black high-school teams in Texas, Kansas, Missouri, and Arkansas." As a junior and senior, he started on Miller's Trojan juggernauts. Douglass swept 31 consecutive games during this era.

Miller was an extraordinary coach. He had played at Langston for Zip Gayles, a high-quality mentor in both basketball and football. "You can rule the mountain if you have that old desire," Miller told his boys. "When you did something wrong, he'd whack the fence with a board he carried," Gautt remembers. "Anybody who ever played for him kept part of his philosophy for themselves. To get a compliment from him was to get a slice of heaven."

Gautt saw football as a means to an end. "I wanted social respect," he recalls. At Douglass he became president of the senior class, made the National Honor Society, won the Civitan Award for scholarship and activities, and won the DHS All-Around Boy Award. But Douglass remembers him most for football.

As a senior, Gautt played in the first integrated high-school game ever staged in Oklahoma, Douglass versus Oklahoma City Capitol Hill, coached by C. B. Speegle. Staged at the Capitol Hill Stadium, the battle drew 10,000 and was televised. Capitol Hill won 13-6. Gautt was just coming off an injury yet bowled up the middle for 30 yards and the Douglass touchdown. "Douglass and Capitol Hill had been scrimmaging each other since 1947," remembers Speegle, "but this was the first game."[3]

"Fighting was feared, but there was none," says Gautt. As usual, the kids themselves got along great, setting an example for the adults. After the game each school named one of its players to go to the other school and spend a full day. Gautt represented Douglass at Capitol Hill. "I took the Capitol Hill boy's classes there and he took mine at Douglass," Gautt says. "We had no trouble."

Gautt also became the first black to play in the Oklahoma High School all-state game. The North had injured both its fullbacks in practice. North coaches Bear Jensen, of Claremore, and Tractor Trent, of Dewey, asked permission from the Coaches Association Board of Control to use Gautt.

[2]C. L. ("Curly") Sloss, Charles Parker, and Jimmy Stewart to author, November 27, 1980.

[3]C. B. Speegle to author, November 12, 1980.

It was granted. Although it was then August, Gautt joined the North on Wednesday, only two days before the game, and learned the signals.

The Douglass power runner scored three touchdowns and sparked the North to a 33-9 victory before 12,000 at Taft Stadium. Gautt boomed 23 yards to the opening touchdown. Then he shocked the South by running 90 yards to score with the second-half kickoff. He was an easy choice as the game's outstanding back.

Meanwhile the Medi-Phar Association, a group of black physicians and pharmacists in Oklahoma City, raised $4,000 for a four-year scholarship for Gautt. They planned to send him all the way through OU.

"Stepping out of a car at the main gate of the university at Norman was both frightening and exciting," Gautt said later. "I was in a place where I had dreamed of playing football, yet I was afraid of all the obstacles."

In October, Wilkinson told the Medi-Phar Association that Gautt wouldn't need the money they had provided. He gave Prentice a full scholarship. Gautt rose to the left-half position on the freshman second team. One afternoon they practiced with the varsity, then climbed on a bus and rode to Tulsa, where they were defeated 33-12 by the Tulsa University frosh.

After the game the Boomers went to a Tulsa restaurant for dinner. Gautt was told they could not serve him. Immediately the entire team got up and walked out. Another café near the turnpike was found, and they were served. Hurt inwardly by the incident, Gautt was cheered by the way his teammates supported him. "I'll never forget how good Jere Durham, Jim Davis, and Brewster Hobby made me feel," he said later. "It was the most joyful moment I had known."

Gautt remembers Wilkinson as "a father figure. Soft-talking, always smiling, patting you on the back, he made you feel like you were a superperson to him." Gautt also appreciated Bob Burris, a student coach. "He always believed in me," says Prentice. 'Hey,' he told me one day, 'you're as good or better than anybody out here.'" Eddie Crowder, then in his second season as varsity assistant coach, was another of his favorites. Gomer Jones? "I always had the feeling that he knew totally what he was doing," says Prentice.

"I always wanted everybody to like me," Gautt says today. "I think that was a flaw. If I wanted people to like me, I would only show them that half of me I thought was most attractive. So I wound up being only half a person in the presence of the very people I most wanted to impress. There were so many parts of me that I was having problems with. I felt like I was walking on eggshells.

"I had such an insecure feeling coming from a black environment into different social conditions. I'd see the signs at the railroad depots and the bus terminals, 'Colored Rest Room' or 'Colored Water Fountain,' like I was an animal. Mose (his coach at Douglass) didn't want me to go to OU. 'Ada Sipuel[4] had a great problem there,' he said."

However, Mrs. Minerva Sloss, Gautt's English teacher at Douglass and wife of the football coach at Dunjee, put it to him beautifully when she said, "Nobody can make you feel inferior without your consent to it."

Wilkinson talked to him frequently, preparing him for the rebuffs ahead. The coach shielded him from occasional alumni opposition and hostility. "My respect for him deepened," says Gautt today. "Oklahoma then was flushed with national championships. He didn't need me, or any kind of a controversy. But he never let me know about the hate mail he received. I found out about that later."

As a sophomore, Gautt did not play well. "I wasn't hitting with any intensity," he remembers. "Bud told me, 'The way you're playing, you're not even going to make our traveling squad.' But behind his words he seemed to be saying, 'I know that you can do better.' I always felt he believed in me."

Gautt gradually became adjusted to living and performing in a white world. Some freshman players did not want to play on the same team with him. One transferred to another school. But as a sophomore he made more progress. "My fears gradually turned out to be, for the most part, only in my head," he sums it up today.

The outlook for 1957 was uncertain. The only returning starters were Stiller, Oujesky, Krisher, and Thomas. The offense had to be altered radically to compensate for the loss of speed, run-pass option threat, and experience. The only encouraging aspect was that the Sooners had a coach who was skilled at crafting strong teams from ordinary talent and experience.

Exciting news came from the rest of the Big Seven Conference that was organizing soundly to reduce Oklahoma's dominance. Missouri installed the Georgia Tech system, hiring Frank Broyles, Bobby Dodd's long-time assistant. Iowa State switched to UCLA's successful single-wing style and hired Jim Myers, Red Sanders's line tutor, to teach it. Nebraska set up the Oklahoma system, moving Bill Jennings, one of Bud's most trusted assistants, into Pete Elliott's head job when Elliott changed to California. And Darrell Royal, Oklahoma's little all-round back of 1946-47-48-49, left the University of Washington post to take the Texas job.

Two-a-day practices in the early September heat can be punishing. I decided to ask Don Stiller, cocaptain from Shawnee, about it.

"Nobody likes 'em," said Stiller. "But they're what make our team. They

[4]Black student Ada Sipuel's admission to the University of Oklahoma after a protracted legal struggle ended desegregation at the institution.

hurt worse the first five days in the heat. You're not used to being hit. Every muscle is sore. You're so tired you can't eat or sleep. Each day after practice we all get empty half-gallon tomato cans from the dining room and fill them with milk, water, lemonade, or orange juice and lots of cracked ice. We carry them around, sipping from them.

"Two-a-days are tough on our coaches, too. Gomer always gets hoarse about the fourth day. Sam Lyle is too tired to gesture when he talks. Ted Youngling gives out a little quicker on the push-ups when he leads our calisthenics. But after five days everybody begins to get used to it."

One of the sophomores who quickly made a mark for himself was Bobby Boyd of Garland, Texas. "He was smart and tough," remembers Clendon Thomas. "He'd try to knock your head off. Of course, we had these in abundance."

Jimmy Carpenter, a little sandy-thatched freshman back from Abilene, Texas, came up that fall to study petroleum land management and play football. Carpenter's town, Abilene, stayed in a football ferment. His fifth-grade team played a ten-game schedule. "We played block and tackle, the good old rough kind," Carpenter says. His seventh- and eighth-grade teams played two games weekly, twenty-five for the year.

"Our ninth-grade team, traveling to San Angelo for a game, became ill from food poisoning on the way," Carpenter remembers. "We played anyhow, and won." His Abilene High School teams won 49 straight games and swept the state 4-A championship his last three seasons.

Why did he come to Oklahoma? "I liked Eddie Crowder, the assistant coach who recruited me," says Carpenter. "I liked Coach Wilkinson. Oklahoma didn't try to recruit us illegally. Other schools would offer to buy our girlfriends a gift. At Oklahoma they took us duck hunting out into the western part of the state, and that was it."

Leon Cross, a guard from Hobbs, New Mexico, High School, came from a losing team. In grade school he played flag football. Despite his high-school team's 11 20 record for three seasons, Cross made all-state. He was recruited for Oklahoma by Gomer Jones.

Another promising freshman was Jerry Payne, end from Breckenridge, Texas. Payne had hurt his knee in the Oil Bowl game and had to have it repaired. He took his revenge out on his textbooks, making A's in everything but military science.

"Once while we were practicing, Carl Dodd called the coach 'Bud' in front of everybody," Ross Coyle remembers. "For a moment there was a great silence on the field. Bud just laughed, relieving the tension."

On a later morning, when the coaches lined up the various teams, Brewster Hobby found himself on the same team as cocaptain Clendon

Thomas. "I thought I'd been promoted to the first team," remembers Hobby. "We'd scrimmaged the day before and I'd looked pretty good. However, both Clendon and I were actually down on the fourth team. Clendon had been demoted because he'd had a bad practice. Bud moved you up and down to get your attention."

The fellow who unseated Thomas that day was Johnny ("the Gnat") Pellow, tiny Enid junior who weighed only 160 when his wallet was full. A sprinter in track, Pellow's speed let him cover widely on pass defense. Besides, he was sharp on his assignments and tough as a picnic egg.

The new players liked and respected their head coach. "He was aloof, yet always approachable," remembers Ross Coyle. "There's a fine line there and he could walk it."

As usual, Wilkinson chose his players for their defensive ability. "I loved to play defense," end Joe Rector says. "Gomer taught us so well that I could play defense in my sleep—how to play a guy's head, how to keep my shoulders parallel with the line of scrimmage, how to fight off the blockers and string out the play."

Wilkinson didn't neglect blocking instruction. Gautt remembers that his first lesson came during a rain. "Coach taught the fullbacks to block by the numbers," Prentice remembers. "First, as you approach your opponent, you step with the inside foot directly toward the center of his body. Second, plant your outside foot on the outside of his outside foot. Third, throw your inside arm across his body. Fourth, push back on your outside foot as you throw your inside arm across his body. You had to get right in the guy's face." Gautt added, "There was a certain sweet sound about it when you did it right, a full impact, a sound like hitting a golf ball."

Gautt was the center of a problem when Oklahoma flew to Pittsburgh to open the season. Ken Farris, the business manager, had cleared him in advance with the hotel. But Gautt had no roommate.

Shortly after Oklahoma checked in, Jakie Sandefer asked Farris what arrangement he had made for Gautt. "I put him in a single," Farris answered.

"That won't be necessary," Sandefer said. "In the future, room him with me."

And that was how it was done. At Norman, Gautt lived in a single room. On the road, he roomed with Sandefer, the wealthy Texas kid.

"We both played left half," Sandefer says. "And it was customary for rivals for a position to room together so they could study the plays together. I roomed with him that year and all of the next year. Prentice was a fine person, a good student, a hell of a nice guy."

What was Gautt's impression of Sandefer? "The only evidence I ever saw that he had money was the little black leather coin purse he carried," laughs

Gautt today. "When he undressed at night, he'd take that little purse out of his pocket and put it on the dresser. It was small. Had room only for nickels, dimes, and quarters. Instead of carrying a roll of bills, he carried only as much change as the average high-school girl."

Once Sandefer, alone, became embroiled in a dispute with three other youths. "You just stay here," he told them. "I'll be back." At the athletic dorm he found Gautt.

"Hey," Gautt remembers he said. "I need you to go with me. I'm having some problems with some guys out here."

Gautt grinned. "Let's go," he said, pleased that Sandefer wanted his assistance. But the opposition had vanished.

Nearly 4,000 Sooner fans made the long trip to Pittsburgh. A crowd of 58,942 packed the stadium. Thousands more stood on a bluff overlooking the south goalposts.

Coach Johnny Michelosen's craggy maulers had also suffered losses from graduation. It was a game between two new teams, a big one and a little one. Clendon Thomas, Oklahoma's big halfback, recalls that "Oujesky was my blocking guard, yet I was bigger than he was. It bothered him some too, but he dug 'em out of there."

In the first half Oklahoma's light forwards bumped it out in the high humidity with Pitt's percherons on the spongy field. The decisive factor was Oklahoma's two teams. Pittsburgh's starters grew fatigued playing against both the Sooner starters and alternates. Once Byron Searcy, Sooner tackle, blocked Charley Brueckman, Pitt center. As Brueckman fell on Searcy, he said, "I wish you guys would call time-out. We've used up all of ours."

On fourth down and 4 from the Pitt 12, Quarterback Carl Dodd pitched to Sandefer going to the right. Sandefer took a quick look into the end zone and saw a white shirt streaking across the goal. Jakie pegged. Joe Rector turned, leaped, and came down with the ball for a touchdown, with a Pitt man on his back. Dodd kicked goal. Oklahoma led 7-0 at the half.

Oklahoma dominated the last half with its forcing defense. Joe Rector struck Bill Kaliden, Pitt quarterback, as he pitched, and Dennit Morris recovered the fumble on the Pitt 20. After Bill Krisher pulled from right guard and splattered the Pitt end, Thomas ran over two tacklers to slash into the end zone. Dodd forward passed to Stiller for the third. Dick Carpenter grabbed a deflected pass and raced to the fourth. Oklahoma won 26-0.

Wilkinson liked the Sooner effort. It was epitomized by David Baker, alternate quarterback, who once punted 40 yards then raced down the right sideline to tackle John Flara, Panther safety.

A new enemy, Asian flu, stalked the Oklahoma squad as they prepared for their 60th straight conference game without defeat, this one against unbeaten Iowa State. The Sooners were fortunate that the disease struck during an off week.

It struck hard. Five starters, cocaptains Clendon Thomas and Don Stiller, Bill Krisher, Joe Rector, and Doyle Jennings, spent most of the week in bed. Also hospitalized were alternates David Baker, David Rolle, and Ross Coyle. Wilkinson himself missed four days of practice during the idle week and, after suffering a relapse, cancelled his Monday appearance before the Oklahoma City Quarterback Club and went back to bed.

"We're 'way behind in our practice," David Baker told reporters from his bed in the University Infirmary, "and in our physical condition too." Had they had many guests? "Not many," Baker replied, "Guess they're afraid of catching it. Mrs. Wilkinson came to see us and I was asleep. I woke up later and saw the radio she left for us."

The 40-14 score by which Oklahoma won in no wise reflected the intensity of the contest. Iowa State's quarterback was Dwight Nichols, a tough little 23-year-old service veteran. The Sooners greeted him inhospitably when Ken Northcutt tackled the ball loose from him, Bob Harrison recovering on the Cyclone 20. Five plays later Carl Dodd slipped across the goal behind blocks by Northcutt and Harrison. Then the Sooners scored twice more, Thomas on a pitchout, Dodd on a fake pitch. Just before the half Nichols did better, flipping a pass to Gibson for 18 and a touchdown.

The decisive play of the game occurred early in the last half when Ross Coyle leaped phenomenally to spear a Nichols pass with one hand and come down with it on the Sooner 41. Oklahoma's alternates marched 59 yards to the decisive touchdown.

With the third quarter nearly over, left end Chuck Latting of the Cyclones walloped a punt 55 yards down to the Sooner 19. Jakie Sandefer drifted beneath it. Instantly, Oklahoma leaped into its blocking pattern along the west sideline. Sandefer cut fast from the sunshine in the field's center into the shade of the stadium along the west boundary. Resounding blocks by Morris and Rector let him gain it. There he found a cordon of red-shirted blockers formed to escort him in that most thrilling expression of team cooperation, a long punt runback.

Down on the Cyclone 25 Sandefer ran out of blockers and also encountered the last Cyclone. He was Nichols, the safety. Jakie pivoted sharply to his left, losing Nichols. The Cyclone didn't abandon the pursuit. He dived and tripped Sandefer just short of the goal, but Jakie had just enough energy left to hurl himself across it, completing an 81-yard run.

224

Darrell Royal was making a distinguished start with a young Texas squad that had finished 1-9 the preceding year and had bowed 0-45 to Oklahoma. He had braced Texas so briskly that the Longhorns would finish 6-3-1 and meet Mississippi at the season's end in the Sugar Bowl.

Quickly, Texas took the initiative. Mickey Smith intercepted a Sooner pass and came back to the Sooner 17. Maneuvering cleverly off the belly series, Texas scored five plays later when quarterback Walter Fondren passed to right end Monte Lee in the end zone.

Rocked by the fiery Texas onslaught, the Sooners braced and using ground plays marched 66 yards to the tying touchdown. Dodd mixed the offense well. Thomas hit fast on the handoff to score from 3 yards out behind blocks by Krisher, Doyle Jennings, and Rector. "Krisher loved to pull so he could get a running start on the guy he was going to unjoint," Ed Gray once said. Dodd kicked the crucial goal. The score was tied 7-7.

A great guard is like an anonymous blood donor. Nobody sees him spend himself as he performs his hard rough job. Bill Krisher, Oklahoma's blond statuesque 218-pounder from Midwest City was such a man. With Texas threatening, Krisher arose to the emergency with two crushing stops.

Joe Clements, Texas quarterback, took the snap and started to drop back to throw. Overpowering the Texas middle, Krisher picked up Clements's legs. On the next play, Krisher charged fast again. This time he propelled the Texas center into the quarterback, causing him to fumble. Dennit Morris recovered the dropped ball on the Sooner 42. The pressure was off.

So were Krisher's shoulder pads. The senior guard was wearing his third pair of custom-mades against Texas and they were "beat up pretty bad," mourned Jack Baer, Sooner equipment man. "He tears the flaps off them and even bends the steel." Krisher's tapering build contributed to the problem. He had shoulders like a stevedore and a waist like a village belle.

In the third quarter the Sooners drove 80 yards to the winning touchdown. From the Texas 1, Byron Searcy, Ken Northcutt, and Bob Harrison blocked, and Sandefer whipped through the torn Texas middle to score. Dodd kicked goal. Sooners 14, Steers 7.

Does a lineman ever get a laugh? Jerry Thompson, Sooner alternate tackle from Ada, grinned. "Sure!" he chuckled. "I was covering a Texas punt. A guy clipped me from behind. I sat down. The referee threw a red flag. It landed in my lap. I tossed the flag away. Another official ran up and also threw a red flag, and it landed in my lap. I threw it away too. On Monday after the game, the coaches ran that part of the movie back and forth. It looked like I was throwing a million flags."

Later, Sandefer intercepted a pass and came back 19 yards to the Steer

Clendon Thomas running through Texas in 1957 as the Sooners won 21-7. Photo by Sports Information Department, University of Oklahoma.

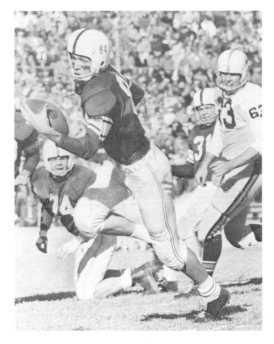

Ross Coyle fielding a pass against Oklahoma A&M in the 1957 game at Norman. Photo by Oklahoma Publishing Co.

Guard Bill Krisher.

Jakie Sandefer finishing his 83-yard touchdown punt runback against Iowa State in 1957.

21. Dodd put the ball over the goal. Oklahoma had won 21-7. "At the finish, head held high as he trudged off the field, grim-jawed Darrell Royal still looked unconvinced," wrote Jack Gallagher of the *Houston Post.*

Like a tough cop returning to walk his old beat, Oklahoma concentrated the following week on establishing law and order in its own Big Seven Conference. Since Bud Wilkinson had become the Sooner police sergeant 11 years earlier, no felonies had been committed against his teams by a conference foe, Oklahoma having gone 60 straight league games without defeat.

Kansas, weakened by influenza as the Sooners themselves had been two weeks earlier, was booked and incarcerated 47-0 at Norman. The Sooner alternates, quarterbacked by David Baker, scored five of Oklahoma's seven touchdowns.

"I don't know how to explain it," Baker told reporters after the melee. "Next week we may not get past the 50." Wilkinson used all 54 men he suited. After sinking to number two in the polls following their 21-7 win from Royal's Texans, the Sooners were back in the top spot following Kansas.

It was typical that Wilkinson, despite his 47-0 victory, could keep the friendship of the opposition coach. Chuck Mather of Kansas wrote in his next alumni letter, "Even though they defeat you 47-0 you cannot find any resentment because of your admiration and respect for the way they play. They have spent many a hard practice day in attaining their perfection."

The Kansas players were equally generous when accosted by the press in their locker room. Tackle Frank Gibson: "How can anyone teach them to hustle like that?" Quarterback Duane Morris: "It's that unity that gets you. They just do everything together. No matter what 11 guys are out there—they play together." Guard Paul Swoboda: "Oklahoma always wants to win real bad."

"The toughest game on the schedule is the first one you play after you're voted number one in the national polls," said Bob Harrison, Oklahoma center. "We found that out when we met Colorado."

Undefeated Colorado had picked up the momentum of a careening ambulance since badly outplaying Washington in a 6-6 opening tie and came into its Oklahoma test with all its pistons pumping powerfully. The crowd was sold out at 61,624, greatest throng ever to see a game in the Big Seven Conference. Coach Dal Ward's Golden Buffaloes were ambitious to sever Oklahoma's record of 44 straight triumphs.

They nearly did it too. As the fourth quarter started, Ward's Buffaloes had pulled ahead 13-7 when Bob Stransky, their fine running back, forward passed to Boyd Dowler for a touchdown while he was falling, after Bill Krisher, Sooner guard, had struck him solidly. Ellwin Indorf had kicked goal.

Indorf kicked off. It was a high boot. With Colorado players sprinting down under it, Sooner fans thought it would never come down. Clendon Thomas, Wilkinson's most-feared back, caught it out of the gloomy sky and cut upfield behind his blockers. Fighting and spinning, Thomas came back 30 yards to midfield, where Colorado's last tackler got him.

That runback fired the Sooners. "You could feel the unity and the determination in our first huddle," said Dennit Morris, Oklahoma's senior fullback. "Everybody was leaning forward. Even before Carl finished calling the signal, our guards, Ken Northcutt and Bill Krisher, each had one foot out of the huddle ready to go. Carl moved us fast. Twice I just barely got back to the huddle in time. I told him not to wait for me, I'd hear it coming in."

But after three plays, Oklahoma had only 9 yards. It was fourth and 1 from the Colorado 45, the most crucial play of the game. Dodd elected to try for the yardage instead of punting. Moreover, he was not afraid to call himself. He came around right end on a keeper and, shearing upfield behind a block by tackle Doyle Jennings, surged 11 yards to a first down on Colorado's 34. The Sooners drove on in. From the Colorado 8, Dodd called

Thomas around the weak side and, pitching out to him, joined Morris in standing off the Colorado end and halfback. Thomas scored in the corner of the field.

A hush fell over the stadium as the antagonists positioned themselves for the extra point try. Dodd, a Norman boy, waved his arms to quiet the crowd. Harrison fired the ball back to Sandefer. With Sandefer holding and the line keeping Colorado out, Dodd thumped the ball cleanly between the posts. Dodd said later, "Naw, I wasn't nervous about it. I figured if I missed it we could get another touchdown." Oklahoma won 14-13.

Earlier in the game Oklahoma needed, and got, two blocked kicks to attain its winning margin. On Colorado's try for point following their first touchdown, Bill Krisher rooted strongly through their defense and shoved a Colorado lineman back into the kick, blocking it. It was a spectacular, vital play. Later, when Colorado tried a field goal, Thomas shot in from right halfback to block it.

Dick Snider, sports editor of the *Topeka Daily Capital,* portrayed the situation pretty well when he wrote, "Oklahoma, a football elephant hanging over the brink of defeat with its tail wrapped around a daisy, pulled up from behind in the final period here Saturday to edge amazing Colorado 14-13."

Seeking the hundredth victory of the Bud Wilkinson regime, the Sooners got it by defeating Kansas State 13-0 at Manhattan.

Dick Corbitt, junior guard from Altus, made possible the last Sooner touchdown when he blocked Wilson's punt. Steve Jennings caught the ball in the air and was tackled on the Purple 43. Oklahoma's alternates drove the distance, Bobby Boyd scoring on the handoff over Thompson, Oujesky, and Davis. The Sooners still remember how fiercely Don Zadnik of the Cats guarded his end.

"The field was wet, and we were all muddy," recalls Oujesky. "Byron Searcy and I played next to each other. Kansas State subbed a lineman. He came on the field wearing a spotlessly clean uniform, purple jersey, white pants. He was playing opposite Searcy. I began kidding him about how muddy he was going to get. Soon Searcy told me to cut it out, 'because he's knocking the hell out of me.'"

In the Big Seven championship clash at Columbia, Missouri, the Sooners faced a Missouri team that stood 3-0 in the conference and had won four straight. The contest was very even all through the first half. Steve Jennings's fumble recovery on the Sooner 43 put the alternates in gear, and Dickie Carpenter ran left, saw all his routes were closed, then swung back right to go 16 yards to a touchdown. Baker booted goal.

Clendon Thomas lifted a long punt out on the Tiger 7 that gave Oklahoma field position and set in motion a 49-yard touchdown drive. Bobby Boyd scored off blocks by Stiller, Searcy, and Northcutt. However, Coach Frank Broyles's Missourians fought back with brilliant aerial play. Quarterback Phil Snowden passed them down to the Sooner 8. The OU starters came in, but Snowden scored on a keeper. It was the first touchdown by rushing yielded by Gomer Jones's forcing defense in 12 consecutive games. At the half Oklahoma led 13-7.

In the last half the Sooners seemed to be recalling, and digesting, the talk Wilkinson made to them Friday afternoon in the hotel at Jefferson City. "The answer lies deep down in your own hearts," the coach said. "You either do or you don't. I know you can if you will. Be poised and go out there and enjoy it. You're a part of something that's great. Are you going to keep the faith? You can't change it after it happens tomorrow. It's something you'll be proud of, or regret, all your lives." Oklahoma won 39-14.

Notre Dame, standing 4-2 over a murderous schedule, faced Oklahoma in a football tiff at Norman falling 50 years to the day after Oklahoma became a state.

The Sooners went into battle trailing three long strings of consecutives behind them like streamers of ticker tape. Wilkinson's red-garbed legions had won 47 straight, gone 48 consecutively without defeat and scored in 112 straight, each an all-time national record. Coach Terry Brennan's Irish were poised to draw from the upset tradition that had been college football's finest.

The crowd, sold out since May, totaled 63,170, an all-time Norman record. Everybody tried to borrow, beg, or steal a ticket from a Norman friend. John Jacobs, long-time Sooner track coach, devised a novel way to meet this pressure. He ordered hundreds of copies of a printed form letter that read as follows: "Dear Mrs. (the men always make the wimmen write): Thanks for your great interest in my welfare and for your congratulations on my all-victorious track team of 1927. It would give me great pleasure if I could make it possible for you to see the Notre Dame–Oklahoma football game, but I can not. Sincerely, your relative, Jake."

Defense was the game's theme. For 57 minutes neither team could drop the bomb that wrote the epilogue. Accustomed to the superb offenses of the Wilkinson teams, the Oklahoma crowd sat astounded as they watched the Irish stand up the Sooner blockers or run over them. Oklahoma had to make three goal line stands and defend ruggedly all over the gridiron.

"Notre Dame was very competitive and emotional," remembers Byron Searcy, Sooner left tackle. "I don't think that either our coaches or players respected them enough," Searcy added. "Before the game everybody sat around as if waiting for somebody to say, 'Well, let's go plow.'

"After defeating Missouri the week before for the conference championship and the Orange Bowl bid, we were flat," Searcy amplified. "We'd been flirting with defeat all year anyhow, barely beating Kansas State and Colorado. And, besides, we'd beaten Notre Dame 40-0 the year before."

The Sooners achieved their longest advance the first time they obtained the ball, marching 58 yards. Dodd ran left and passed to Dennit Morris for 11 yards. Dodd burst around the Irish left flank for 12 more and a first down. Defensive holding cost Notre Dame a penalty back to their 20. Thomas whipped around the Irish right side for 7 and a first down on the Irish 13. But the Irish held and Ecuyer broke up a fourth down pass.

Later, Notre Dame went on offense. Quarterback Bob Williams passed them down the field to the Sooner 3, but Oklahoma threw back four rushes. Early in the fourth quarter the contest's most dramatic moment was at hand. On the ninth play Thomas's long punt bounced across the goal and it was Notre Dame's ball on its 20.

An Irish drive of heroic power and continuity followed. With true precision and team effort, they moved 80 yards in 20 plays to the game's only touchdown. Nineteen of the plays were rushes with Pietrosante, or Reynolds, or Lynch bucking to first downs. One was a pass, Williams to Royer, for 10. Down on the Oklahoma 12 the Sooners again knocked the ball loose from Williams but he fell on it. Finally it was fourth down and goal to go from the Sooner 3. There was 3:50 left to play.

It was here that the Sooner crowd was yelling so vociferously that Williams, the Irish quarterback, couldn't make his players hear his signals. The referee couldn't quiet the crowd either. Several Oklahoma players stood and, although their backs were to the wall, motioned to their spectators to be quiet and give the visitors their chance. And the crowd obeyed them. Lindsey Nelson, who with Red Grange was televising the game from coast to coast, noted this and pointed it out to his millions of listeners. Then came the play.

"They were in tight, real tight," said Williams later from the Irish dressing room, "just waiting for me to give the ball to Pietrosante, or Nick the Greek God, as we call him. Well, I faked to Nick into the line and then tossed out to Dick Lynch going wide to the right. It worked like a charm and there we had it."[5]

---

[5] Notre Dame finished 7-3 that year. They closed their season by demolishing Southern California 40-12 and Southern Methodist 54-21.

With 1:22 to go, Oklahoma had the ball on its 39. Wilkinson sent in some of his reserves. "I just thought they might do better," Bud explained later. "You have to have quickness at the end of the game and they were fresh." Johnny Pellow caught two passes, one a 40-yard deflection he carried to the Irish 36. But another pass was intercepted.

When the game ended, and the crowd milled in disbelief, Jack Ogle, stadium public-address announcer, assured everybody over the P.A., "Come back next Saturday, folks. That's when the new winning streak starts."

Wilkinson closed the Sooner dressing room to everybody and talked to his tearful squad. "You have done something no other major college football team has ever done before or will ever do again," he said. "You won 47 straight football games. I am proud of you. You have been just as much a part of this as any other Oklahoma team. The only ones who never lose are the ones who never play."[6]

Ross Coyle, Sooner end, remembers that the crowd stayed long after the game to greet and cheer the Oklahoma players after they showered and dressed. "I was so upset," Coyle remembers. "After the game I was going home to Marlow in my old '53 Ford coupe. Some guy tried to cut in front of me and I almost ran over a highway patrolman."

After the game Brennan said, "Oklahoma took the loss graciously. Bud Wilkinson congratulated me warmly and sincerely and told me we played a better game and deserved to win. It's tough to lose after a streak like that, but they were strictly big league about it."

Later, the Oklahoma coach shouldered the blame for the defeat, disclosing that the Sooner strategy was to try to win by letting the Irish play their way into defeat. "Notre Dame had been fumbling five or six times in every game, up to that one, and I felt we should emphasize forcing them into errors," Wilkinson said. "I did not make any special offensive preparation. When Notre Dame made only one error, a fumble on their 4 that they re-covered, our game plan was frustrated. If I had made special offensive preparations, we might have won."

On Monday noon at the regular weekly meeting of the Oklahoma City Quarterback Club, when Wilkinson arose to speak, the entire assemblage of three hundred fans stood and began counting slowly in unison, "one—two—three—four—five—six—seven . . ." and on through "forty-seven." It took a long time to finish the count. It was tremendously moving and impressive.

With Nebraska next, people were wondering how well Oklahoma would play after its first defeat in nearly five years. Wilkinson challenged his

---

[6] Jakie Sandefer to Tim Cohane, October 1, 1964.

squad when he talked to them Friday afternoon in the Cornhusker Hotel.

"Nobody remembers the team that gets beat," the coach began. "Who did Caesar ever beat? You don't know, do you? Who did the Yankees beat all those years they won the World Series? The defeated teams aren't remembered. The world belongs to the people who win.

"An awful lot of people care about this team. Let's don't let them down. Last week you lost and you took it with lots of sportsmanship. But I don't think you ought to get carried away about being a good sport. Let's get our mind back on winning. This is the most important game we've ever played."

Before the Oklahoma squad had left Norman, Brewster Hobby, Oklahoma's third string right half, had been promoted to the alternates when Bobby Boyd was hurt. "In practice Monday I had the most miserable day of my life," Hobby remembers. "On Thursday I scrimmaged with the fourth and fifth teams, feeling I had lost forever the chance to prove myself."

Dejected, Hobby began walking to the dressing room. Wilkinson called him back. "He put his arm around me and walked that 100 yards with me," Hobby recalls. "He related how bad I had looked, how I'd stumbled over my own feet and screwed up everything. 'I'm going with you at left half on the alternates against Nebraska,' Bud went on. 'I know in my own mind that you can do the job.'"

"That incident gave me the confidence to compete at Oklahoma," Hobby says today. "I scored two touchdowns against Nebraska, rushed 57 yards, didn't get beat on a pass play, supported well. Next year I became a starter at right half. Coach Wilkinson never made you feel that you were a lesser member of the team no matter how poorly you played."

The Sooners had practiced excellently all week and it showed. In the last half Morris kicked off into the end zone. "The ball was trickling along the ground unclaimed," Joe Rector recalls. "Two Nebraska players hovered over it, arms held out. One wouldn't let the other cover it. 'Get away from it,' he yelled. He almost had me convinced that I shouldn't touch it either," Rector remembers, "but instead of thinking, I reacted, covering it in the end zone with a long dive." Dodd kicked goal. Oklahoma won 32-7.

Although Oklahoma State stood 6-2-1 for the season and had bowl aspirations, the Sooners kept the Aggies' feet to the fire with no letup of effort, a continuity of exertion that always pleased the coach. Final score 53-6. Oklahoma had one game remaining, the Orange Bowl tussle against Duke's Blue Devils, coached by Bill Murray.

After the Aggie game Cliff Speegle, Aggie coach, said, "Thomas made them click. They wouldn't be half as good without him."

Asked later how it felt to score 36 touchdowns, rush 2,120 net yards, and amass 216 points during his three-year career at Oklahoma, all of them modern times school records, the halfback grinned and said, "That's what a great line will do for you."

Oklahoma led the nation that year in punt runbacks with 648 yards, tied for first in interceptions with 23, placed second in interception yardage with 338, third in penalty yardage with 78 a game, fifth in scoring with 28.5 a game, fifth in rushing offense with 297 a game, seventh in total offense with 360 yards a game and seventh in defense against scoring with yields of 6.8 a game. Oklahoma was voted number four in both the AP and UP polls.

Guard Bill Krisher and halfback Clendon Thomas made first All-America. Jakie Sandefer ranked third nationally in punt runbacks with 249 yards. Notre Dame placed four men on Oklahoma's first all-opponents' team and four on the second.

Duke, the Orange Bowl opponent, was a veteran bowl team. Coach Bill Murray's Blue Devils had trimmed Nebraska 34-7 in the Orange three years earlier. Duke had also beaten Alabama 29-26 in the Sugar. The Blue Devils had played twice in the Rose Bowl, losing each by a narrow margin, 20-16 to Oregon State in 1942 and 7-3 to Southern California in 1939.

"Duke is a big team, widely recruited," Bud told the Sooners at the Bal Harbour Hotel the day before the game. "Don't misunderstand me. They are a fine school with a fine coach and fine boys.[7] But if you will play them so hard and fast that in the last half they tire and have to play on their willpower, I honestly think you'll beat them. I think you can outgame them. If you don't, you don't deserve to win anyhow."

In the first quarter George Harris, Duke quarterback, shot a pass down the field. David Baker plucked it out of the ozone on the 6-yard line and ran it back 94 yards down the sideline to a touchdown. It was the longest interception runback of all bowl history.

Midway of the second quarter each team scored. The Sooners tallied first. With Clendon Thomas lined up at right end, Dodd pitched out to Sandefer. Sandefer handed off to Thomas who reversed wide to his left and, helped by blocks by Harrison and Doyle Jennings, strode across the goal. Dodd booted the conversion. Oklahoma led 14-0.

Aroused, the Blue Devils did something rarely accomplished against Oklahoma, scored on a 65-yard drive in seven plays from kickoff. McEl-

---

[7] Jay Wilkinson, younger son of the Oklahoma coach, later went to college at Duke and became an All-American.

haney plunged for the touchdown. Carlton goaled. Oklahoma's margin had been cut to 14-7.

In the third period each team scored. Dodd's 36-yard punt runback and his quarterback sneak over guard brought Oklahoma's. Duke retaliated magnificently, powering 85 yards in 11 plays with Dutrow shredding Oklahoma tacklers right and left as he swept the weakside to score. As the antagonists entered the fourth quarter, Oklahoma led 21-14, but the game was still a dogfight.

The fourth quarter belonged decisively to Oklahoma. Making deadly capital of Blue Devil errors, the Sooners scored four touchdowns. On a Duke quick kick, their center snapped the ball off the kicker's knee, Dennit Morris recovering on the Duke 24. Dodd passed to Sandefer for 12, then pitched out to Sandefer for the touchdown.

Northcutt recovered a Duke fumble on the Duke 38. Hobby passed to Baker for a touchdown. "They stopped me last time in the flank. I'll be over the middle this time," Baker told Hobby in the huddle. Then Ross Coyle blocked Williams's punt. On the first play Baker called the spread left, spun out wide, and hit Hobby for a touchdown.

Before each of these last touchdowns Wilkinson had told Baker, "Keep it on the ground and hammer it out. Stay in your straight-T." "Yes, sir," said Baker. But each time Baker disobeyed the order, called a pass off the spread, and scored. On the sideline, Wilkinson threw up his hands and grinned. "I might as well let him call them," he said.

Later, I asked Baker why he had twice gone against the coach's orders. "I dunno," he replied. "It just seemed to me both plays would work." Oklahoma led 41-14.

Duke launched another fighting rally. It ended disastrously when Bennett Watts intercepted Brodhead's pass, ran 40 yards, pitched a lateral to Dick Carpenter, threw a block, and lying on his stomach watched Carpenter score on the 73-yard play. Although Oklahoma that day would be red-flagged for 165 yards in penalties, many of them for clipping as the Sooner downfield blockers flattened everybody in sight, Oklahoma won 48-21.

With six minutes left and the Oklahoma third team on the field, Jakie Sandefer, on the bench, leaned over to get a drink of water. "Don't tank up on water," Wilkinson warned. "This game isn't over yet."

Sandefer grinned and looked at the scoreboard. It read 41-21. "I thought to myself that if Duke overcame that lead in the few minutes we had left, they'd need a stronger drink than I was taking," he said.

Red Smith, New York columnist, wrote, "For the football fan, watching Oklahoma is a treat. Going at top speed and employing their talents with

David Baker finishing his 94-yard pass interception runback against Duke in the 1958 Orange Bowl. Ross Coyle (84) protects from the rear. Photo by Sports Information Department, University of Oklahoma.

confidence and polished precision, Bud Wilkinson's operatives create excitement. It is all very well to point out that their winning margin stemmed from Duke errors but that is an essential part of their game. Wilkinson trains opportunists to seize and exploit every chance."

Ed Cope, *Miami Herald* sportswriter, watched Wilkinson. "He danced, yelled, grinned, groaned, and slapped the broad backs of his Oklahomans as they streamed in and out of a riotous fourth quarter," Cope wrote. "'Get another one!' Wilkinson shrieked after Jakie Sandefer wheeled the Sooners into 28-14 command.

"'Hold 'em!' he hollered, tugging at his Oklahoma red necktie as Duke swept to its final futile touchdown. . . . Then, in the white heat of the windup, Wilkinson turned coach again—mannerly, dignified, professional. He walked over to a clot of Sooner players and said softly, 'No conversation about those penalties. What's done is done. No complaining, understand?'"

236

Bob Harrison, Sooner center, throwing Bob Brodhead, Duke quarterback, for a 14-yard loss in the 1958 Orange Bowl.

Bob Harrison.

Bill Krisher, Sooner guard, knocks the ball loose from Larry Rundle, Oklahoma A&M back in the 1957 game at Stillwater.

The game statistics illustrated the completeness of the Oklahoma preparation. The Sooner defense ran back two Duke forward passes for touchdowns and blocked two Duke punts, one for a touchdown. Oklahoma ran back six punts for 128 yards. They outpunted Duke, 34.7 net yards to 28.1. They scored two touchdowns by forward passing. They were outrushed 231-165 but averaged 3.7 yards a rush to 3.2. They played all 44 men they brought. That the Sooners could score 48 points despite the distraction of 165 yards in penalties seems proof that they were indeed in a meticulous state of readiness for the game.

238

1957 SENIORS TODAY

Carl Dodd is a real-estate broker in Dallas, Texas. He also breeds and raises quarterhorses at a farm near Denton, Texas.

Doyle Jennings is agent for the Equitable Life Assurance Society of the United States in West Monroe, Louisiana.

Bill Krisher is executive director of Meaningful Life, Inc., a Christian organization at Wendy's Meadow Ranch, Ben Wheeler, Texas.

Ken Northcutt is dock supervisor for Consolidated Freightways of Oklahoma City, Oklahoma.

Buddy Oujesky is real-estate manager of Winn-Dixie Super Markets, of Fort Worth, Texas. He is also a Missouri Valley Conference football official.

Byron Searcy is a partner in Ferree-Searcy, Inc., a commercial-real-estate firm in Fort Worth, Texas.

Clendon Thomas is owner and president of Chemical Products Corporation of Oklahoma City, Oklahoma.

13. BREAKTHROUGH OF PRENTICE GAUTT

Most interesting of the new rules for 1958 was the one awarding the team scoring a touchdown the right to try for two extra points with either a scrimmage run or forward pass anywhere behind the opponent's 3-yard line.

Wilkinson liked it. "It should bring great strategic and dramatic interest to what has been the most routine play in football," he said. He was a member of the National Rules Committee that passed it. He would suffer his only 1958 defeat because of it. Another coach on Oklahoma's schedule, Darrell Royal of Texas, disliked the rule yet would win his biggest victory of the season by using it.

Wilkinson's athletic directorship was attracting attention. "The athletic department is the most solvent division of the university," President George Cross told the press while announcing that a new athletic dormitory would be built and financed entirely by football funds. "It is retiring stadium bonds well ahead of schedule and since 1950 has contributed $365,000 to university enterprises not related to intercollegiate activities."

In spring practice Wilkinson's new team seemed sprocketed for offense. The Whites riddled the Reds 49-36 in scrimmage the week before the Varsity-Alumni game, with Prentice Gautt, who had been switched to fullback, butting down the defenses for 194 net yards rushing. Gautt had straightened out his thinking, achieved his racial breakthrough, and begun hitting the white boys who were his teammates as hard as they were hitting him.

Injuries, as usual, dotted the proceedings. The worst happened to Leon Cross, alternate team guard who was all set for his sophomore season when a 600-pound iron air compressor broke loose from its moorings in the back of a pickup truck and smashed his arch, necessitating a summer operation. Guard Jerry Thompson fractured a hand.

A new wave of freshmen had been recruited. They chose Oklahoma for a variety of reasons. Phil Lohmann had gone to Oklahoma City when Wilkinson called on him at his home in Pauls Valley. "The coach talked to my mother for two hours before I got home," Phil recalls. "After that, there was no question in her mind where I was going to school." Paul

Benien, a fullback at Tulsa Cascia Hall High, was recommended to Wilkinson by Jack Santee, a rival coach at Tulsa Marquette.

Jim Byerly, 230-pound all-state center from Crane, Texas, an oil-field town in the mesquite country south of Odessa, recalls Wilkinson, accompanied by assistant coaches Crowder and Rudy Feldman, flying to Crane in a university plane to visit him.

"Bud talked to us in the living room of our home," Byerly remembers. "When Bud talked to a group, each one of us felt that he was talking to him alone. Afterwards he took us all to dinner. Mom said later that she'd never had so many people opening doors for her and trying to hold her chair."

Full of run and eager for work, Oklahoma's twelfth squad coached by Wilkinson and Jones broke fast from the barrier. Center Bob Harrison and end Joe Rector were elected captains. Although the Sooners kept only three starters from 1957, Wilkinson's team was, as usual, a short-priced entry with a well-squared nose. Two national magazines touted the Sooners to win their fourth national championship.

Meanwhile a controversy had arisen over the recruiting of Mike McClellan of Stamford, Texas, High School. The young man had won the Texas 100-yard and broad jump championships in track and was also a quality football player. Oklahoma was one of several schools that courted him, but the boy chose Baylor. However, he soon became disenchanted with the hazing there.

"There was just something about licks with a board, shining untold numbers of shoes, and washing cars that didn't appeal to me," he explains today. Withdrawing at the end of the term with a B scholastic average, he transferred to Oklahoma. Baylor, through Coach Sam Boyd and Abner McCall, dean of the Baylor law school and chairman of the Baylor athletic council, charged that Oklahoma had encouraged McClellan to leave Baylor.

Wilkinson denied this. So did McClellan. However, Boyd and McCall kept the media in an uproar. "Boyd was mad," McClellan says, "and McCall wanted to be president of Baylor and was using me in his pursuit of the office." Wilkinson refused to give McClellan an athletic scholarship.

McClellan packed up again and returned home to Stamford. In February he obtained a job in the Texas oil fields. Thus Wilkinson made it possible for other schools to recruit McClellan, if they could, or for McClellan to change his mind and return to Baylor, as his family wished.

McClellan remained steadfast. He made it plain that he would not enroll anywhere except at Oklahoma. Wilkinson gave him a scholarship. In September, 1958, he enrolled at Oklahoma in petroleum land management.

241

"Spring training of 1959 was the end of the ordeal," McClellan concludes the episode today. "I was now where I wanted to be."

At Oklahoma a freshman player's first duty was to learn and obey the rules laid down by Port Robertson, the freshman coach. "I loved Port," asserts Phil Lohmann. "The first day we had a meeting Port talked to us. He told us that we would be extremely well disciplined in our football, our studies, and our behavior. And that if we didn't get along with him on all those points, we would be the ones who would be gettin' along— down the road."

"I reported in at OU that fall weighing 256 pounds," resumes Jim Byerly. "Ken Rawlinson told me I had to drop to 207 pounds by spring. You know what? I made it! I played handball a lot with Pricer and Krisher. All they ever did was see who could hit me the hardest with the ball. At Jeff House they had a 'Fat Boy Table.' We ate spinach, hard-boiled eggs and all the soup we wanted. Port stood guard nearby."

Port was the freshman "dorm mother" as Byerly called him. "He inspected our rooms," Byerly says. "He'd come in, look around, shake his head, and walk out again. Next Sunday he'd call a meeting in the third floor film room. 'Gentlemen,' he'd say in that little whiney voice of his, 'We've provided you with a wonderful place to live. You'll notice that there aren't any mice or rats in this building. You know why? Because the place is so darned messy that no self-respecting rat would live in it.'"

The players knew that if they broke Robertson's rules they had to arise at 6, meet the coach on the varsity football field, and run the stadium steps. "One morning," remembers Byerly, "Port told us to be there at 6. We were there. But Port wasn't. We waited until 6:15 then went back to the dorm for breakfast. That afternoon he called us into his office and assigned each of us 25 more flights of stadium steps."

"But we couldn't get into the stadium," we told him. "You weren't there. The gate was locked."

"You should have climbed the fence and run 'em on your own," said Port.

Two weeks after the 1958 practice started, a group of freshman players were sitting in Jefferson House. The question arose about who was the strongest man in the dormitory. Port walked by and stopped to listen. "Gentlemen," he said, "we can find that out very quickly. I want you to elect the five strongest guys on the squad. Then we'll see if they can hold me down." Port was forty-four years old but worked out daily with his wrestlers. He had on his sweat clothing. The freshmen wore regular campus clothing. They elected five muscular linemen.

They went into the east upstairs hallway. Port lay down on the floor. It

242

was all very good-natured. Everybody was laughing and giggling. One of the electees sat on the coach's right arm, another on his left arm. A third man sat on his right leg, a fourth on his left leg. The fifth man sat astride the coach's stomach. The rest of the squad pleaded with Robertson not to go through with it. They liked him and were afraid he might be hurt. Paying no attention to them, Robertson turned to Phil Lohmann who was present. "You're the starter," he said. "When they're ready, holler 'go!'"

"Go!" yelled Lohmann. The coach erupted off the floor. *Boom! Bang!* The stack of players gyrated up and down. In a few seconds the coach was on his feet, festooned with bodies. "Everybody was laughing," recalls Lohmann, "but soon Port had 'em all in a pile and was sitting on 'em."

"Gentlemen, don't worry about it," Robertson said. "We'll get along."

"They still hadn't figured out how in the world he did it but none of them wanted a replay," Lohmann laughs today. "They were all on time at study hall that night, and afterwards too."

A coolness had sprung up between Wilkinson and Bill Jennings, the new Nebraska mentor who had been a capable assistant to Bud on the Sooner staff. It began in May, 1957, and resulted in another probation for Oklahoma by the NCAA. Wilkinson protested the eligibility of two Nebraska freshmen who had received grants-in-aid[1] from Jennings. Wilkinson, the Sooner director, sent a letter of inquiry to Bill Orwig, Nebraska director. Earl Sneed, Sooner faculty representative, sent another to Earl Fulbrook, the Cornhusker faculty man.

"Bud should have called me first instead of going over my head to my athletic director and faculty man," says Jennings. "The accusations were false," he adds, "but my Nebraska bosses warned me to 'go straight.'" Both Wilkinson and Eddie Crowder, then the Sooner assistant in charge of recruiting, disclaim any knowledge of this event today. "I don't recall anything about that," says Bud. "The incident that created the misunderstanding with Bill was over Monte Kiffin."

Kiffin, a Lexington, Nebraska, High School boy, was a tackle who later would be voted the outstanding high-school athlete in Nebraska. The boy wrote Wilkinson that he wanted to come to Oklahoma. Kiffin's coach had first written Bud about Kiffin. Wilkinson was reluctant, preferring not to invade the recruiting territory of a rival conference school. "I'd rather not recruit in Nebraska without Coach Jennings's permission," Bud wrote back.

That statement circulated widely in Nebraska. Jennings says it brought him much criticism and eventually was published in Nebraska newspapers.

[1] George Lynn Cross, *Presidents Can't Punt* (Norman: University of Oklahoma Press, 1977), pp. 316-20.

Its implication, he says, was that the Nebraska program he headed was not good enough for Kiffin.

Meanwhile Crowder persuaded Wilkinson to accompany him on a recruiting trip in a university plane. One of their stops was at Lexington, Nebraska, to meet Kiffin. "Monte was a tall, lean lineman, our type," Crowder remembers today. "We met his parents."

Jennings was furious. "Nebraska people thought that I thought that Monte should go to Oklahoma," says Jennings, "that I had given Bud permission to recruit him."

He wrote Wilkinson a letter, threatening that if Bud continued to recruit Kiffin he (Jennings) would turn over to the NCAA full information about all the Oklahoma infractions that occurred while he (Jennings) was on the Sooner coaching staff, including some not reported. "I knew that the Nebraska job was the only opportunity I would ever have in coaching," Jennings says today. "I was trying to survive."

One of these infractions dealt with an incident Jennings says happened in 1954, after he had left the Sooner staff. Oklahoma football was being investigated by the NCAA. Jennings says that Wilkinson telephoned him, asking him to come to Norman and testify before the NCAA infractions committee that he knew nothing of any Sooner recruiting irregularities and that he did not know Arthur Wood, the Oklahoma City accountant who had furnished funds to Jennings with which to finance visits of outstanding high-school athletes to the Norman campus. Jennings says that he consented to Wilkinson's request, traveling from Fort Worth to Norman in a University of Oklahoma plane.

Wilkinson regarded the 1958 Jennings letter as blackmail. With President Cross's approval, he sent a copy of Jennings's letter to Walter Byers, NCAA executive director, suggesting that if Jennings had such information that he release it at once to Byers and also to Chancellor Hardin of Nebraska. Later in the year Byers would delve further into the matter.

"Monte Kiffin was an innocent victim of all this," Jennings points out. "He just happened to be involved." Always a formidable recruiter, Jennings signed Kiffin for the Cornhuskers. "For us, he was a good tough player, a tackle," says Jennings today.

West Virginia, coached by Art ("Pappy") Lewis, was fresh from romping over Richmond 66-22 and also from measuring Pittsburgh, Wake Forest, and Syracuse in the last three games of the previous season. Oklahoma, in its final scrimmage, had looked wretched during a 0-0 tie. "The summer publicity we've been getting is a great tribute to our 1957 team but our 1958 team hasn't yet made a first down," Wilkinson fretted.

With 55,432 fans jamming the stadium, the Sooners played sloppily.

But the defense, as usual, was as solid as an oaken stump. On one Mountaineer series, Steve Jennings, Sooner left tackle, got four tackles in five plays. Finally Edward ("Wahoo") McDaniel, alternate end from Midland, Texas, blocked a punt in midfield and that was the game's pivotal point.

Six plays later fullback Prentice Gautt broke down the middle and cut to the outside. One after another, three Mountaineer tacklers bounced off Gautt's hitting shoulder and his thick thighs like grasshoppers off a speeding automobile. Running 27 yards, Gautt scored standing. "He had finally found himself and had the confidence he needed," recalls halfback Brewster Hobby. "I was so glad for him that I grabbed him by the legs and tried to chair him around the field."

The big crowd gawked with surprise when Oklahoma lined up for the extra point. The Sooners elected to go for 2 by taking the ball across the goal from the 3-yard line. They did it too, Baker running wide to his right with Gautt throwing a shattering block on the end. For the first time at Owen Field, the big electric scoreboard registered an 8 after a touchdown and conversion.

Oklahoma completed 264 yards in forward passes with Bobby Boyd, alternate quarterback who flung his forward passes sidearm like a man pegging at a dart board, throwing two touchdowns, one of them to McDaniel for an 86-yard gain. After the 47-14 Sooner victory Oklahoma was rated number one in the nation by both the AP and UP polls.

Football occasionally made fine friends of former high-school enemies. Oklahoma had proof of this in quiet reserved Dick Corbitt of Altus and long-jawed Jim Lawrence of Sayre who played side by side in the starting Sooner line. In their last Altus-Sayre high-school game, both were ejected for fighting. "We just started slugging it out," Corbitt says. "We weren't mad. Just keyed up. Later, when I heard that Lawrence was going to Oklahoma, I went there too. I wanted him on my side."

Len Casanova, coach of Oregon's Ducks, the next Sooner opponent, had played 11 with Wilkinson's Sooner Sugar Bowl champions of 1948 and 1949 while coaching Santa Clara.

In its subjugation of West Virginia the week before, Oklahoma had used a new formation that flankered ends, tackles, and backs in both directions. But the Yellow and Green had two sharp-eyed scouts at that game. One of them, backfield coach Johnny McKay, said, "This Oklahoma offense is the wildest thing I've ever seen. You need three hands to write it down." But Casanova needed only one brain to plot a defense that fettered Sooner feet all afternoon. Oklahoma got only 129 yards rushing, 27 forward passing, and scored only one touchdown. It won the game 6-0.

The crowd of 61,300 saw the lone Sooner touchdown scored in the

245

second quarter when Jere Durham and Jerry Tillery hit Sandy Fraser, Oregon's ballcarrier, forcing Oregon's only fumble of the game. On fourth down and one from the Oregon nine, quarterback Bobby Boyd rolled out to his left and forward passed to Dick Carpenter for the touchdown. The Sooners tried a two-point conversion on a run by Boyd but it failed by a yard.

"It was my habit on defense," remembers Brewster Hobby, "to force some rival ballcarrier to the sideline then lower my head and put him up in the nickel seats. As a result I sometimes missed because when I hit him I'd have my head and eyes down. Coach Wilkinson got on me several times about this.

"In the Oregon game it happened in front of the Sooner bench. I unloaded on an Oregon guy, missed him, and slid under Coach Wilkinson's feet. He reached down and grabbed me by the shoulder pads. 'How many times have I told you not to lower your head and shut your eyes when you tackle?' he scolded me. All the time he was talking my feet were flying as I tried to get away from him and back on the field. Everybody was laughing at me."

Oregon recovered field position by breaking Willie West, their black speedster, loose through the Sooner left side. Prentice Gautt swung in behind him and after a thrilling race of 53 yards pulled him down from behind on the Sooner 36, saving a touchdown.

"Look at our colored boy catch that Oregon nigger from behind," somebody yelled from the stadium, and Gautt says the remark was a good indication of how integration was progressing in Oklahoma. "My toleration of white-black relationship in our state had grown so greatly that I enjoyed the remark too," Gautt chuckles softly today.

"I'm mighty glad the game's over," West said later from Oregon's dressing room. "I bet I sleep all the way back to Eugene."

Coach Casanova lauded the defensive play of Sooner quarterback David Baker. "I think that David Baker is the best back I've ever seen on defense," Casanova told the press. "He's simply a terrific behind-the-line defensive man, capable of catching you from any angle at any time."

Texas hadn't beaten Oklahoma in seven seasons. But they had a new coach, Darrell Royal, former Sooner quarterback. And now Royal was clashing a second time with Wilkinson, his former coach. Texas's record was 3-0. They had beaten Georgia, Tulane, and Texas Tech.

The game was decided by the new two-point conversion rule just legalized by the National Rules Committee of which Wilkinson was a member. In the second quarter Vince Matthews, Texas reserve quarterback who was playing despite a bad cold, forward passed the Orange down to the Oklahoma 10 where Rene Ramirez ran left and flipped a halfback pass to George Blanch for a touchdown.

In spite of Royal's opposition to the new two-point rule, he used it, and Texas led 8-0 when left guard R. G. Anderson blocked fullback Don Allen across the goal.

"Texas came to play, and I might add, not only to play but to win," wrote Homer Norton, *Houston Post* special correspondent. "The young coach Darrell Royal has learned a lot of lessons from the old master, Bud Wilkinson."

In the third period Oklahoma scored on a weak-side pass, Bobby Boyd to Dick Carpenter. Oklahoma also tried a two-point conversion but Boyd was rushed and couldn't get the ball off. Texas led 8-6. Texas's two-point conversion loomed larger and larger.

Then Oklahoma scored on an unusual play. Max Morris, reserve center, broke through and attacked a Lackey-Dowdle handoff. The ball popped loose and rested for a moment on Dowdle's hip. Jim Davis, Sooner right guard, snatched it and ran 24 yards to a touchdown. When Boyd passed to Tillery for two extra points, Oklahoma led, 14-8.

With the final moments flying, Texas showed its heart. Vince Matthews, the quarterback with a touch of influenza, began to zip his forward passes. He took them down to the goal. With the ball on the Sooner 5, Royal sent in Bobby Lackey, the starting quarterback. "Lackey is a big, tall boy and I wanted somebody who could see over the Oklahoma line," Royal explained afterwards. Lackey shot a jump pass to Bob Bryant for the touchdown. Lackey also kicked the extra point. Texas won 15-14.

Dr. George L. Cross, the Oklahoma president, went to the Texas dressing room to congratulate Royal. The jubilant Texas players were celebrating, but the young Texas coach was nowhere in sight. The president found him outside leaning against the building. "His face was colorless, except for a sort of greenish-blue tint around his mouth," said President Cross. "He was obviously ill; it was apparent that he had lost at least part of his lunch."[2]

When the president congratulated him, Royal said that it somehow "just didn't seem right to beat Mr. Wilkinson," his old coach. Back in the Texas dressing room, he felt better. "No team ever gave a coach so much to be happy about," he declared. Vince Matthews, who had hit 8 of 10 passes, bubbled, "How can you have a cold when you feel as good as I do?"

Wilkinson said from the Oklahoma dressing room, "Their fourth-quarter finish was the finest I've ever seen."

[2]George Lynn Cross, *Presidents Can't Punt,* pp. 300-303.

Long-nosed Jimmy Carpenter looked more like a tennis champion than a halfback. You cringed every time he came up from the secondary to tackle the other side's fullback. He weighed only 165 and had such a nice set of pearly white teeth.

But when Jakie Sandefer had to sit out a game or two because of injury, Wilkinson moved Carpenter to left half. He was the only sophomore on the starting eleven. "He's a tenacious little guy," Wilkinson described him. The Sooner coach had never hesitated to use a Lilliputian. Some of his better known ones were Royal, Bobby Goad, Buddy Jones, Jack Ging, Gene Calame, Sandefer, and Don K. Brown. Others followed.

Like all of Bud's teams, this one improved steadily. After yielding two touchdowns each to West Virginia and Texas, the '58 Sooners shut down hard on all others, surrendering only four touchdowns in the last eight games.

Blanked in the first quarter by Kansas, coached by Jack Mitchell, former Sooner quarterback, the Sooners drove to a touchdown in five plays. Then the Sooners began a second drive. Gautt launched it by shooting through a hole opened by Jim Lawrence and Dick Carpenter and rolling 42 yards to the Kansas 12, running out of the arms of two Jayhawkers riding him piggyback. Boyd passed to Tillery for the touchdown. Jackie Holt, Gainesville, Texas, junior, circled right end for two extra points when Gautt threw a smashing block ahead of him.

"I felt as proud as if I'd scored," Gautt said later on the team plane coming home.

On a fourth and two situation from the Sooner 36, Kansas gambled, but Gilmer Lewis tackled McKown for no gain. Then the Sooners drove 64 yards to score, Baker hitting Hobby with a fourth-down pass. Baker optioned to Jackie Holt for two extra points.

But Kansas did not fold. From midfield Morris whipped a pass to Homer Floyd. As Floyd ran down the east sideline Jimmy Carpenter turned him back toward the middle, and Bob Harrison, Sooner center who had followed the play hard all the way, was somehow able to lasso him on the 6. Morris tried another pass but Gautt, playing linebacker, leaped high to spear the ball one-handed. "A Willie Mayes catch," the *Daily Oklahoman* called it.

With eight minutes to play, Wilkinson sent in his third team and Johnny Pellow of Enid fielded a Kansas punt on the run and reversing the field sped 38 yards to a touchdown. Then Kansas tried a pass but Pellow flashed in front of the ball, caught it, and turning on his fresh speed ran 78 yards to another touchdown. Just before the game ended, Pellow nearly scored again, returning Morris's punt 50 yards to the Kansas 20. The final Sooner

248

margin was 43-0. Pellow's feat of streaking 166 yards in the last eight minutes and scoring two touchdowns was the talk of the press box.

Steve Jennings, Ardmore senior, blocked the fourth punt of his career to set up a touchdown during Oklahoma's 40-6 triumph over Kansas State on Band Day. Sandefer's 15-yard pass to Tillery fetched it. Bobby Boyd's 10-yard pass to Ronnie Hartline, Lawton sophomore, produced the second. Baker's buck over blockers Harrison, Corbitt, and Thompson brought the third. When Thompson blocked Lee's punt into the end zone, Ross Coyle, preying along the flank, recovered for the fourth touchdown. Carpenter's 45-yard punt runback produced number five. Hobby hit over Jim Lawrence for the sixth.

Bus Mertes, Kansas State coach, said after the game, "Oklahoma, as Bud's folks well know, possesses the quality of getting better as they go along in the season. You'll get better against Colorado too, but I say that's going to be a hell of a ball game."

Oklahoma's 12-year defeatless record in conference play held no terrors for Colorado's Golden Buffaloes. Boulder had always been a barrier for Bud. Never had the Sooners won by more than one touchdown on the frowning heights of Folsom Field.

Ward of Colorado was the conference coach whom Oklahoma feared most. The silver-thatched Buffalo preceptor and his men annually accepted the Oklahoma challenge with joyful truculence. "The kids like playing against Oklahoma. They get up for it," Ward told Bob Hurt of the *Topeka Capital.*

Folsom Field had been sold out at 48,264. Eight thousand more saw the fracas on closed circuit television at Norman, Boulder, and from two auditoriums in Denver. The big crowd was colorful in the bright sunshine.

It was a game of towering punts. Bob Cornell, whom Wilkinson started at quarterback, booted a 50-yarder which tackle Gilmer Lewis covered in racing stride, driving back George Adams, the receiver.

Boyd Dowler, Buffalo quarterback, brought a cry of awe from the stands when he lifted a magnificent punt out of bounds on the Sooner 1, the ball soaring 57 yards. The Buff defense forced a Sooner punt and when Ward's wingback, Eddie Dove, ran it back 40 yards to the Sooner 35, Hartline, the last tackler felled him, and Colorado was in position to score.

But in Bob Harrison, Oklahoma had another in Gomer Jones's long queue of excellent centers. Reversing, Dove swept the weak side for 6, Harrison tackling. Cook tried a strong-side sweep, but Harrison covered fast, tackling for no gain. Colorado bucked down to the Sooner 17 and tried Dove again, but Harrison shot the gap and dropped him for a loss of 5. Dowler passed to fullback Chuck Weiss for 10. The Sooners were penalized for defensive holding to their 2. Cook squirmed over for the touchdown. Ellwin Indorf kicked goal. The Buffs led 7-0.

Proud as peacocks, the Sooners showed what they could do. Storming back from kickoff, they put together a 48-yard touchdown play. It was an off tackle buck to the left with Gautt carrying. Lewis, Thompson, Corbitt, and Harrison drove their opponents out of the play. Jimmy Carpenter picked up the end, Lawrence screened the safety, and Rector blocked the off linebacker.

Gautt bolted through the hole, cut sharply to his right, and outran the last defender to the goal. Faking a kick for point, Baker stood and rolled out behind Gautt to throw a perfect pass for two points to Jimmy Carpenter, alone in the end zone. Oklahoma led 8-7.

The kicking remained fantastic. Jim Davis booted the kickoff over the goal. Oklahoma stopped them, and Dowler belted the ball 52 yards out of bounds on the Sooner 23. McDaniel punted back equally far, and Tillery covered so fast that he nailed Cook for no return on their 25. Cook himself quick-kicked 52 to the Sooner 20. The crowd gasped, watching the punts soar against the snowy profile of the peaks.

The goal was 76 yards away but Oklahoma went the distance. Hobby hit off the handoff to the 1-foot line. Baker scored off right tackle behind Corbitt, Lawrence, Rector, and Hobby. Baker ran the option for two extra points. Now Oklahoma led 16-7.

Again Dowler dropped back to punt. This time there was a double detonation. Ross Coyle, Sooner end from Marlow, streaked in from the outside and blocked the ball. "Lewis and I decided we might block it," Coyle remembers. "Dowler kicked slowly. Lewis went inside, carrying two Colorado guys before him. I went outside and got it."

On fourth down Baker plunged over from one foot out. Baker kicked goal. Oklahoma won 23-7.

After the final gun Ward, the Colorado coach, walked to both Sooner team buses, each full of sweaty players, complimenting the Sooners. He was looking for Bob Harrison, Sooner cocaptain and center. The Sooners finally found Harrison for him and Ward congratulated the big pivot warmly. That gracious gesture by the losing coach typified the sportsmanship under which the Colorado-Oklahoma games were played.

In spite of seven lost fumbles, which tied their all-time record, the Sooners defeated Iowa State 20-0 at Ames. Iowa State lost only two fumbles but each set up an Oklahoma touchdown. Joe Rector introduced the first by hitting Mike Fitzgerald so hard on the second half kickoff that he drove the ball out of his hands, Hobby covering for Oklahoma on the Cyclone 19. Four plays later Jimmy Carpenter scored on the handoff.

The other Iowa State fumble came in the fourth quarter, Bobby Boyd recovering it on the Cardinal and Gold 8. Boyd scored behind blocks by Durham and Payne with Sandefer boring in ahead of him to widen the hole. "Wahoo" McDaniel, Oklahoma's junior end, once quick-kicked 91 yards to the Cyclone 4, longest Oklahoma punt in modern Sooner football history.

Ross Coyle, Sooner end, broke his wrist in this game. "I fell wrong after a tackle and it doubled under me," he says. "On Monday Ken Rawlinson, our trainer, fixed me up with a makeshift deal. He soaked strips of tape in something that made them rigid but still legal. The officials okayed it. The swelling went down and there was no pain. I didn't miss a game."

The next opponent was Missouri, tutored by Dan Devine who in the previous season had coached Arizona State to an all-victorious year. Devine's Sun Devils had led the nation in total offense with 445 yards averaged a game. A Sooner Homecoming Day throng of 54,268 saw the Tigers and Sooners butt it out for the conference championship, the Orange Bowl bid and severance or continuation of Oklahoma's feat of having played 69 consecutive Big Seven games without defeat.

Employing a multiple offense, Devine's powerhouse from the persimmon country had puckered Colorado 33-9 the week before, running their conference record to 4-0. That was Oklahoma's record, too. The Sooners alternated two teams which were named after girls, the starting "Abigails" and the alternate "Belle Starrs" after the infamous female outlaw.

The "Abigails" got their appellation in an odd way. When Oklahoma came to the scrimmage line with a play called, and quarterback David Baker saw an opening for a sneak, he would tap center Bob Harrison on the rump and Harrison in turn would warn the Oklahoma guards that a wedge block was needed by calling out a girl's name. One day in practice the situation arose and Harrison, stumped, blurted out "Abigail," a girl's cognomen popular in the last century but seldom used in the present. It nearly broke up the scrimmage. The Sooners rolled on the ground.

Devine announced Wednesday that he was asking Oklahoma to put the Missouri team benches at Owen Field farther away from the noisy Sooner crowd. At Norman, Wilkinson replied that home and visiting team benches were exactly the same distance from the stands. However, he added, "Of course we'll do whatever we can to make them more comfortable."

Oklahoma quickly complied with Devine's request but business manager Ken Farris pointed out that the change would place the Tigers farther away from their own fans. "We always locate seats for visiting fans in the first eight rows directly behind the visiting team's bench," Farris disclosed.

It was surprisingly warm, 68 degrees, for football in mid-November. On only their fourth play of the game the Sooners fumbled to the Tigers and thus got it out of their system. There were no more lost Sooner fumbles that day.

Oklahoma struck suddenly with a long forward pass. Baker rolled out and pitched to Hobby going to his left. It looked like a sweep until Hobby saw Ross Coyle, his left end, behind the Missouri secondary. Hobby pulled up and fired long to Coyle who outran a Tiger secondaryman to score. It was a 74-yard play. Baker kicked goal. Oklahoma led 7-0.

The Sooner forward passing was sharp that day, Oklahoma completing 10 of 13 for 160 yards. Five Sooners, Boyd, McDaniel, Rolle, Cornell, and Bill Noble intercepted Missouri passes for 68 yards in runbacks. Boyd ran back a punt 38 yards to score. Hobby played both battery positions brilliantly, catching four passes and completing three of three. Coyle lost another touchdown on a completed pass when Gautt clipped, nullifying the 65-yard play. Gautt led the rushing table.

Missouri began the last half by marching 62 yards to the Sooner 13. On fourth down Snowden tried a sneak but Corbitt outcharged his man and, helped by Harrison, held Snowden to inches. The Sooners scored four more touchdowns and won 39-0.

Bill Jennings returned the following week to his hometown of Norman, Oklahoma, as head coach of a foreign football power—Nebraska. Fresh from a 14-6 upset of Pittsburgh, which had beaten Notre Dame, Jennings's Cornhuskers were closing their conference season at Norman. It was Dad's Day and a crowd of 44,740 came.

Every day had been Dad's Day when Jennings, still a boy, watched Ad Lindsey's Sooners play at Owen Field in the late 1920s and early 1930s. Bill's dad was Bud Jennings, Cleveland County sheriff, who spirited his son past business manager Bill Cross's gendarmes by flashing the silver star pinned to his galluses.

Fired by these frequent views of college football, young Bill became the scourge of the Jefferson Elementary School team. He also played for "Snorter" Luster's Norman High School Tigers and Tom Stidham's Oklahoma Sooners. And now he was walking through the gates of Owen Field in a new capacity, as the head coach of the Cornhuskers. He was still getting in the home park free.

When his Scarlet team, famous for upsetting national powers, lost five in a row, Bill was hanged in effigy on his own campus. He replied by inviting his student executioners to report for football. When he beat

Prentice Gautt, Sooner fullback, butts over three West Virginia tacklers, one after another, during his 27-yard run at Norman in 1958. Here he flattens a third man. Photo by Oklahoma Publishing Co.

Prentice Gautt, Sooner fullback.

Brewster Hobby, Sooner halfback, runs back a Missouri punt to start Oklahoma on its first touchdown drive.

Joe Rector, Sooner end.

Pittsburgh the week before the Oklahoma game, the Nebraska kids burned their ropes.

Oklahoma ranked number four nationally that week in both polls. Gautt was averaging approximately six yards per carry, blocking murderously, and, teamed with Bob Harrison, was linebacking ruggedly. For the first time black spectators began to dot the crowds at Owen Field.

The Sooners spanked Nebraska 40 to 7. Oklahoma played its sharpest first quarter of the year, driving 55, 51, and 55 yards to touchdowns. After Larry Naviaux of Nebraska picked off a Sooner pass and ran it back 93 yards down the west sideline for a touchdown, the longest interception return against the Sooners in modern times, Oklahoma put the game away.

The victory assured Oklahoma of a spot in the Orange Bowl despite the fact the Sooners had played Duke there the year before. It was the twenty-fifth anniversary of the Orange Bowl, and they asked the Big Seven Conference to let its true champion play by special dispensation. The Big Seven granted the request.

Oklahoma, 8-1, a bowl certainty, and Oklahoma State, 7-2, a bowl possibility, clashed at Stillwater in the annual battle of the bell clapper. Wilkinson's Sooners didn't have to win the game, and therein lay the danger. For Coach Cliff Speegle's Cowboys, it was the biggest opportunity of the year. They had rested two weeks and on the preceding Saturday had watched the Oklahoma-Nebraska game at Norman. They would be playing at home before a throng of 37,014. Scouts from both the Sugar and Cotton Bowls would be there to watch them. And that wasn't all.

When the Sooners arrived at the Aggie stadium after spending the night before at nearby Guthrie, a dismal sight met their eyes. Not only was the gridiron wet as a swamp from melting snow but an intramural game was being played on it, cutting it up even more. When the storm was forecast three days earlier, Wilkinson had offered to lend the Cowboys the Sooner field tarp, transporting it to Stillwater by truck. The Cowboys refused.

Although the field was a quagmire, game day dawned beautifully. The sun shone brightly and the thermometer at kickoff stood at 60 degrees. Most of the fans sat with their feet in the melting snow after it had been swept off the seats.

The game of fumbles and thrilling goal-line stands stood 0-0 when, with six minutes left to play, the Aggies entrenched themselves and from their 1-yard line threw the Sooners back four times to take the ball on downs. When Jim Wood punted out safely, it looked like a scoreless tie. Wilkinson sent in the "Belle Starrs."

254

They stole the game with one dramatic sortie. It was third down and 7 from the Cowboy 31. The Sooners were in their regular split-T offense. Bobby Boyd, the alternates' junior quarterback, called a weak-side buck by the fullback. But when the Sooners came up to the scrimmage front, Boyd took another look and saw that the Cowboys were in a loaded defensive alignment, poised to shoot all the gaps. So he checked to the quarterback option play to the right.

The Sooner blockers in front of him did their job. Jere Durham and Jerry Tillery double-teamed the tackle. Jim Davis fenced in the guard. Boyd faked the handoff to the right half, kept the ball and faked a pitch to the left half going wide to the right.

He faked it so well that the Aggie linebacker and left end flared out, playing the pitch. Boyd cut back through the hole, stepped around the middle safety and ran 31 yards to a touchdown. With Boyd holding, McDaniel kicked goal. Oklahoma won 7-0.

As usual, the rival players got along fine. The Sooners not only picked tackle Jim Howard and fullback Larry Rundle on their all-opponents' eleven, but gave Howard more votes than any other lineman. They picked end Jim Wood and back Forest Campbell of the Cowboys on their second team.

At the close of the regular season Oklahoma was voted fifth place in both the Associated Press and United Press polls. Thus the Sooners performed the unmatched feat of placing in the nation's top ten for the eleventh consecutive year, convincing proof of Wilkinson's winning consistency. No other school has ever done this. Michigan State and Notre Dame each had achieved it for seven years.

Oklahoma's defense, directed by Gomer Jones, topped the nation in defense against scoring, yielding only 4.9 points a game. The Sooners ranked second in rushing with 257.4 net yards a game. Bob Harrison was a wide choice for All-American center and he also was voted the outstanding lineman of the nation by the United Press.

The campus was shocked three weeks before the Orange Bowl game with Syracuse when David Baker, Oklahoma's starting quarterback, was dropped from the university because of failure to attend class and maintain a satisfactory scholastic standing. In 1958 he was the Sooners' ranking signal caller, punter, placekicker, and best defensive back.

The boy had been a good student, logging an A and four B's in his first freshman semester. He later declared that his troubles at OU "were my own fault." He called Wilkinson "the finest man I ever met . . . he got more out of me than was there. . . . He's done as much for me since I left the university as he did while I was there." He quickly transferred to

Bethany Nazarene College of Bethany, Oklahoma, and in 1959-60-61 played professional football as a defensive back with the San Francisco '49ers. In 1960 he was selected for the Pro-Bowl game.

Bobby Boyd, quarterback of the alternate unit, the "Belle Starrs," was the logical one to succeed Baker but Boyd didn't punt. Neither did anybody else in the starting backfield. Besides, Boyd was accustomed to the relieving unit and they to him. They had scored 17 touchdowns to the starting team's 18. On defense they had given only two touchdowns all season to the starters' three. Bob Cornell, Oklahoma City sophomore, was moved from the third team to the starting group.

How did Cornell feel about the promotion? "When you find a red shirt in your locker, you know it's a challenge but you think you're as good as anybody else and you play like a Sooner," he asserted.

Cornell says that Wilkinson, on the sideline, knew what play his quarterback would call before the team ever left the huddle. "On each play he knew the down, the yard line, the time left, the score, and what he had taught us to call under all those situations," said Cornell. "If we were inside our own 30, the quarterback kept the ball or faked a handoff and kept, or ran the option and kept. He didn't want us to risk pitchouts or handoffs.

"If it was second and eight in midfield, we'd run the fullback off tackle because the defense would probably be spread out to stop us from making eight. If it was second and a foot to go from there, we'd call a reverse or a counter and if they moved in the wrong direction we might score. From the thirty on in—four down territory—we kept trying to make first downs and eventually score.

"Half our plays were either the option pass or run. But most of these were runs because the defensive halfback on the side we ran toward usually stayed back to cover our receiver, leaving us room to run. This was why Oklahoma had the reputation of seldom passing."

"We practiced a lot harder than most bowl teams," remembers Ross Coyle, "and afterwards we did sprints up and down Collins Avenue in front of our Miami hotel. Bud's workouts always paid off. They gave us confidence."

"Bud had given us a new trick play," recalls Bob Cornell, "and also two new passes that Syracuse hadn't seen in our films. In the trick play our quarterback faked a quick pitch to our left half running wide to the left. Meanwhile Prentice Gautt, our fullback, also took two steps to the left, then stopped and looked back. The quarterback turned and faked a handoff

---

Bud Wilkinson demonstrates that football is a game of emotion as well as of coaching.

Photo by sports Information Department, University of Oklahoma.

Photo by C. Ned Hockman

to the right halfback bucking up the middle. Then the quarterback turned and tossed a long, low pitch to Gautt who exploded into sudden motion around our left end. The right side of our line swung across the field to block for Gautt."

In the Orange Bowl game Oklahoma tried to play to the right the first time it got the ball. Gautt got 10 yards. On the next down Cornell called the same play to the left and Gautt, starting, stopping, then bursting into sudden action with all his fresh speed turned on, fielded Cornell's long lateral and ran 42 yards to a touchdown with Rector throwing a block on the goal. Cornell's pass for two extra points was blocked by Mautino but Oklahoma led 6-0.

Late in the first quarter the Orangemen drove 53 yards on Zimmerman's forward passing before fumbling on the Oklahoma 19, Harrison recovering. On the second play thereafter Hobby forward passed to Ross Coyle for 79 yards and a touchdown with Gautt blocking out Zimmerman on the Syracuse 25 and Rector throwing two more blocks along the route.

"Before the game, Bud had changed the pass route for our ends and halfbacks," Coyle remembers. "All year, our ends had been our deep receivers and our halfbacks received shallowly. But against Syracuse Bud reversed this. Our ends ran a shallow out pattern and our halfbacks took the deep routes. Cornell pitched to Hobby and Hobby threw the option pass to me." The Sooners added two extra points when Cornell pitched to Sandefer who passed to Hobby crossing the goal. Oklahoma led 14-0.

Syracuse, coached by Ben Schwartzwelder, didn't fold. "Our program," remembers Joe Rector, "was to run them into the ground, make them tired. But in the second half they came back hard on us and we got tired."

Late in the third period Oklahoma raised its margin to 21-0. Syracuse was back on its 13. They jumped offside and were penalized back to their 8. Cornell threw Baker for a loss of 5. Davis and Thompson held Zimmerman to 2. Harrison batted down a pass. From his own 5, Gilburg punted. Hobby ran it back 40 yards to a touchdown.

"It was a low, line-drive punt, and Hobby took it on the right hash mark," recalled Cornell. "We didn't have a chance to block for him. He fielded it and took off down the sideline and scored." Boyd kicked goal.

As the fourth period began, Syracuse marched 69 yards to a touchdown in seven plays. The Saltine Warriors ran over the strong Sooner defense. In fact, they outrushed Oklahoma 239 to 152 net yards in the game. All their plays were runs. Weber's 15-yard buck brought the score. Their pass for two extra points failed. Oklahoma won 21-6.

1958 SENIORS TODAY

David Baker is State Farm Insurance agent, Norman, Oklahoma.

Dick Corbitt is superintendent of buildings and grounds, Moore Public Schools, Moore, Oklahoma.

Ross Coyle is editor and publisher of the *Blanchard News,* Blanchard, Oklahoma.

Bob Harrison owns and manages a 1,500-acre farm near Stamford, Texas.

Jim Lawrence is owner of the Lawrence Department Store, Cordell, Oklahoma.

Joe Rector is president and broker of Rector Realty, Inc., Muskogee, Oklahoma.

Jakie Sandefer is president and chairman of the board of Sandefer Oil and Gas Corporation, Inc., of Houston, Texas.

14. THE CHICAGO FOOD POISONING

Oklahoma opened in 1959 against Northwestern, a Big Ten Conference colossus coached by Ara Parseghian. In the previous season the Wildcats had drubbed Ohio State 21-0, annihilated Michigan 55-24, and bowed only 20-26 to Iowa's Rose Bowl champions. From that northern powerhouse, Parseghian kept 29 of his top 33 players.

Texas, coached by Darrell Royal, only club to defeat Oklahoma in 1958, still kept 14 of its top 22 hands to infiltrate with an all-victorious freshman crop. Army, tutored by Dale Hall, retained its nifty Joe Caldwell to Bill Carpenter "Lonely End" passing alliance and a lot more besides. The Big Seven clubs wouldn't lie down either. "We'll have to play at a fierce level of intensity to survive," Wilkinson warned his 1959 squad.

Most of the pressure that fall fell on Gomer Jones. The squat Sooner line boss was hard at work with the greenest forwards of his 13-year career at Norman. In the coaches' locker room after practice, Jones would relax with a cigarette. "The freshmen are all scared of me," he soliloquized softly. "Hell, I'm not a tough guy. When they get to be sophomores and juniors, I'm scared of them."

They all liked him. "Gomer was the guy with the shirt unbuttoned and the hair rumpled," remembers Jim Byerly. "He was the one who would chew you out. Bud would smile and whisper in that low voice that only you could hear. But Gomer hollered and the whole world heard him. He was like a nagging wife. I loved him.

"In spring, during the off season, old earthy Gomer liked to keep in touch with his linemen," Byerly went on. "He'd ask us to come by his office for a little fireside chat. 'How're your grades?' he'd ask and so on. Once when Bill Winblood, another of our centers, and I were sitting there, Gomer began slapping his pockets. 'God damn!' he burst out. 'I'm out of cigarettes.' Turning to Winblood, he said, 'Bill, I know you smoke. Gimme one.' Grinning, Winblood handed it over."

They all liked Wilkinson too. Jim Byerly recalls, "Once I got a letter from Bud inviting me to come to his home and have dinner with him and Mrs. Wilkinson. I was surprised and nervous until I got there and found 40 other players there, too. There was nothing formal about it. We all had a good time. He just wanted to have us over for dinner."

Quarterback Bob Cornell was slowed that fall by his studies in the architectural school. "I was down in grade points and wanted to drop architecture," says Cornell today. "But Port wouldn't let me. 'No!' he said. 'Stick it out. We'll get after it.' He made me take a summer correspondence course, Math 14, analytical geometry. If it hadn't been for Port, I'd never have got my degree."

There was much change. The players moved into Washington House, their new athletic dormitory. It had sunken living rooms, seven-foot bunks, and cork bulletin boards for glamour pinups, but no air-conditioning. Assistant coach Clive Rush had resigned to return to Ohio State. In his stead Wilkinson hired Bob Blaik, son of Earl ("Red") Blaik, former Army coach.

The game was livened that fall when the College Rules Committee eased the substitution restriction and lengthened the goal posts. The crossbar was widened for the first time in history from 18 feet 6 inches to 23 feet 4 inches to encourage field goal attempts. But the committee was most pleased with its revision of the substitution statute. Basically, one player at one time could reenter a game as many times as his coach wished, provided the game clock was stopped.

Wilkinson predicted that college offenses would continue to stress the broken formations so popular the last two years, the slot, flanker, man in motion, and split ends. He believed that those devices would do to the secondary what the splits did to the defensive line, spread it.

"Novelty is important," Bud believed. "If you do something different you don't have to do it real well."

The Sooners still rewarded rockem-sockem defensive play. The "Ug" Award was introduced that fall. It went to the player who performed most outstandingly on defense in each game. The "Ug" was sponsored by Tim Cohane, sports editor of *Look* magazine, and by Willard Mullin, *New York Herald-Tribune* sports cartoonist who painted the trophy pictograph. Jerry Thompson, Sooner tackle from Ada, won it four times that fall.

Thompson, a stubby little Scotch-Choctaw, maintained that the most fun about a football pileup was to be on the bottom. "If you're on the bottom," he explained, "you probably got the first tackle and started the whole thing. That oughta make you feel proud."

Monte Deere, a small wiry farm boy living near Amarillo, Texas, was offered a scholarship that fall. "OU was the only major university that came after me," says Deere. "They really wanted my friend, Duane Cook, Amarillo tackle who had several major offers. I'd been full of Boomer Sooner ever since high school. Duane soon came across too." The Sooners called Deere "John Deere" and no wonder. He had lived and worked on a farm nearly all his life.

261

Another freshman who signed that fall was Melvin Sandersfeld, a rangy tailback from Hobart. In the 1958 finale at Clinton, Sandersfeld was calling signals. With Clinton leading Hobart 6-0 and Hobart possessing the ball back on its 20, the game was nearly over. Sandersfeld began calling himself on short punches over guard 80 yards up the field. He scored the touchdown. Then he bucked over right guard for two extra points and the 8-6 win.

Afterwards, Tex Bartlett, his coach, had a giant-sized picture of Sandersfeld installed in the lobby of the Hobart High School gymnasium. Abashed, Sandersfeld wouldn't enter that edifice for months.

Port Robertson, Oklahoma's freshman coach, had 140 men report that fall, 103 of them walk-ons. One of the walk-ons had just returned from a lion hunt in Africa. "Now, men," Port told the squad that first day, "we've got a lot of fellows. We're going to do some hitting and sprinting to find out who's got it."

He selected the two biggest fullbacks, James Parker of Sweetwater, Texas, and Gary Wylie of Whitesboro, Texas, and lined them up facing each other. Robertson blew his whistle. *Bam!* Parker and Wylie crashed into each other so hard that white chips flew off their helmets. That one lick reduced the squad from 140 to 130. The lion hunter and nine others quit on the spot.

In the spring of 1959 the NCAA's investigation of Oklahoma football was reopened. Walter Byers, NCAA executive director, asked Bill Jennings, the Nebraska coach, to appear before the NCAA infractions committee to answer questions. Jennings did. Byers was very interested in how much financial help Art Wood, the Oklahoma City accountant, had given Sooner football.

Meanwhile, President Cross had queried Wood about the matter. The accountant admitted freely that he had handled such a fund, and that he had asked close friends and clients in his firm to partially reimburse him. He pointed out that the Touchdown Club or any other organization was not involved and that he had operated on an individual basis. He said that Jennings was the only Sooner coach who knew of this and that Jennings was not involved in misdoings of any consequence. The total expended during the three-year period did not exceed the sum of $6,000, Wood said.

President Cross relayed this information to Walter Byers. Byers asked Wood if the NCAA could examine the records of the funds—bank statements and cancelled checks—on a confidential basis. It was his view that a fund might still exist and that the quickest way to clear up the matter was to permit a confidential inspection of the records. Wood declined, explaining that it would be a violation of professional ethics and also of a federal statute that could bring a year's imprisonment and a $1,000 fine.[1]

Wood's explanation did not satisfy the NCAA, and early in January of 1960 Oklahoma was placed on indefinite suspension with the added provision that the football team could not appear in postseason games or on television. This was not damaging then, since Oklahoma had neither the team nor the record to be invited. Meanwhile, Wood maintained a close contact with Byers, the two meeting twice at Kansas City to discuss the situation.

Oklahoma suffered a costly casualty in scrimmage the Saturday before the Northwestern game. Leon Cross, who for three days prior to the accident had been on the Sooner starting eleven at guard, tore knee ligaments while making a pass protection block. Two days later the knee was operated on by Dr. Don O'Donoghue in Oklahoma City.

Depressed, Cross went to Wilkinson and offered to surrender his scholarship. "I felt like I was taking a handout," says Cross. "I wanted to get a job, work my way through. Bud wouldn't hear of it. 'We're not taking you off scholarship,' he said firmly. 'The percentage of those who return to the university after losing their scholarship is very low.' He told me that my first duty was to get a good education."

Wilkinson moved Phil Lohmann, most versatile player on the squad, into Cross's position. As a senior, Lohmann remembers, "The OU football brochure designated my utility position with a 'u.' My friends all said that meant 'useless.'"

Wilkinson flew the Sooners to Evanston on Wednesday night so they could work out Thursday in a secluded spot, go to the theater and retire early. They had dinner at the Chez Paree, famous for its cuisine, its popular entertainers, and its early show.

I had been in Chicago all week calling on newspapers and broadcasting stations, helping to publicize the game. On Thursday afternoon when I returned to my Chicago hotel, Fred Russell, sports editor of the *Nashville, Tennessee, Banner* who did the college football preview for the *Saturday Evening Post,* phoned from Nashville. He had picked Oklahoma to finish number one in the nation that year.

Russell revealed that Oklahoma had just dropped from a six-point to a

[1] Section 7216 of the Internal Revenue Code forbade any person engaged in the business of preparing tax returns from disclosing any information furnished to him for, or in connection with, the preparation of any such return or declaration, "or from using any such information for any purpose other than to prepare, or assist in preparing, any such return or declaration." It provided that those who did "shall be guilty of a misdemeanor, and, upon conviction thereof, shall be fined not more than $1,000, or imprisoned not more than one year, or both, together with the costs of prosecution."

three-point favorite in the betting odds against Northwestern. "As I recall," says Russell today, "we ran the point spread in Friday's paper and usually got it from a Nashville bookie. My guess is that the guy who gave us the odds on Thursday must have phoned back later to report the sudden change —and ask if we had any news of an Oklahoma injury or anything."

I told him that aside from the loss of Leon Cross a week earlier, I knew of none, and that our team was then working out at Evanston. After the workout, there was no injury or illness. The Sooners showered, dressed, and went by bus to the Chez Paree. It was early.

"Then something odd happened," remembers halfback Brewster Hobby. "The waiters began spot-serving the fruit cocktails, instead of going down the line. It was organized." Fullback Prentice Gautt and end Wahoo Mc-Daniel didn't go the Chez Paree. "Something cautioned me to stay in the hotel and rest," Gautt says today. "I still had in mind not being served in some restaurants because of my color. Besides, I was trying to put on my game face, to think about the game."

Later Ron Hartline, Gautt's roommate, came into the room. "He looked pale and sick," Gautt says. "He told me that he and several other of our players had become violently ill from the fruit cocktail served them at the supper club and had just had their stomachs pumped out. All night he kept getting up and going to the bathroom."

Gautt soon found out what had happened. Within 30 minutes after being served the fruit cocktail, 13 Sooner players, including 10 on the starting and alternate teams and Jimmy Harris, student assistant coach, became very queasy. "Feeling a sudden inclination to vomit, I ran to the rest room and found lots of competition," says Hobby. "So many of our players were chucking their food that the fluid on the floor was as thick as my shoe soles." "I was nauseated," recalls left end Paul Benien, "and ran downstairs to get some fresh air."

Taxicabs were summoned to transport them back to the hotel. The sick players piled into them. However, the cabs had to stop several times en route so that the players could get out and regurgitate. It was decided to take them to a hospital in Evanston. "I was so sick," remembers halfback Jimmy Carpenter, "that when I leaned out the cab door to vomit, I would have fallen into the street if Brewster Hobby hadn't grabbed the back of my belt."

Quarterback Bobby Boyd was so ill that he lay prostrate on the ground. Bob Page, another quarterback, suffered a circulatory collapse which was of deep concern to Dr. D. G. ("Mike") Willard, the Sooner team physician who hurried to the Louise Weiss Memorial Hospital where many of the players had been taken.

"At the hospital I was told by hospital personnel that the boys were ill with food intoxication," Doctor Willard said. "Seven of the players were put to bed there and nine stomachs were washed out. The affected boys were given hypodermics for nausea."

"Many of us were too weak to work out Friday," Carpenter remembers. "Bob Page, who had gone into shock at the hospital, wasn't released until 9:30 Saturday morning, the day of the game." "On Friday I still felt like I'd gone through a bad case of the flu," says Hobby. "I had no strength in my legs. This persisted up to game time." Left end Paul Benien says, "In the dressing room before the game I weighed only 179. My playing weight was 192."

As was his custom, Wilkinson didn't make a big issue of the incident in the newspapers. However, when he talked to the squad Friday night at the Orrington, he told them, "Don't tell yourself when it gets tough, 'I've got the best excuse in the world in the food poisoning.' Forget that. The record won't say 'food poisoning.' It'll just give the score."

On Saturday the game began under dark, fast-moving banks of clouds blown by a strong south wind. A crowd of 50,813 filled Dyche Stadium, 6,250 of them Oklahomans. Dick Thornton of Northwestern booted a punt into the wind that rolled out on the Sooner 9. Boyd called the correct play, a quick kick. However, the center snap struck another Oklahoma player's leg. McDaniel snatched up the ball and tried to punt anyhow but Joe Abbatiello, Wildcat guard, blocked it, and Gene Gossage, Wildcat tackle, recovered on the Sooner 9, Purdin scoring three plays later.

The sky darkened and it began to rain, then stopped. The spectators began putting on their raincoats. The Sooners weren't playing well. Their alternates, a green untried array, came in, were stopped, and punted only 9 yards. Thornton ran wide then cut back to score standing up. Stock missed goal and the Sooners trailed 0-13. Hobby ran the kickoff back 30 yards to the 43, then fumbled.

The rain began to fall in sheets, drenching the crowd. So savage was the cloudburst that writers in the press box could not see the players on the field. The Sooners kept driving. Jimmy Carpenter swept his right end, saw Hobby open in the end zone and fired a short pass through the downpour for a touchdown. Jim Davis kicked goal. Score 13-7.

Oklahoma's alternates went in. On Northwestern's first scrimmage play after the kickoff, Burton dashed 62 yards to their third touchdown. The Sooners fumbled on their 7, and Northwestern scored on a pass, Thornton to right end Paul Yanke. Northwestern led 25-7.

The Oklahoma alternates, with Bob Page moving them well, threatened. With 50 seconds left in the half, Jackie Holt made a tremendous catch of

265

Page's pass for a 35-yard gain to the Northwestern 10. But the Sooners fumbled on the next play, and time ran out.

Those fumbles were fatal. The Sooners fumbled 12 times to Northwestern's 2, losing 5, donating Northwestern the ball on the Sooner 9, 8, 20, and 37, besides tossing a pitchout into a Wildcat's hands. Northwestern quickly cashed those five miscues into five touchdowns.

There was no rain in the last half but the turf was awash. Marshall York charged hard to blunt two plays but Thornton's blooper punt rolled weirdly to the Sooner 2 and stopped as if thumbing its nose at the Oklahomans. Oklahoma's alternates marched 50 yards to the game's final score, a buck by Jackie Holt with Billy White, Jerry Payne, and Benien blocking ahead. Northwestern won 45 to 13.

With the game almost over, Parseghian, the winning coach, looked across the field at Wilkinson. "Bud had been my idol," Parseghian said later. ". . . The thing that impressed me was seeing Bud Wilkinson moving up and down the sidelines, shouting encouragement to his team, assuming that the contest was still very much alive."[2]

Oklahoma's players gave Northwestern full credit. Of Pete Arena, Wildcat guard, tackle Jerry Thompson said later, "Real tough boy. Best lineman I've played against." Gene Gossage, Purple tackle, also sold the Sooners. Gautt was asked after the game whether the slippery ball had any effect on the outcome. "It wasn't that slippery," he replied sadly.

Why did the odds on Oklahoma change so suddenly Thursday afternoon prior to the food poisoning three hours later? Gamblers had somehow penetrated the supper club's security and adulterated the fruit cocktail. The Chicago police showed very little interest in the matter. Two weeks later at Los Angeles, Occidental College cancelled a game when its team was laid low with symptoms of food poisoning.

At his press conference at Norman the following Monday noon, Wilkinson was asked why Oklahoma played the game "with upset tummies." Bud explained, "In college football you play under whatever circumstances exist at that time. If you win, you do so with humility. If you lose, you try to lose the same way." His reply was an expression of his creed.

The only humorous treatment of the food poisoning episode was that of John Cronley, veteran sports editor of the *Daily Oklahoman* of Oklahoma City. In his column a few days later, Cronley wrote of two Oklahoma doctors. One went to Evanston to see the game. The other stayed home to watch it on TV. The latter, when the game ended, wired his friend, "Dammit! You poisoned the wrong team."

[2] Ara Parseghian to Tim Cohane, July 16, 1964.

There was no letdown in Sooner fan enthusiasm following the Northwestern defeat. At midnight, when the Sooners finally arrived at the Oklahoma City airport, 3,000 students and fans had driven the 40-mile round trip from Norman to greet them.

Despite the torrential rains that fell at Norman the last three days and nights before the Colorado game, 53,745 people fought the weather and somehow arrived at Norman for the contest, many of them during the first and second quarters.

Oklahoma's 42-12 victory over Colorado's young team was due to errorless play and the fact that the Sooners had recovered their physical sharpness. Mike McClellan, 180-pound Baylor transfer starting his first game, intercepted a Colorado pass and turning on all his fine speed came back 29 yards. McClellan then took Oklahoma down to the goal with a 37-yard ramble to the Buffalo 10. Bobby Boyd dove to a touchdown over the backs of Davis, Lewis, and Thompson. McClellan had replaced his roommate, Jimmy Carpenter, who was lost for the season after rekinking a leg muscle in the Northwestern game.

Bob Scholl, Oklahoma's alternate center, left the game at the half with an injury, and Wilkinson replaced him with Jim Byerly, the sophomore third-stringer. "I want you to do a good job, Jim," said Wilkinson.

"Man!" says Byerly today. "That fired me up. Although I was a Baptist, Bud had always seemed like the Pope to me." Byerly played sensationally, making 13 tackles in the last half alone.

During the week of the Texas game, it was always Port Robertson's custom to convene his freshman squad and warn them not to go to Dallas and sell their complimentary tickets. One of the freshmen that year was John Tatum, a lineman from Heavener.

"Three weeks into my first season and school year," Tatum recalls the incident, "I would make my first journey to Dallas, the Cotton Bowl, the OU-Texas shoot-out, and the Dallas County jail."

Tatum and two other freshman players, Don Dickey and Dean Bass, arrived in Dallas at 7 o'clock Friday night and stopped at a restaurant. "We sat at the counter and ordered," Tatum describes it. "Dean whipped out two Texas-OU tickets and said he needed to sell them. A gentleman at the counter overheard him and approaching him, asked the price. Dean quoted him a price of $25-30 per ticket. The gentleman said fine and that he would go around the corner to his hotel room and be back with the money.

"Meanwhile, Dean went to the rest room. He gave Don the tickets and said if the guy comes back to make the deal. The guy came back, Don handed him the tickets and Don handed me the money. The next thing

I knew we were under arrest. This was about 7:20 P.M. which must have been some kind of freshman football team record at OU. Arrive in Dallas at 7 P.M., arrested 20 minutes later."

Dean Bass called Coach Robertson that night, 24 hours after Port's "stay out of trouble" speech and asked him to get Don and John released. Port did get them released—at 12:45 the next day—just before the Cotton Bowl kickoff. On Sunday evening Tatum found a note on his door at the dorm back in Norman. It read: "Mr. Johnny Edward Tatum: Be at my office at 7 A.M. tomorrow. Incidentally, that is when the little hand is on the 7 and the big hand is on the 12. Port."

"Little did I know," Tatum resumes the account, "that at 7 next morning my destiny in life would be altered by a man I would learn to despise, then respect, then love—Port G. Robertson. The theme of the meeting was that we had strayed off the beaten path and Port now would 'take us under his wing.'" An hour later Max Morris, varsity tackle and Tatum's room-mate told him what being under Port's wing really entailed. "I was terrified," Tatum says.

"The first thing I did was a G.I. on our dorm room in readiness for Port's noon inspection. My mother would not have believed the cleanliness of our room that day. Everything was spotless. I'll always remember the frustrated look on Port's face when he couldn't find any dirt or dust anywhere. A feeling of inner triumph raced through me as Port turned to leave. I had won the first battle, I thought.

"As Port passed my desk he suddenly stopped and pointed at a bottle of aspirin on a desk shelf. 'Are those your aspirin?' he asked with a satisfied tone to his voice.

"Yes, but can't you have aspirin on your desk?" I snapped back.

"Port turned toward me and with an almost brutal stare that I felt cut into me said, 'Mr. Tatum, it is all right to have aspirin on your desk, but look what a very messy person you are. The aspirins are not stacked neatly inside the bottle. That will cost you 100 trips up and down the stadium steps."

"It seemed to me in the months that followed everything I did was wrong. I wanted to rebel against Port but I became determined that he could not run me off. As I became more and more disciplined, the hate I had formerly felt toward Port changed to respect. I learned from him that everything has a price tag. The academic side of college had become easier for me since Port had confined me to mandatory study hall three or four nights a week throughout my entire freshman year.

"Through all my mental warfare with Port I learned that he was a man who patronized no one. His word was his bond. If Port said it, it would

268

come to pass. I never remember Port being wrong about anything. He always seemed to know what I was up to well in advance. I was dazzled. He had gotten my attention.

"Today, I still think about Port and his Portisms. The Great One taught me the most important secret in life, to give freely of myself in order to help others. His willingness to help me was the basic foundation upon which my respect, admiration, and love for him would be built."[3]

The forearm shiver game, Oklahoma vs. Texas, was next. The Oklahoma practices that week were magnificent. The Texas boys on the Sooner squad wanted to play well against their former high-school teammates aligned with the Longhorns.

Loss of three Sooner starters caused the coaches to make more adjustments than a chiropractor. Jimmy Carpenter and Brewster Hobby, starting half-backs, and Billy Jack Moore, starting guard, were out with injuries. Despite that, Hobby was so fired up that he insisted on wearing his full uniform anyhow and sitting on the Oklahoma bench.

Not only did Oklahoma play with several whites and a black, but Wilkinson also suited two Indians, left end "Wahoo" McDaniel, a Choctaw-Chickasaw born at Bernice, Oklahoma, and Jerry Thompson, a part-Choctaw from Ada. Kirk Kickingbird, the Cherokee-Ojibway student mascot from Anadarko who was known as "Little Red," danced along the sidelines in full war regalia.[4]

Oklahoma's practicing fervor spilled over into the game. After the Texas kickoff soared into the end zone, Prentice Gautt rushed 19 yards off guard and 14 off tackle before Texas stopped the advance. Jerry Thompson was trap-blocking the Texas guard, Jim Davis, senior center, was mucking the other guard to the outside, while ends McDaniel and Ronnie Payne went down for the halfbacks. This became Oklahoma's most effective play of the game.

"I remember Gautt running that trap," Darrell Royal, the Texas coach, says today. "He just raced up and down the field. He must have made 150 yards on us that day." (Actually, Gautt rolled 135 and Ronnie Hartline, alternate fullback, 54.)

Midway through the first quarter, Texas surrendered its only fumble, Jackie Holt recovering on their 32. The Sooner alternates were in. Bob Cornell, their quarterback, made an excellent call. It was third down and one on the Texas 23. Cornell faked to fullback Ron Hartline who himself

---

[3] John Tatum to author, October 22, 1980.
[4] Today Kickingbird is an attorney in Washington, D.C., and director of the American Indian Law Institute.

excellently faked the trap buck, drawing in the Texas defense. Jackie Holt slipped behind their secondary and Cornell passed to him for the first touchdown. Davis missed goal but Oklahoma led 6-0.

"Bud had just put the play in that week," Bobby Boyd recalls. "Everybody had been setting their defense to stop our fullbacks."

The Sooner starters came back in. On a Texas sweep, Boyd, who would lead tacklers of both teams with eight clean stops, came up fast to tackle Collins for no gain. Then he slapped down a pass. Texas punted. The Sooners had field position on their 41. Boyd skillfully moved them 59 yards to a touchdown in seven plays, pitching out to Dick Carpenter who broke 33 yards to a touchdown while almost trodding the sideline chalk. The Sooner try for two extra points failed. But Oklahoma led 12-0.

Texas rallied fiercely. They drove 73 yards, Rene Ramirez tossing the halfback pass to Larry Cooper for the touchdown. Bob Lackey's try for point was too low but struck a Sooner player and ricocheted weirdly between the posts. The Oklahoma lead was cut to 12-7.

Again Texas put a strong drive into gear and swung 61 yards in nine plays for another touchdown. Marshall York, Sooner right tackle, sustained a bruised hip on this drive and was withdrawn.

Amid the wildest excitement, Dowdle, the Texas fullback, hammered 5 yards to the Sooner 1. There were only 18 seconds left in the first half and the clock was running. With players of both teams still tangled on the ground, there wasn't time for Texas to get up, retreat to the huddle, hear the signal, return to the scrimmage line, and launch a play. However, Gilmer Lewis, Sooner captain and left tackle, had been hurt on the preceding play and the officials called time, stopping the clock.

After Wilkinson substituted for Lewis, Texas still had time for one more play. They scored on a buck by Dowdle. That marked the first time in five years that the Orange had scored through Oklahoma with a rush. Mickey Jackson, substitute tackle who had been a former high-school quarterback but loyally accepted his switch to the line, blocked Lackey's try for point but Texas led 13-12. When the Sooners reached their locker room, they learned they must play the last half without both York and Lewis, their starting tackles.

With four sophomores now in the starting lineup, Oklahoma gave it a terrific try. In the last half the Sooners launched four threatening drives but twice self-destructed with lost fumbles and were stopped twice. Later, Texas scored on a pass, Mike Cotten to Collins, the play going 61 yards. They failed to convert but won 19-12. In his letter to the alumni Wilkinson praised his team which had contended fiercely although going most of the way without five starters.

270

Oklahoma's gaudy record of conference invincibility went on target the next week before 38,561 at Missouri. Gilmer Lewis and Marshall York, Oklahoma starting tackles, stayed home to take treatment. Lewis had a knee sprain, York a hip-pointer. Thompson was switched from guard to left tackle. Vernon Lang, Wichita Falls, Texas, sophomore, went to left guard. Two sophomore alternates, right guard Karl Milstead and right tackle Tom Cox, advanced to the starting eleven. Billy Jack Moore and big Bill Watts moved into the alternate line.

The Missouri defense was so sinewy that Oklahoma led only 6-0 at the half. Jackie Holt's pass interception run to the Mizzou 36 launched that touchdown. Mike McClellan scored it behind a block by Gautt but McDaniel missed goal.

In the last half Oklahoma came back strongly. The Sooner margin grew to 9-0 after Jim Davis booted a field goal. As the fourth quarter started, the Sooners wheeled 77 yards to a second touchdown on Boyd's 14-yard cutback. Danny LaRose, Tiger end, came up fast to stop him but Gautt cut him down at the corner. Boyd pitched to Hobby for two extra points and Oklahoma led 17-0.

Later, the starters drove to the Tiger 39 and Wilkinson sent in the third team. Bob Page, its quarterback, scored on a 3-yard keeper. Page's keeper for two extra points was barely short. Final score, 23-0.

Coach Jack Mitchell's Kansas Jayhawkers failed by only the thump of the ball off the cranium of the head linesman to shatter Oklahoma's 13-year record of never having lost a conference game under Wilkinson. Bobby Boyd's punt runback, a darting, twisting weave of 44 yards, and Boyd's smash across the goal behind blocks by Thompson, Lang, and Jim Davis had brought the Sooner touchdown. Davis kicked the vital extra point. Then Dave Harris, Kansas's third-string halfback, broke for 60 yards and a touchdown, faking the last Sooner tackler out of his socks. Mitchell chose to go for an 8-7 victory rather than a 7-7 tie.

"It was a rollout running pass into the flat," the Jayhawk coach recalls today. "Our kid [halfback Jim Jarrett] was reaching out to catch the ball when it hit the official in the back of the head."

The ball rebounded into the arms of Bob Cornell, Oklahoma's defensive half, and Cornell promptly touched it down in the end zone. So Oklahoma won 7-6, but the Big Seven was closing in on the shining Sooner string of 74 conference games without defeat.

In the fourth period a record punt was born. John Hadl, big Kansas halfback whose last name looked like a typographical error, walked back into the end zone. The north wind blew behind him. The ball detonated off Hadl's toe and lifting monstrously soared far over the Sooner safety's head

271

then bounded in long leaps to the Oklahoma 2-yard line. The punt measured 94 yards.

Mitchell's assistant at Kansas was Bobby Goad, lightweight Sooner end of 1946–49. I liked something Goad said before the game. The Sooners had lost to Northwestern and Texas and looked a cut below their usual quality. A sportswriter asked Goad how he felt about the Kansas-Oklahoma game. "I hope we beat Oklahoma," Bobby said, "but I don't want anybody else beating 'em."

When Oklahoma last lost a conference football game, 13-16 to Kansas at Lawrence in 1946, Jim Tatum was coach, Harry Truman was president, and the current crop of Sooner freshmen hadn't yet started first grade.

Nebraska, the old champ, coached by Bill Jennings, the Norman boy who had been an assistant at Oklahoma under Wilkinson, put together its best game of the season to upset Oklahoma 25-21 at Lincoln and stop the Sooners' undefeated conference string at 74 straight games.

"The only thing we felt we could beat OU at was our kicking game," says Jennings today. "We punted seven times, sometimes on third down when we had the wind. We never gave them the ball in Nebraska territory all afternoon."

Wilkinson's postgame statement agreed. "We extend our most sincere congratulations to the Nebraska squad and Coach Bill Jennings," he said. "They prepared well for the game and played well."

Bud took the blame for the defeat. "Although our assistant coaches are doing a fine job, it must be that I am not," he said in his alumni letter. "If I were, our team would not continue to make the same type of basic mechanical errors so repeatedly in every game. We allowed Nebraska to block a quick kick and run it back for a touchdown. We allowed them to return one of our punts 61 yards to our 4-yard line. With three men back, we let another Nebraska punt drop without fielding it."

The Sooners started off well, driving the opening kickoff 72 yards for the touchdown. Most of their plays were sweeps right and left off an unbalanced spread with Gautt putting the Cornhusker cornerman on the ground so often that Oklahoma scored in 2 minutes and 50 seconds elapsed time. On his first carry of the game Gautt bucked off tackle for the touchdown and Jim Davis kicked goal.

Then Nebraska showed what it could do. After Harry Tolly's punting gave them field position on the Sooner 43, Jennings's men drove to a touchdown, scoring on a jump pass, Tolly to Dick McDaniel. Ron Meade missed the conversion. Oklahoma led 7-6.

A few minutes later, the Sooners tried a quick kick. But the center snap was high. Cornell tried to kick it anyhow and center Jim Moore of Nebraska blocked it. Guard Leroy Zentic picked it up and ran 30 yards to a touchdown. Again Meade missed the conversion but now Nebraska led 12-7.

Aroused, the Sooner alternates marched 54 yards to a touchdown after Jerry Tillery returned the short kickoff to the Sooner 46. From the Cornhusker 6, Cornell called the fullback slant but seeing Nebraska overshifted to stop it, he sneaked up the middle to score. Davis kicked goal.

Nebraska never slackened in the last half. Soon, Tolly's punts gave them field position on the Sooner 33. Tolly twice dropped back to pass. Each time the Sooners rushed fiercely, forcing him to run. He ran well, darting to the Sooner 6. Oklahoma held. Meade kicked a 22-yard field goal at an angle and Nebraska, putting up a spirited fight, had regained the lead, 15-14.

As the fourth quarter began Nebraska continued to control the game. McDaniel punted 54 yards, but Pat Fischer, Nebraska's speedy little half, ran out of the arms of a Sooner tackler and sped 61 yards to the Sooner 4 before Hobby caught him from behind. On the third Nebraska play, Tolly scored. Meade kicked goal. Now Nebraska led by eight, 22-14.

Three plays later, the Cornhuskers built their lead to 11 on a field goal when Meade bored the ball between the posts from 33 yards out. The score was 25-14 with 6:50 left to play.

In the game's dying moments Oklahoma, now fully alive to its peril, spurred itself into a desperate effort. The Sooners marched 67 yards to a touchdown in nine plays from kickoff, using only 2:44 off the clock. Gautt began it with a 19-yard thrust over Payne, York, and Hobby and ended it with a scoring slant on fourth down from the 3. Davis kicked goal. Now Nebraska led 25-21 with 4:06 remaining.

Davis kicked off and Ronnie Payne tackled Dyer back on Nebraska's 18. Oklahoma's defense held. Nebraska punted dead to the Oklahoma 41. Only 2:25 was left to play.

The Sooners attacked with desperate fury. Boyd passed to McDaniel for 11. The Nebraska crowd stood, shouting encouragement to the Cornhuskers. Gautt slashed off tackle for 8. Boyd passed to Hobby for 9. Gautt bucked 3 yards to a first down on the Cornhusker 27. But time was almost gone, forcing Oklahoma to pass. Meade intercepted Oklahoma's third one in the end zone, and the game was over.

"That destroyed everybody," Bob Cornell recalls, still melancholy about it 23 years later. With the Nebraska students carrying their victorious coach off on their shoulders, Wilkinson had to run 100 yards to overtake them so that he could shake Jennings's hand.

And so college football's longest conference undefeated string was halted

273

Wilkinson walks in defeat from the field at Lincoln in 1959 after Nebraska's 25-21 upset win. It was Oklahoma's first conference loss under Bud in 13 years. Photo by Don M. Wright, UPI.

Guard Karl Milstead leading quarterback Bobby Boyd on a run again Kansas at Norman in 1959.

Fullback Ron Hartline running against Texas at Dallas in 1959.

at 74 games and 13 years. That Sooner skein took its hallowed place in football's paradise alongside three other Wilkinson feats, 47 straight wins (no ties) 1953-57, 48 games undefeated (one tie) 1953-57, and eleven consecutive years placing in the top ten of the Associated Press poll 1948-58.

In their dressing room after the game, the Sooners sat gloomily staring down at the concrete floor while truckers loaded the baggage. Bud asked the boy Nebraska had sent to help the Oklahoma student managers to leave. Then, standing in his shirt sleeves, bareheaded, his face drawn, he talked to the squad.

"I must be a sorry coach, men," he began, "because I can't seem to get through to you that if you have discipline you'll never make the ridiculous mistakes you made out there today. If I were doing my job correctly, you'd have that discipline. I've told you over and over what's the matter but I didn't sell you, I guess. I just don't know how to get on people's backs."

He described the mistakes they had made. "I don't ask you to win," he went on. "All I ask you to do is play as well as you can. That's all. If you'd just do that, I'd be the happiest guy in the world. Even if we lost."

Later, seated in the bus with Mr. Dowell and myself, he said, "We're not a hungry team. When we get behind, we eat 'em up. But we don't play well when we're ahead. It's my fault or we wouldn't do that. I feel so bad about it that I could cry."

At the Lincoln airport a high fence separated the Oklahoma team plane from the terminal area. The Sooners had started to board the plane. A Nebraska student wearing a yellow sweater drove up in a car with several companions. "Yeah, you're the great Oklahoma team," he chided, "but you can't beat Nebraska. Go on back and get yourselves some more oil wells."

The Sooners just looked at him stonily, then got on the plane. Another Nebraskan, a muscular little man who looked intoxicated, joined in the abuse. "Yeah," he jeered, "you Oklahoma guys can't take it, can you?"

A man who had driven to the airport with his family got out of his car. He'd seen and heard it all. "Don't pay any attention to them," he called to the Sooner coaches who, standing behind the players, hadn't yet boarded the plane. "They're not Nebraska. We're sorry about this. You're great sports and you have a fine team." Wilkinson walked over to the fence. Grinning, he shook hands with the man and thanked him.

With a doff of their white helmets to the Cornhuskers, Oklahoma regrouped and tried to save the one conference record still alive when they clashed with Kansas State at the Wildcat homecoming. Deadlocked with Kansas for the conference top at 3-1, the Sooners could cinch a tie for the flag by defeating Kansas State and Iowa State in their remaining conference games. And if Kansas should be defeated or tied by Colorado or Missouri, the Sooners could win the championship outright, their 12th consecutive league diadem.

As was his custom when the team played poorly, Wilkinson promoted and demoted. Four sophomore forwards crouched in the starting line, Byerly at center, Milstead at right guard, Cox at right tackle, and Ronald Payne at right end. Mike McClellan at right half was the fifth sophomore starter that week.

The Wildcats played so aggressively that Oklahoma led only 7-0 until late in the third quarter when key interceptions by Jim Davis, Bob Cornell, Bennett Watts, and Dale Perini changed the game around. Oklahoma won 36-0.

Army's football bluebloods, an enduring eastern power for more than 60 years, came to Owen Field next for an intersectional combat that had been sold out at 61,716 since August. It was a tilt of tarnished Titans. Coach Dale Hall's Black Knights, 4-2-1 and suffering terrible casualties while being speared off their horses in early season by Illinois 20-14 and Penn State 17-11, had regained most of their wounded and hadn't lost a joust since. Notwithstanding the 28-degree temperature and the northeast wind, the sun shone brightly and the field was dry and fast. The Sooners wore long stockings.

Army took the opening kickoff and skipped 58 yards to a touchdown in seven plays. Bill Carpenter, their "Lonely End" who on every play stayed out almost to the right sideline and never came into the huddle,[5] and Joe Caldwell, their gifted forward passer who had pegged the Cadets to the number one rank in the nation in aerial play the year before, were the main figures in this advance. Caldwell's flat trajectory pass to George Kirschenbauer brought the touchdown on a 37-yard play with Carpenter throwing the vital block.

Army kicked off, stopped the Sooners, and forced a punt. Again the Black Knights came majestically up the field and had reached the Sooner 35 when Jim Byerly made a timely interception of a deflected pass. That play changed the initiative to Oklahoma. Starting from their 30, the Sooners thrust 70 yards in 16 plays. Bobby Boyd cut off tackle, was hit, and alertly

---

[5] On every down Carpenter lined up facing the huddle. If Caldwell's feet were squared, a run was indicated. If either of the quarterback's feet was advanced, it was a pass. When the Army wingback ran from the huddle to his position, he flashed Carpenter a signal indicating which of five routes he (Carpenter) would run, on each of which he either blocked or became a pass receiver. Thus the defense was compelled to cover him on every play. Coach Earl Blaik to Tim Cohane, July 10, 1978.

pitched out to Mike McClellan, going wide. Mike crossed the goal untouched. Jim Davis booted the goal that moved Oklahoma ahead, 7-6.

Each team scored once in the second quarter. "Wahoo" McDaniel's 37-yard punt that rolled dead on the Army 7 gave the Sooners field position for theirs. Army tried a run to the right. Jim Davis and Billy White hit Kirschenbauer so solidly that the ball was driven back into the Army end zone. Paul Benien recovered it there for a Sooner touchdown. "I dove for it, got it, lost it, dove for it again," Benien recalls the play. Davis kicked goal. Oklahoma 14, Army 6.

The Black Knights stayed cool. Moving with confidence and precision, they drove 73 yards to a touchdown from kickoff, scoring on an 11-yard pass down the middle, Caldwell to Don Usry. Army was threatening again when, on the last play of the first half, Tom Cox, Oklahoma's ever-trying sophomore tackle from Amarillo, made a play that the Sooners still talk about. Caldwell faded and cocked his arm. Cox rushed him and was knocked off his feet by Caldwell's protection. Jumping up, he chased Caldwell to the east sideline and was flattened a second time. Scrambling to his feet, Cox nailed Caldwell for an 8-yard loss.

On the second play of the last half, Rushatz tried a buck but Jerry Tillery hit him, Hobby recovering the ball on their 9. On the next play, Boyd, dodging and twisting cleverly, crossed the goal. Davis converted. Oklahoma led 21-12.

On the final play of the third quarter, Thompson hit Henry Minor, forcing a fumble, and Davis recovered it on the Army 20. Oklahoma scored, Boyd squirming to a touchdown from one yard out. Davis kicked goal. Now Oklahoma led, 28-12.

Army had too much morale to let Oklahoma make a rout of the game. Stung, they again drove all the way from kickoff with Caldwell's passes zipping through the cold air on target. He hit four straight to the 1. Rushatz plunged for the touchdown. Caldwell also used the pass for two extra points, spearing Kirschenbauer over the goal. Final score, Oklahoma 28, Army 20.

Wilkinson said later, "Army, coached by Dale Hall, was a magnificent opponent. I was as much impressed with their morale on the field and their graciousness in defeat as with their rugged play."

Caldwell said, "Oklahoma was as tough a team as we have met. They're clean, tough, and we like to play a good clean-playing team."

Iowa State's "Dirty Thirty," a spirited band of fighters with a 7-2 record, had given up only two touchdowns in their last five games. The Sooners scored first from the Cyclone 23, with Bobby Boyd cutting and dodging and tearing free until he was over the goal. Oklahoma put the game away in the fourth period. Gautt bucked powerfully for the first touchdown. Gautt also ran 48 yards for the second, breaking through the line and reversing sharply to the left. Winning 35-12, the Sooners bagged their twelfth straight Big Seven championship. Kansas had been upset by Colorado.

Despite Oklahoma's advantage in depth and speed, the "Dirty Thirty" gave a good account of themselves. "They sure hit hard," praised Ronnie Hartline. "They would hit me and say, 'Kinda hurts, doesn't it?'" Coach Stapleton of Iowa State said, "Oklahoma was up for us today. That's darned sure a change when they get up for Iowa State."

Oklahoma closed its season at 7-3 with a come-from-behind defeat of Oklahoma State at Norman, 19-7. For three quarters the Cowboys led with Tony Banfield intercepting three Sooner passes and Don Hitt, their center, playing a raging defensive game. Dick Soergel whipped a quick pass to Billy Dodson for their touchdown. Dodson kicked goal. Oklahoma's field goal came with 53 seconds left in the first half. Jim Davis, Sooner center, booted a 21-yarder at an angle. The Cowboys led 7-3.

They led 7-3 at the start of the fourth period too, as the rival defenses fought it out. Once "Wahoo" McDaniel, who led the tackling chart for the Sooners with eight clean stops, kicked out of bounds on the Cowboy 8. The play was recalled, and a 5-yard offside penalty was levied against Oklahoma. This time McDaniel duplicated his feat from farther back, again toeing the punt out on the Cowboy 8.

Oklahoma scored twice in the fourth period. Boyd, who quarterbacked both Sooner teams because of an injury to Cornell, handed off to Hartline, and when Paul Benien brush-blocked the linebacker and then blocked the safety off his feet, Hartline ran through two other tacklers on a 31-yard scoring ramble. Later, Boyd scored on a sneak. Final score, 17-7, Sooners.

Oklahoma fell off in the 1959 national statistics, ranking fourth in rushing with 273.5 yards per game, ninth in forward pass interceptions with 20, and tenth in total offense with 340.5 net yards.

Northwestern, Army, and Texas each landed eight positions on Oklahoma's all-opponents' eleven. Bill Carpenter, Army's "Lonely End," collected every one of the 27 votes cast by the Sooners and was voted the outstanding player Oklahoma had met.

1959 SENIORS TODAY

Bobby Boyd owns a restaurant in Baltimore and is a partner with Johnny Unitas in another restaurant there. They also jointly own an airfreight company.

Dr. Prentice Gautt is assistant commissioner of the Big Eight Athletic Conference.

Brewster Hobby is president of the First National Bank West, Norman, Oklahoma.

Edward ("Wahoo") McDaniel is a professional wrestler based in Charlotte, North Carolina. He also books and promotes professional wrestling.

Dr. Jerry Payne is a physician engaged in family practice in Hereford, Texas.

Jerry Thompson is a land man for the Harrell and Bradshaw Oil Company of Denver, Colorado.

15. THE RISE OF THE SEVEN DWARFS

Oklahoma's supporters were cheered when the *Saturday Evening Post's* summer preview and also that of *Street and Smith* predicted that Oklahoma's 1960 team would finish sixth in the nation. Actually, the 1960 season was to have more square corners than any Wilkinson had experienced. "Our line has adequate potential but our backfield situation is the weakest I can recall since coming to Oklahoma," Wilkinson said in the summer brochure.

Sports Illustrated asserted that the Big Eight would not that season be known as "Oklahoma and the Seven Dwarfs." Nearly everything was changing. "There are more high-school teams," Wilkinson told the magazine, "better coaches and bigger and faster players. I believe you win games by setting a novel tempo, but first you have to hang tough and kick well. It's getting harder to contain teams like Kansas, Nebraska, and Colorado."

With Oklahoma forbidden to play in bowl games because of its NCAA probation, Wilkinson needed a recruiting allurement to attract good high-school players. He sought to schedule a home-and-home series with the University of Hawaii, but the Big Eight by a 5-3 vote refused to grant the Sooners a recruiting advantage during a probationary period.

Oklahoma's indefinite NCAA probation still hurt although the Sooners had their defenders too. Among them was *Sports Illustrated,* when in its issue of January 18, 1960, commented that "Bud's well-behaved Sooners, perennial champions of the Big Eight Conference, had just been slapped with one of the heaviest penalties in the NCAA records, and seemingly for no crime whatever."

Oklahoma's coaches had just been paid a supreme compliment by Ray Graves, who for 13 years was Bobby Dodd's line coach at Georgia Tech. "I've visited practices all over the country," Graves told Bill Connors, *Tulsa World* sports editor, at the Gator Bowl press party, "and I think Oklahoma does the best job on the field of any staff in America. . . . They sell their kids and in turn their kids believe in their style and play their hearts out. . . . We were grateful to Bud and Gomer for giving us their 5-4 defense," Graves added. "They developed it and it became the international defense. They've really done a great service for football."

Bob Ward, an All-American guard at Maryland for Coach Jim Tatum, came on the Sooner staff that season. Ward was a very intense person and a competitor. When he found something he didn't like in a spring practice film, he would go to Washington House, find the player, and admonish him, "This has got to improve. Don't let yourself play like that any more."

Ward was a contrast to Wilkinson's soft-voiced staff. Usually his was the only voice raised on the practice field. Once Ward was coaching a circle drill near the intersection of two nearby streets, Lindsey and Jenkins. "You're not hitting!" the coach berated. Suddenly two automobiles collided nearby with a loud crash. Tires squealed and glass flew.

"Did you hear that?" Ward yelled. "That's the way I want you to hit! Knock his motor out!"

Spring practice in 1960 brought one physical problem after another. The most uncommon was suffered by Melvin Sandersfeld, big Hobart sophomore. Spring vacation interrupted football so Sandersfeld went home to plow. The tractor he was driving caught fire, burning his arms and singeing his hair and eyebrows.

Sandersfeld somersaulted backwards off the seat. He drove a pickup truck to Rocky, summoned the volunteer fire department, beat it back to the blaze, and was pumping water furiously from a nearby well and hurling it on the fire when the fire department pumper arrived. Returning to Norman, he resumed spring practice although his arms were covered with scabs.

Jimmy Carpenter, who played left halfback in 1958, was being groomed at quarterback. He rehurt his leg in spring practice and got in only half the 20 days. Bob Page, Borger, Texas, junior, would have been formidable at the position but dislocated his shoulder and was benched for the year.

The report was better on Leon Cross, the Hobbs, New Mexico, guard who had battled through three spring and two autumnal practices without ever having played a down in a game. His knee and arch stood up fine. On the night before the return contest with Northwestern, Cross was running across a new parking lot north of Washington House when he stumbled over a concrete bumper block and fell. But he jumped up grinning. "I think I'm going to make it this fall," he laughed. "I'm really looking forward to this season."

The best-conditioned athlete on the squad was Monte Deere, wiry little Amarillo, Texas, sophomore. Every day Deere ran to the river bridge and back, played handball, lifted weights, and on the odd days ran 15 100-yard dashes. He did most of it all summer, besides running with the Amarillo Palo Duro High School team. "After one look at the Oklahoma squad of 1959, I felt that the only way I'd ever make that team was to be in better physical condition than any other man on it," said Deere.

Port Robertson, freshman coach and academic counselor, reported a few days late that fall. He was busy coaching the American Olympic freestyle wrestling team at Rome. Russia, usually a power in Olympic wrestling, made no gold medal moon shots at the Rome Olympiad. Robertson's American team trounced four world champions, three of them Soviets. They won three Olympic gold medals and probably missed winning a fourth because of an injury to one of their men. They placed in five additional weights. It was a smashing performance by a green team struggling with an unfamiliar style directed by a man who was probably the finest catch-as-catch-can style coach in the nation but had known nothing about the Olympic vogue.

One of the freshmen that fall was John Garrett, 190-pound single-wing tailback from Stilwell who was part-Cherokee Indian. "I loved that tailback," says Garrett today, "It was the glory spot." At Norman he soon ran into trouble with Robertson. If an athlete let his grades decline too dramatically, Robertson made him return to Norman the day after Christmas and spend the holidays studying. Garrett fell in this category.

"I wanted to be home all of Christmas so I told Port that I'd quit before I'd come back to Norman to study," Garrett added. He tried to transfer during the holidays to the University of Arkansas, but Merrill Green, former Sooner halfback who was then a Razorback assistant, told him, "John, you'd make the biggest mistake of your life to leave OU."

So Garrett returned to Norman although he didn't return until classes resumed. As his punishment, Robertson assigned him to cutting salads in the athletic dining hall two hours every morning for two months. Then Robertson summoned him to his office. "Have you learned your lesson?" asked the coach. Garrett grinned. "Yes, sir. You win. Now I understand the system."

When Garrett graduated, Robertson congratulated him. "John Garrett, I'm glad that you stayed. You're a better man than I thought you were." Garrett grinned. "If I am," he told himself, "it's because you made me that way." "Port was the greatest asset OU had," Garrett says today. "He was the drill sergeant."

Respect for the freshman coach was widespread. "We had a lot of discipline at Oklahoma," says Jimmy Carpenter, "But a lot of our guys would never have graduated if it hadn't been for Port." Charley Mayhue said, "Port was rough and stern, but when my grades came in, I loved him like a father."

Billy White, varsity left tackle, could imitate Robertson's voice. White phoned Ron Payne, varsity left end. "Report to my office," he ordered, copying Robertson's vocal style. Payne hurried to the coach's office, but Robertson wasn't there and hadn't been there, the secretary told him. Payne knew that he'd been had. He returned to his room. The phone rang again. Payne picked it up. "You dirty so and so," he said and hung up.

Presently the phone rang a third time. Payne had no difficulty identifying the caller. The coach cleared his throat gently and ominously. "Mr. Payne," he said, "I don't think I heard what I think I heard. Get your little fanny over here and five minutes ago is too late for you to arrive." Payne hurriedly returned and tried to explain. Port let him squirm, then dismissed him. Payne began looking for the talented White. "When the rest of the squad heard about it, they laughed until they rolled on the floor," remembers Leon Cross.

Later White paid for his mischief. He was deathly afraid of snakes. Somebody tossed a gartersnake into his room. White jumped out the second story window of Washington House. Luckily he landed in a bush that broke his fall.

A crowd of 61,289 came for the return opener against Northwestern. Coach Ara Parseghian's Wildcats still had Dick Thornton, their fine quarterback, and he forward passed both of their touchdowns. Fullback Mike Stock kicked two field goals. But Gomer Jones's junior line of Ron Payne, Billy White, Leon Cross, Jim Byerly, Karl Milstead, Tom Cox, and Jerry Tillery prevented Northwestern from scoring on the ground. Milstead kicked a 35-yard field goal. Northwestern won 19-3.

"I had missed a lot of football and didn't play very well," Leon Cross remembers. "The fact that I even started the game showed how we were hurting in depth and talent."

Biggest surprise to Gary Wylie, Oklahoma's 6-foot 4-inch sophomore fullback from Whitesboro, Texas, was the fact that the Sooners lost. At Whitesboro, ten miles south of the Oklahoma line, Wylie had never played on a winning team. His high school won only five games his sophomore season, three his junior year, and two his senior campaign. "I came to Oklahoma to play on the winning side and we got racked 19 to 3," he said, shaking his head rucfully.

Pittsburgh's rugged rhinos moved menacingly against Oklahoma at Owen Field on an 86-degree day with the south wind blowing hard and the sky partly overcast. The Panther-Sooner clash embodied all the elements that made college football dramatic and colorful. Each team made two successful goal line stands. Both moved the ball surprisingly well. Pitt put together sustained drives of 70, 98, 79, and 56 yards. Oklahoma marched 49, 43, 87, and 65 yards. Neither side lost a fumble.

Oklahoma scored first when, from the Panther 30, Carpenter faked smoothly to Hartline who realistically feigned a buck into the line. Carpenter palmed the ball until he saw Ron Payne racing behind the Pittsburgh secondary and threw to him for the touchdown. Milstead kicked goal.

Bursting with power, Pitt drove back 70 yards from kickoff to the Sooner 10. The Sooner line slowed them, and when the Panthers twice tried the rollout pass, Billy Meacham, Clinton sophomore, each time attacked Mike Ditka, Pitt's All-American end, so fiercely that he prevented Ditka from catching the ball.

With great fighting spirit, Pitt stormed back up the field 98 yards to score their first touchdown. Pitt elected to go for two extra points by sending Sharockman wide around the Oklahoma left end. However, McClellan and Billy White covered fast, meeting Sharockman very hard on the Sooner 2 and bumping him out of bounds. Oklahoma led 7-6 at the half.

With Pitt leading 14-7 in the fourth period, their brawny operatives moved 73 yards to within 18 inches of a third touchdown. It was fourth down. They elected to go wide, sending Traficant around Oklahoma's left end. Ronnie Payne covered fast, fought through their blocks, and getting a hand on Traficant, slowed him until the Sooner pursuit swarmed in to hold the play for no gain. It was Oklahoma's ball on downs.

That play changed the complexion of the game. The Oklahoma starters drove 65 yards. Then Wilkinson sent Oklahoma's fuzz-faced alternates into the game. Pittsburgh's percherons had manhandled them so mercilessly that Wilkinson had used them in only 14 plays to the starters' 71. But not this time. York stopped John Yaccino for no gain. Lang held Mike Frasca to one yard. Traficant flat-passed to Chuck Reinhold, but the Sooner seconds ganged him for a loss of 3. Fred Cox dropped back to punt.

H. O. Estes, Sooner guard from Lindsay, blocked open a lane for Phil Lohmann, Sooner left end. With great effort Lohmann got both his hands in front of the kicked ball, blocking it. York recovered on the Pitt 11.

Still fiercely fevered, Oklahoma's young rogues scored in two rushes. Wylie hit for 6. On the handoff Don Dickey, Phillips, Texas, sophomore, hit for 5 and the touchdown over Vernon Lang, Tom Cox, and Paul Benien. Pitt still led 14-13. The Sooners faked a conversion kick, Milstead swinging his leg in the kick motion. Bennett Watts arose with the ball and swung wide behind Milstead's crashing block on Ditka to score the two points standing. Oklahoma won 15-14. Billy Meacham was voted the "Ug" Award.

Monte Deere, Amarillo, Texas, sophomore and lightest man on the squad, hadn't played in either the Northwestern or Pittsburgh games. "I wasn't used to sitting on the bench," he says. "I went to Bud's office. They called him out of a coach's meeting to talk to me. 'Coach,' I told him, 'I'm going to leave OU and go someplace where I can play.'

"For five minutes he talked to me so kindly, patiently, and logically that when he finished I would have mopped out the Student Union twice a day if he had asked me to. He told me I was doing a real fine job but that

McClellan and Sandersfeld were bigger and that if either didn't play well against Texas, I'd get my shot. I didn't play a down against Texas. However, next week Billy Meacham split his toe on the corner of a door and it had to have stitches. Bud moved me to right half, and I started the fourth game, against Kansas.

"What do I think of Bud? The awe I held him in ranked someplace between mortal man and the Supreme Being. Ability to motivate was his biggest talent. He was like E. F. Hutton. When he talked, we all listened."

Texas trimmed Oklahoma in the big game at Dallas, 24-0. Wilkinson gave them full credit. "The Longhorns, ably coached by Darrell Royal and his staff, outsped us, outhit us, outfought us and totally outplayed us," Bud wrote in his letter to the alumni.

And then he wrote something else. Like a soothsayer, he read the remainder of Oklahoma's season infallibly. "It is difficult to know what will be in store for our team the rest of the season," he said. "Each week we will meet an excellent opponent who has waited years for Oklahoma to be somewhat below par. For years they have been looking forward to defeating us decisively, just as Texas did. We do not have a bad team; neither at this stage do we have a good one. We must learn to make a total, all-out, unrelenting effort on every play of every remaining game if we expect to survive."

Brother played against brother in the Texas game. They were Marshall York, Sooner tackle and cocaptain, and brother Tommy, Texas sophomore left end. It was the first collegiate view of Tommy by their parents, Mr. and Mrs. A. B. York of Amarillo. They had driven to Norman to see Marshall play against both Northwestern and Pittsburgh. "Norman is only 290 miles from Amarillo but Austin is about 480," the father explained.

Wayne Lee, sophomore center from Ada, threw ten unassisted tackles and four assisted. Ronnie Hartline and Karl Milstead were close behind. Hartline won the Sooner "Ug."

The 9½ points by which the odds makers favored ninth-ranked Kansas over Oklahoma in the Sooners' first defense of their conference championships was the greatest wagering reject of all time against a Wilkinson-coached Oklahoma team. And yet the gamblers were eminently correct about the class of the Jayhawkers. Kansas, defeated only by Syracuse, later won the Big Eight championship then was made to surrender it because Bert Coan, their fine halfback, had been taken by a Kansas graduate on a trip to Chicago to see the All-Star game.

The Sooners poured out all their energy with long touchdown drives at the start of each half, then fought furiously to avoid engulfment by Coach Jack Mitchell's Kansans. But the wheel of fortune spun away from the

Jayhawks who in the final moments fumbled twice to mar advances that had reached the Sooner 15- and 25-yard stripes and with 20 seconds left in the game missed a point-blank field goal from the one-yard line by the best placekicker in the conference, John Suder, who had hit 21 of 21 extra points before the Oklahoma game. Suder's kick rose high in the air like a blooper shot in golf.

With the 13-13 tie, the Sooners ended what John Cronley, *Daily Oklahoman* sports editor, called their "monstrous month" with a 1-2-1 record. Only conference games remained, and by winning all six, Oklahoma could still win or tie for the flag.

Hartline, Sooner fullback, had lamed his knee on the second kickoff but trainer Ken Rawlinson strapped him up and he returned to outrush the entire Kansas team, 110 to 109 net yards. Mike McClellan cracked off tackle behind White, Payne, and Cross to score Oklahoma's first touchdown. Milstead kicked goal.

McClellan also scored Oklahoma's last touchdown. It came on a brilliant ruse, a fake field goal. The play started like the one in which Bennett Watts ran for two points to win the Pittsburgh game. Carpenter rose with the ball and circled wide to the right with the Jayhawkers in hot pursuit. Then he introduced the new wrinkle, pegging a screen pass back over their heads to McClellan who picked up blocks by White, Cross, and Byerly and raced down a narrow corridor along the west sideline to score. Tackle Stan Kirsham blocked Milstead's kick. Billy White won the "Ug" Award.

Coming home on the team plane, Jimmy Carpenter was asked why Oklahoma played so well. "Well, we were such big underdogs that we just decided we'd try to beat 'em," he grinned.

In his press conference the following Monday, Wilkinson was asked if there was any possibility of developing an Oklahoma forward passer who threw from a pocket instead of off the option. "If we had one," answered Bud, "we'd be using him. When a team is losing, everybody gets highly technical about what we'd better use."

Frank Boggs, *Daily Oklahoman* writer, described the Kansas State game well when he wrote, "Not one single thing happened that indicated that the Sooners are embarking on another of those so-called 'Monster Months.' Instead, this was a typical 'Serene Saturday,' like normal."

Ronnie Hartline and Mike McClellan didn't play because of injuries, but 52 other Sooners did. Hartline, whose soft, high voice belied his ferocious fullbacking, sat out a game for the first time in his life.

"It was just terrible," fretted the 213-pound Lawtonian. "I wouldn't have felt so bad if I hadn't been suited up." White was voted his third "Ug" Award. Oklahoma won 49 to 7.

The 49-point harvest did not change Wilkinson's opinion of his squad. "We're just a good old normal team, that's all," he grinned from Oklahoma's locker room.

Although Wilkinson never complained that the altitude at Boulder affected his team's play, he usually took the Sooners to the high country two or three days early. "On Thursday we practiced hard at Denver, did lots of wind sprints," recalls Paul Benien, today an Oklahoma City physician. "It takes time for your red blood cells to adjust to altitude."

Bob Blaik, Sooner scout, had told the Sooners earlier that "Colorado's greatest forte now is defense. They have a superb middle linebacker in guard Joe Romig. They have two fine defensive ends in Mel Semenko and Jerry Hillebrand. Their tackles, Chuck Pearson, 215, and Bill Eurich, 224, will put tremendous pressure on our offensive guards. Nobody has moved the ball very well against them."

The crowd at Folsom Field, sold out at 45,281 since summer, began hurriedly to don raincoats and slickers as cold rain started spitting down just as the rival captains walked out for the coin flip. The temperature was 45, a stiff north wind blew off the nearby mountains, and the day grew so dark, even at 2:00 P.M., that the electric scoreboard shone almost as brightly as if the contest were being played at night.

The second quarter had just started when Coach Everett ("Sonny") Grandelius's Coloradoans began a 61-yard march that won the contest. The Sooners fought so furiously that Colorado went into the air, with quarterback Gale Weidner throwing.

Jim Byerly, Sooner linebacker, got a hand on the pass, deflecting it. Hillebrand made a difficult catch of the deflection for a first down on the Sooner 19. Then he made another superclutch of his own deflection on the Sooner 1. Because of a previous penalty, it was second down and goal to go.

They shot Weiss up the middle but Wayne Lee, Ada sophomore, met him in the air as he dove, stopping him. Weidner tried a sneak but Milstead, Cross, and Lee piled him. On fourth down Weiss twisted across the goal. Hillebrand kicked the extra point. Colorado won 7-0, administering to the Sooners their first shutout by a conference opponent since 1942 and virtually eliminating them from the conference race.

At his press conference back at Norman on Monday, Wilkinson was asked why Hartline wasn't used when the Sooners got a first down on the Colorado 5-yard line following a 68-yard run by Bennett Watts. "Colorado was defending Hartline on every play," Bud answered. "That was their first responsibility. Their defense was packed to stop him first. In that situation I think it was better to fake to Hartline and call on other players."

Then Wilkinson added, "As a coach you try to do the very best you can. Since coaches are subject to the human quality, the same as anyone else, this is no guarantee that what you think is best is always correct. You make the decision in light of your best judgment. When you win, you gain confidence in your judgment. When you lose, you do some soul-searching. The validity of your judgment is then not so apparent."

"They all just want to beat our brains out, every team we play. They just can't wait to play us. Nobody can wait." Karl Milstead, Oklahoma's muscular guard, was talking to Volney Meece, *Daily Oklahoman* dressing room writer, about Iowa State which had just defeated Oklahoma at Ames, their first triumph over the Sooners in 28 years.

Milstead was right. Every opponent seemed to play its best game of the season against Oklahoma. The six Sooner foes combined had given Oklahoma a total of only four fumbles all season, had yielded an average of only one intercepted pass a game, and had been penalized an average of only 31 yards a contest.

With only eight minutes left to play and Oklahoma leading 6-3, Coach Clay Stapleton's single-wingback outfit from Iowa State drove 71 yards to the winning touchdown. On fourth and 1 from the Sooner 1, fullback Tom Watkins wedged across the goal. Cliff Rock converted and Iowa State had its winning count of 10-6. Three minutes later its students spilled joyously onto the field.

With the Cyclone fans demonstrating happily after the game, the stadium public-address man intoned that "President James H. Hilton has authorized me to announce that because of the outstanding victory over Oklahoma, classes will not meet Monday morning but will resume Monday noon."

Whereupon John Cronley, *Daily Oklahoman* sports editor busy hammering out his story in the press box, let out a growling roar, "What in the hell do you have to do in this town to get a full day off?"

That defeat definitely eliminated Oklahoma from the Big Eight derby. On the bus coming home from the Oklahoma City airport, Wilkinson grinned and tried to hearten his young charges. "Cheer up, Marshall," he told York, his right tackle and cocaptain, "nothing to lose now. Let's go for broke. Have some fun."

Coming home on the team plane from Ames, I talked to Jimmy Carpenter, our sorrel-thatched little quarterback who wore a 16½ collar ("I've run into so many people they've jammed my neck down like an accordion."). He leaned forward from an aisle seat and answered questions in a soft, polite voice.

"When you get beat, it's just hard to face people," Carpenter said. "When I played two years ago [on the 1958 Oklahoma team that won nine of ten

288

and defeated Syracuse in the Orange Bowl], we were always well respected. Our opponents seemed to think, way down in their hearts, that they'd lose. We need to get the psychological advantage of winning. We haven't really been run off the field yet. We never quit. We still think we can beat anybody we play."

Carpenter settled back into the folds of his tan leather jacket and looked thoughtful. "I'll never get used to losing, ever," he said, very seriously. "It's such a discouraging feeling. We get letters from people chiding us. Sometimes we get booed on our own field."

Ken Rawlinson, Sooner trainer, came through the plane carrying a small box of paperback novels. "Who wants a book?" he called out.

Carpenter craned his "accordion" neck, perusing the titles in Rawlinson's box. "Where's that horror story?" he asked, as if he hadn't already suffered football horror enough.

Missouri, 8-0 and ranked number two in the nation by the AP poll, led the country in defense against rushing. Their goal line hadn't been crossed by an enemy rush all season.

Coach Dan Devine's Tigers, boasting five home-state halfbacks who were noted for their zooming speed off guard-pulled power sweeps, were favored by 8½ points. A crowd of 53,369 jammed the stadium at Owen Field to watch the Bengals battle a four-times defeated Oklahoma squad that Wilkinson said "has come so close to winning that it's painful."

The early pain was applied by the Sooners and felt by the Tigers. On Thursday Wilkinson's squad had been paid an impromptu visit by 2,000 students who stayed and watched the workout. On Saturday, just before the kickoff, the red-garbed Oklahoma band, carrying its instruments, ran across the field and surrounding the Sooner huddle played "Boomer Sooner." Intoxicated by all this, the Oklahoma team lost no time.

Billy White, junior left tackle from Amarillo, was the man who opened the gates of statistical horror on the visitors as the Oklahomans rushed 323 net yards on the country's top-ranked defense, scored three touchdowns, and contended so fiercely that they punted only once.

On the third play Oklahoma shocked everybody by jetting 70 yards to a touchdown. The play looked like a buck by Hartline who faked realistically, drawing part of the defense with him. Byerly, Lang, and Tom Cox blocked their men in. Ronnie Payne took his opponent out. The Sooners let the tackle through, and when Estes pulled to cross-block him, Carpenter handed off to Mike McClellan gushing through the gap.

White sprinted across the secondary from his left tackle position and blocked flat the man who should have stopped the play, Missouri's left defensive halfback. McClellan whirled through the hole and flew down the

289

Billy White, Sooner tackle (73) at bottom of picture, came across the field to block out Norm Beal, Missouri defensive half, to set up this 70-yard touchdown run by Mike McClellan against Missouri. Inset: Billy White.

west sideline, outspeeding everybody to the goal. It was the first touchdown by rushing Missouri had yielded all year. Hartline missed the extra point but Oklahoma led 6-0.

Devine later gave White full credit. "Our Norman Beal was in McClellan's path," Devine said, "Our movies show that White threw a block that sent Beal ten feet into the air. Beal was still up there when McClellan went past."

Missouri didn't lose its poise. The proud Tigers roared back to score 24 straight points. It looked like Oklahoma would be crushed.

The Sooner alternates had yielded that last touchdown, but Wilkinson left them in, and they proved that they were ready to play as partners to the starters.

In five crisp plays they drove 59 yards to score. Their touchdown maneuver was the same play off which McClellan had scored. Byerly, Tatum, and York blocked their opponents in, Dale Perini took his out. Cook,

290

Amarillo, Texas, sophomore, threw a stunning trap block. Benien and Claude Hamon went across for the secondary. Melvin Sandersfeld knifed through the hole, cut back, and reversed his field while going 36 yards to score. The Sooners tried a rush for two points but it failed. Missouri led 24-12 but Oklahoma was back in contention.

The Sooners came back for the last half in a fighting mood, McClellan intercepting a pass on his 29. Using all rushes, Oklahoma moved up the field with their crowd in thunderous outcry. Hartline's 26-yard power rush after Byerly, Lang, and Estes cut him into the secondary reached the Missouri 37. Now the going was tougher and Carpenter called on Hartline for the key gains. Carpenter clawed his way over the backs of Byerly and Lang for the touchdown. Hartline kicked goal and Missouri's lead had been whittled to five points, 24-19. "I don't believe I have ever been prouder of an Oklahoma team than I was at this critical point," Wilkinson said later.

Heartened by the roaring of their crowd, the Sooners kicked off to Missouri and stopped them on tackles by Tatum, Perini, and Jim Parker. Danny LaRose's short punt rolled dead on the Tiger 35. This was Oklahoma's golden opportunity to take the lead, but the Sooners fumbled a pitchout, Missouri recovering.

Then Missouri broke through with excellent offensive execution. On the first play of the fourth quarter, Stevenson swung wide to his left on a sweep, dashing 60 yards to a touchdown. The Sooners wild-pitched another lateral. Recovering on Oklahoma's 30, the Tigers were stopped and called on Tobin to boot a 29-yard field goal. Oklahoma tossed away another pitchout. Three plays later Donnie Smith bucked for the final Missouri touchdown. Tobin kicked his twenty-first straight conversion. Missouri led 41-19.

Even then, Oklahoma didn't fold. The starters drove 65 yards for another touchdown which Cornell scored on the game's last play with an 8-yard run. But a backfield in motion penalty erased it and the score stayed 41-19.

Missouri's errorless play was the difference. The Tigers' only mistakes were one pass interception and one 5-yard penalty. Their deadly cashing of Sooner bobbles contributed to the score. The Sooners came into possession twelve times. They yielded seven turnovers, four times on fumbles, three on pass interceptions. Even then, they outrushed Missouri 323 net yards to 300. It was Oklahoma's first conference defeat at Norman since 1942 and her first loss to Missouri in 14 years.

"That was a helluva offensive battle," Devine said from the Bengal dressing room. "We don't have anyone who can keep up with Mike McClellan. I've got a whipped team physically. Our squad is dead tired." Center Wayne Lee led the Sooner tackling chart. He had eight unassisted stops, two assisted. Billy White won his fifth "Ug" of the season.

291

The Nebraska-Oklahoma clash that year had an odd motif. Although the Sooners and Cornhuskers together had won 26 conference championships in the last 32 years, their mingling at Norman was a go-for-broke duel for sixth place in the Big Eight.

Nebraska stood only 3-6 overall and Oklahoma had stumbled to 2-5-1 but each had occasionally risen to the heights. Coach Bill Jennings's Scarlet had beaten Texas 14-13, Army 14-9, and lost with honor to Minnesota 26-14.

The Sooners won the first half 14-0. They first scored on a weak-side handoff with Lohmann, White, and Estes opening a hole through which Mike McClellan darted 23 yards to a touchdown. Later Carpenter correctly read the Cornhusker defense and lined a long forward pass to Ronny Payne 49 yards for a touchdown.

The tide of battle changed shockingly in the last half. Nebraska won it, 17-0, quickly proving that its morale was of the 60-minute variety. Bill ("Thunder") Thornton, their big fullback, bucked to the first touchdown. Pat Fischer, their quarterback, faked a placekick and circled the Sooner left end for two points. Now Oklahoma led only 14-8.

When Bob Cornell quick-kicked 70 yards out on the Nebraska 17 in the fourth quarter, Oklahoma had fine field position. But on Nebraska's fourth play Thornton struck off tackle and ran 68 yards to score. "They had a quick trap up the middle," remembers Monte Deere, Sooner defensive halfback. "I saw it and red-dogged it [shot the gap]. I met Thornton just as he got the handoff and he was so big and strong and fast that he ran over me and scored the touchdown. Nobody blocked me. He just flat ran over me. As I picked myself up, I saw Gomer shaking his head over on our bench."

Ronny Payne charged fast to block Ron Meade's try for point and the score stood 14-14. But the Sooners misplayed another pitchout, and Meade booted a 22-yard field goal that won the game, 17-14.

In spite of the six defeats, the Sooners still liked and respected their coaches tremendously. "Bud was a perfectionist who inspired young men to play above their ability," says Bob Page, reserve quarterback. "He reminded me lots of a minister who after giving a tremendous sermon made you feel good about yourself and those around you.

"Gomer enjoyed keeping a close relationship with all the players," Page went on. "We all loved him, that was the biggest thing. Even if he chewed you out, you knew that back of it all he still liked you a lot. You were sure of it. I never heard a player bad-mouth Gomer."

By defeating Oklahoma State 17-6 at Stillwater, the Sooners of '60 closed their only losing season under Wilkinson at 3-6-1 and salvaged fifth place in the Big Eight.

With three frontline backs, Mike McClellan, Melvin Sandersfeld, and Jimmy Carpenter, all injured early in the hostilities, Bob Cornell, senior quarterback from Oklahoma City, rose to the heights of his sophomore Orange Bowl performance. Cornell sat in the Sooner sulky and coolly slapped the reins out along Sooner backs during both Oklahoma touchdowns. He scored the second touchdown himself and emerged the game's top rusher.

Wilkinson was gratified that the Sooners originated 65 rushing plays without losing the ball a single time on fumbles. "When a team is losing," he wrote in his alumni letter, "it is very easy for the players, particularly the seniors, to lose some of their morale and incentive. I am pleased to report that our men never surrendered to this attitude. They continued to practice well."

Sandersfeld's strong-side sweep gave Oklahoma a 7-0 halftime lead. Then Carpenter went out with a rib bruise. When both McClellan and Sandersfeld also were hurt, the Sooner backfield ranks were thinned. Monte Deere was moved from right to left half. Jerry Pettibone, fourth team left half, was jumped to the starting eleven. OU drove 77 yards to a touchdown from the last half kickoff. Cornell called the quarterback sneak and struck fast over Byerly and Lang to score from 3 yards out. Milstead kicked goal.

Trailing 0-14, Coach Cliff Speegle's Cowboys answered with the best gesture a fighting club can make, driving 80 yards from kickoff. Fullback Jim Dillard, State's "Fairfax Freight," highballed through the Sooners for the touchdown. Their try for two points failed.

The Cowboys kicked off. Jerry Pettibone, the Sooner fourth-stringer who had been given a battlefield promotion to left half, prayed the ball wouldn't come to him. But it did, "I ran up the middle," he remembers. 'I saw some daylight and broke to the left. I passed the Sooner bench in midfield. Bud ran along the sideline with me. 'Run, Jerry, run!' he yelled. They finally knocked me out of bounds. That was my all-time thrill!" It was Pettibone's senior year, and he had never played a down. But he had never missed a minute of practice either.

Phil Lohmann, Sooner left end, won the "Ug" Award that day. "Best time I ever had on the football field," Lohmann chuckles today. "Bud and Gomer had designed a ten-man defense in which I was the corner man, free to roam. The reason I was allowed to wander was because the position of their wingback told us exactly what the play was going to be. We'd got this out of their films. The night before the game my son Jeff was born, so I didn't miss a day of practice. That was kind of a high week for me."

Oklahoma's most sensational player in 1960 was Billy White, its 197-

pound junior pharmacy major from Amarillo. Because of his raised eyebrows, the Sooners called him "Clown." But no matter what they called him, White was a terrific fighter in every game. He was the only Sooner chosen on an All-Big Eight Conference eleven, and he made them all. Missouri's Orange Bowl Champions even gave him an 8-7 edge over Joe Romig, Colorado's All-American guard. The Sooner coaches voted White five "Ug" Awards. After the disastrous 1960 season the Sooners elected him captain. It was the first time in 15 years that the players had elected only one.

The end-over-end roll of the once imperial Sooners was due to several things. Looking back on it, the players have their own ideas. "We didn't have the hosses," says Monte Deere. "Lack of depth, especially quality depth," opines Bob Page, "and the competition was stiffer. The calibre of opposition players was catching up." "Our overall attitude wasn't quite as good," says Leon Cross.

"The recruiting fell off," believes Charley Mayhue. "Just the name OU wasn't raising goose bumps on high-school kids as it once had." "Bud's enthusiasm for coaching seemed to be declining some and after all those years, who could blame him?" says Bob Cornell. "When we'd go to his home for meetings, he talked lots about history and politics."

Assistant coach Eddie Crowder says, "We had been drawing our players from Oklahoma and northwest Texas, but this wasn't sufficient any more. So we started going outside. Also, the Texas schools began to recruit more intensely. I felt that after our 47-game winning string ended, our entire staff underwent a decline in their motivation. And I thought I could discern in Bud a waning of his usual coaching exuberance."

Wilkinson and Gomer Jones, whom Bud always saluted and treated as his "cohead coach," deserve everybody's plaudits for invigorating Big Eight Conference football, making it a power in the nation. "We've dominated the Big Eight, not because we're that much better, but because they have not worked as hard as we have," Bud told Tim Cohane, sports editor of *Look* in 1954. "They've got to get to work."

They did get to work, and this was Bud's great contribution to his conference—he forced it to build up to Oklahoma's level, lifting the Big Eight to the same horizon with other major football leagues in the land.

1960 SENIORS TODAY

Bob Cornell is an architect in Oklahoma City and vice-president of RGDC, an architectural engineering planning firm of Oklahoma City.

Ron Hartline is football coach at MacArthur High School, Lawton, Oklahoma.

Jerry Tillery is a heavy-equipment broker in El Reno, Oklahoma.

Marshall York owns a tire and supply store in Amarillo, Texas.

16. NOVEMBER RALLY

The 1961 schedule was thorny—Texas, Army, and Notre Dame—plus a revitalized Big Eight bursting with muscle and a new sense of freedom after striking the Sooner shackles that had held an entire conference prisoner for twelve long years.

Just before spring practice started, Wilkinson threw Oklahoma fandom into a fearful funk by agreeing to become Special Consultant on Youth Fitness to John Kennedy, President of the United States. Many Oklahomans believed that they were losing Wilkinson. Others doubted if he had time to handle both jobs.

President Kennedy had a great conviction about the need of a physical fitness program for the nation's young people and was looking for somebody to head it. Ted Reardon, a Massachusetts politician who was a close friend of the President, first phoned Wilkinson about it, asking him if he would visit the President at the White House to discuss the matter. Wilkinson did. After the usual courtesy conversation Wilkinson asked the President how important the program was to him.

"His reply," says Wilkinson today, "remains vivid in my memory. He said, 'I don't believe there is anything more important. The mechanization of our society has virtually eliminated for the majority of our citizens enough physical activity in their daily lives to maintain physical fitness. Escalators, lawnmowers, automobiles are all developments of the last sixty years. We have reached a state where muscular activity has been virtually removed from our lives. School children no longer walk to school. They are bussed.

"I do not consider myself a great student of history, but from my reading I have reached the conclusion that nations do not respond to challenges unless the population as a whole has great vigor and vitality. These qualities are based on the individual physical well-being of the citizen.'"[1]

The president asked Wilkinson if he would accept the position. "I told him yes, I would be very pleased to do it," Wilkinson says today. Kennedy suggested that Wilkinson resign his Oklahoma position and come to Wash-

[1] Bud Wilkinson to author, March 19, 1982.

296

President John Kennedy and Bud Wilkinson shortly after the President appointed Wilkinson his special consultant on youth fitness in 1961. Photo courtesy of Sports Information Department, University of Oklahoma.

ington full-time to serve as the consultant on physical fitness. "I explained to him," says Wilkinson, "that I felt my ability to address the problem with the proper media and public support was enhanced by the fact that I was an active coach and suggested that I handle the situation part-time so as not to lose this important asset. He readily agreed."

But first Wilkinson returned to Norman and cleared the matter with President Cross and the university regents, assuring them that the commitment would not interfere with his coaching responsibilities. The regents gave unanimous approval. He also wrote a letter to each member of

297

Here's how Jim Lange, *Daily Oklahoman* cartoonist, saw it, mirroring Sooner fandom's early fear. Oklahoma Publishing Co.

the Touchdown Club. "The government understands the limitations on my time," his letter said. "Briefly, I will be here for our spring practice sessions. After spring practice I will be on call to the government until the first of August at which time I will again devote my efforts to our team in preparation for the coming season." This eased, somewhat, the general anxiety. The coach went vigorously to work on both fronts. He had always been able to handle two jobs efficiently.[2]

Jim Byerly, senior center, passed up his last season of football with the Sooners. "I realized for the first time that college football was big business and that a dad-gummed scholarship was cheap wages," Byerly explains today. "Our former players who had turned pro would return to the campus

[2]At one of his speeches in behalf of fitness, Wilkinson was asked, "What is a football game?" And Bud replied, "A football game is 22 people on a football field desperately needing rest and 100,000 people in the stadium desperately needing exercise."

298

driving a new car but with no money in their pockets. In those days a pro lineman got only seven or eight thousand dollars a year. This led to my decision to quit and go to work for my father-in-law in Oklahoma City. He owned several restaurants and I helped manage some of them. I didn't tell Bud. I didn't want anybody to talk me out of it."

Then a stroke of good fortune fell. On January 9, 1961, the NCAA announced at its annual meeting in Pittsburgh that Oklahoma's indefinite probation had lifted. It had lasted one year and three days. After several meetings, Walter Byers, NCAA executive director, and Art Wood, the Oklahoma City accountant who had moved to Reno, Nevada, agreed upon a modified approach that released the logjam. This was accomplished without Wood's violating the disclosure provision of the Internal Revenue Code by revealing the names of his clients.

"After our give and take, we got along fine," Byers says today. "He once entertained me and an NCAA committee at his home at Lake Tahoe. We had a meeting in the area and he invited us to come by for cocktails. We did."[3]

Crippling player losses, the worst in the 67 years of Sooner football, hit Oklahoma that summer and fall. Not only Byerly but also Jerry Goldsby, number two left tackle behind Captain Billy White, decided not to play. Married and a father, Goldsby had financial problems. But he stayed in school. In 1963 he returned to Sooner football. Fullback Billy Stone, Lindsay sophomore, became a scholastic casualty. Halfback Billy Meacham gave up football because he couldn't get his injured knee and thumb in shape to play. Don Dickey, who scored the winning touchdown against Pittsburgh, was lost because of a lame knee. Johnny Smith, promising Tulsa sophomore back, sustained a displaced neck vertebra while running back a punt and never played again.

Two new assistant coaches joined the staff. Assistant Bob Blaik resigned to enter private business. Replacing him was Jay O'Neal. Chet Franklin, former Utah guard, was also hired full-time.

The injury misfortune continued. Just before the Notre Dame game, quarterback Bill Van Burkleo, promising Tulsa sophomore, was idled with a sprain of an ankle ligament. Melvin Sandersfeld sprained his back and didn't play against the Irish. Charles Mayhue, Ada sophomore, wrecked a knee and was red-flagged for the season. Johnny Tatum needed knee surgery after a freak accident. After an operation on July 8, he worked so diligently on his rehabilitation that he didn't miss a game.

Bob Page, the ranking quarterback who was forced to miss the 1959

[3] Walter Byers to author, October 10, 1980.

and 1960 seasons because of shoulder injuries, joined the wounded. On photo day preceding fall practice he backed up to throw a dropback pass at the request of a cameraman and sprained his ankle. He had forgotten to tape it. He also missed the Notre Dame game.

At the first freshman meeting Coach Robertson looked around at his squad. "Our equipment man's name is spelled B-A-E-R," Robertson said, "but if you bother him about equipment just before practice starts, he's B-E-A-R." Half an hour later, after putting them through their paces, the coach's voice became deceivingly soft, maddeningly polite. "You're so slow I can't tell whether you're movin' or growin'," he told them.

The Notre Dame game, played in 81-degree heat at Notre Dame, showed that Oklahoma's green alternate eleven could neither move nor grow on defense. Coach Joe Kuharich's Irish won 19-6.

Wilkinson summed up the battle's salient points in his alumni letter when he wrote, "Our starting team played approximately 80 percent of the time in the heat and came close to getting a standoff. Our second team, in the game for only 11 plays on defense, gave up the astonishing total of 160 net yards, 14.5 yards a carry. With a defensive yield like that, it is almost impossible to win."

But the Sooner seconds showed a surprising aptitude for offense. Notre Dame's kickoff sailed short and high against the gale. Gary Wylie fielded it and, shooting straight down the middle behind excellent blocking, cut to the right sideline and ran 48 yards to the Irish 28 before their last tackler got him.

The Sooner alternates scored in seven plays. Bucks by Wylie and Dan Jordan, Amarillo sophomore, and sweeps by Van Burkleo to right and left put the ball on the Irish 4. From there halfback Jackie Cowan, Oklahoma City sophomore, scored on a pitch from Van Burkleo, with Wylie coming back from the end zone to throw a block. Milstead missed goal and the score stood 6-6.

There was no more Sooner scoring. Meanwhile Notre Dame marched 74 yards to its second touchdown and quickly powered to a third on the running of Dabiero. Deere's interception of Lamonica's pass on the Sooner 7 prevented a fourth.

The low-water mark, as Wilkinson called it, of Oklahoma football during his period occurred in the first quarter of the Iowa State game at Norman. The Cyclones scored three touchdowns and led 21-0. The Sooners surrendered five of six fumbles and threw a pass interception, and Coach Clay Stapleton's sound little club made rich capital of them.

Oklahoma gained the wind in the second quarter and recovered its poise. Wilkinson inserted Bob Page, Borger, Texas, senior, at quarterback. Be-

ginning as an eighth grader back at Borger, Page had started every game
he ever played at the position. Cool and poised, he halted the Sooner panic,
pulled them together and piloted them 76 yards to a touchdown in 19
plays, scoring it himself on a 3-yard keeper around the Cyclone right end,
Payne and White throwing blocks. George Jarman, 5-foot-7-inch Tulsa
sophomore, kicked goal. Now Iowa State led 21-7.

In the third period the Sooner defense became so staunch that Iowa
State was held without a first down and managed only nine yards rushing.
Meanwhile Oklahoma launched another drive. Wilkinson sent in Page and
he steered them 80 yards, handing off to Carpenter for the touchdown
behind blocks by White and Gilstrap.

On the conversion Page boldly went for two points and got them. The
Sooners faked a kick for goal, Carpenter rising with the snap and throwing
a short screen pass to Page who broke across the goal behind blocks by
Payne and White. Iowa State's lead was cut to five, 21-15. "Now I was
convinced we would win," Wilkinson said later.

With 5:16 left Oklahoma had its chance but, after moving 41 yards to
the Cyclone 31, lost it by dropping another fumble which Kidd of Iowa
State covered just before the final gun.

Page was asked how it felt to lose that one. "It was like a death in the
family," he replied. "We all felt sorry for Bud because we knew he hated
to lose worse than anybody. But we never quit. When you don't get annihilated, you suck it up and practice hard for the next game."

Texas, with a winning percentage of 1.000, and Oklahoma with one of
.000, met at Dallas in the battle of the contrasting ciphers. It was the
first time in the history of the series that one team was all-victorious
while the other had lost every start.

Coach Darrell Royal's orange speedmobile made the Sooners pay costly
penance for three turnovers by transforming a blocked kick, a pass interception, and a fumble into touchdowns while winning 28-7. However, the
Sooners battled hard. Against three previous opponents Texas had averaged
504 total yards on offense. The Sooners held them to 272 and compelled
them to punt seven times. The Steers broke no long plays.

Oklahoma's touchdown came early in the fourth quarter when the Texas
second team was on the field. Van Burkleo, the sophomore quarterback,
directed the Sooners 68 yards to the 1-yard line. The longest play of this
march came on a trap play up the middle. When Claude Hamon, Oklahoma
City Harding junior, trap-blocked the Texas guard, Lohmann broke into the
open and ran 35 steps to the Texas 16. Page came in and handed off to
Lohmann for the touchdown. Jarman kicked goal. At the battle's close
Wilkinson embraced Royal, his former quarterback, in the gridiron's center.

"Texas had a superteam," Jimmy Carpenter summed it up later. Royal's outfit finished 9-1, beat Mississippi in the Cotton Bowl, and finished number three nationally in the AP poll.

When Dale Perini was hurt in practice, Wilkinson moved Jim McCoy, fifth-team end from Okmulgee, to the alternates. Although McCoy was a senior, it was his first road trip ever with his team.

"The worst thing about staying home when your team leaves on a road trip is having to face everybody when you go to class," said McCoy. "You feel humiliated." In the excitement of playing right end for the alternates before 75,504 at Dallas, McCoy forgot his previous embarrassment.

On the succeeding Saturday, Coach Jack Mitchell's Kansas Jayhawkers smothered Oklahoma with defense, holding the Sooners to 98 yards of total offense and six first downs. No other opponent had choked off a Wilkinson team that thoroughly. The Sooners got across the 50 only twice with the ball. It was the first conference whitewash Oklahoma had ever suffered under Wilkinson at Norman.

Yet Kansas won the game only 10-0. There was a reason for that. The fierce, never-quitting Sooners themselves played elegant defense, blunting seven Kansas drives that reached the Oklahoma 2, 3, 12, 22, 30, 40, and 44-yard lines. But no farther.

Oklahoma's best opportunity to score came almost as the first quarter ended. Geary Taylor, sophomore halfback from Amarillo, lofted a punt 54 yards downfield that stranded Kansas back on its 23. McClinton reversed wide but Jim McCoy, the new right end, overpowered the play, tossing him for a loss. McFarland bucked off tackle but McCoy piled that play too, after it gained 3. John Hadl punted strongly, the ball carrying well against the breeze to the Sooner 45.

Paul Lea, Terrell, Texas, junior, fielded it. He faked to Van Burkleo, then came back to his left, along the west sideline, where the Sooners had formed their blocking wall. Thus Mitchell's old play was used against him. A Kansas tackler bore down upon Lea before he reached that wall but John Benien, Tulsa sophomore, erased him from Lea's path. "Best block I ever saw in my life," praised Johnny Tatum later. "Benien never did leave his feet. He just ran through him." With the Sooner crowd roaring, Lea wove back 41 yards before the last Jayhawk tackler nailed him on the Kansas 14. But Mitchell's defense stopped everything, and when Milstead tried a field goal into the gale, the wind blew it wild.

Mitchell, the Kansas coach, said from the Crimson and Blue locker room, "Oklahoma is exactly the opposite of what many people think. They have very little line depth or backfield speed. Yet they gave as fine a team effort as anybody we've played. They played like the devil. They never quit."

But it was the fourth straight Sooner defeat. Next morning John Cronley, sports editor of the *Daily Oklahoman,* wrote a column critical of Wilkinson. Asked to comment on it in his press conference Monday, Wilkinson defended the sports editor, saying, "I think people are too critical of the press. A columnist's number one priority is to be read. If he doesn't write something controversial or interesting, he won't be read. A columnist has as hard a job as a football coach. He has to go to the wall every day and write something people will read. That is not easy."

All-victorious Colorado, ranked number nine in the nation in the United Press poll and tenth in the AP balloting, came to Owen Field. A crowd of 45,117 cheered itself hoarse as the action ebbed and flowed. The Sooner feat of allowing only two touchdowns in the last half all season had kept the fans loyal.

With quarterback Bob Page moving them smartly, the Sooners went 60 yards in ten plays against the wind for the game's first touchdown. Page bucked hard on a quarterback sneak behind Lee, Hamon, and White to score. Jarman kicked goal.

"Bud always had a gimmick play," Page recalls that touchdown today. "On this one, McClellan raised up and took a step backwards. 'Hold it!' he yelled, raising both arms. 'What do I do on this play?' Colorado's players relaxed, Joe Romig too. The ball was snapped. Our blockers had the edge and I scored over Romig." However, the Sooners say that was the only time all day that they blocked the spirited Colorado All-American.

Colorado fought back hard. Soon they led 10-7. Hillebrand kicked off with the wind, booting strongly and low. The ball bounced wickedly, Oklahoma barely covering it on their 6. The situation looked very bleak at this point. Wilkinson substituted his alternates, a practice he had followed steadfastly despite that unit's greenness at the start of the season. He kept Page at quarterback and Carpenter at left half.

When Page, aided by a block by fullback Dick Beattie, Tulsa sophomore, shot around Colorado's right end for 20 yards, the Sooners were out of the hole and on their way. Carpenter threw the halfback pass to Wylie for 20 yards and Oklahoma was nearly at midfield. Page kept moving the attack. On the Buffalo 20, Page set himself and, passing carefully into the treacherous crosswind, hit John Porterfield, Bixby sophomore, for 19 yards and a touchdown. Jarman's unerring boot was good. Now Oklahoma led 14-10.

Scenting an upset defeat that would cost them the Big Eight leadership, Colorado rallied and surged ahead 16-14. And the lead in the thrilling game had changed hands four times.

Then misfortune struck Oklahoma at a critical time. Trailing by two points, the Sooners had the strong wind and 11 minutes in which to score either a touchdown or a field goal. Hillebrand's kickoff twisted low and to the right against the gale. The green Sooner linemen failed to cover it. Jim Hold, Colorado end, dove for it on the Sooner 31. Exploiting this break, Colorado drove on in, Schweninger bucking across the goal. Wylie broke up their pass for two points but Colorado had won 22-14.

Asked at his Monday press conference to comment on Oklahoma's failure to cover Hillebrand's short kickoff, Wilkinson said, "On this situation, linemen think first of their blocking duty. They figure it's a normal kickoff. Usually when this happens, the ball goes much deeper than this did. It happens once a year someplace and it finally happened to us."

It was Oklahoma's fifth straight defeat. They had lost nine of their last ten games and had won only three of their last 15. "It was very frustrating," Leon Cross says. "We'd played well enough to win some of them." Phil Lohmann remembers that he felt very low. "Until you play at Oklahoma and lose five in a row, you don't know what *low* is," he said. Virgil Boll, Sooner halfback, said, "There was something intangible about that season. We were fighting everybody real good but we didn't know how to win." Jay O'Neal, who had just signed on full-time that fall as Sooner assistant coach, shook his head in consternation. "Boy!" he told himself, "this coaching ain't worth a damn."

Sonny Grandelius, Colorado's young coach, said, "You can say for me that Oklahoma is the best 0-and-5 team I've ever seen." Frank Boggs, *Daily Oklahoman* writer, saw fun in the unfortunate kickoff situation. "The final Colorado touchdown was different, at least," Boggs wrote. "The Buffs kicked off to themselves, which isn't easy."

The Sooners felt like kicking themselves until Wilkinson told them in the Sunday morning squad meeting that they would win all five remaining games despite the fact the first four would be played on the opponents' home fields. He repeated the prediction statewide on his Sunday television show. That was so unlike Bud that it braced the team remarkably. "He saw that we were improving and we could sense it too," says Bob Page. "We were becoming more consistent. Our offense could sustain drives. We made fewer errors."

Page, aeronautical engineering senior from Borger, Texas, had beaten off all quarterback competition. But it was costly. Page wanted to drop his engineering courses. "I was passing but having to work my tail off with that and football too," he recalls.

Robertson, the academic counselor, would have none of it. "Young man —peahead—you're not going to do anything of the kind," Robertson said. So Page stayed with the engineering and in spite of the distraction of football he earned a B.S. and later an M.S. in aeronautical engineering and lacked only a dissertation to harvest a Ph.D. in chemistry as well.

Coach Doug Weaver's Kansas State Wildcats, who had beaten both Indiana and Air Force, tore out after the Sooners very aggressively on November 4 at Manhattan. With 4:19 left to play, the Sooners led by only four points, 10-6. "It was neck and neck," said Phil Lohmann. "Kansas State played great. We were terrified. You've never been terrified until you're neck and neck with Kansas State after you've already lost five."

In the fourth period a Sooner back ran the wrong way, bumping into a teammate, and there was nobody to take the pitchout. Luckily, Carpenter bird-dogged it for a 9-yard loss back to the Sooner 18. It was second and 19, a great spot for a quick kick.

There was only 4:09 left to play. Wilkinson had added a fake quick kick to the Sooner offensive repertoire that week. On their regular quick kick Page would take the snap and toss it back to Carpenter who would retreat a step, then step forward and boot the ball end over end to get all the roll. Page called the fake boot. The Sooner linemen yelled, "Quick kick!" Carpenter took the pitch from Page, backed up, swung his leg, but handed off behind his back to Mike McClellan reversing wide to the left.

Milstead and George Stokes, sophomore lineman from Madill, swung left also and threw telling blocks to help McClellan turn the corner. Page led him upfield and blocked out the Wildcat safety. McClellan blazed 82 yards to a touchdown. That dramatic play changed the game's tide completely. Oklahoma won 17-6, breaking its losing streak. Leon Cross said later, "I doubt if there's ever been an OU team that appreciated a victory as much as we did that one."

Missouri had installed a new wide-end six-man line defense that blanked four opponents that season and yielded only 5.7 points—less than a touchdown each game—to its whole schedule. Using that, Coach Dan Devine and Al Onofrio, his defensive assistant, had developed a team that finished 7-2-1.

But Oklahoma had been playing rugged defense, too. "We're going to win this game," Wilkinson told the Sooners. "In every football game a team gets the ball, first and ten, twelve to fourteen times. If you can stop Missouri fourteen times, not let them score, make them give up the ball, we'll win."

It seemed a bold statement with Captain Billy White, Oklahoma's cyclonic left tackle, out of the game with an ankle sprain and a hip-pointer he had sustained against Kansas State. Dennis Ward, Bartlesville junior, started in place of White. Behind Ward was rangy George Stokes of Madill, a good mover and talker-upper. "It ain't agonna work!" he'd call across the scrimmage line to the opposition.

White wore street clothing when he walked to the middle of the field at Columbia for the coin flip. He won it and chose to receive. A misting rain was falling but Missouri's field tarp had kept the field dry. A record crowd of 45,146 came.

When Ron Taylor, Missouri quarterback, passed 40 yards in the first quarter to end Conrad Hitchler to the Sooner 3, Oklahoma's defense met its acid test. Tobin hit over left tackle. The play made 2 yards before Oklahoma closed the hole. Taylor tried a quarterback sneak but the Sooners pinched it off for no gain as safety Paul Lea came up fast to bump the ballcarrier back. Tobin tried the right side. No gain.

On fourth down the Tigers hit over their right side with left half Vince Turner carrying. Dennis Ward made a strong knifing charge, broke through, and tackled Turner for a 2-yard loss. Oklahoma had won the ball on downs.

After a 44-yard punt runback by Jimmy Carpenter and a touchdown-saving tackle by Mike McClellan kept pressure on the Tigers, Missouri fumbled, and Wayne Lee, Sooner center, covered the ball on the Tiger 43. It was touchdown time for Oklahoma.

Leon Cross and Tom Cox blocked Dick Beattie forward for 3. McClellan struck off 5 on the handoff and 3 on a sweep and the Sooners had first down on the Tiger 32. After Missouri stopped two plays, Bill Van Burkleo came in for one down only and pegged a swing pass to Paul Lea who ran 15 yards to the Tiger 14. Oklahoma tried a sweep but Crawford of Missouri derailed it after a yard gain.

Page was back at quarterback and he called the halfback option pass, pitching to Carpenter sweeping Missouri's left flank. Carpenter shot a pass to McClellan who broke through a Missouri tackler on the 5 and scored. "I caught the ball from Page and threw it to Mac all in one motion because the Missouri defensive end was all over me," says Carpenter today. "I never did see Mac catch it." Jarman kicked goal and Oklahoma led 7-0.

That was the final score as the rival defenses made the offenses eat the football all afternoon. "It was a tremendously satisfying victory over a strong opponent," remembers Leon Cross. "A rich reward for our coaches and players. We'd won a big one."

With statuettes of Babe Ruth, Lou Gehrig, and Miller Huggins looking on from center field, Oklahoma joined battle with Army at Yankee Stadium on a cold afternoon in November. Army brought a 6-2 record into the game and also a cheering corps of 2,200 gray-clad cadets who roared encouragement to the Black Knights all through the contest. Army had won five straight in New York where they had long been the favorites of Gotham fans.

Bob Ward, Sooner assistant who had scouted Army's recent triumphs over Detroit and William and Mary, had brought back one extremely valuable piece of information. Army's defense huddled in a closed circle well behind the scrimmage front and came back slowly to the ball. So Wilkinson designed a bit of bunko, a quick play run without a huddle. All week before the game the Sooners worked on it with enthusiasm as they always did on one of Wilkinson's specials.

The play had two phases. First, quarterback Page handed off to left half Carpenter who cross bucked to the right and, after gaining 2 or 3 yards, went down purposely, letting Army tackle him. The Sooners didn't want a first down which would necessitate moving the markers forward and delay the play's second phase, the coup de grace, or death blow.

However, no Army tackler challenged Carpenter, so after running 11 yards he dropped to the turf for a first down which was what the Sooners didn't want. Page was equal to the emergency. Summoning the Sooners into a huddle, he recalled the same play. This time Carpenter stumbled forward 3 yards and dutifully went down. Army retreated casually into its defensive cluster.

As Carpenter arose, he handed the ball to the referee whom Page had forewarned about the strategy. The Sooners pretended to walk slowly back to their huddle. Except there wasn't any huddle this time. The Sooners quickly deployed into a 6-1 offensive line that was strong to the wide, or left, side of the field. When the referee set the ball down, center Wayne Lee crouched over it, Carpenter squatting behind him. When the referee dropped his arm, Page waited two seconds, as the rules stipulated, then yelled his snap count, "Set! Hike!"

Lee lifted the ball to Carpenter whose season of quarterbacking in 1960 had taught him how to handle the long lateral. Just as Army emerged from its defensive retreat, Carpenter shoveled the ball diagonally to his left, a long pitch to McClellan. Ron Payne and Karl Milstead blocked in. Leon Cross and Tom Cox pulled out and joining fullback Dick Beattie swung ahead of the sprinting McClellan as a blocking shield. Page threw a block downfield.

McClellan had two speeds—fast and where did he go? Although Army pursued gamely, Oklahoma's blockers protected Mike neatly. McClellan zoomed 75 yards, pulling away from halfback Joe Blackgrove, the last Army pursuer, and crossed the goal. Jarman converted. Oklahoma led 7-0.

Army came back hard. Blackgrove fielded a pitchout and circled the

The Sooner quickie against Army at New York in 1961. On a play run without a huddle, Mike McClellan zooms 75 yards to the opening touchdown. Sports Information Department, University of Oklahoma.

Welcome home! Three thousand students and townspeople crowd Norman's Max Westheimer airport to greet the Sooners after the Army victory.

Sooner left side for 33 yards to the Oklahoma 31. But the Sooner defense stopped that nonsense.

The hard-fought game delighted the New York crowd of 39,952. The tackling was hard and crisp. Once Army drove to the Sooner 30, but McClellan came up fast to rock Paul Stanley, and the Sooners gained the ball on downs. Still fighting hard, Army began the last half with a 43-yard advance that reached the Sooner 38. They pitched to Blackgrove, their best runner, but Monte Deere came up fast to nail him for no gain.

Oklahoma's 76-yard march to its second touchdown followed. The alternates were in except that Page quarterbacked them and Carpenter was at left half. Page pitched to Carpenter for 10. Lohmann bucked powerfully for 24 to the Army 42. Page, getting a decisive block from Carpenter, ran the bootleg reverse pass for 17 more. An Army penalty for piling on took the Sooners to the 11. Three plays later Wylie, running to his left, hit Carpenter with a 7-yard pass to the Cadet 1-yard line.

Army's 2,200-man cadet corps roared bad-manneredly, refusing the officials' effort to gesture them into some semblance of quiet so Oklahoma could hear Page's signals. "Army's players were very disciplined, ready to jump right at you," Page recalls today. "When I went to a delayed count, they jumped offside twice. On the half-yard line we used our quick count and scored." Page drove over Tatum and Gilstrap for the touchdown. Jarman goaled. Oklahoma led 14-0.

Army refused to fold and scored a touchdown of its own when Blackgrove passed to Paul Zmuida, their "Lonely End." When Lewis passed to Zmuida for two points, Oklahoma led only 14-8. There was still 4:37 to play.

Lohmann ended the Black Knights' last threat when, playing linebacker, he tipped Lewis's pass. The ball slid behind him but juggling it behind his back he pulled it around in front and ran 37 yards to the Army 17. On a keeper Page bucked 11 to the Army 6. With 1:02 left Page ran two plays into the line but didn't try to score. He concentrated on handling the ball carefully. Oklahoma won 14-8.

"That night, the coaches told us to take the night off, have fun," remembers Paul Benien. "We were so excited. Three wins in a row." Dr. Mike Willard, Sooner team physician, went with the coaches to Jack Dempsey's restaurant for a steak. "Tell Dempsey that Willard's here," Mike growled amiably to a waiter as they entered.

Red Smith, the noted sports columnist, saw the game on a 21-inch television screen at his home. "Chances are," he wrote next day, "the military leaders of tomorrow learned more last Saturday about the value of surprise to an attacking force than they had absorbed in three years of lectures at the Academy.

"For the television viewer who happened to be out in the kitchen opening a can of Brand X and was caught woolgathering, like Army, the play was rerun on video tape between halves. Though Oklahoma this year hasn't got the terrific overall speed that used to characterize Bud Wilkinson's teams, the Sooners were still too soon for the military. And the give-and-take in the line proved the unwisdom of training combat troops on a marshmallow diet."

The Nebraska game was played on the same field at Lincoln where Coach Bill Jennings's Cornhuskers had upset the Sooners of 1959, fracturing an Oklahoma string of 74 consecutive conference games without defeat. It was warm and clear, and the Scarlet turf, softened by the previous week of snow and rain, was dried by four days of warm south wind.

Jennings's Nebraskans seemed totally unimpressed with Oklahoma's November comeback. Led by Dennis Claridge, 200-pound sophomore, they led 14-0 at the half and their lead could have been 28-0 had not a receiver lost one of Claridge's passes on the Sooner 10 and had not another receiver dropped a Claridge throw on a fake field goal. "Bud chewed us out at the half, the worst we ever got chewed," remembers Jimmy Carpenter.

Carpenter looked like he'd been physically chewed. "He'd had his helmet jammed down on his nose, cutting it," remembers Leon Cross. "He was sitting forlornly on the bench with his nose bleeding. Bud singled him out, telling us Jimmy was busting a gut trying to win and not getting any support from us linemen. We geared it up."

The last half was a totally different game. Receiving the kickoff, Oklahoma scored in three plays, Page forward passing to Ron Payne for 30 yards and a touchdown. Jarman kicked goal. Then Monte Deere returned a punt 19 yards to the Cornhusker 33, running to their last tackler.

That positioned the white-garbed Sooners for their second touchdown. The first team came in. Page faked flawlessly to Lohmann and pitched to Carpenter who slipped around right end for the touchdown. Jarman kicked goal. Score 14-14.

Two minutes later Claridge blasted a 70-yard punt that rolled dead on the Sooner 2. "We were in a delicate, crucial situation," Wilkinson described it later in his alumni letter. But the Sooners of '61 possessed much of football's basic ingredient—courage.

Page moved the alternate team out of the hole with three straight keepers. The alternate blockers kept clearing them out and the Sooners began unspooling a memorable march. Nobody knew it then but Oklahoma was on its way to a fantastic exhibition of ball control.

310

As the antagonists changed goals for the start of the fourth period, Page kept mixing the plays. Page pitched to Carpenter for a first down on Oklahoma's 33. Beattie bucked to another on the 48. Lohmann burst off tackle, and the ball squirted from his grasp, but Page had the good luck to cover it on the Nebraska 38. Payne, Ward, and Milstead blocked Lohmann ahead 8 yards more. Page rolled out to pass but, since nobody was open, he ran and, picking up a block by Perini, dodged 14 yards to the Nebraska 12. Every spectator in the Nebraska stadium was getting a close-up view as the ground-gobbling Oklahomans crossed every yard line on the field and passed every section in the stadium during their march.

Carpenter bucked three times for a first down on the Scarlet 1. Twice Page tried quarterback sneaks but Jennings's defense thwarted both. Then Page faked to Lohmann and pitched to Carpenter who scored around right end without going off his feet. Jarman kicked goal. It was a drive of 98 yards in 25 plays and burned up 13 minutes of time. The game soon ended and the Sooners carried Bud and Gomer off the field on their shoulders.

Carpenter had scored the last two touchdowns but he always laughed that off. "I was up to 170 pounds my senior year," he said proudly.

Jennings, the Nebraska coach, joked 19 years later, "I used to say that we beat OU two and one-half years in a row because we led 14-0 at the half."

Oklahoma, winner of four straight road games but loser of five consecutive home tilts, contended next against both that enigma and resurgent Oklahoma State. The final game of the season was played at Norman. The Sooners hadn't won at home since October 22, 1960, when they flogged Kansas State 49-7.

The Cowboys led 2-0 when Bob Adcock, their fullback, tackled Jimmy Carpenter for a safety. On the ensuing free kick, Jim McCoy, Sooner end, raced down and recovered the ball on the bounce on the Cowboy 43. The rules provided that, same as for a kickoff, the free-kicking team can recover the free ball. The Cowboys didn't know that, but McCoy did.

Oklahoma moved 43 yards to a touchdown, Page faking well and keeping around right tackle for the score. Jarman kicked goal and the Sooners led 7-2. Later, Ted Davis, Cowboy placekicker, booted a 22-yard field goal and the lead was cut to what looked like the score of a tennis match, 7-5.

Virgil Boll's recovery of a Cowboy fumble on the State 39 put Oklahoma's alternates in business, and they pushed to a touchdown on a buck by Page. Jarman's goal kick left Oklahoma leading 14-5. The Cowboys lost a touchdown on a drive from kickoff when halfback Jim Dillard ripped off 13 yards to the Sooner 1 then fumbled when Mike McClellan jolted him with a saving tackle, center Wayne Lee recovering for a Sooner touchback.

Oklahoma also cashed that break, driving 80 yards in seven plays for their third touchdown. McClellan's 50-yard sweep to the Cowboy 23 was the longest gain, and Carpenter scored the touchdown on a pitch from Page.

Winning 21-13, the Sooners picked up their fifth straight victory and gained undisputed possession of fourth place in the Big Eight. Page, the quarterback, said later, "After the season ended we thought we could play with anybody. We would even have liked another shot at Texas."

In his alumni letter, Wilkinson paid tribute to "the basic qualities of manhood that our seniors possess. The foundation of a football team is leadership from within the squad itself," Bud added. "Coaches, to a degree, help individuals and the team develop physical skills and coordination, but the basic elements of character have usually been established in the hearts and minds of college men."

Guard Leon Cross and end Ron Payne each won two "Ug" Awards that season, Cross in the Texas and Iowa State games, Payne in the Notre Dame and Army contests. Other "Ug" winners were Kansas-game tackle Billy White, Colorado-game tackle Tom Cox, Kansas State–game tackle Dennis Ward, Missouri-game end Dale Perini, Nebraska-game tackle Duane Cook, and Oklahoma State–game center Johnny Tatum.

After the season Wilkinson resumed his duties as special consultant to President Kennedy. He began conferring with government agencies, private organizations and groups outside the government in his zeal to form a widespread youth fitness program. But when he would return to Norman, he always seemed discouraged by these meetings.

"He reported that those with whom he talked had been more inclined to discuss the congressional appropriations needed to finance the project than to discuss the project itself," President Cross revealed. "They spoke in terms of millions of dollars. Wilkinson's idea was that a successful program could be launched with relatively little federal money. He was critical of many agencies of the federal government that he thought had been wasteful of federal funds, and he was emphatic that the citizens should make an effort to reduce the waste in Washington.

"For the first time he mentioned that he might be interested in entering politics. He suggested one day, partly in jest, that he might change his registration to the Republican party and run for the United States Senate sometime."[4] Thrift and prudence had always been salient features of Wil-

[4] George Lynn Cross, *Presidents Can't Punt* (Norman: University of Oklahoma Press, 1977), p. 326.

kinson's makeup and were annually reflected in virtually every phase of the athletic department finances he controlled.

The Sooner rally through their last five games attracted wide attention. In the Associated Press's annual poll at the end of the year, sports editors and sportscasters from coast to coast voted Oklahoma's November rally the greatest comeback of 1961 in any sport.

Darrell Royal, the Texas mentor, always gave his old coach high credit for that feat. "I believe that was probably the best coaching job Bud Wilkinson has ever done at Norman, more so than when the Sooners were winning 40 straight."[5]

In 1981 Royal enlarged a bit on his premise. "The measure of a good coach," he said, "is how he reacts to losing. Can he keep the respect and confidence of his players in what he is trying to do? Will they believe that losing is only a temporary situation and that if they stay with what they are doing things will get better?

"A coach grows strong and mature when he encounters defeats, repeated defeats. It's not hard to coach a winning football team, handle the press, keep the players happy, keep the staff together. If you win your first five games, it's lots easier to come back and win the second five. But to lose the first five and then come back and win the last five tells me that under the most trying circumstances a coach has maintained control of the whole situation. It takes leadership to do that."[6]

[5] "Darrell Royal Talks Football" (Englewood Cliffs, N.J.: Prentice Hall, 1963), p. 66.
[6] Darrell Royal to author, February 27, 1981.

1961 SENIORS TODAY

Dr. Paul Benien is an osteopathic physician and surgeon in Oklahoma City, Oklahoma.

Jimmy Carpenter is an independent oil-and-gas operator in Edmond, Oklahoma.

Tom Cox is coowner of a real estate firm in Crested Butte, Colorado. In 1981 he was elected mayor of Crested Butte.

Phil Lohmann is president of Apex Energy, Inc., a public oil-and-gas firm in Norman, Oklahoma, and owner and chairman of the board of Lohmann and Associates, a petroleum engineering consulting firm, also in Norman, Oklahoma.

Mike McClellan is a partner in McClellan, Massey and Marshburn, Inc., real estate consultants in Dallas, Texas.

Karl Milstead is an independent oil producer in Wichita Falls, Texas.

Bob Page is president and owner of the Stokes Canning Company of Denver, Colorado, and of the Ellis Foods Corporation, also of Denver.

Ron Payne owns the Ron Payne Development Company of Breckenridge, Texas.

Billy White owns and operates a charter fishing boat at Freeport, Texas.

17. THE SOPHOMORE TEAM

Sap green but eager, Oklahoma's 1962 team inherited only two starters, guard Leon Cross and center Wayne Lee. The squad promptly elected them cocaptains.

Lee, a rugged linebacker, had fought his way to a defensive starting position as a sophomore and in 1961 became a fine offensive pivot as well. In fact, line coach Gomer Jones later said of him, "He's as fine an offensive blocker as we've had since I've been here."

Cross had lost two years, 1959 and 1960, because of unfortunate injuries. When he overcame them and played in both 1961 and 1962, the Sooners began calling him "Old Rugged Cross" or just "Old Rugged." Dan Parker, the *New York Mirror* sports columnist, wrote the week of the Army game that the "Sooners' Old Rugged Cross is a He, not a Hymn." Paul Benien, an end of that period, said of Cross, "He was here before I got here and left after I left."

With nine starters gone, prospects looked as dreary as last year's cornstalks. But nobody was throwing in anything. A mettlesome sophomore crew that ranked a cut above any Wilkinson had ever recruited infiltrated the 1962 varsity and helped it tan the Alumni 47-24 in the spring game.

It was plainly a transition year at Norman, a developing period for green, spirited youngsters who in their first four games must cut their football eyeteeth on Syracuse's Liberty Bowl champions, Texas's Cotton Bowl kings, Kansas's Bluebonnet Bowl monarchs and Notre Dame.

"The only thing we didn't like was our new dorm, Washington House," remembers Charley Mayhue. "Although it was designed for air-conditioning, none was ever installed and meanwhile we were left with the small windows and the bad acoustics. A lot of the guys got married not only because they found the right girl but to get away from that dorm."

Dennis Ward, who had spelled Billy White at left tackle when White was injured, was given another year of competition when the conference ruled his sophomore season a hardship case. "Ward," says Leon Cross, "was a tall, lanky kid who got knocked around a lot. He became a classic example of determination, dedication, and hard work. I respected him as much as any OU player who ever lived."

A new kickoff time, 1:30 P.M., was born that fall. Many Oklahoma fans

315

drove long distances to see the Sooners play. An earlier kickoff would let them start home earlier, eliminating much night driving. A new assistant coach joined the staff. He was George Dickson who had quarterbacked Notre Dame's national champions of 1949.

The sophomore crop that fall was as strong as horseradish. Among the ends was Glen ("Moose") Condren, a 227-pounder from Muldrow. He was the squad's "Lil Abner." He decked more people in scrimmage than anybody else.

Rick McCurdy, Purcell High School's big Scots tailback who had a 3.9 grade point average, wanted OU's medical school so badly that he passed up offers from all three military academies and several Ivy League schools. He was big, intelligent, could maneuver well and played like a senior.

John Flynn, an Irish-Catholic end from Washington, D.C., St. John's, was tough, hard-nosed, and didn't like to wear shoes. "He played with the gusto of a street fighter," Leon Cross sketched him. "He was the most exceptional athlete I've ever been around," added Rick McCurdy. "He had a quick forearm shiver, was the fastest of all our ends, could always make the catch, and could do all this without much training. Even when he was in the wrong defense, which was often, he would sometimes make the interception because he had a great feel for where the ball would be in the air."

Ralph Neely of Farmington, New Mexico, a tackle whose sweatshirt would almost have fit around the Marland mansion, had intelligence, desire, and superior size and speed. "He was a hell of a prospect but like all sophomores still made sophomore mistakes," Gomer Jones described him. Then there was Eddie ("No Quarter") McQuarters, 230-pound black tackle and state heavyweight wrestling champion from Tulsa Washington. He had first impressed Sooner coaches when they saw him outrun one of their halfbacks during a wind sprint at the all-state game training camp. "Eddie and I roomed together on the road trips," recalls John Garrett. "He was a superhuman, one of the finest."

The politest boy on the squad was Lance Rentzel of Oklahoma City Casady, a big, versatile youngster whose piano playing had won the gold medal at the Oklahoma Music Festival and who made the Dean's Honor List at OU. But football was what he liked best. He became a corking runner-receiver.

Another fine prospect who was quick to sign was Tommy Pannell who had quarterbacked Norman High to the state championship. In the freshman game with Tulsa University, Pannell ran back a punt 60 yards to a touchdown, bucked 6 yards off tackle for another, and returned a kickoff 67 yards.

Jim Grisham, first sophomore to start at fullback since Leon Heath in

316

1948, had Texas written all over him. He wore flowery shirts, big belt buckles, blue jeans, and a cowboy hat. He majored in mechanical engineering and in spite of football somehow fought his way through long afternoon labs in physics, chemistry, and engineering. "Anytime you want something bad enough, you can get it," he said he learned from Bud and Gomer.

As a sixth-grader at Olney, Texas, Grisham made the junior-high team, and "we played eight night games with out-of-town opponents." Wilkinson twice visited the fullback in his home at Olney where Grisham remembers that Bud was very fond of Mrs. Grisham's hot biscuits and fresh-churned butter. "I wanted to play for Bud," Grisham says. "I liked the way he coached."

Other sophomores who had been coached as freshmen by Robertson and Norman McNabb, his assistant, were Butch Metcalf of Garland, Texas, and Allen Bumgardner of Putnam City.

Then there was Ron Fletcher, a Cinderella quarterback prospect who stood only 5-9, weighed 159, and could throw the football out of sight. As a freshman, Fletcher had sold hot dogs for the OU concessions department at OU's 1961 games and waited tables at the student union. Then he walked on as a sophomore and, liking his progress, the coaches gave him a full scholarship. The Sooners called him "Mother Fletcher."

Another new player that fall was the only junior-college transfer Wilkinson had ever accepted, Joe Don Looney from Cameron Junior College of Lawton. Looney had punted and run Coach Leroy Montgomery's Cameron outfit to an all-victorious season and a 28-20 Little Rose Bowl triumph over Bakersfield, California, Junior College. Looney had swept Bakersfield's end for the winning touchdown. "He was as good a kid as I ever coached," Montgomery later told Dan Lauck of the *Manhattan,* Kansas, *Mercury,* when Montgomery was an assistant at Kansas State.

Since Cameron was in recruiting territory assigned to Jay O'Neal, Sooner assistant coach, O'Neal went to Lawton to make inquiries and study film. "The films showed that Looney had lots of talent," says O'Neal. "He was a polite, handsome, pleasant kid. He came from a fine family. His father, Don, a Texas Christian end, had been Davey O'Brien's favorite pass receiver there. Joe Don had attended one semester each at Texas and Texas Christian, going out for track. He didn't stay at either place."

Looney's grades at Cameron were a problem at first. "He wanted to play at Oklahoma but first he had to graduate from junior college," remembers O'Neal. "He needed to make 19 hours of B at Cameron in the spring and summer semesters to graduate. We told him that if he did that we'd take him. So help me, he did it, and some of them were A's. The boy was intelligent. We had very little trouble with him his first year at Norman."

317

When Looney showed at Oklahoma's fall practice in 1962, Wilkinson had never seen him. It was photo day. O'Neal was standing near Bud. Looney ran by, wearing Oklahoma's red regalia. He weighed a trim 207 and ran with a light elastic gait, his feet spurning the Owen Field turf. "Bud blinked," O'Neal remembers. "'Who in the world is that?' he asked.

It soon became evident that the new arrival had lots of rebellion in him. He avoided going to the training room for treatment. He was sometimes late for practice. He didn't want to pose for publicity pictures. "He had a negative reaction to the team concept of accepting various things expected of everybody if the team did well," assistant coach Eddie Crowder explained it.

Eight days before the Syracuse opener, Tommy Pannell, the cotton-thatched sophomore quarterback from Norman whom sports writers had voted the outstanding player of the Varsity-Alumni game the preceding spring, fractured his ankle in scrimmage and was lost for the year. Two days earlier Pannell had moved the scrimmaging varsity to four touchdowns in five possessions and completed 12 of 15 passes. He had the part down cold. Wilkinson had never started a sophomore at quarterback in his previous 15 years at Oklahoma, but the fiery little Norman blond had that tradition ground into powder when he broke his ankle.

Volney Meece, *Oklahoma City Times* columnist, put it neatly when he wrote, "The footballers toiling in Norman, Indian Territory, lost their Tom-Tom Monday."

Wilkinson and his staff began to work diligently with Monte Deere, Amarillo senior, who had played primarily at defensive halfback. They also schooled two other sophomores, Bobby Page of Wolfe City, Texas, and Norman Smith of Monahans, Texas.

In the first game of the season Syracuse led Oklahoma 3-0 and was driving for a 10-0 victory. With only inches to gain on fourth down from the Sooner 27, they gave the ball to Jim Nance, their 225-pound black fullback who had battered the Sooners all day with his power plunges. Nance started wide, then cut up the middle. The Sooner alternates were in. There was 2:57 left to play.

Johnny Tatum, Sooner center, came up fast, like a bantam gamecock, and nailed Nance solidly around the legs, stopping him in his tracks. However, Nance had only to fall forward for the first down. Paul Lea, Sooner safety, prevented this by coming up behind Tatum to hit Nance high with a supporting tackle. Thus the Sooners held the Orangemen for downs and came into possession on their own 27. Without this Tatum-Lea double whammy, time probably would have run out before Oklahoma could gain possession of the ball.

Near the Sooner bench Joe Don Looney, the Cameron transfer, was pacing the sideline like a caged leopard. Suddenly, he walked up to Wilkinson. "Coach, put me in and I'll score a touchdown for us and win the game," he said.

"Bud sent him in and with him a play," remembers assistant coach Eddie Crowder. "It was a good play against the type of defense Syracuse was using."

"Looney walked into our huddle wearing a one-day stubble of beard and with his arms bulging beneath his red jersey sleeves," recalls quarterback Monte Deere. "We called him 'Bluto' after the character in the Popeye cartoon strip. His eyes were glazed. It looked like fire was coming out of them.

"'Gimme that damned ball. I'm gonna score a touchdown,' he growled to me. Shoot!" laughs Deere today, "I couldn't wait to give it to him."

The play went left. "The defensive end crashed and took me as I pitched to Looney," Deere recalls. "Neely got a great block." Dennis Ward got one too, on the end. John Flynn's on the linebacker was also decisive. Joe Don turned upfield, Syracuse men swarming around him. He seemed engulfed by their orange and blue jerseys.

Running with power and balance, the newest Sooner phenom somehow fought out of all their clutches, stumbling but refusing to go down. Suddenly he found himself free. Turning on all his fine speed, he burst down the east sideline and, with the roaring Sooner crowd wondering who he was but perfectly willing to accept him, he sped 60 yards to the game's winning touchdown. With Deere setting up the ball, George Jarman kicked goal. The Sooners took their first lead of the game, 7-3. There was still 2:07 left to play.

Jarman's kickoff against the south breeze gave the Sooners time to follow the ball with full momentum. The receiver, Bill Hunter, the Orange's fastest back, cradled the leather under one arm and started back up the field. Neely, the young sophomore Titan who played left tackle for the Sooner alternates, flattened him with an open field smash that left him prone on the turf. "With that tackle, Neely made the team," the Sooners remember. The game ended soon after.

Rick McCurdy, alternate right end, recovered three fumbles in the contest, one of them on the Oklahoma 10 after Coach Ben Schwartzwalder's visitors had powered 70 yards.

Red Smith came to Norman to cover the game for the *New York Herald-Tribune*. In his lead paragraph he wrote, "The fearless football forces of Syracuse invaded the Indian Territory yesterday for the first time in history. It was a hair-raising experience."

Oklahoma went for its seventh straight victory the following week but instead lost for the fifth time in six outings to Notre Dame, the opponent that had always won the close ones from the Sooners.

The Irish won 13-7, but the Sooners blew a golden opportunity in the final moments by driving 71 yards to a first down on the Irish 3. Recognizing their opportunity to tie the score 13-13 on a touchdown and win 14-13 if George Jarman could kick goal (the squat little Tulsan had booted 18 straight), the Sooners grappled with the problem but were held for downs. "I just made a bad pitch," Deere described his fourth down toss to Wylie that misfired.

Oklahoma's cocaptains talked right to the point in the dressing room afterward. Center Wayne Lee said, "It sure is somethin' to get down there and not score. It's something we've got to learn—how to score." Guard Leon Cross added, "I think we learned a lot today but that sure is a helluva way to learn it. We just lost our poise."

Grisham, a rugged linebacker, topped the Sooner tackling chart with 12 unassisted stops. John Flynn was voted the "Ug" Award. Professor Leonard Haug, Sooner bandmaster for 25 years, directed his final halftime show at this game. Dr. Gene Braught had succeeded him the year before.

Next week Oklahoma moved to Dallas to confront the third, and most thunderous, challenge of its new season—Texas. Coach Darrell Royal's all-victorious Steers were then ranked number one in the nation by the UPI Coaches' Poll and had lost only one game of their last 19. However, Oklahoma might have won had they not given Texas the ball on the Sooner 27 and later on the Sooner goal with wild pitchouts that resulted in fateful fumbles and Texas touchdowns.

The game became a defensive bash. Texas had to punt ten times, Oklahoma eleven. All the scoring was compressed into the second quarter. Early in that period the Sooners misplayed a pitchout, and Duke Carlisle of Texas recovered on the Sooner 27. Green and muscular through two units, the Sooner defense dug in and stopped them, whereupon Tony Crosby, their placekicker, toed a 26-yard field goal. Texas led 3-0.

A short time later Koy lofted a windblown punt that Lea fair-caught on the Sooner 9. On Oklahoma's first scrimmage play the Sooners made another tragic fumble of a pitchout. For a moment the ball bounded crazily along the white chalk of the goal line. Then Perry McWilliams, Texas center, recovered it in the end zone for a touchdown. Now Oklahoma trailed 9-0.

Texas tried a scrimmage play for two points but the Sooners smothered it. There was only 3:30 left in the first half and it looked like the scoring was over.

But with all-out effort, the Sooners refused to concede even that. The alternates were in. Oklahoma owned the ball on its own 27. Wilkinson substituted two sophomores, Ron Fletcher, the little quarterback born in Eufaula, and Lance Rentzel, the halfback from Casady. Fletcher was on the fourth team, Rentzel on the fifth. Neither had played a down of college football.

Fletcher, who had good upper body strength, strong wrists, and a quick release, could throw the ball 85 yards. Back at Norman, when the Sooners had concluded practice and Wilkinson was jogging around the field, as was his custom, Fletcher and Rentzel contrived to impress the coach by practicing what they called "58-Special," a long pass. With only 1:36 left in the half at Dallas, Wilkinson remembered that impromptu play.

"My tongue had been cut badly in scrimmage so Bud moved me to halfback because I couldn't talk," recalls Fletcher. Rentzel had almost failed to get into the stadium for the game. Wilkinson had told him that he would have to furnish his own transportation to Dallas but that Jack Baer, the equipment man, would pack his gear. Rentzel started to Dallas with a friend, but the friend's car had broken down at Marietta.

Carrying his suitcase, the halfback hitchhiked the rest of the way, participated in some of the pregame parties, went to sleep at 4 A.M., and arose at 8. With nothing else to do, he visited the state fair and ate some hot dogs and cotton candy before reporting at the stadium gate where Fletcher had to vouch for him before he was admitted to the Sooner dressing room. Neither expected to play.

Quarterback Norman Smith pitched to Fletcher, running to his right. Rentzel, the flankered right end, ran downfield. "I was hung over, tired as hell, legs hurting, dizzy, and scared out of my mind," Rentzel later recalled it. The defensive back was deeper than usual. "I stopped short," Rentzel resumes, "turned, and the ball hit me in the chest." The play gained 39 yards to the Texas 34. The clock was running.

"We started to leave the field," Fletcher adds, "but we could hear Coach hollering, 'Turn it over! Turn it over!' So we told Norman Smith and he called the same play to the left with Rentzel the flankered left end." The Texas defensive back there was Jim Hudson who later performed with the New York Jets' professional team. Hudson played Rentzel closer than had the other defender. So Rentzel—hangover and all—just flat outran Hudson and fielded Fletcher's bomb as he crossed the goal. Touchdown!

"The referee told Rentzel that if he didn't give him the ball he was going to penalize us," Fletcher laughs today. "Rentzel just kept showing it to the fans."

Jarman's try for point was blocked by Johnny Treadwell. Texas led 9-6. And neither team could score thereafter.

321

Comment from the Texas dressing room was generous to Oklahoma. "We won on the breaks," said Coach Royal. "That was the toughest, hard-fisted fight I can remember." Cocaptain Pat Culpepper said, "They like to hit. That 77 (Neely), 51 (Wayne Lee), Cross, and Looney were all good." Center Perry McWilliams said, "Duane Cook hit me as hard today as I've ever been hit." Guard Johnny Treadwell said, "This Oklahoma-Texas game is quite an experience. It's nothing like anything you've been in before."

Jim Grisham and Charley Mayhue led the Sooner tackling chart. Joe Don Looney was the game's top rusher with 81 net yards and averaged 43 yards on seven punts. Mayhue, Paul Lea, and Virgil Boll, Sooner pass defenders, held Texas to 21 yards through the air. Leon Cross was voted the "Ug" Award. The next week Lance Rentzel was moved to the third team.

After the Texas game Wilkinson heard that Looney, the Cameron transfer, was quitting school. The boy had a strange affinity for academic wandering. Oklahoma was his fourth college in three years. The Sooner players found Looney packing his clothing. They asked him why he was leaving.

"The grass is growing up around my feet," Joe Don answered. "I've got to be moving on."

Wilkinson invited Looney to his home.

"Do you like Norman?" Bud began.

"Oh, yes, coach. I like it very much," Looney replied.

"Do you like the University of Oklahoma?"

"Oh, yes. It's the best school I've ever attended."

"Do you like the boys you play with?"

"I sure do. I've been around a lot of teams but these are the best boys I've ever been with."

"Do you like to play football, Joe Don?"

"Yes, sir. I enjoy it more than anything else I've ever done."

"Well, then, Joe Don," pursued Wilkinson, "why in the world are you talking about leaving?"

The boy's eyes began popping out of his head. "I can't stand going to class," said Looney. "I don't have time to get my laundry out."

At Wilkinson's suggestion, they agreed that Looney would stay at Norman five more days. "Then if you want to leave on Sunday," said Bud, "go right ahead. I'm with you." Looney agreed.

Wilkinson sympathized profoundly with the athlete. "The boy has curtains in his mind," the coach summed him up. "He's not violent. With just a little help, he'd be okay. A good psychiatrist could straighten this kid up in three or four months.

"The boy has so much pride that he can't take any kind of defeat," the coach went on. "He's really not a superplayer, and this complicates things.

The best way to play him is to hold him out until we take the sting off the opposition then put him in when they're half a step slow. Of course, if we did this, the newspapers would start getting critical. That wouldn't bother me, but it would bother him."

Three more sophomores were elevated to the Oklahoma first team before the Kansas game, left end John Flynn, left guard Newt Burton, and right end Rick McCurdy. "Flynn and McCurdy were already the best ends in the conference," says Leon Cross.

Meanwhile, Gomer Jones was busy recasting John Garrett, a tailback in high school, into a center. "I'd had a knee operation in 1961 that hurt my tailbacking speed," remembers Garrett. "Every day Gomer and I and a quarterback would go out 20 minutes early and he'd work with me, teaching me how to snap the ball and block with the same motion. "Keep your butt down!" he kept telling me.

The Oklahoma-Kansas game at Lawrence was another defensive fight. Kansas was a slight favorite because of its talented backfield which featured sophomore Gale Sayers. So good was Coach Jack Mitchell's Jayhawk line that Oklahoma didn't make a first down in the first quarter. Meanwhile Kansas scored its touchdown on a 38-yard pass, Rodger McFarland to Tony Leiker. Duff kicked goal.

"At halftime," Leon Cross remembers, "Coach Wilkinson told us we had a great opportunity to do something for ourselves and that we were the only ones who could do anything about it. He said he thought we could still win if we went out and played a strong second half." Monte Deere recalls that Wilkinson grasped Looney by the shoulders and shook him.

"Joe Don, you're not playing as well as you can," the coach told Looney. "Now get with it." And Deere says that again Looney's eyes assumed their phosphorescent gleam.

In the last half Oklahoma's two lines took command on the game. Deere called a trap play. McQuarters manhandled the guard, Wayne Lee blocked his man left, and Larry Vermillion pulled to trap the middle linebacker, who was drawn out of position by Grisham's fake. Deere handed off to Looney who shot through the hole and broke 16 yards to a touchdown. Butch Metcalf, Garland, Texas, sophomore, kicked goal. Score, 7-7.

In the fourth quarter Leiker punted dead to the Sooner 44. It was then that Oklahoma mounted its game-winning drive. Deere passed to Flynn who caught the ball over his head for 29 yards. The alternate line came in. Looney slashed 7 yards, and then Grisham bucked four times to the Kansas 3. After faking again to Grisham, Deere broke clean around the Kansas right wing to score. Metcalf had no chance to kick goal when the snap sailed far over his head.

323

"On the play before," Deere explained, "I saw that nobody was keying me. The Kansas cornerman was coming in on our fullback. So I called Grisham's off-tackle buck, faked to him and kept."

It was a fitting comeback for the Amarillo senior who had been widely abused by die-hard fans for errant ball-handling in the other games. Had he received any crank letters or phone calls, I asked him on the plane coming home.

Deere grinned. "Yessir! It was the worst after the Texas game. I could hear people talking around the campus. They said the final score was "Deere 9, Oklahoma 6." Some fellow from Houston wrote me a three-word letter. It said, 'Buddy, you stink,' But our players and coaches weren't down on me and that's the only thing that counts."

The postgame comment of Coach Jack Mitchell of Kansas was a tribute to the coaching of Gomer Jones. "The Sooner line whipped us," said Mitchell. "They seemed to be everywhere we wanted to go."

Of Gomer's tutoring of the Sooner forwards, guard Newt Burton said, "He's crankiest of all about wasted motion. He wants you to make every step count. You must gain ground every step you take. When you pull, you take your first step in the direction you're going. Don't ever lift one foot and put it down in the same place. If you step wrong, you've lost two steps."

Grisham's linebacking ferocity won him another "Ug" Award. "He doesn't tackle 'em, he gores 'em!" enthused Clay Cooper, Missouri scout.

Oklahoma's sophomores met a different kind of psychological trial in the Kansas State game at Norman. The Wildcats, 0-5, had scored only one touchdown all season. It was hard for the young Sooners to get up for such an opponent. Wilkinson suited 55 men and played them all as Oklahoma won 47-0. Bud Dempsey, Fort Worth, Texas, senior, rushed 96 yards and scored two touchdowns during his service with the third unit.

Kansas State's longest gain caught Oklahoma flat-footed. Quarterback Doug Dusenberry faked a punt from the end zone but instead threw a forward pass. Fullback Willis Crenshaw leaped to spear the ball one-handed and ran to the Sooner 32 before halfback Bert Gravitt, Denver City, Texas, sophomore, tackled him after a 60-yard gain. This prevented a touchdown.

Defense and punting were Oklahoma's main strengths as Wilkinson's scuffling sophomores, now tied for first in the Big Eight, clashed with Colorado at Boulder.

It was an interim year for Colorado. The Buffaloes were almost totally without physical ability, talent, and experience. Bud Davis, the interim coach, tackled the situation courageously and after defeating Air Force 29-12 in the final game was carried off the field by his players. But Oklahoma had too much speed and power. The Sooners won 62-0.

324

Wilkinson congratulates Monte Deere, his new quarterback, after Deere directed Oklahoma to a 13-7 victory over Kansas at Lawrence. Photo by Richard Clarkson, *Topeka Capital-Journal,* Topeka, Kansas.

Gomer Jones and Bud pass each other without speaking after Kansas went ahead 7-0.

Joe Don Looney, convoyed by Gary Wiley (37) and Larry Vermillion (62), sprints 60 yards to the winning touchdown against Syracuse at Norman in 1962. Photo by Richard Clarkson, *Topeka Capital-Journal,* Topeka, Kansas.

Deere, the Sooner quarterback, always belittled his own forward passing skills. "I was a terrible passer," he laughs today. "The guys teased me about it. They said the reason they couldn't intercept opposition passes was because they weren't used to catching spirals. They said my passes looked like dead quail falling out of the sky." In the five games previous to Colorado, Deere had completed a total of only six passes for 74 yards.

Colorado was undoubtedly aware of this, and so was Oklahoma. Consequently, when Deere began to fire his fatal aerials through the mountain atmosphere, both teams regarded him with much the same awe with which the Aztecs first heard the booming blunderbusses of Cortez.

Right from the opening kickoff Deere came out throwing. He faked to Grisham and hit Boll for 25 yards. Then he overshot Boll who was open. He faked again to Grisham and hit Boll for 32 yards and a touchdown after only 1:07 had been played. Later in the period, after Colorado had marched 74 yards to the Sooner 1 only to fumble, Deere, from the Sooner 17, faked to Grisham and pegged to Boll for 83 yards and another touchdown. "I threw one of my rare spirals," Deere chuckles today, "and overshot him. But he jumped up and tipped the ball twice, caught it, and ran to the goal."

Early in the second quarter, from his own 16, Deere lined a pass to John Flynn who ran 62 yards to the Colorado 23 before Bill Harris, Colorado's last tackler, overtook him. Two plays later Deere fired again to Flynn, this time for a touchdown. Deere didn't play in the last half. The first half statistics showed that his receivers fielded five of his "dead quail" for 246 yards and three touchdowns.

Looney lofted four punts for an average of 46.5 yards and took first place in the nation. The Sooner thirds played half the game and scored three touchdowns, Dempsey plunging for one, Rentzel sweeping for the second and third. The Sooner starters played only the first five minutes of the last half, then saw no more action.

"Bud was a gentleman," says Deere. "He'd let the starters come out for the last half and break through them once, then we were through for the day."

On the plane flying the Sooners to Ames, Iowa, for the Iowa State game, Leon Cross, Oklahoma's soft-voiced cocaptain and right guard who fretted over the team like a mother robin over her young, was worried about the Sooner mental attitude.

"I can't tell whether we're up or down," Cross frowned, puckering the slight lattice of stitches healing on his forehead. "We have so many sophomores. I tell myself, 'Well, it's liable to blow apart any day now.' Yet we keep hanging in there."

326

Before a crowd cut to 16,000 by the opening of the pheasant-hunting season, Oklahoma won 41-0. The pheasant hunters wouldn't have enjoyed the game anyhow. The Cyclones had just lost tailback Dave Hoover from a practice injury, and Tom Vaughn, their fine sophomore fullback, lamed a knee on their first possession.

Paul Lea, Oklahoma's senior safety from Terrell, Texas, set up three of the first four Sooner touchdowns with sparkling defensive plays. He ran back a punt 30 yards to the Cyclone 19 and Grisham pounded 8 yards into the end zone. Lea intercepted a Cyclone pass to introduce an Oklahoma scoring trek of 71 yards climaxed by Grisham's successful run from the 5. Lea flitted back 36 yards with another punt, and 11 plays later Deere faked neatly, pitched to Looney going wide, and Looney scored. Gaining confidence from his passing show against Colorado, Deere completed 9 of 13 for 93 yards against the Cyclones.

Missouri, unbeaten in ten consecutive games and ranked number six in the nation, moved menacingly on Owen Field. Coach Dan Devine's Bengals led the nation in rushing with 287.6 net yards per contest. Their defense was flinty too, having given only 4.5 points per game. At the end of the year Missouri defeated Georgia Tech in the Bluebonnet Bowl.

A sellout throng of 61,826 that included a contingent of 4,000 fans from the persimmon country came to see the bruising defensive scuffle. A cold drizzle was falling, the temperature stood at 40, and the wind blew from the northwest. Oklahoma's attitude was apparent from the opening kickoff. Looney fielded the low, driving kick on the Sooner 4 and ran it back strongly to the 44 before he was hit and fumbled. Guard Newt Burton recovered for the Sooners.

On the second play Deere threw a screen pass to Virgil Boll who picked up a key block from Dennis Ward and sped 42 yards to the Tiger 9 before Daryl Krugman, their last tackler, felled him. From the Tiger 3 Looney faked a sweep then cut back through a hole opened by Leon Cross and Duane Cook. Metcalf kicked goal. With the game only 2:30 old, Oklahoma led 7-0.

The fired-up Sooners began the last half as they had the first, navigating 80 yards to a touchdown from kickoff. On the first play Jim Grisham surged 30 yards to midfield. Boll reversed for 10. A 5-yard penalty hurt but Grisham bucked 10 more and, with the Sooner line enjoying a slight edge on Missouri's, Grisham, in short punches, rammed it down to the goal. Deere scored from the 4 by faking cleverly to Grisham then following him through the hole as the Mizzou linebacker tackled the fullback. McCurdy, Cook, Cross, and Lee blocked the hole open. Metcalf's kick veered wide of the post but now Oklahoma led 13-0. That was the final score.

327

Looney's punts averaged 44.6 yards. Grisham rushed 116 net yards, 6 more than the entire Missouri team. Ralph Neely and Melvin Sandersfeld led the tackling chart. The coaches voted the "Ug" to Wayne Lee.

Johnny Roland, Missouri's fine halfback, said of Oklahoma after the game, "I think the thing that's outstanding about them is that every player is doing something."

Nebraska had hired a new coach, Bob Devaney, a Michigander who came from Wyoming, where his five-year coaching record was 35-10-6 and four Skyline Conference championships. Devaney's Cornhuskers stood 8-1 and had defeated Michigan and North Carolina State. They later laced Miami in the Gotham Bowl.

It was a game between teams that had risen from hickdom to high hat in one short season. Devaney's Cornhuskers had made an astonishing climb from Nebraska's 3-6-1 status of the preceding season. Oklahoma, now 6-2, ranked tenth in both the AP and UPI polls. Oklahoma's defense had blanked four straight foes through 19 consecutive quarters and held the opposition to an average of 4 points a game.

John Flynn, Oklahoma's combative left end, jumped the Sooners into a 7-0 lead when he blocked Jim Baffico's first punt back to the Scarlet 1, Newt Burton recovering. On the next play Burton and Wayne Lee blocked Grisham over. Butch Metcalf kicked goal.

Although both antagonists preferred to run with the football, and could, all five of the remaining touchdowns were scored by forward passing. "Dead quail" were still falling out of the sky for Monte Deere. He fired three touchdown aerials.

One of them came on a morsel of skulduggery. Deere pitched to Looney who reversed to give the ball back to Deere. End John Porterfield leaped in a corner of the end zone to palm Deere's pass.

In the third period Deere hit three passes in a row, to Looney in the flat for 5, to Flynn who made a great catch back over his nose downfield for 40, and to Porterfield in the end zone for the touchdown. "John Flynn is the only guy I ever saw who can make the catch by rotating his head like an owl," Wilkinson laughed later.

On Oklahoma's next possession Deere passed to Allen Bumgardner, Putnam City sophomore, for the touchdown. Nebraska counted when Claridge passed to Mike Eger in the end zone, the first scoring that Oklahoma's pass defense trio of Sandersfeld, Mayhue, and Lea, had surrendered for 21 straight quarters. Oklahoma's third team blinked the scoreboard for the final tally when Norman Smith passed to Wylie. Final score, 34-6.

"You deserve that ride, Bud," Devaney told Wilkinson in midfield as the Sooners carried their coach off the field. The victory brought Oklahoma

John Flynn, Sooner left end, blocks Jim Baffico's punt in the 1962 Nebraska game at Norman, setting up the Sooners' opening touchdown.

Sooner cocaptains of 1962, center Wayne Lee and guard Leon Cross.

Back on top and happy are Sooner assistant coaches Gomer Jones (left) and Eddie Crowder.

the conference championship and put the Sooner striplings in the Orange Bowl. It was Deere's birthday and he got a nice present from *Sports Illustrated,* which voted him National Back of the Week. Ralph Neely was voted the "Ug" Award.

Oklahoma, which had risen to eighth in both national polls, scored the first four times it got the ball to defeat Oklahoma State 37-6 in the finale at Stillwater. Not only did Deere lay out three touchdown passes, but the Sooners further proved their mastery of aerial play when Mike Miller, Cowboy passer, pegged into the hook zone, and Grisham leaped to snare the ball one-handed and run 40 yards to the fifth touchdown.

Grisham led the rushing table with 156 yards. The "Ug" Award was voted to tackle Dennis Ward. For the third time that season Deere fired three touchdown passes. "Don't aim the ball, just throw it," Deere says Wilkinson told him. Despite Deere's disparagement of his own passing, his 1962 seasonal totals were impressive. He completed 38 of 63 for 768 yards and nine touchdowns, dropping "dead quail" all over the premises. His completion percentage was 60.3. He threw no interceptions.

On defense that season the Sooner lines had stopped four great backs, limiting Sayers of Kansas to 23 yards in 9 carries, Hoppmann of Iowa State to 23 yards in 16 carries, Roland of Missouri to 9 yards in 12 carries, and Bill ("Thunder") Thornton of Nebraska to 32 yards in 11 carries.

In national team statistics the Sooners ranked second in rushing (265.9 net yards), third in total offense (470.7 net yards), third in scoring defense (4.4 points per game), fourth in total defense (201.8 yards), fifth in punting (40 yards), seventh in pass defense (71.8 yards a game and three touchdowns), and tenth in punt returns (13.5 yards). Oklahoma was ranked seventh in both national polls.

Looney led the nation in punting with his average of 43.4 yards. Looney finished fifth in rushing with 852 yards for an average of 6.21. Paul Lea ranked fifth in punt runbacks with 17 for an average of 14.9 yards. Leon Cross made the first All-American team, Wayne Lee the second. Cross, Lee, and Looney were selected on Roger Stanton's *Football news* 33-man All-American squad.

Alabama, the defending national champion coached by Paul ("Bear") Bryant, was a senior aggregation (eight seniors, two juniors, and one sophomore) who showed Oklahoma's youngsters the wide room they had for improvement. Bryant had coached the 1950 Kentucky team that shaded Oklahoma 13-7 in the 1951 Sugar Bowl.

In their dressing room before the game the Sooners were thrilled when Wilkinson came through the door escorting John Kennedy, President of the

United States, who spent part of his winters in Florida and frequently saw the Orange Bowl game.

"He was smiling and joking and shook hands with several of the players," cocaptain Leon Cross recalls. "Everyone was kinda stunned, but he put us all at ease. He mentioned that he wanted to see if his physical fitness man was keeping his own men in shape. He spotted Larry Vermillion, our alternate guard who had a slight paunch. The President went over and patted Larry on the stomach and asked, 'Is this man okay?' and the Sooners roared. Then he smiled at Vermillion, saying, 'How are you? Good luck!'"

Right from the start it became evident that Oklahoma would need that luck. Melvin Sandersfeld of the Sooners halted Alabama's first advance when he dove on his nose to intercept the first forward pass flung by quarterback Joe Namath, only sophomore on the 'Bama starting team. Swarming to the ball and revealing a superb linebacker in Lee Roy Jordan, Bryant's defense stopped three Sooner plays, and Looney punted 49 yards.

Jordan was a typical Bryant leader, an unheralded high-school player from the small town of Excel, Alabama. Tough as nails, he loved football.[1] "He was so at home backing the line that he looked like he was asleep before the play started," Glen Dobbs, Tulsa coach, told Nick Seitz, *Norman Transcript* sports editor. "Jordan wasn't blocked all afternoon," Rick McCurdy remembers. "Quickness was his main strength."

Then 'Bama showed what it could do on offense. Namath brought the Tide up the field. In nine plays they arrived at the Sooner 25. "It was hard to stop their rollout," recalls John Garrett, Sooner linebacker. After David Voiles, Hooker sophomore, tackled Namath for no gain, Namath forward passed to Richard Williamson, their split end, for a touchdown. "I think we had a flanker formation in the other direction," remembers Coach Bryant.[2] "And Joe was throwing on a two-second count, which is pretty quick. He threw to Williamson on a short-Z route which went for a score."

Then came an even more dramatic Oklahoma forward pass, masked with typical Wilkinson artfulness. Bud sent the tiny Fletcher into the game. The Sooners had gone into a series in which they didn't huddle. They just lined up and went. On the previous play Jim Grisham had bucked 24 yards to a first down on the 'Bama 36, and the 'Bama players began crowding the scrimmage front. The third play was this pass.

"We jumped over the ball as Alabama went into their defensive huddle,"

[1] Bill Connors, *Tulsa World,* December 15, 1963.
[2] Paul Bryant to author, January 23, 1981.

recalls Fletcher. "We snapped the ball. Allen Bumgardner got behind their halfback and was wide open. The ball went 55 to 60 yards in the air. Allen caught it. Ernie Versprille of Alabama caught Allen at the Alabama 6. When I came off the field, President Kennedy and Jackie were standing and applauding. Big day for me!"

Bumgardner says, "Fletcher's pass was perfectly thrown. I stayed in full stride running down the sideline. The Alabama back had an angle on me as he came straight across the field. Had I stopped, he would have gone straight past me, and I could have walked in. How'd I feel? Terrible, terrible!"

Jim Grisham, Sooner fullback, had separated his shoulder during a work-out at the University of Miami before the game. Working against a seven-man blocking sled, he hit it with his shoulder. But it had no recoil springs like the sleds at Norman. Grisham's right shoulder had to be strapped down for the game. He couldn't raise it very high and had little strength to hold the ball.

From the 'Bama 6, Deere called Grisham over guard. Billy Piper of Alabama met him in the hole and put his helmet right on the football. The ball went straight up into the air. Mike Hopper of Alabama recovered it on the 6. 'Bama's ball!

The Sooners threatened again when Versprille fumbled, and Porterfield recovered for Oklahoma on the 'Bama 31. Grisham hit for 4 and 2, Jordan tackling both times. Grisham hit over Jordan for 5 and a first down on the 'Bama 20. Two plays later Grisham bucked over Jordan for 10 yards to the 'Bama 8. "My forward motion was stopped," Grisham recalls the play. "I was sliding laterally. I heard a whistle blow and I dropped the ball to return to our huddle. Alabama covered the ball. I asked the referee about that whistling blowing. He said that he didn't hear anything."

After Cotton Clark punted out on Oklahoma's 8, and there was an exchange of punts, Alabama drove 34 yards to its second touchdown, Namath flicking a pitchout to Clark who ran 13 yards to the goal. Later, Tim Davis added a field goal. 'Bama won 17-0.

The Sooners moved the ball well, penetrating to the 'Bama 6, 8, 15, and 10-yard lines. In the final seven minutes of the game, Deere drove them 50 yards to the 'Bama 15 and later 55 yards to the Alabama 10, but they couldn't score.

Grisham rushed 107 net yards on the Tide. At the players' party that night, as the Sooners were introduced, one by one, Coach Bryant of Alabama walked clear across the stage to shake hands with Grisham.

After the game Wilkinson stood in the churchlike calm of the Sooner dressing room and told the press, "Their line was quicker offensively and defensively than ours. Our line didn't give our quarterbacks enough time to pass or execute our fakes properly while theirs did. They were much better prepared, no question about it. Everything they did was excellent. Bryant brought them along perfectly."

Bryant said, "I think the quickness of our first unit line, and our passing, made the difference."

President Kennedy saw the game from a stadium box seat. His sympathies seemed to lean toward the team coached by the director of his physical fitness program, reported Stephen Trumbull of the *Miami Herald.* "He jumped to his feet only once," Trumbull wrote, "in the first quarter when Oklahoma completed a 56-yard pass play to the Alabama 7-yard line. He slumped noticeably when the scoring chance ended in a fumble."

As the game was ending, the President told Farris Bryant, governor of Florida who sat beside him, that he thought that the better team had won. "But his smile appeared to be a little broader when Oklahoma was on the move," Trumbull wrote.

1962 SENIORS TODAY

Duane Cook is a mechanical engineer and manager of maintenance for the Sun Refining and Marketing Company, Tulsa, Oklahoma.

Leon Cross is associate athletic director in charge of fund raising and public relations in the University of Oklahoma.

Monte Deere is president and chief executive officer of the United Bank and Trust Company, Norman, Oklahoma.

Dr. Paul Lea is a dentist in Plano, Texas.

Wayne Lee is an architect in Boulder, Colorado.

Melvin Sandersfeld is accounting supervisor at Western Electric of Oklahoma City, Oklahoma.

Lt. Col. Dennis Ward is stationed at Fort Benjamin Harrison, Indianapolis, Indiana.

333

18. FINAL SEASON

Bud Wilkinson's final Oklahoma team operated from the momentum of having won 13 of its last 16 games in its comeback under the imaginative Minnesotan. But it would also have its difficulties. Not only had it lost two fine assistant coaches, Eddie Crowder and Rudy Feldman who had accepted the first and second positions at Colorado, but it would also have to cope with an unfortunate disciplinary problem.

For the second consecutive season the squad elected a center and guard for its captains, John Garrett of Stilwell and Larry Vermillion of Chickasha. Assistant coach Bobby Drake Keith was hired from Alabama.

The 1963 schedule was as tough as hickory. The Big Eight, bristling with coaching and playing talent, would never again be the romp it once was. In 1962 three Big Eight teams were invited to play in bowls. Missouri and Nebraska won theirs.

Oklahoma's preponderantly junior team would risk its untested sophomore quarterbacking and new pass defense against the usual murderous early schedule—Clemson, which had swept its last four games, Texas, which had beaten Oklahoma five straight years, and Southern California's national and Rose Bowl champions who kept 29 lettermen from their all-victorious team that blanked Notre Dame 25-0 in its last regular season contest. Nobody ever accused Wilkinson of booking soft nonconference slates.

In August, two weeks before the start of practice, assistant coach Jay O'Neal had a long-distance telephone call from Joe Don Looney. "Is it all right if I come back weighing 227?" Looney asked. He explained that he had worked all summer on a weight program prescribed by the Louisiana State trainer. "We had given him a weight of 205 to come back to, and I told him 227 would make him slower," O'Neal says. "No," Looney insisted, "I'm faster than ever." "And he was," concludes O'Neal. "He looked slimmer and was kicking the ball better than ever."

As usual, reports from the registry office documented the academic excellence of the squad motivated by Wilkinson and by Port Robertson, his academic counselor. Leon Cross, 1962 cocaptain and All-American guard, set the pace with a straight 4-point average (all A's) in biological science. Nine other lettermen scored in the A-B (3-point or better) range. They

334

were 1963 cocaptain Larry Vermillion (mathematics) 3.67, end Rick Mc-
Curdy (premedicine) 3.57, tackle Duane Cook (mechanical engineering)
3.32, quarterback Monte Deere (biology) 3.29, halfback Virgil Boll (accounting) 3.17, end John Porterfield (education) 3.13, halfback Charley
Mayhue (social studies) 3.07, fullback Bud Dempsey (business management), and center David Voiles (premedicine) 3.0.

Other lettermen shooting close to a B average were center Johnny Tatum
(physical education) 2.93, quarterback Norman Smith (business) 2.89,
guard Newt Burton (predental) 2.87, halfback Joe Don Looney (education)
2.86, tackle Dennis Ward (petroleum land management) 2.81, tackle Ralph
Neely (business) 2.74, end John Flynn (business) 2.69, fullback Jim Grisham (mechanical engineering) 2.63, and tackle George Stokes (radio and
television) 2.61. Best students among the 1963 sophomores were guard
Carl Schreiner (predental), who logged a 3.76 and had already won the
Jay Myers Memorial Award given to the best freshman student-athlete
based on first semester grades, and quarterback John Hammond (business),
Tulsa, 3.58.

Clemson's rugged Tigers from the Blue Ridge foothills of South Carolina who had finished 5-1 for runner-up honors in the Southeastern Conference, opened the season at Norman. "We play that old ugly kin' of
football," bubbled Frank Howard, their balding tutor. "We ain't dirty or
nuthin' but we play tough and mean. We like to keep control of the ball.
Then *they* ain't got it."

In the first half Howard's troops played "tough and mean" no matter
who had it, spurting into a 14-0 lead when Jim Parker fired a touchdown
pass to Lou Fogle, and left half Hal Davis later bucked across from the 3.

That seemed to exasperate the Sooners. Lance Rentzel galloped back 50
yards with the next kickoff to provide field position but Oklahoma lost
a fumble to ruin that opportunity. Virgil Boll's 40-yard punt runback gave
Oklahoma another chance. From the Clemson 26, the game changed dramatically. The alternate line was in. On a fullback buck guard Ed Mc-
Quarters, center Carl McAdams, White Deer, Texas, sophomore, and tackle
Jerry Goldsby handled the men over them to open a hole.

Grisham broke through cleanly. Allen Bumgardner swung across from
right end and blocked the inside safety. Grisham cut around them and,
turning on his speed spigot, outran the halfback to score in the corner
of the field. George Jarman kicked goal. Oklahoma trailed 14-7 but seemed
to be coming on.

In the second half the Sooners scored the first three times they possessed
the ball. The first time Mike Ringer of Pauls Valley, first sophomore ever
to start a season at quarterback for Wilkinson, called the option, faked to

Grisham, kept the ball, and pitched out to Rentzel just before being hit by a Clemson end. "I was always nervous in every game until I got hit and by that time Clemson had hit me plenty," Ringer laughs today. Grisham's fine fake momentarily froze the Clemson interior, giving Rentzel a good start around the weak side. Lance broke down the east sideline, cut back behind blocks by Bumgardner and Glen Condren, and ran 49 yards to score. Jarman's kick tied the count at 14-14.

John Flynn set up Oklahoma's go-ahead touchdown by blocking Bob Fritz's punt, David Voiles fielding it and running to the Tiger 5. Ringer hit twice over Neely, Schreiner, and Garrett to score. It was extremely hot, 90 degrees with no wind. "When we thought we were wearing them down, we'd run straight at them," remembers Ringer. Oklahoma's third line put so much pressure on Clemson that they fumbled, Robert Vardeman, Still-well sophomore, recovering on their 14. After three running plays failed, Jarman kicked a 22-yard field goal, with Ringer holding.

Neely, Oklahoma's left tackle, just a broth of a boy, as the Irish say, had barely turned 20, wore a size 8 helmet, stood 6-6, hefted 243, and had a jaw as indestructible as a hitching stone. But he could run like a wild rhino. Early in the fourth quarter he broke behind the Clemson secondary and on a tackle-eligible forward pass fielded Ringer's perfect heave over his shoulder and, with his long strides devouring the landscape, outran the safety for a touchdown. Jarman's toemanship was perfect. Oklahoma won 31-14. David Voiles led the tackling chart and was voted the "Ug" Award.

Howard, Clemson's coach, took the defeat good-humoredly. "I don't feel bad," he spoke from the Tiger dressing room. "Gomer's line just whipped ours."

I always liked Neely's portraiture of Gomer Jones. "He can sit there and chew you out," said Neely, "and before it's over have you laughing at yourself. He doesn't try to make you do it. He wants you to want to do it right. And to have the responsibility and pride of doing it right. I don't think there's a player out there who wouldn't give his right arm for the man."

Southern California, coached by John McKay, was next, the game to be played at Memorial Coliseum in Los Angeles. The Trojans, rated number one, kept nearly all of their national championship squad including their smooth aerial battery of quarterback Pete Beathard to Hal Bedsole, the All-American end. The Trojans rated as one of the half-dozen most formidable antagonists Wilkinson would face in his 17-season career. The contest was the NCAA's nationally televised game of the week.

Arriving at Los Angeles a whole day early so that they could work out Thursday in a Los Angeles all-time record heat wave of 110 degrees did not exempt the Oklahomans from the colorful expostulations of the California newspapermen. Jim Murray wrote, "The Oklahoma Sooners, who came to L.A. Thursday, are the only team in football with a head coach who looks more like a poet than a punter. Bud Wilkinson looks like he got lost on the way to a Browning lecture. In fact, most parents think he's recruiting for the choir when he first comes around."

Wilkinson's choristers found out quickly that they could run up and down the scale on the Trojans. McKay, the Trojan coach, was so concerned about the inordinate heat that he urged Wilkinson to postpone the game six hours and play it that night, but Bud declined. "Their 115 degrees down on the field wasn't any worse than our 100 back home,"says Charley Mayhue. "They built wicker wall shades over both benches." "They tried to cool the field by installing big fans in each end zone," remembers John Garrett, "but they caused a dust storm and had to be dismantled."

Said Wilkinson to Dan Jenkins of *Sports Illustrated* the night before the game, "We know them pretty well, I think. We both know each other. It should come down to the players' talents, and the breaks. I only know that we're going to have a lot of people where they plan to be."

"Our warm-up before the game was one of Bud's gems," remembers Rick McCurdy. "He sent us out wearing light pads and white T-shirts off which the sun's rays would reflect. We left our helmets, shoulder pads, and game jerseys in the dressing room. Southern Cal came out fully dressed. How hot they looked and how enviously they stared at us. I think they were impressed."

Bobby Page drove the Sooners 34 yards before they fumbled. The defending national champions fumbled too, Goldsby recovering on the Sooner 35. From there Mike Ringer came in and drove the Sooners 65 yards in 15 plays to a touchdown. Looney scored it up the middle on a 19-yard double reverse. "There wasn't anybody around," Looney described the play later. "Everybody was layin' down." Jarman kicked goal.

Southern California sped back gamely 67 yards to score a touchdown of their own on a buck by Ernie Pye but lost the extra point on a wild center snap. "We took it to 'em but they stuck with us," said Jim Grisham.

Early in the second quarter Ringer quarterbacked the Sooners 53 yards to another touchdown. This time Oklahoma used Southern California's chief weapon, aerial play. Boll passed to Looney who had first handed off to him on a double reverse, the play gaining 19 yards. Rentzel passed to Porterfield for 10. Ringer passed to McCurdy who dove for the ball on the Trojan 4. "Coming right over you, Number 78," Neely told the Trojan tackle opposite him and sure enough the Sooners did, Ringer faking to Grisham and scoring over Porterfield, Neely, and Schreiner. Jarman kicked another goal. Just before the half Jarman added a 43-yard field goal with Ringer holding. The Sooners led 17-6. "Oklahoma was wonderfully prepared," wrote Dan Jenkins.

The Sooners kept assaulting the Californians with their ground game. With Bobby Page at quarterback, they drove 79 yards with the last-half kickoff to the Trojan 1. There Grisham, hitting with the drive of tandem engines, rammed across the goal for the touchdown that would have given Oklahoma a 23-6 lead but a motion penalty negated it, and Bedsole, big Trojan wingman, blocked Jarman's try for a field goal.

The Trojans fought their hearts out. Late in the game, after Schreiner covered Looney's punt on the Trojan 3, McKay's team rolled 97 yards to their second touchdown with Beathard completing three short passes to Brown. Beathard's pass for two extra points sailed wild.

Still keeping the ball away from the dangerous Trojans, Oklahoma prolonged its control through the last two and one-half minutes on a fake field goal pass, Ringer to McCurdy, who grabbed the tipped ball on the Trojan 13 for a first down.

"We felt we had to control the ball to win," Wilkinson told the writers after the game. "It was no superstrategy. It was pretty obvious to everybody." The Sooners did control it, originating 97 offensive plays to 51 for the Trojans.

McKay, the Trojan coach, was white-faced and grim as he met the press after the game. "There's no use passing if you can't catch them," he snapped. "I don't see how Pete could have thrown better. But we kept putting him and the line in the bind by dropping the stinking passes."

The Sooners felt they contributed importantly to that. "We played a zone pass defense that day," remembers McCurdy. "If Bedsole came into your zone, you hit him before the quarterback threw." Even when the Trojan All-American didn't have the ball he was constantly being bumped hard by Mayhue, Boll, Bumgardner, Porterfield, Flynn, or McCurdy. They kept him off balance, blanked him without a single catch.

Mayhue, who won the game's "Ug" Award as the Sooner who most distinguished himself on defense, said, "Jay O'Neal did a tremendous job preparing our secondary. From films of their previous games he saw that Willie Brown ran mostly deep routes and Bedsole short ones — curls, hooks, and sideliners. So we covered loose on Brown and tight on Bedsole. And we got a real good pass rush. Goldsby played a great game, also McQuarters and Burton."

Mayhue scythed the elusive Trojan backs off their feet all afternoon. He postponed the first Trojan touchdown by tackling Mike Garrett on the Sooner 13 after Garrett ran 21 yards. Mayhue was the last Sooner tackler.

338

When Beathard whipped a quickie to Ron Heller in the right flank, Mayhue, covering fast, hit Heller quail high, knocking the ball loose from him.

Jim Grisham, the game's top rusher with 86 net yards, says, "There was lots of smog in the air. Hard to get a deep breath. We got along good with the Trojans. Mike Garrett and I kidded a lot. Ringer, our new quarterback, played well. He was a good field general. He controlled the team well."

McKay's Trojans outpassed Oklahoma 116 to 53 yards. Wilkinson's Sooners outrushed the Trojans 307 to 121. Oklahoma ran back kicks for 147 yards. Rentzel's 59-yard kickoff return gave the Sooners field position for their second touchdown. Looney later added a 50-yard kickoff return. Jackie Cowan brought back a Trojan punt 38 yards. Newt Burton made the best grades offensively, the coaches decided after grading the film. Jarman's five points by placekicking provided the statistical difference. The final score was 17-12.

For the first time in history the big Dallas game had the first and second teams of the land. The number two outfit looked by far the readier when the rivals came out for the kickoff. A Dallas sportswriter, Blackie Sherrod of the *Times-Herald*, caught the Texas exhilaration when he wrote that "the second-ranked Longhorns burst from the entrance tunnel just before the game, gathered in front of their bench and leaped constantly in the air, hopping up and down in the same spot with a hypnotic frenzy to get the thing started."

Darrell Royal, their young coach, says today, "We had a big psychological advantage because we were scared to death after watching Oklahoma beat Southern Cal on television. Oklahoma deserved to beat Southern California. But it came out of it with a problem." The Texas coach was referring to Joe Don Looney. Word of Looney's noncompliance was spreading.

If ever a football team translated fear into fury, it was Texas that day. The Orange received the opening kickoff, and blocking and running with determination locomoted 68 yards in 13 plays to a touchdown. On fourth down from the Sooner 2, quarterback Duke Carlisle swung left and cut back inside for the touchdown. Crosby kicked goal.

"We ran surprisingly well off tackle that day," Royal remembers. "Tommy Ford ran well off a new wrinkle we put in. We went from a tight wing to a tight slot." Wilkinson said, "Our tackles could not seem to hit them squarely enough to stop them cleanly."

In the second quarter Ford of Texas skirted right end for 12 yards and a second touchdown. Crosby's conversion left Texas leading, 14-0.

Oklahoma went the whole game without Mike Ringer, its sophomore quarterback who had moved the Sooners to all 48 of their points against

339

Clemson and Southern California. While studying in the Sooner dormitory the Sunday before the Southern California game, Ringer had accidentally thrust his elbow into a 14-inch rotating electric fan, the blade cutting into the elbow's bursa sac. He played well against the Trojans but next day the elbow developed fluid. It was so sore that if you drew a piece of gauze across it he was in pain. After three operations Ringer played no more that year. "First time I ever lost a quarterback from studying," deadpanned Bud. Against Texas, Mayhue and Flynn were both knocked out in the second quarter and sat out the rest of the game.

Texas surged ahead 21-0 early in the third period when Rentzel fumbled a pitchout, and Scott Appleton, Texas tackle, recovered it at the Sooner 18. Texas scored when Carlisle tossed a long lateral to Phil Harris who outran the Sooner end and tackle to score in the corner of the field. And Bill Connors, covering for the *Tulsa World*, later wrote of Wilkinson's "solemn, almost glazed stare, with head down" as he watched the game from the sideline.

The Sooners countered with a 62-yard scoring drive during which quarterback John Hammond spun forward passes of 14 and 11 yards to Bumgardner and McCurdy. Grisham broke off tackle for 14. Then Hammond faked to Grisham, and himself whipped off tackle for the touchdown. Jarman kicked goal with Hammond holding. Now Texas led 21-7.

Texas drove 63 yards for their fourth touchdown. Marvin Kristynik, their sophomore quarterback, shot a touchdown pass to George Sauer, Jr., in the end zone. "I was behind the receiver," Virgil Boll recalled later, "but we were 14 points behind. Deciding to gamble for a touchdown interception I cut in front of him and their passer lofted it over me for a touchdown. I felt like I was ten feet tall. Every one of those 75,000 people was watching me."

"Losing Ringer hurt," recalls Charley Mayhue. "He was an excellent quarterback. He'd had a supergame against the Trojans." Jim Grisham said, "Every game we went into, we had a new quarterback." Texas won 28-7.

Grisham led all rushers with 74 net yards in nine plays for an average of 8.2 yards a carry. Hammond hit three of four passes for 48 yards. After grading the films, Oklahoma's coaches decided that no Sooner played well enough on defense to merit the "Ug" Award.

"We were unaggressive, totally flat," Wilkinson summed it up in his alumni letter. "I do not wish to detract in any way from Texas's magnificent performance. They were well prepared. They played like champions." Royal's team played that way all year, finishing all-victorious, torpedoing Navy in the Cotton Bowl and winning the national championship.

The Looney matter came to a head after the Dallas game. All fall the halfback had created problems while trying to force OU football to conform to his way of life. "He became more independent, harder to get along with," recalls Leon Cross, then a student coach. "He was a strange kid," remembers Bob Page, also a student coach. "In practice, the first time you told him to do something, he'd do it great. The second time, it bored him." Monte Deere remembers that Looney would say, "My legs are tired. I'm not going to work out today. And he wouldn't!"

"Bud didn't want Joe Don back in 1963," remembers Mayhue, "but Joe Don begged and saw a psychiatrist and maintained that he had a changed attitude. He worked hard early in the fall, then fell back into his old groove."

"Bud wanted to dismiss both Looney and John Flynn early but he left it to the squad, and they said keep them for awhile yet," recalls coach Jay O'Neal. "Joe Don and Flynn were gunrunning buddies. Neither was good for the other. Everybody knew that Flynn didn't train. But the players liked and respected Flynn for the great job he did on Saturday."

"Bud called me into his office after the Texas game," says cocaptain John Garrett, "and told me to go tell Joe Don that he was off the squad. Bud always delegated tough jobs to other people. I found Looney lying on the bed in his room. He seemed sincerely shocked. 'Who did it? Why?' he asked. I told him the coaches and players felt he was more of a detriment to the team than an asset. 'What can I do to get back on the team?' he asked. I told him I didn't have the answer, to talk to Bud." But the decision stood and the team became much the better for it.

Alternating Jackie Cowan and Larry Shields, Wichita Falls, Texas, sophomore, in the departed Looney's left half position, Wilkinson braced the Sooners for seven straight conference games. Kansas, coached by Jack Mitchell, was the first, and a loyal crowd of 61,000 came to Owen Field to see the action.

Gale Sayers, Jayhawker tailback, dismayed them in the first quarter when he broke off tackle, cut back sharply, and ran 61 yards to score. Gary Duff kicked goal. But Charley Mayhue, crack Sooner defensive back, cheered them by intercepting Dave Crandall's pass and returning it to the Kansas 15. Oklahoma's starting line of Porterfield, Neely, Schreiner, Garrett, Burton, Stokes, and McCurdy blocked the Sooners to a touchdown in three plays, quarterback Norman Smith bucking for it. Jarman kicked goal.

A 30-yard field goal by Duff, after Allen Bumgardner and George Stokes with timely tackles stalled a 44-yard Jayhawker drive, gave Kansas a 10-7 halftime lead.

The Sooners forged ahead 14-10 when Bumgardner wrecked a Sayers sweep, separating the Jayhawk star from the ball, Flynn recovering on the Kansas 47. Bobby Page came in at quarterback and working behind the

341

alternate line of Flynn, Goldsby, McQuarters, McAdams, Vermillion, Condren, and Bumgardner moved the Sooners to the touchdown, faking a buck and passing to McCurdy in the end zone. A Kansas defender wrestled McCurdy for the ball, but the Purcell boy took it away from him.

A 52-yard Sooner offensive in the fourth period, that ended with Smith keeping for the touchdown and Jarman booting the goal, moved Oklahoma into a 21-10 margin. With only 5:39 left to play, quarterback Steve Renko looped a completion to Sayers for 8 yards and a touchdown. Still deadly, Renko shot another aerial to Sayers for two points and Oklahoma led only 21-18. That was the final score. Sooner coaches voted the "Ug" Award to guard Eddie McQuarters.

Newt Burton, Oklahoma's burr-headed junior guard, continued his habit of usually registering the highest grades of any Sooner lineman after coaches graded the Kansas film.

Burton knew all about railroads—the chatter of the telegraph, the click of the rails, the creosote smell of the ties. "I can even remember seeing a few steam trains," he reminisces with nostalgia. Because of his father's progression of jobs with the Frisco railroad, from telegrapher at Neosho, Missouri, to superintendent of claims at Springfield with in-between employment at one smoky gray depot after another, Newt had played high-school football in many towns.

"I had to change schools so many times that I never had any close friends," said the Sooner guard. "Just as I'd start to get acquainted in one town, Dad would take off to another. But it taught me to get along with new people. It cured my shyness."

John Flynn regained the starting left end position against Kansas State, whom the Sooners laced 34-9. Rushing 441 net yards, the Sooners scored four touchdowns on ground plays. Jim Grisham bucked for one, Bobby Page for another, and Jackie Cowan fielded a pitch from Page and got a piece of the red flag while sprinting to the corner.

With three minutes left to play the Kansas State student section began to chant, "We want Looney! We want Looney!" Grisham silenced them when on his twentieth and final carry he ran 56 yards to a touchdown after Gordon Brown blocked down on the tackle to give him running room.

Lance Rentzel, late in the first period, took a punt on the Sooner 29. Quickly, he broke for the west sideline where he knew that friends were waiting. Voiles got the first downfielder. McQuarters, Stokes, Vermillion, and Cowan each expunged opponents. Rentzel ran behind end Ron Harmon who wiped out the last tackler. The runback went 71 yards. The "Ug" Award was voted to Allen Bumgardner.

His broken ankle much improved, Tommy Pannell, third team quarterback, led the drive to Oklahoma's fifth touchdown during the 35-0 rout of Colorado. Pannell bucked twice for first downs. Then while in the grasp of a tackler, he coolly drilled a touchdown pass to Jon Running, Tulsa sophomore. Jarman's extra point ended the day's scoring. Coach Eddie Crowder's Buffaloes had to play without injured halfback Bill Harris, who had the highest rushing average in the Big Eight. Carl McAdams, alternate center, won the "Ug" Award.

Runbacks of kicks and interceptions surpassed anything in the history of Big Eight football in the Oklahoma-Iowa State game. The Sooners gained 209 yards in this manner compared to 198 yards rushing and passing. Iowa State gained 180 on runbacks as opposed to 75 rushing and passing.

Coach Clay Stapleton's Cardinal and Gold battlers shot into a 14-0 lead. When a Sooner fumble presented them the pigskin on the Oklahoma 14, the Iowans needed eight downs to score, Tom Vaughn, their fine fullback, wiggled across by inches. A little later Vaughn ran back McCurdy's punt 73 yards to a touchdown.

With 7:59 left in the half Bobby Page moved Oklahoma 70 yards to its first touchdown. Page executed a screen pass perfectly, retreating to draw the defense to him, then throwing in the left flat to Ron Harmon who ran 27 yards to score. Grisham, the contest's leading rusher, scored the tying touchdown with a 4-yard smash over Neely and Schreiner with Cowan leading the play. Jarman's boot made it 14-14.

Two sparkling runbacks by Virgil Boll proved the difference. In the third quarter Boll fielded Balkovec's high punt on the Sooner 9, fled across field to the security of the Sooner blocking phalanx, and turning upfield ran it back 55 yards. Vaughn, their last defender, tackled him on the Cyclone 36. Stopped by the fighting Iowans, Oklahoma took a 17-14 lead on a field goal by George Jarman.

Later, Bunte of the Cyclones hurled a long pass. Boll gauged the ball perfectly, gliding in to make the interception then using downfield blocks by McCurdy, Harmon, and Voiles, returned it 46 yards to the touchdown that finalized the Oklahoma victory at 24-14. Carl Schreiner won the "Ug."

"Tom Vaughn, their fullback, and I went head-to-head," Grisham grins today. "He played all their offense. I played all of ours and any time they got down to our 10, I'd go in and lineback. That's where I met Vaughn. After the game we got together and had a talk. We had met while going to New York to the *Look* magazine All-American party. I fractured my ankle in that game."

At his press conference on Monday, Wilkinson said, "A fellow who is playing well for us on both offense and defense, whom nobody seems to notice, is Virgil Boll."

343

Boll, senior opportunist from Wichita, Kansas, ran his right halfback position the way he ran his paint-spraying business in summer. Oklahoma's Dutch flanker back demanded the same competence from his employees as he asked of himself in football. "Sure helped me get through school," said Boll who had a wife and infant son. One summer Boll saw seven men come and go before he found the helper or two he liked. "Guess I'm hard to work for," laughed the proprietor of the Boll Painting Company, flashing a grin so wide that he looked like he was gasping for breath.

Larry Shields scored two touchdowns and intercepted two forward passes in the fourth quarter, as Oklahoma defeated Missouri 13-3 at Columbia in the season's eighth game. Late in the first period, Krugman of Missouri booted a long, high punt against the wind. Shields fielded the kick on his 35 and set sail for the east sideline where blocks by Rentzel and Boll let him gain it. Then, one by one, other Sooner blocks sprouted in his path like dandelions in spring. "We had almost diagrammed execution by all eleven people," Wilkinson wrote in his alumni letter. "This is rare. It was our best play of the year."

Larry Brown, Jenks sophomore who played fullback in the last half when Grisham's injured ankle stiffened, contributed a steamy 35-yard buck on a later drive and led everybody in rushing with 74 yards. It was Oklahoma's 90th conference victory under Wilkinson. Guard Eddie McQuarters was voted the "Ug."

Nebraska, 8-1, was next and it looked as if Jim Grisham, Oklahoma's fine fullback who made the first All-American team that year, might not play. But he did. With his twisted ankle wrapped in a soft plaster cast, he didn't practice the week of the Nebraska game, or the Missouri contest before it either. "I played less than half the game against Nebraska," says Grisham today. "I couldn't push off my foot. You need your ankle and knee for driving power."

Something else disturbed the Oklahoma team far more. When they returned after practice Friday to the Cornhusker Hotel in Lincoln, they heard from business manager Ken Farris the shocking news that President John Kennedy had been assassinated at Dallas, Texas.

Wilkinson telephoned Ted Reardon, the president's executive assistant in Washington, asking him to consult the president's family about their wishes concerning postponement of the game. Within an hour and one-half Reardon phoned Wilkinson back. "He reported that Bobby [Kennedy] told him that the family felt strongly that we should play the game rather than delay it," Wilkinson says.

"I relayed this information to Dr. Cross (who was at Lincoln with the team), who talked with the president of Nebraska. They decided that we

344

Vicki McNeeley, freshman Ruf-Nek queen, leads the "interference" on Larry Shields' 65-yard punt runback that won the 1963 Missouri game at Columbia. The forlorn fellow in the middle is a Missouri cheerleader who saw nothing to cheer about. Photo by Arnold Crank, *Kansas City Star.*

should play the game even though other games about the country were being canceled." The final consultation also involved Big Eight executive director Wayne Duke and Governor Frank Morris of Nebraska.

"Most of us wanted to come home and reschedule the game two weeks later," remembers right end Rick McCurdy. "The game was a dream state to me. I felt like I'd been knocked unconscious and could recall the game but no specifics of it."

"Bud had always brought back some personal word from the president wishing us good luck," recalls Jim Grisham. "This always thrilled us. We felt like we knew him personally."

345

Fullback Jim Grisham crossing the goal on his 28-yard touchdown dash against Clemson at Norman in 1963.

Rick McCurdy, Sooner end, leaps to glove a deflected pass late in the Southern California game of 1963.

"After I heard about the shooting of the president, I couldn't get my mind on football," says cocaptain John Garrett. "We were just college kids, and Kennedy was our president. Most of us had met him personally in our Orange Bowl dressing room, and we all liked him and felt close to him. He was a friend of Bud's, and that made him a friend of ours. He was such a young president to die so soon. You just can't go out and play a football game after your president has been assassinated." The Nebraska squad was undoubtedly disconcerted too, as were many of the other teams about the nation. Many games that day were canceled, including the Kansas State-Oklahoma State contest at Stillwater and the Iowa State-Drake game at Des Moines.

In his talk to the Oklahoma team late Friday afternoon at the Cornhusker Hotel, only six hours after the president's assassination, Wilkinson told the Sooners that he knew it was difficult for them to get ready to play when all they could hear was the radio and television broadcasting details about the president's death. He told them that unless they could discipline themselves to concentrate they wouldn't win.

"Life goes on," Wilkinson concluded. "It's short. We don't have much time to do the things we want to do. About all there is to life is what you do with your opportunities. If you'll go after this team hard, reducing the game to a test of heart and courage, these guys can't stay up with you."

But the team that did the most with its opportunities was Nebraska. The Cornhuskers that season finished 9-1 and defeated Auburn in the Orange Bowl. They defeated the Sooners too. The score was 29-20. The Scarlet triumph severed a Sooner string of 16 consecutive conference victories.

Field position is vital in football. On five of six occasions in the first half Nebraska came into possession of the ball after Sooner turnovers on the Oklahoma side of the 50-yard line, yet the OU defense always stopped them short of the goal. Theisen of Nebraska did kick a field goal and the Cornhuskers led at the half 3-0. Both teams were guilty of faulty mechanical performance. Oklahoma yielded seven turnovers, Nebraska five.

In the last half Coach Bob Devaney's Cornhuskers proved themselves deadly opportunists. When Oklahoma fumbled a punt on the Sooner 15, Nebraska recovered and scored in six plays. When the Sooners fumbled on their 32, Nebraska scored in 12 plays. Twice Nebraska intercepted Sooner passes and after long runbacks by Theisen and McCloughan scored touchdowns.

Meanwhile Oklahoma had scored on a 58-yard drive. Page screen passed to John Porterfield for 36 yards. Then Wilkinson sent in Ron Fletcher who started a sweep action to the right, stopped, and threw back across the field to John Flynn who ran for the touchdown.

With Nebraska leading 29-7 and time ticking away, the Sooners rallied fiercely, scoring two touchdowns. Tommy Pannell, Norman junior, took over the quarterback controls when Page was hurt. Pannell whipped forward passes to Flynn and McCurdy to the Nebraska 31. Then he called a deep reverse, and Wes Skidgel, junior halfback from Cleveland, broke for 27 yards and a touchdown. Jarman kicked goal. There was 1:57 left to play.

A Cornhusker fumble, recovered by Bumgardner on the Scarlet 25, provided another opportunity. Pannell shot a pass down the middle to Skidgel for the third Sooner touchdown and Jarman kicked goal. "They had a good team," says Mayhue. Flynn was voted the "Ug" Award.

"Sooner coach Bud Wilkinson, long-reigning king of the conference, took the defeat with the dignity of a champion," wrote Tom Allan in the *Omaha World-Herald*. "Standing legs apart, his elbows cradled in his hands, the white-haired Sooner coach said, 'I think Nebraska is a very fine team. They are big and strong and quick and well coached and determined. They play extremely well. We have no excuses of any kind.'"

The Bluebonnet Bowl invited the Sooners. "I don't particularly want to go but if the team wants to go, I'll go," Wilkinson said while discussing it with his captains, Vermillion and Garrett, on the plane coming home. At Norman the squad voted against going and began preparations for the final game of the season with Oklahoma State, which under its new coach Phil Cutchin had extended Nebraska 20-16 the week before Oklahoma's clash with the Cornhuskers.

"If we can win," Bud told the squad, "we will finish the season 8-2 which in these times of evenly matched teams is a good record. It is possible," he added, "that we could be in the top ten teams in the country."

Jim Grisham was back in form at Stillwater after sitting out much of the Missouri and Nebraska battles. He set a new school rushing record of 218 yards and counted four touchdowns. "I didn't wear a cast and my ankle felt pretty good," says the fullback today. "That was the first college game my folks saw me play. I tried to do a good job for them."

Cutchin's Cowboys led 10-7 in the third quarter. Wilkinson said that the Sooners played their best football of the entire season in the game's final 22 minutes. With Page mixing his plays shrewdly, the Sooners scored four touchdowns, dispatching the Cowboys 34 to 10.

The Sooner coaches voted the "Ug" Award to Carl McAdams, sophomore center. At his Monday press conference later, Wilkinson said that the mark of a great running back was his ability to start one place, taking the defense with him, then to cut into an open spot. "This is what Jimmy Brown [the pro standout] does so well," said Wilkinson. "This is what Jim Grisham does real well, too."

Wilkinson's last Sooner team did finish 8-2. "If we'd have done that well in high school, we would have thought we had a most wonderful season, but the Wilkinson standard had been so high," recalls Rick McCurdy.

Oklahoma was voted eighth in both national polls. Wilkinson's feat of coaching Oklahoma teams that were voted in the nation's top ten for 11 consecutive years, 1948-58, has never been equalled by any coach to this writing. Their achievement of placing in the top ten 13 times during Wilkinson's 17 seasons as head coach is also praiseworthy.

In the 1963 national statistics the Sooners placed fourth in rushing, fifth in punt returns, eleventh in scoring and forward pass defense, twelfth in total defense, and tied for second in fumbles lost with 25. In pass interception returns Shields tied for second in the nation. Grisham was fifth in rushing. Jarman placed seventh in extra point proficiency with 29 of 32 for .906.

During Wilkinson's 17 years as head coach, his Oklahoma teams won a total of 139, lost 27, and tied 4 regular season games for .837 percent. They averaged 29.1 points a game, yielded 10.1 a contest. His bowl record was 6-2 although conference rules prevented two of his finest teams, 1952 and 1956, from playing in bowls. They won 23 consecutive games on foreign fields.

After tying for the conference championship in 1947, his first year as head coach, Wilkinson's teams won the league flag the next 12 years in succession. They won 44 straight conference games, 1952-59. They played 74 straight conference games, 1947-59, without defeat. Only five games of the 74 were real close, tied or decided by one point. Oklahoma shut out the opponent in 24 games, held them to one touchdown in 25 additional games, held them to two touchdowns in 15 others, the opponent usually scoring against the Sooner reserves.

The most notable accomplishment of his career was the 47 straight victories his teams scored, 1953-57. Starting with the Pittsburgh tie, they went 48 in a row without a defeat during the same period. His teams of 1947-57 scored in 112 consecutive games. His ground attacks were the most consistently devastating in college football. For 13 straight years, 1947 through 1959, Sooner rushing offenses never fell below ninth nationally. They led the nation in 1953, 1955, and 1956 and placed second in 1949, 1952, 1958, and 1962. Yet Wilkinson always regarded defense as even more important.

On February 5, 1964, Wilkinson announced as a candidate for the United States Senate after first resigning as Oklahoma football coach and later as athletic director. His decision required considerable courage. As of July 1, 1964, there were 1,058,465 Democrats (80.68 percent) registered in Oklahoma compared to only 248,458 Republicans (18.93).[1] I asked Bud why he decided to run in the face of these odds.

He replied that had he not served as consultant to President Kennedy, he probably would not have made the race. "While in Washington," he explained, "I had a close association with the functioning of the federal government—I became concerned about some of the directions in which the country was moving—and thought that if I could get elected, I might be able to have an effect on the future."

In the 1964 national popular vote for President, Democrat Lyndon John-

[1] Lee Slater, Oklahoma State Election Board Secretary, to author, June 15, 1981.

son carried Oklahoma over Republican Barry Goldwater by 107,169 votes. In the Senate race in Oklahoma, Democrat Fred R. Harris won the state over Wilkinson by 21,390 votes, a splendid showing for the football coach. Thus Republican Wilkinson's total was nearly double that of all the Republicans registered in the state. Somewhere along the line, he picked up a great many Democratic votes.

The first person he telephoned after it became definite that he had lost was his stepmother, Ethel. "Don't be too disappointed," he told her, because I'm not. I think I made a good try."

Even professional football acknowledged the excellence of this college coach. "Last week at the Pro-Bowl game," wrote Melvin Durslag of the *Los Angeles Herald-Examiner*, "Sid Gillman, the coach of the San Diego Chargers and one of the top-rated clinic men in the business, was delivering a quiet discourse on Wilkinson. 'There have been outstanding technical men in the game,' said Gillman, 'and great inspirational leaders. But there has never been one who has combined technique and spirit and leadership as skillfully as Wilkinson. I can't recall a coach as well rounded in all departments as he.'"[2]

[2] Melvin Durslag, *Los Angeles Herald-Examiner,* January 19, 1964.

1963 SENIORS TODAY

Virgil Boll owns and operates a 6,000-acre ranch in Frio County, Texas. He also owns a 967-acre irrigated farm adjoining the ranch, where he grows seed peas, corn, and wheat. He also maintains a working interest in oil.

Jackie Cowan is distributive education coordinator in the Odessa, Texas, schools.

Dr. George Jarman is a dentist in Dallas, Texas.

John Porterfield is assistant superintendent of the Owasso, Oklahoma, schools.

George Stokes is a warrant officer with the United States Army in Germany.

Larry Vermillion owns and operates Vermillion Enterprises, a computing firm in Woodland Hills, California.

THE COACH TODAY

Bud Wilkinson is chairman of the board of Public Employees Benefit Services Corporation, in Saint Louis, Missouri. He is also a college football announcer for the ESPN cable television network, chairman of the National Advisory Committee on Juvenile Justice and Delinquency Prevention, president of the United States Gymnastics Federation, and codirector with Duffy Daugherty of Coach of the Year Football Clinics.

Appendix

WILKINSON FOOTBALL LETTERMEN, 1947-1963

Allen, Sam	Burris, Paul	Depue, Dale
Allison, Carl	Burris, Robert	Derrick, Robert
Allsup, John	Burton, Newt	Dickey, Donald
Anderegg, Dan, Jr.	Byerly, James A.	Dinkins, Merle
Anderson, Frank G.	Bynum, Chet	Dodd, Carl
Andros, Dee	Calame, Gene Dan	Dodson, Teddy
Arnold, Claude	Carnahan, Sam	Donaghey, Jerry
Baker, David	Carpenter, Dick	Dowell, Charles
Ballard, Hugh	Carpenter, Jimmy	Durham, Jere
Bayles, Marion	Carroll, Tom	Ellis, Dick
Beattie, Richard	Catlin, Tom	Emerson, Tom
Beckman, William	Clark, Bert	Estes, H. O.
Bell, John Herman	Cockrell, Gene	Evans, Richard
Benien, John	Cole, J. W.	Ewbank, Bob L.
Benien, Paul	Condren, Glen	Feagan, Jimmy
Bodenhamer, Bob	Cook, Duane	Fischer, Max
Bolinger, Virgilee	Corbitt, Dick	Flynn, John T.
Boll, Virgil	Cornelius, George	Garrett, John C.
Bookout, Billy	Cornell, Bob	Gaut, Bob
Bowman, Chuck	Covin, Bill	Gautt, Prentice
Bowman, Dick	Cowan, Jackie	Gaynor, Joe
Boyd, Bobby	Cox, Tom S.	Gilstrap, Jimmy R.
Boydston, Max	Coyle, Ross	Ging, Jack
Bradley, Lester	Cross, Delbert Leon	Goad, Bobby
Brewer, George	Crowder, Eddie	Goff, Duane
Brown, Bill	Cunningham, Glenn	Goldsby, Jerry
Brown, Don	Cunningham, Joe	Gravitt, Bert W.
Brown, Gordon	Darnell, Bob	Gray, Edmon
Brown, Larry	Davis, Eddy	Gray, Tommy
Brown, Melvin	Davis, J. H., Jr.	Greathouse, Myrle
Broyles, Henry J.	Davis, Jim	Green, Merrill
Bumgardner, Allen	Davis, Samuel A.	Greenlee, Wayne
Burris, Kurt	Deere, Monte	Grigg, Larry
Burris, Lynn	Dempsey, Jackie	Grisham, Jimmie

352

Gwinn, Dick
Hale, Earl
Hallum, Ken
Hammert, B. W., Jr.
Hammond, John
Hamon, Claude
Harmon, Ronald
Harris, Bill
Harris, James
Harrison, Bob
Hartline, Ronnie
Hayden, Jerry
Heape, Gene
Hearon, Darlon
Heath, Leon
Heatly, Richard
Herndon, Bob
Hill, Howard
Hobby, Brewster
Hogan, Pat
Holland, Lonnie
Holt, Jackie
Hood, Fred
Horkey, Joe
Hughes, Jack
Husak, John
Ingram, Austin
Ingram, Jerry
Inman, Richard
Jackson, Mickey
Janes, Charles
Jarman, George
Jennings, Doyle
Jennings, Steve
Johnson, Mickey
Jones, Wilbur
Keadle, Dale
Keller, Kay
Kreick, Edward
Krisher, Bill
Ladd, Benton
Lane, Lester
Lang, Nolan
Lang, Vernon
Lawrence, Jim

Lea, Paul
Leake, John ("Buddy")
Lear, Alvin
Lee, William
Levonitis, Bill
Lewis, Gilmer A.
Link, Emery
Lisak, Ed
Littlejohn, Wray
Lockett, David M.
Lohmann, Phil
Long, Delbert
· Looney, Joe Don
Loughridge, Eldon
McAdams, Carl
McClellan, William
    Michael
McCoy, James P.
McCurdy, Rick
McDaniel, Edward
McDonald, Tommy
McGee, Reece
McNabb, Norman
McPhail, Coleman
McQuarters, Eddie
Manley, Willie Leon
Marcum, Delton D.
Martin, Bob
Mayes, Clair
Mayhue, Charles D.
Meacham, Billy
Mears, Gene
Metcalf, Lawrence
    Butch
Milstead, Karl
Ming, Leslie
Mitchell, Jack
Mobra, Joe
Moore, Billy Jack
Moore, Harry
Morford, Bob
Morford, Brent
Morris, Bill
Morris, Cecil
Morris, Dennit

Morris, Max
Needs, Al
Neely, Ralph E.
Nelson, Don
Nelson, George
Nelson, Roger
Northcutt, Kenneth
O'Neal, Benton
O'Neal, Jay
O'Neal, Preston, Jr.
Oujesky, Buddy
Owens, Jim
Pace, Harry
Page, Bobby W.
Page, Robert
Paine, Charles
Paine, Homer
Pannell, Larry A.
Pannell, Tom
Pannell, William H.
Parker, James L.
Parker, Kenneth
Payne, Gerald
Payne, Ronny
Pearson, Lindell
Pearson, Tom
Pellow, John
Perini, Dale A.
Pettibone, Gerald
Porterfield, John
Powell, Raymond
Powell, Roland
Price, Bill
Pricer, Billy
Rapacz, John
Rector, Joe
Reddell, John C.
Remy, Bill
Rentzel, Lance
Roberts, J. D.
Rolle, David
Rowe, Jared
Rowland, Ed
Royal, Darrell
Salmon, Elton Dale

353

Sandefer, Jakie
Sandersfeld, Melvin
Santee, Jack
Sarratt, Charles
Scholl, Robert
Schreiner, Carl
Schreiner, Carl S. III
Schreiner, Henry
Scott, B. W.
Searcy, Byron
Sherrod, Dale
Shields, Benny
Shields, Larry
Shilling, Cloyd
Silva, Frank
Simmons, Milton
Skidgel, Wesley A.
Smalley, Harley
Smith, Dean
Smith, Fred

Smith, Norman
Stiller, Don
Stokes, George H.
Sturm, Billy
Talbott, George
Tatum, John
Taylor, Loyd Geary
Thomas, Clendon
Thomas, George C.
Thompson, Jerry
Tillery, Jerry
Tillman, Pete
Timberlake, Bob
Tipps, Kenneth
Trotter, Jess
Tubbs, Jerry
Vallance, Chad Y.
Van Burkleo, Bill
Van Pool, Jack
Vardeman, Robert

Vermillion, Larry D.
Vessels, Bill
Voiles, John David
Walker, Wade
Wallace, Dave
Ward, Dennis
Ward, Stanley
Watts, Bennett
Watts, Bill
Weatherall, James
Wells, Ben
West, Stanley
White, Billy
Winblood, Bill
Woodworth, Calvin
Wright, Curtis Truman
Wyatt, Bobby
Wylie, Gary
York, Marshall

INDEX

356

Forty-Seven Straight,

designed by Bill Cason, was set in 11-point Garamond by the University of Oklahoma Press and printed offset on 55-pound Glatfelter Smooth Antique D-10, a permanized sheet, by Cushing-Malloy, Inc., with case binding by John H. Dekker & Sons.